MANHATTAN GMAT

Foundations of GMAT Math

GMAT Strategy Guide

This supplemental guide provides in-depth and easy-to-follow
explanations of the fundamental math skills necessary for a strong
performance on the GMAT.

Foundations of GMAT Math, Fifth Edition

10-digit International Standard Book Number: 1-935707-59-0
13-digit International Standard Book Number: 978-1-935707-59-2
eISBN: 978-0-979017-59-9

Note: *GMAT, Graduate Management Admission Test, Graduate Management Admission Council,* and *GMAC* are all registered trademarks of the Graduate Management Admission Council, which neither sponsors nor is affiliated in any way with this product.

Layout Design: Dan McNaney and Cathy Huang
Cover Design: Evyn Williams and Dan McNaney
Cover Photography: Alli Ugosoli

INSTRUCTIONAL GUIDE SERIES

GMAT Roadmap
(ISBN: 978-1-935707-69-1)

Fractions, Decimals, & Percents
(ISBN: 978-1-935707-63-9)

Algebra
(ISBN: 978-1-935707-62-2)

Word Problems
(ISBN: 978-1-935707-68-4)

Number Properties
(ISBN: 978-1-935707-65-3)

Geometry
(ISBN: 978-1-935707-64-6)

Critical Reasoning
(ISBN: 978-1-935707-61-5)

Reading Comprehension
(ISBN: 978-1-935707-66-0)

Sentence Correction
(ISBN: 978-1-935707-67-7)

Integrated Reasoning
(ISBN: 978-1-935707-83-7)

SUPPLEMENTAL GUIDE SERIES

Math GMAT Supplement Guides

Foundations of GMAT Math
(ISBN: 978-1-935707-59-2)

Advanced GMAT Quant
(ISBN: 978-1-935707-15-8)

Official Guide Companion
(ISBN: 978-1-937707-33-0)

Verbal GMAT Supplement Guides

Foundations of GMAT Verbal
(ISBN: 978-1-935707-01-9)

MANHATTAN
GMAT

November 15th, 2011

Dear Student,

Thank you for picking up a copy of *Foundations of GMAT Math*. Think of this book as the foundational tool that will help you relearn all of the math rules and concepts you once knew but have since forgotten. It's all in here, delivered with just the right balance of depth and simplicity. Doesn't that sound good?

As with most accomplishments, there were many people involved in the creation of the book you're holding. First and foremost is Zeke Vanderhoek, the founder of Manhattan GMAT. Zeke was a lone tutor in New York when he started the company in 2000. Now, eleven years later, the company has Instructors and offices nationwide and contributes to the studies and successes of thousands of students each year.

Our Manhattan GMAT Strategy Guides are based on the continuing experiences of our Instructors and students. For this *Foundations of GMAT Math* book, we are particularly indebted to a number of Instructors, starting with the extraordinary Dave Mahler. Dave rewrote practically the entire book, having worked closely with Liz Ghini Moliski and Abby Pelcyger to reshape the book's conceptual flow. Together with master editor/writer/organizer Stacey Koprince, Dave also marshalled a formidable army of Instructor writers and editors, including Chris Brusznicki, Dmitry Farber, Whitney Garner, Ben Ku, Joe Lucero, Stephanie Moyerman, Andrea Pawliczek, Tim Sanders, Mark Sullivan, and Josh Yardley, all of whom made excellent contributions to the guide you now hold. In addition, Tate Shafer, Gilad Edelman, Jen Dziura, and Eric Caballero provided falcon-eyed proofing in the final stages of book production. Dan McNaney and Cathy Huang provided their design expertise to make the books as user-friendly as possible, and Liz Krisher made sure all the moving pieces came together at just the right time. And there's Chris Ryan. Beyond providing additions and edits for this book, Chris continues to be the driving force behind all of our curriculum efforts. His leadership is invaluable.

At Manhattan GMAT, we continually aspire to provide the best Instructors and resources possible. We hope that you'll find our commitment manifest in this book. If you have any questions or comments, please email me at dgonzalez@manhattangmat.com. I'll look forward to reading your comments, and I'll be sure to pass them along to our curriculum team.

Thanks again, and best of luck preparing for the GMAT!

Sincerely,

Dan Gonzalez
President
Manhattan GMAT

HOW TO ACCESS YOUR ONLINE RESOURCES

If you...

⊗ ### are a registered Manhattan GMAT student

and have received this book as part of your course materials, you have AUTOMATIC access to ALL of our online resources. This includes all practice exams, question banks, and online updates to this book. To access these resources, follow the instructions in the Welcome Guide provided to you at the start of your program. Do NOT follow the instructions below.

⊗ ### purchased this book from the Manhattan GMAT online store or at one of our centers

1. Go to: www.manhattanprep.com/gmat/studentcenter.

2. Log in using the username and password used when your account was set up.

⊗ ### purchased this book at a retail location

1. Create an account with Manhattan GMAT at the website: www.manhattanprep.com/gmat/register.

2. Go to: www.manhattanprep.com/gmat/access.

3. Follow the instructions on the screen.

Your one year of online access begins on the day that you register your book at the above URL.

You only need to register your product ONCE at the above URL. To use your online resources any time AFTER you have completed the registration process, log in to the following URL: www.manhattanprep.com/gmat/studentcenter.

Please note that online access is nontransferable. This means that only NEW and UNREGISTERED copies of the book will grant you online access. Previously used books will NOT provide any online resources.

⊗ ### purchased an eBook version of this book

1. Create an account with Manhattan GMAT at the website: www.manhattanprep.com/gmat/register.

2. Email a copy of your purchase receipt to gmat@manhattanprep.com to activate your resources. Please be sure to use the same email address to create an account that you used to purchase the eBook.

For any technical issues, email techsupport@manhattanprep.com or call 800-576-4628.

Please refer to the following page for a description of the online resources that come with this book.

YOUR ONLINE RESOURCES

Your purchase includes ONLINE ACCESS to the following:

> ### *Foundations of GMAT Math* Online Question Bank

The Bonus Online Drill Sets for FOUNDATIONS OF GMAT MATH consist of 400+ extra practice questions (with detailed explanations) that test the variety of Foundational Math concepts and skills covered in this book. These questions provide you with extra practice beyond the problem sets contained in this book. You may use our online timer to practice your pacing by setting time limits for each question in the bank.

> ### Online Updates to the Contents in this Book

The content presented in this book is updated periodically to ensure that it reflects the GMAT's most current trends. You may view all updates, including any known errors or changes, upon registering for online access.

TABLE *of* CONTENTS

Chapter 1
of
Foundations of GMAT Math

Arithmetic

In This Chapter...

Chapter 1:
Arithmetic

Our goal in this book is not only to introduce and review fundamental math skills, but also to provide a means for you to practice applying these skills. Toward this end, we have included a number of "Check Your Skills" questions throughout each chapter. After each topic, do these problems one at a time, checking your answers at the back of the chapter as you go. **If you find these questions challenging, re-read the section you just finished.**

In This Chapter:

- Quick Start rules of numbers
- PEMDAS
- Combining like terms and pulling out common factors

Quick-Start Definitions

Whether you work with numbers every day or avoid them religiously, give a good read to this first section, which gives "quick-start" definitions for core concepts. We'll come back to many of these concepts throughout the book. Moreover, **bolded** terms in this section can be found in the glossary at the back of the book.

Basic Numbers

All the **numbers** that we care about on the GMAT can be shown as a point somewhere on the **number line**.

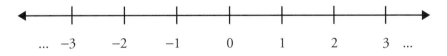

Another word for number is **value**.

Counting numbers are 1, 2, 3, and so on. These are the first numbers that you ever learned—the stereotypical numbers that you count separate things with.

Digits are ten symbols (0, 1, 2, 3, 4, 5, 6, 7, 8, and 9) used to represent numbers. If the GMAT asks you specifically for a digit, it wants one of these ten symbols.

Counting numbers above 9 are represented by two or more digits. The number "four hundred twelve" is represented by three digits in this order: 412.

Place value tells you how much a digit in a specific position is worth. The 4 in 412 is worth 4 hundreds (400), so 4 is the *hundreds digit* of 412. Meanwhile, 1 is the *tens digit* and is worth 1 ten (10). Finally, 2 is the **units digit** and is worth 2 units, or just plain old 2.

412	=	400	+	10	+	2
Four hundred twelve	equals	4 hundreds	plus	1 ten	plus	2 units (or 2).

The GMAT always separates the thousands digit from the hundreds digit by a comma. For readability, big numbers are broken up by commas placed three digits apart.

1,298,023 equals one million two hundred ninety-eight thousand twenty-three.

Addition (+, or "plus") is the most basic operation in arithmetic. If you add one counting number to another, you get a third counting number further out to the right.

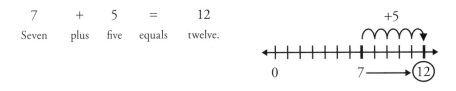

7	+	5	=	12
Seven	plus	five	equals	twelve.

12 is the **sum** of 7 and 5.

You can always add in either order and get the same result.

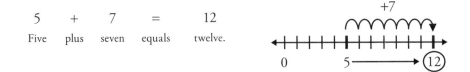

5	+	7	=	12
Five	plus	seven	equals	twelve.

MANHATTAN
GMAT

1

Subtraction (–, or "minus") is the opposite of addition. Subtraction undoes addition.

Order matters in subtraction. $6 - 2 = 4$, but $2 - 6 =$ something else (more on this in a minute). By the way, since $6 - 2 = 4$, the **difference** between 6 and 2 is 4.

Zero (0) is any number minus itself.

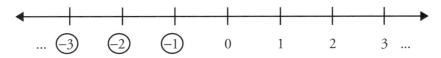

Any number plus zero is that number. The same is true if you subtract zero. In either case, you're moving *zero* units away from the original number on the number line.

$$8 + 0 = 8 \qquad\qquad 9 - 0 = 9$$

Negative counting numbers are –1, –2, –3, and so on. These numbers, which are written with a **minus sign** or **negative sign**, show up to the left of zero on a number line.

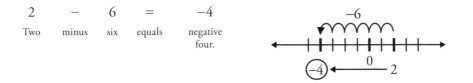

You need negative numbers when you subtract a bigger number from a smaller number. Say you subtract 6 from 2:

Negative numbers can be used to represent deficits. If you have \$2 but you owe \$6, your net worth is –\$4.

If you're having trouble computing *small minus BIG*, figure out *BIG minus small*, then make the result negative.

$$35 - 52 = ? \qquad {}^{4}\cancel{5}2 \qquad \text{So } 35 - 52 = -17$$
$$\underline{-35}$$
$$17$$

Positive numbers are to the right of zero on a number line. Negative numbers are to the left of zero. Zero itself is neither positive nor negative—it's the only number right in the middle.

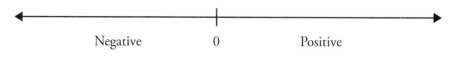

The **sign** of a number indicates whether the number is positive or negative.

Integers include all the numbers discussed so far.

- Counting numbers (1, 2, 3, …), also known as **positive integers**
- Negative counting numbers (−1, −2, −3, …), aka **negative integers**
- Zero (0)

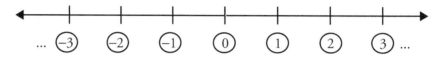

Check Your Skills

Perform addition & subtraction.

1. 37 + 144 =
2. 23 − 101 =

Answers can be found on page 47.

Greater Than and Less Than

"Greater than" (>) means "to the right of" on a number line. You can also say "bigger" or "larger."

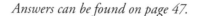

Careful! This definition of "greater than" means that, for negative numbers, bigger numbers are closer to zero. This may be counterintuitive at first.

Don't think in terms of "size," even though "bigger" and "larger" seem to refer to size. Bigger numbers are simply *to the right of* smaller numbers on the number line.

The left-to-right order of the number line is *negatives, then zero, then positives*. So any positive number is greater than any negative number.

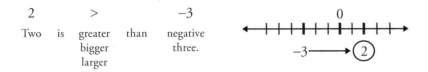

| 2 | > | −3 |
| Two | is greater bigger larger | than negative three. |

Likewise, zero is greater than every negative number.

| 0 | > | −3 |
| Zero | is greater bigger larger | than negative three. |

"Less than" (<) or "smaller than" means "to the left of" on a number line. You can always re-express a "greater than" relationship as a "less than" relationship—just flip it around.

| 7 | > | 3 |
| Seven | is greater bigger larger | than three. |

| 3 | < | 7 |
| Three | is less smaller | than seven. |

If 7 is greater than 3, then 3 is less than 7.

Make sure that these "less than" statements make sense:

−7 is less than −3	−7 < −3
−3 is less than 2	−3 < 2
−3 is less than 0	−3 < 0

Inequalities are statements that involve "bigger than" (>) or "smaller than" (<) relationships.

Check Your Skills

3. What is the sum of the largest negative integer and the smallest positive integer?

Quickly plug in > and < symbols and say the resulting statement aloud.

4. 5 __ 16
5. −5 __ −16

Answers can be found on page 47.

1

Adding and Subtracting Positives and Negatives

Positive plus positive gives you a third positive.

7   +   5   =   12
Seven   plus   five   equals   twelve.

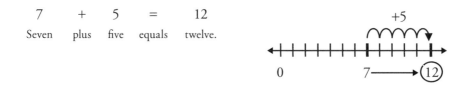

You move even further to the right of zero, so the result is always bigger than either starting number.

Positive minus positive could give you either a positive or a negative.

BIG positive – small positive = positive

8   –   3   =   5
Eight   minus   three   equals   five.

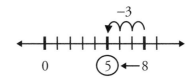

small positive – BIG positive = negative

3   –   8   =   –5
Three   minus   eight   equals   negative five.

Either way, the result is less than where you started, because you move left.

Adding a negative is the same as subtracting a positive—you move left.

8   +   –3   =   5
Eight   plus   negative three   equals   five.

Negative plus negative always gives you a negative, because you move even further to the left of zero.

–3   +   –5   =   –8
Negative three   plus   negative five   equals   negative eight.

Subtracting a negative is the same as adding a positive—you move right. Think two *wrongs* (*subtracting* and *negative*) make a *right*. Add in parentheses so you keep the two minus signs straight.

$$7 \quad - \quad (-5) \quad = \quad 7 \quad + \quad 5$$

Seven   minus   negative   equals   seven   plus   five,
                five

$$= \quad 12$$

which equals   twelve.

In general, any subtraction can be rewritten as an addition. If you're subtracting a positive, that's the same as adding a negative. If you're subtracting a negative, that's the same as adding a positive.

Check Your Skills

6. Which is greater, a positive minus a negative or a negative minus a positive?

Answers can be found on page 47.

Multiplying and Dividing

Multiplication (×, or "times") is repeated addition.

$$4 \quad \times \quad 3 \quad = \quad 3 + 3 + 3 + 3 \quad = \quad 12$$

Four   times   three   equals   four three's added up,   which equals   twelve.

12 is the **product** of 4 and 3, which are **factors** of 12.

Parentheses can be used to indicate multiplication. Parentheses are usually written with ( ), but brackets [ ] can be used, especially if you have parentheses within parentheses.

If a set of parentheses bumps up right against something else, multiply that something by whatever is in the parentheses.

$$4(3) = (4)3 = (4)(3) = 4 \times 3 = 12$$

You can use a big dot. Just make the dot big and high, so it doesn't look like a decimal point.

$$4 \bullet 3 = 4 \times 3 = 12$$

You can always multiply in either order and get the same result.

$$4 \quad \times \quad 3 \quad = \quad 3 + 3 + 3 + 3 \quad = \quad 12$$
Four   times   three   equals   four three's added up,   which equals   twelve.

$$3 \quad \times \quad 4 \quad = \quad 4 + 4 + 4 \quad = \quad 12$$
Three   times   four   equals   three four's added up,   which equals   twelve.

Division (÷, or "divided by") is the opposite of multiplication. Division undoes multiplication.

$$2 \quad \times \quad 3 \quad \div \quad 3 \quad = \quad 2$$
Two   times   three   divided by   three   equals   two.

Order matters in division. $12 \div 3 = 4$, but $3 \div 12 =$ something else (more on this soon).

Multiplying any number by **one (1)** leaves the number the same. One times anything **is** that thing.

$$1 \quad \times \quad 5 \quad = \quad 5 \quad = \quad 5$$
One   times   five   equals   one five by itself,   which equals   five.

$$5 \quad \times \quad 1 \quad = \quad 1 + 1 + 1 + 1 + 1 \quad = \quad 5$$
Five   times   one   equals   five one's added up,   which equals   five.

Multiplying any number **by zero (0)** gives you zero. Anything times zero is zero.

$$5 \quad \times \quad 0 \quad = \quad 0 + 0 + 0 + 0 + 0 \quad = \quad 0$$
Five   times   zero   equals   five zero's added up,   which equals   zero.

Since order doesn't matter in multiplication, this means that zero times anything is zero too.

$$0 \quad \times \quad 5 \quad = \quad 5 \times 0 \quad = \quad 0$$
Zero   times   five   equals   five times zero   which equals   zero.

Multiplying a number by zero destroys it permanently, in a sense. So you're not allowed to undo that destruction by dividing by zero.

Never divide by zero. $13 \div 0 =$ undefined, stop right there, don't do this.

You *are* allowed to divide zero by another number. You get, surprise, zero.

1

$$0 \div 13 = 0$$

Zero   divided by   thirteen   equals   zero.

Check Your Skills

Complete the operations.

7. $7 \times 6 =$

8. $52 \div 13 =$

Answers can be found on page 47.

Distributing and Factoring

What is $4 \times (3 + 2)$? Here's one way to solve it.

$$4 \quad \times \quad (3 + 2) \quad = \quad 4 \times 5 \quad = \quad 20$$

Four   times   the quantity   equals   four times five,   which   twenty.
                 three plus two   equals

Here, we turned $(3 + 2)$ into 5, then multiplied 4 by that 5.

The other way to solve this problem is to **distribute** the 4 to both the 3 and the 2.

$$4 \quad \times \quad (3 + 2) \quad = \quad 4 \times 3 \quad + \quad 4 \times 2$$

Four   times   the quantity three   equals   four times   plus   four times
                 plus two   three   two,

$$= \quad 12 \quad + \quad 8$$

which   twelve   plus   eight,
equals

$$= \quad 20$$

which   twenty.
equals

Notice that you multiply the 4 into *both* the 3 and the 2.

Distributing is extra work in this case, but the technique will come in handy down the road.

Another way to see how distributing works is to put the sum in front.

1

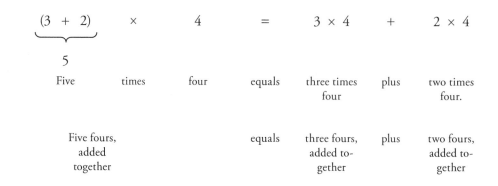

(3 + 2)	×	4	=	3 × 4	+	2 × 4
5						
Five	times	four	equals	three times four	plus	two times four.
Five fours, added together			equals	three fours, added together	plus	two fours, added together

In a sense, you're splitting up the sum 3 + 2. Just be sure to multiply both the 3 and the 2 by 4.

Distributing works similarly for subtraction. Just keep track of the minus sign.

6	×	(5 − 2)	=	6 × 5	−	6 × 2
Six	times	the quantity five minus two	equals	six times five	minus	six times two,
			=	30	−	12
			which equals	thirty	minus	twelve,
			=	18		
			which equals	eighteen.		

You can also go in reverse. You can **factor** the sum of two products if the products contain the same factor.

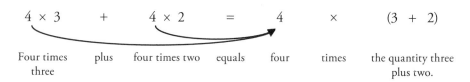

4 × 3	+	4 × 2	=	4	×	(3 + 2)
Four times three	plus	four times two	equals	four	times	the quantity three plus two.

Here, we've pulled out the **common factor** of 4 from each of the products 4 × 3 and 4 × 2. Then we put the sum of 3 and 2 into parentheses. By the way, "common" here doesn't mean "frequent" or "typical." Rather, it means "belonging to both products." A common factor is just a factor in common (like a friend in common).

You can also put the common factor in the back of each product, if you like.

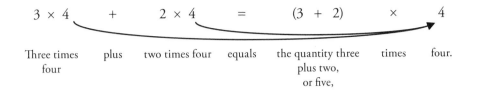

3×4	$+$	2×4	$=$	$(3 + 2)$	$\times$	4
Three times four	plus	two times four	equals	the quantity three plus two, or five,	times	four.

Like distributing, factoring as a technique isn't that interesting with pure arithmetic. We'll encounter them both in a more useful way later. However, make sure you understand them with simple numbers first.

Check Your Skills

9. Use distribution. $5 \times (3 + 4) =$

10. Factor a 6 out of the following expression: $36 - 12 =$

Answers can be found on page 47.

Multiplying Positives and Negatives

Positive times positive is always **positive**.

3	$\times$	4	$=$	$4 + 4 + 4$	$=$	12
Three	times	four	equals	three four's added up,	which equals	twelve.

Positive times negative is always **negative**.

3	$\times$	-4	$=$	$-4 + (-4) + (-4)$	$=$	-12
Three	times	negative four	equals	three negative four's, all added up,	which equals	negative twelve.

Since order doesn't matter in multiplication, the same outcome happens when you have **negative times positive**. You again get a **negative**.

-4	$\times$	3	$=$	$3 \times (-4)$	$=$	-12
Negative four	times	three	equals	three times negative four	which equals	negative twelve.

What is **negative times negative**? **Positive**. This fact may seem weird, but it's consistent with the rules developed so far. If you want to see the logic, read the next little bit. Otherwise, skip ahead to "In practice…"

Anything times zero equals zero.	-2	$\times$	0	$=$	0
	Negative two	times	zero	equals	zero.

$0 = 3 + (-3)$

Substitute this in for the
zero on the right.

-2 × [3 + (−3)] = 0

Negative   times   the quantity three   equals   zero.
two   plus minus three

Now distribute the −2
across the sum.

-2×3 + $-2 \times (-3)$ = 0

Negative   plus   negative two times   equals   zero.
two   negative three
times three

-6 + something = 0

That "something" must be positive 6. So $-2 \times (-3) = 6$.

In practice, just remember that **Negative × Negative = Positive** as another version of "two wrongs make a right."

All the same rules hold true for dividing.

Positive ÷ Positive = Positive
Positive ÷ Negative = Negative
Negative ÷ Positive = Negative
Negative ÷ Negative = Positive

Check Your Skills

11. $(3)(-4) =$

12. $-6 \times (-3 + (-5)) =$

Answers can be found on page 47.

Fractions and Decimals

Adding, subtracting, and multiplying integers always gives you an integer, whether positive or negative.

Int	+	Int	=	Int
Int	−	Int	=	Int
Int	×	Int	=	Int

(*Int* is a handy abbreviation for a random integer, by the way, although the GMAT won't demand that you use it.)

However, dividing an integer by another integer does not always give you an integer.

MANHATTAN
GMAT

$$\text{Int} \quad \div \quad \text{Int} \quad = \quad \begin{array}{l}\text{sometimes an integer,}\\ \text{sometimes not!}\end{array}$$

When you don't get an integer, you get a fraction or a decimal—a number between the integers on the number line.

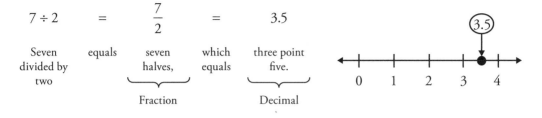

$$7 \div 2 \quad = \quad \frac{7}{2} \quad = \quad 3.5$$

| Seven divided by two | equals | seven halves, | which equals | three point five. |

Fraction   Decimal

A horizontal **fraction line** or bar expresses the division of the **numerator** (above the fraction line) by the **denominator** (below the fraction line).

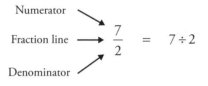

Numerator

Fraction line ⟶ $\dfrac{7}{2}$ = $7 \div 2$

Denominator

In fact, the division symbol ÷ is just a miniature fraction. People often say things such as "seven *over* two" rather than "seven halves" to express a fraction.

You can express division in three ways: with a fraction line, with the division symbol ÷, or with a slash (/).

$$\frac{7}{2} \quad = \quad 7 \div 2 \quad = \quad 7/2$$

A **decimal point** is used to extend place value to the right for decimals. Each place to the right of the decimal point is worth a tenth ($\dfrac{1}{10}$), a hundredth ($\dfrac{1}{100}$), etc.

$$3.5 \quad = \quad 3 \quad + \quad \frac{5}{10}$$

Three point five   equals   three   plus   five tenths.

$$1.25 \quad = \quad 1 \quad + \quad \frac{2}{10} \quad + \quad \frac{5}{100}$$

One point two five   equals   one   plus   two tenths   plus   five hundredths.

1

A decimal such as 3.5 has an **integer part** (3) and a **fractional part** or **decimal part** (0.5). In fact, an integer is just a number with no fractional or decimal part.

Every fraction can be written as a decimal, although you might need an unending string of digits in the decimal to properly express the fraction.

$$4 \div 3 \quad = \quad \frac{4}{3} \quad = \quad 1.333\ldots \quad = \quad 1.\overline{3}$$

| Four divided by three | equals | four thirds (or four over three), | which equals | one point three three three dot dot dot, forever and ever, | which equals | one point three repeating. |

Fractions and decimals obey all the rules we've seen so far about how to add, subtract, multiply and divide. Everything you've learned for integers applies to fractions and decimals as well: how positives and negatives work, how to distribute, etc.

Check Your Skills

13. Which arithmetic operation involving integers does NOT always result in an integer?
14. Rewrite 2 ÷ 7 as a product.

Answers can be found on page 47.

Divisibility and Even and Odd Integers

Sometimes you do get an integer out of integer division.

$$15 \div 3 \quad = \quad \frac{15}{3} \quad = \quad 5 \quad = \quad \text{int}$$

| Fifteen divided by three | equals | fifteen thirds (or fifteen over three), | which equals | five | which is | an integer. |

In this case, 15 and 3 have a special relationship. You can express this relationship in several equivalent ways.

15 is **divisible** by 3.
        15 divided by 3 equals an integer   15 ÷ 3 = int
15 is a **multiple** of 3.
        15 equals 3 times an integer   15 = 3 × int
3 is a **factor** of 15.
3 **goes into** 15.
3 **divides** 15.

Even integers are divisible by 2.

14 is even because 14 ÷ 2 = 7 = an integer.

All even integers have 0, 2, 4, 6, or 8 as their units digit.

Odd integers are not divisible by 2.

15 is odd because 15 ÷ 2 = 7.5 = not an integer.

All odd integers have 1, 3, 5, 7, or 9 as their units digit.

Even and odd integers alternate on the number line.

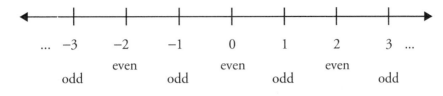

Zero is even because it is divisible by 2.

0 ÷ 2 = 0 = an integer.

Only integers can be said to be even or odd.

Check Your Skills

15. Fill in the blank. If 7 is a factor of 21, then 21 is a _____ of 7.

16. Is 2,284,623 divisible by 2?

Answers can be found on page 47.

Exponents and Roots (and Pi)

Exponents represent repeated multiplication. (Remember, multiplication was repeated addition, so this is just the next step up the food chain.)

In 5^2, the **exponent** is 2, and the **base** is 5. The exponent tells you how many bases you put together in the product. When the exponent is 2, you usually say "squared."

5^2	=	5×5	=	25
Five squared	equals	two fives multiplied together, or five times itself,	which equals	twenty-five.

When the exponent is 3, you usually say "cubed."

1

4^3	=	$4 \times 4 \times 4$	=	64
Four cubed	equals	three fours multiplied together, or four times four times four	which equals	sixty-four.

For other exponents, you say "to the ___ power" or "raised to the ___ power."

2^5	=	$2 \times 2 \times 2 \times 2 \times 2$	=	32
Two to the fifth power	equals	five two's multiplied together,	which equals	thirty-two.

When you write exponents on your own paper, be sure to make them much tinier than regular numbers, and put them **clearly up** to the right. You don't want to mistake 5^2 for 52 or vice versa.

By the way, a number raised to the first power is just that number.

7^1	=	7	=	7
Seven to the first power	equals	just one seven in the product,	which equals	seven.

A **perfect square** is the square of an integer.

25 is a perfect square because $25 = 5^2 = \text{int}^2$.

A **perfect cube** is the cube of an integer.

64 is a perfect cube because $64 = 4^3 = \text{int}^3$.

Roots undo exponents. The simplest and most common root is the **square root**, which undoes squaring. The square root is written with the radical sign ($\sqrt{\ }$).

5^2	=	5×5	=	25,	so	$\sqrt{25}$	=	5
Five squared	equals	five times five,	which equals	twenty-five	so	the square root of twenty-five	equals	five.

As a shortcut, "the square root of twenty-five" can just be called "root twenty-five."

Asking for the square root of 49 is the same as asking what number, times itself, gives you 49.

$\sqrt{49}$	=	7	because	7×7	=	7^2	=	49
Root forty-nine	equals	seven,	because	seven times seven,	which equals	seven squared,	equals	forty-nine.

The square root of a perfect square is an integer, because a perfect square is an integer squared.

$$\sqrt{36} \quad = \quad int \quad because \quad 36 \quad = \quad int^2$$

The square root of   is   an integer,   because   thirty-six   equals   an integer
thirty-six   squared.

The square root of any *non*-perfect square is a crazy unending decimal that never even repeats, as it turns out.

$$\sqrt{2} \quad \approx \quad 1.414213562\ldots \quad because \quad (1.414213562\ldots)^2 \quad \approx \quad 2$$

Root two   is   one point four one four   because   that thing squared   is   two.
                about   two blah blah,   about

The square root of 2 can't be expressed as a simple fraction, either. So usually we leave it as is ($\sqrt{2}$), or we approximate it ($\sqrt{2} \approx 1.4$).

While we're on the subject of crazy unending decimals, you'll encounter one other number with a crazy decimal in geometry: **pi** (π).

Pi is the ratio of a circle's circumference to its diameter. It's about 3.14159265… without ever repeating.

Since pi can't be expressed as a simple fraction, we usually just represent it with the Greek letter for *p* (π), or we can approximate it ($\pi \approx 3.14$, or a little more than 3).

Cube roots undo cubing. The cube root has a little 3 tucked into its notch ($\sqrt[3]{}$).

$$\sqrt[3]{8} \quad = \quad 2 \quad because \quad 2^3 \quad = \quad 8$$

The cube root of eight   equals   two,   because   two cubed   equals   eight.

Other roots occasionally show up. The **fourth root** undoes the process of taking a base to the fourth power.

$$\sqrt[4]{81} \quad = \quad 3 \quad because \quad 3^4 \quad = \quad 81$$

The fourth root of   equals   three,   because   three to the   equals   eighty-one.
eighty-one   fourth power

Check Your Skills

17. $2^6 =$

18. $\sqrt[3]{27} =$

Answers can be found on page 47.

Variable Expressions and Equations

Up to now, we have known every number we've dealt with. **Algebra** is the art of dealing with *unknown* numbers.

A **variable** is an unknown number, also known simply as an **unknown**. You represent a variable with a single letter, such as x or y.

When you see x, imagine that it represents a number that you don't happen to know. At the start of a problem, the value of x is hidden from you. It could be anywhere on the number line, in theory, unless you're told something about x.

The letter x is the stereotypical letter used for an unknown. Since x looks so much like the multiplication symbol $\times$, you generally stop using $\times$ in algebra to prevent confusion. To represent multiplication, you do other things.

To multiply variables, just put them next to each other.

What you see	What you say	What it means
xy	"x y"	x times y
abc	"a b c"	The product of a, b, and c

To multiply a known number by a variable, just write the known number in front of the variable.

What you see	What you say	What it means
$3x$	"three x"	3 times x

Here, 3 is called the **coefficient** of x. If you want to multiply x by 3, write $3x$, not $x3$, which could look too much like x^3 ("x cubed").

All the operations besides multiplication look the same for variables as they do for known numbers.

What you see	What you say	What it means
$x + y$	"x plus y"	x plus y, or the sum of x and y
$x - y$	"x minus y"	x minus y
$\dfrac{x}{y}$	"x over y" or "x divided by y"	x divided by y
x^2	"x squared"	x squared, which is just x times x
$\sqrt{x}$	"the square root of x"	the square root of x

By the way, be careful when you have variables in exponents.

What you see	What you say	What it means
$3x$	"three x"	3 times x
3^x	"three to the x"	3 raised to the xth power, or 3 multiplied by itself x times

Never call 3^x "three x." It's "three **to the** x." If you don't call 3^x by its correct name, then you'll never keep it straight.

An **expression** is anything that ultimately represents a number somehow. You might not know that number, but you *express* it using variables, numbers you know, and operations such as adding, subtracting, etc.

You can think of an expression like a recipe. The result of the recipe is the number that the expression is supposed to represent.

Expression	What you say	The number represented by the expression
$x + y$	"x plus y"	The sum of x and y. In other words, the recipe is "add x and y." The result is the number.
$3xz - y^2$	"3 x z minus y squared"	First, multiply 3, x, and z, then subtract the square of y. The result is the number.
$\dfrac{\sqrt{2w}}{3}$	"The square root of 2 w, all over 3"	First, multiply 2 and w together. Then take the square root. Finally, divide by 3. The result is the number.

Within an expression, you have one or more **terms**. A term involves no addition or subtraction (typically). Often, a term is just a product of variables and known numbers.

It's useful to notice terms so that you can **simplify** expressions, or reduce the number of terms in those expressions. Here are the terms in the previous expressions.

Expression	Terms	Number of Terms
$x + y$	x, y	Two
$3xz - y^2$	$3xz, y^2$	Two
$\dfrac{\sqrt{2w}}{3}$	$\dfrac{\sqrt{2w}}{3}$	One

If the last step in the expression recipe is adding or subtracting, then you can split the expression up into more than one term. Plenty of expressions contain just one term, though (just as that last one did).

An **equation** sets one expression equal to another using the **equals sign** ($=$), which you've seen plenty of times in your life—and in this book already.

What you might not have thought about, though, is that the equals sign is a *verb*. In other words, an equation is a complete, grammatical sentence or statement:

Something   *equals*   something else.

Some expression   *equals*   some other expression.

Here's an example:

$$3 + 2x \qquad = \qquad 11$$

Three plus two *x*   equals   eleven.

Each equation has a **left side** (the subject of the sentence) and a **right side** (the object of the verb *equals*). You can say "is equal to" instead of "equals" if you want:

$$3 + 2x \qquad = \qquad 11$$

Three plus two *x*   *is equal to*   eleven.

Solving an equation is solving this mystery:

What is *x*?

or, more precisely,

What is the value (or values) of *x* that make the equation *true*?

Since an equation is a sentence, it can be true or false, at least in theory. You always want to focus on how to make the equation *true*, or keep it so, by finding the right values of any variables in that equation.

The process of solving an equation usually involves rearranging the equation, performing identical operations on each side until the equation tells you what the variable equals.

$3 + 2x$	$=$	11	Three plus two *x*	equals	eleven.
-3		-3	Subtract 3		Subtract 3
$2x$	$=$	8	Two *x*	equals	eight.
$\div 2$		$\div 2$	Divide by 2		Divide by 2
x	$=$	4	*x*	equals	four.

The solution to the original equation is $x = 4$. If you replace *x* with 4 in the equation "$3 + 2x = 11$," then you get "$11 = 11$," which is always true. Any other value of *x* would make the equation false.

If the GMAT gives you the equation "$3 + 2x = 11$," it's telling you something very specific about *x*. For this particular equation, in fact, just one value of *x* makes the equation work (namely, 4).

MANHATTAN
GMAT

Check Your Skills

19. What is the value of the expression $2x - 3y$ if $x = 4$ and $y = -1$?

Answers can be found on page 48.

PEMDAS

Consider the expression $3 + 2 \times 4$.

> Should you add 3 and 2 first, then multiply by 4? If so, you get 20.
> Or should you multiply 2 and 4 first, then add 3? If so, you get 11.

There's no ambiguity—mathematicians have decided on the second option. **PEMDAS** is an acronym to help you remember the proper **order of operations**.

PEMDAS Overview

When you simplify an expression, don't automatically perform operations from left to right, even though that's how you read English. Instead, follow PEMDAS:

Parentheses	Do P first
Exponents	Then E
Multiplication	Then either M or D
Division	
Addition	Then either A or S
Subtraction	

For $3 + 2 \times 4$, you do the M first (multiply 2 and 4), then the A (add 3 to the result).

$$3 + 2 \times 4 \qquad = 3 + 8 \qquad = 11$$

If you want to force the addition to go first, add parentheses. P always goes first:

$$(3 + 2) \times 4 \qquad = 5 \times 4 \qquad = 20$$

Multiplication and Division are at the same level of importance in PEMDAS, because any Multiplication can be expressed as a Division, and vice versa.

$$7 \div 2 = 7 \times \frac{1}{2}$$

In a sense, Multiplication and Division are two sides of the same coin.

Likewise, Addition and Subtraction are at the same level of importance. Any Addition can be expressed as a Subtraction, and vice versa.

1

$$3 - 4 = 3 + (-4)$$

So you can think of PEMDAS this way:

$$PE^M/_D {}^A/_S$$
$$\longrightarrow$$

If you have two operations of equal importance, do them **left to right**.

$$3 - 2 + 3 \qquad = 1 + 3 \qquad = 4$$

Of course, **override this order** if you have parentheses:

$$3 - (2 + 3) \qquad = 3 - 5 \qquad = -2$$

Now let's consider a more complicated expression:

$$3 + 4(5 - 1) - 3^2 \times 2 = ?$$

Here is the correct order of steps to simplify:

$$3 + 4(5 - 1) - 3^2 \times 2$$

Parentheses $3 + 4(4) - 3^2 \times 2$

Exponents $3 + 4(4) - 9 \times 2$

Multiplication or **D**ivision $3 + 16 - 18$

Addition or **S**ubtraction $3 + 16 - 18 = 19 - 18 = 1$

Let's do two problems together. Try it first on your own, then we'll go through it together:

$$5 - 3 \times 4^3 \div (7 - 1)$$

P

E

M/D

A/S

Your work should have looked something like this:

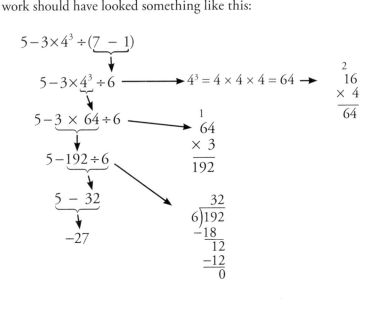

Let's try one more:

$$32 \div 2^4 \times (5 - 3^2)$$

P

E

M/D

A/S

1

Here's the work you should have done:

$$32 \div 2^4 \times (5 - 3^2)$$

$$32 \div 2^4 \times (5 - 9)$$

$$32 \div 2^4 \times (-4)$$

$$32 \div 16 \times (-4)$$

$$2 \times (-4)$$

$$-8$$

Check Your Skills

Evaluate the following expressions.

20 $-4 + 12/3 =$

21. $(5 - 8) \times 10 - 7 =$

22. $-3 \times 12 \div 4 \times 8 + (4 - 6) =$

23. $2^4 \times (8 \div 2 - 1)/(9 - 3) =$

Answers can be found on page 48.

Combining Like Terms

How can you simplify this expression?

$$3x^2 + 7x + 2x^2 - x$$

Remember, an expression is a recipe. Here's the recipe in words:

> "Square x, then multiply that by 3, then separately multiply x by 7 and add that product in, then square x again, multiply that by 2 and add that product into the whole thing, and then finally subtract x."

Is there a simpler recipe that's always equivalent? Sure.

Here's how to simplify. First, focus on **like terms**, which contain very similar "stuff."

Again, a term is an expression that doesn't contain addition or subtraction. Quite often, a term is just a bunch of things multiplied together.

"Like terms" are very similar to each other. They only differ by a numerical coefficient. Everything else in them is the same.

The expression above contains four terms, separated by + and − operations:

$$3x^2 \quad + \quad 7x \quad + \quad 2x^2 \quad - \quad x$$

Three x squared   plus   seven x   plus   two x squared   minus   x

There are two pairs of like terms:

Pair one: $3x^2$ and $2x^2$

Pair two: $7x$ and $-x$

Make sure that everything about the variables is identical, including exponents. Otherwise, the terms aren't "like."

What can you do with two or more like terms? Combine them into one term. Just add or subtract the coefficients. Keep track of + and − signs.

$$3x^2 \quad + \quad 2x^2 \quad = \quad 5x^2$$

Three x squared   plus   two x squared   equals   five x squared.

$$7x \quad - \quad x \quad = \quad 6x$$

Seven x   minus   x   equals   six x.

Whenever a term does not have a coefficient, act as if the coefficient is 1. In the example above, "x" can be rewritten as "$1x$":

$$7x \quad - \quad 1x \quad = \quad 6x$$

Seven x   minus   one x   equals   six x.

Or you could say that you're adding $-1x$.

$$7x \quad + \quad -1x \quad = \quad 6x$$

Seven x   plus   negative one x   equals   six x.

Either way is fine. A negative sign in front of a term on its own can be seen as a −1 coefficient. For instance, $-xy^2$ has a coefficient of −1.

Combining like terms works because for like terms, everything *but* the coefficient is a **common factor**. So we can "pull out" that common factor and group the coefficients into a sum (or difference). This is when factoring starts to become really useful.

For a review of factoring, see pages 21 through 23.

In the first case, the common factor is x^2.

$$3x^2 \quad + \quad 2x^2 \quad = \quad (3 + 2)x^2$$

Three x squared   plus   two x squared   equals   the quantity three plus two, times
x squared.

The right side then reduces by PEMDAS to $5x^2$. Of course, once you can go straight from $3x^2 + 2x^2$ to $5x^2$, you'll save a step.

By the way, when you *pronounce* $(3 + 2)x^2$, you should technically say "the quantity three plus two…" The word "quantity" indicates parentheses. If you just say "three plus two x squared," someone could (and should) interpret what you said as $3 + 2x^2$, with no parentheses.

In the case of $7x - x$, the common factor is x. Remember that "x" should be thought of as "$1x$."

$$7x \quad - \quad 1x \quad = \quad (7 - 1)x$$

Seven x   minus   one x   equals   the quantity seven minus one,
times x.

Again, the right side reduces by PEMDAS to $6x$.

So, if you combine like terms, you can simplify the original expression this way:

$$3x^2 + 7x + 2x^2 - x \quad = \quad (3x^2 + 2x^2) + (7x - x)$$

$$= \quad 5x^2 + 6x$$

The common factor in like terms does not have to be a simple variable expression such as x^2 or x. It could involve more than one variable:

$$-xy^2 + 4xy^2 = (-1 + 4)xy^2 = 3xy^2 \qquad \text{Common factor: } xy^2$$

Remember that the coefficient on the first term should be treated as -1.

Be careful when you see multiple variables in a single term. For two terms to be like, the exponents have to match for every variable.

In $-xy^2 + 4xy^2$, each term contains a plain x (which is technically x raised to the first power) and y^2 (which is y raised to the second power, or y squared). All the exponents match. So the two terms are like, and we can combine them to $3xy^2$.

Now suppose we had the following series of terms:

$$2xy \quad + \quad xy^2 \quad - \quad 4x^2y \quad + \quad x^2y^2$$

Two x y   plus   x y squared   minus   four x squared y   plus   x squared y squared

None of the terms above can combine to a single term. They all have different combinations of variables and exponents. For now, we're stuck. (In the next section, we'll see that there's *something* you can do with that expression, but you can't combine terms.)

The two terms in the following expression *are* like:

$$xy^2 \qquad + \qquad 3y^2x$$

x y squared   plus   three y squared x

The order of the variables does not matter, since you can multiply in any order. All that matters is that the variables and exponents all match. If you need to, flip around $3y^2x$ to $3xy^2$. So we can combine:

$$xy^2 \quad + \quad 3y^2x \quad = \quad 4xy^2 \quad = \quad 4y^2x$$

x y
squared   plus   three y squared x   equals   four x y squared,   which also
equals   four y
squared x.

In general, be ready to flip around products as you deal with numbers times variables. The order of multiplication does not matter.

$$x(-3) \qquad = \qquad -x(3) \qquad = \qquad -3x$$

x times
negative three   equals   negative x times
three,   equals   negative three x.

The last form, $-3x$, is the standard form. You can encounter the others as you rearrange terms.

The common factor in the like terms could be the square root of a number:

$$\sqrt{2} + 3\sqrt{2} = 1\sqrt{2} + 3\sqrt{2} = (1+3)\sqrt{2} = 4\sqrt{2} \qquad \text{Common factor: } \sqrt{2}$$

Or the common factor could include π:

$$2\pi r + 9\pi r = (2+9)\pi r = 11\pi r \qquad\qquad \text{Common factor: } \pi r$$

When terms are *not* like, tread carefully. Don't automatically combine them. You may still be able to pull out a common factor, but it won't be everything but the coefficients.

As you practice simplifying expressions, keep in mind that your main goal is to reduce the overall number of terms by combining like terms.

PEMDAS becomes more complicated when an expression contains terms that are not like and so cannot be combined. You especially need to be careful when you see terms "buried" within part of an expression, as in the following cases that we'll come back to:

1

Terms inside parentheses

$$-3(x-2) \qquad x \text{ and } 2 \text{ are not like}$$

Terms in the numerator or denominator of a fraction

$$\frac{1}{1-x} = 2 \qquad x \text{ and } 1 \text{ are not like}$$

Terms involving exponents

$$\frac{x^{-3} + \left(x^2\right)^4}{x^5} \qquad x^{-3} \text{ and } (x^2)^4 \text{ are not like}$$

Terms under a root sign

$$\sqrt{x^2 + y^2} \qquad x^2 \text{ and } y^2 \text{ are not like}$$

Terms in parentheses, with the parentheses raised to an exponent

$$(x + y)^2 \qquad x \text{ and } y \text{ are not like}$$

Check Your Skills

Combine as many like terms as possible in each of the following expressions:

24. $-3 + 4\sqrt{2} + 6.3$
25. $4\pi r^2 - 3\pi r + 2\pi r$
26. $8ba + ab^2 - 5ab + ab^2 - 2ba^2$

Answers can be found on page 48.

Distribution

As we mentioned at the end of the last section, things become more complicated when multiple terms are found within a set of parentheses.

For a quick review of distribution, go to page 21.

We'll start by distributing the example from the previous section: $-3(x-2)$. Remember that you're multiplying -3 by $(x-2)$. To keep track of minus signs as you distribute, you can think of $(x-2)$ as $(x + (-2))$. We'll put in the multiplication sign ($\times$) to make it clear that we're multiplying.

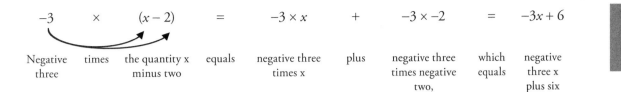

1

Remember that the negative sign (on −3) distributes.

When you do all this on your paper, you shouldn't use × to show multiplication, because you could confuse it with *x*. Use a big dot or nothing at all. You might also put parentheses around the second product, to help keep track of sign.

-3		$(x-2)$	$=$	$-3\,x$	$+$	$(-3 \cdot -2)$	$=$	$-3x+6$
Negative three	times	the quantity x minus two	equals	negative three times x	plus	negative three times negative two,	which equals	negative three x plus six

How can you simplify this expression?

$$4y^2 - y(5 - 2y)$$

First, distribute negative *y* (−*y*) to both terms in the parentheses:

$$4y^2 - y(5 - 2y) = 4y^2 - 5y + 2y^2$$

Notice that −*y* times −2*y* becomes +2y^2.

Then combine 4y^2 and 2y^2 because they are like terms:

$$4y^2 - y(5 - 2y) = 4y^2 - 5y + 2y^2 = 6y^2 - 5y$$

Sometimes the term being distributed involves a root or pi. Consider this tougher example:

$$\sqrt{2}\,(1 - x\sqrt{2}\,)$$

The principle is the same. Distribute the first root two to both terms in the parentheses.

$\sqrt{2}$	$\times$	$(1 - x\sqrt{2}\,)$	$=$	$\sqrt{2} \times 1$	$+$	$\sqrt{2} \times -x\sqrt{2}$	$=$	$\sqrt{2} - 2x$
Root two	times	the quantity one minus x root two	equals	root two times one	plus	root two times negative x root two,	which equals	root two minus two x

Remember, root two times root two is two. $\sqrt{2} \times \sqrt{2} = 2$.

For a more in-depth look at multiplying roots, go to page 125.

Here's an example with pi:

$$\pi(1 + r)$$

Distribute the pi:

π	$\times$	$(1 + r)$	$=$	$\pi \times 1$	$+$	$\pi \times r$	$=$	$\pi + \pi r$
pi	times	the quantity one plus r	equals	pi times one	plus	pi times r,	which equals	pi plus pi r

Check Your Skills

27. $x(3 + x)$

28. $4 + \sqrt{2}(1 - \sqrt{2})$

Answers can be found on page 48.

Pulling Out a Common Factor

Let's go back to the long expression on page 36:

$$3x^2 + 7x + 2x^2 - x$$

This expression has four terms. By combining two pairs of like terms, we simplified this expression to $5x^2 + 6x$, which only has two terms.

We can't go below two terms. However, we can do one more useful thing. The two terms left ($5x^2$ and $6x$) aren't "like," because the variable parts aren't identical. However, these two terms do still have a common factor—namely, x. Each term is x times something.

x is a factor of $6x$, because $6x = 6$ times x.

x is also a factor of $5x^2$, maybe a little less obviously.

$x^2 = x$ times x

So $5x^2 = 5x$ times x

Since x is a factor of both $5x^2$ and $6x$, we can factor it out and group what's left as a sum within parentheses.

$$5x^2 \qquad + \qquad 6x \qquad = \qquad (5x + 6)x$$

Five x squared   plus   six x   equals   the quantity five x plus six, times x.

If in doubt, distribute the *x* back through and verify that you're back where you started.

$$(5x + 6)x \qquad = \qquad 5x^2 \qquad + \qquad 6x$$

The quantity five x plus six,   equals   five x squared   plus   six x
times x.

$(5x + 6)x$ can also be written as $x(5x + 6)$. Either way, it may or may not be "simpler" than $5x^2 + 6x$. However, pulling out a common factor can be the key move when you solve a GMAT problem.

Sometimes the common factor is hidden among more complicated variable expressions.

$$x^2y \qquad - \qquad xy^2 \qquad = \qquad xy(x - y)$$

x squared y   minus   x y squared   equals   x y times the quantity x minus y.

Here, the common factor is *xy*.

Sometimes the common factor involves a root or pi.

$$\sqrt{2} \qquad + \qquad \sqrt{2}\,\pi \qquad = \qquad \sqrt{2}\,(1 + \pi)$$

Root two   plus   root two times pi   equals   root two times the quantity one plus pi.

Here, the common factor is $\sqrt{2}$. Notice that the first term ($\sqrt{2}$) is the same as the common factor. Whenever the factor you are pulling out is the same as the term, leave a 1 in its place (in the parentheses).

$$\pi r^2 \qquad - \qquad \pi \qquad = \qquad \pi(r^2 - 1)$$

pi r squared   minus   pi   equals   pi times the quantity r squared minus one.

Here, the common factor is π. Again, when you pull π out of the second term (which is π), leave a 1 behind in its place. You can check that this works by distributing π back through.

You might only factor out an integer, or even a negative sign.

$$2 \qquad + \qquad 4x \qquad = \qquad 2(1 + 2x)$$

Two   plus   four x   equals   two times the quantity one plus two *x*.

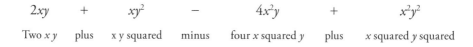

$$3 \quad - \quad x \quad = \quad -(x-3)$$

Three   minus   x   equals   the negative of quantity x minus three.

Remember this monster from a couple of sections ago?

$$2xy \quad + \quad xy^2 \quad - \quad 4x^2y \quad + \quad x^2y^2$$

Two xy plus xy squared   minus   four x squared y plus x squared y squared

What is the common factor that you can pull out?

Answer: xy

$$2xy + xy^2 - 4x^2y + x^2y^2 = xy(2 + y - 4x + xy)$$

Check Your Skills

29. Factor a negative x out of the expression $-2x^3 + 5x^2 + 3x$
30. Factor the following expression: $4x^2 + 3xy - yx + 6x$

Answers can be found on page 48.

Long Multiplication

Let's review the basics of long multiplication.

When multiplying two numbers, always put the smaller number in the bottom row. You would write 8×57 as

$$\begin{array}{r} 57 \\ \times\ 8 \\ \hline \end{array}$$ $7 \times 8 = 56$
Put the 6 underneath, then carry the 5.

$$\begin{array}{r} {}^5 57 \\ \times\quad 8 \\ \hline 6 \end{array}$$ $5 \times 8 = 40$, + the 5 we carried = 45. Because we're at the end, put the 45 underneath.

$$\begin{array}{r} 57 \\ \times\ 8 \\ \hline 456 \end{array}$$

You should also be comfortable multiplying two two-digit numbers. $36 \times 85 =$

$$\begin{array}{r} {}^3 85 \\ \times\ 36 \\ \hline 0 \end{array}$$ Start with the 6. $5 \times 6 = 30$

Put the 0 underneath, then carry the 3.

$$\begin{array}{r} {}^{3}85 \\ \times\ 36 \\ \hline 0 \end{array}$$

$8 \times 6 = 48$, + the 3 we carried = 51. Because we are done with the 6, place the 51 underneath.

$$\begin{array}{r} {}^{\cancel{3}}85 \\ \times\ 36 \\ \hline 510 \end{array}$$

Now deal with the 3. Remember that the 3 actually represents 30. Place a 0 underneath the right most column, then multiply. Don't forget to cross out the 3 you carried last time!

$$\begin{array}{r} {}^{3}85 \\ \times\ 36 \\ \hline 510 \\ 0 \end{array}$$

$5 \times 3 = 15$. Place the 5 underneath then carry the 1.

$$\begin{array}{r} {}^{1}{}^{3}85 \\ \times\ 36 \\ \hline 510 \\ 50 \end{array}$$

$8 \times 3 = 24$ + the 1 we carried = 25. Place the 25 underneath.

$$\begin{array}{r} 85 \\ \times\ 36 \\ \hline 510 \\ 2550 \end{array}$$

Now add the rows underneath.

$$\begin{array}{r} 510 \\ +{}^{1}2550 \\ \hline 3060 \end{array}$$

$85 \times 36 = 3,060$

Don't let multiplication slow you down on the GMAT. Do multiplication drills to become quick and accurate.

Long Division

$$13\overline{)234}$$

13 goes into 23 one time.

$$13\overline{)234} \quad \overset{1}{} \\ -13 \\ \overline{104}$$

Place a 1 on top of the digit farthest to the right in 23.

1×13 is 13, so subtract 13 from 23, and bring down the next digit (4).

What is the largest multiple of 13 less than or equal to 104?

$$\overset{18}{13\overline{)234}} \\ -13 \\ \overline{104} \\ -104 \\ \overline{0}$$

If necessary, list multiples of 13 or try cases until you find $13 \times 8 = 104$.

The number may not always divide evenly, in which case you will be left with a remainder. E.g. $25 \div 2 = 12$ with a remainder of 1.

In the previous example, the answer was an integer ($234 \div 13 = 18$). However, the answer will not always be an integer.

Let's try dividing 123 by 6.

$$6\overline{)123}$$

6 doesn't go into 1, but it does go into 12 two times.

$$\overset{2}{6\overline{)123}} \\ -12 \\ \overline{03}$$

Place a 2 on top of the digit farthest to the right in 12.

$2 \times 6 = 12$, so subtract 12 from 12, and bring down the next digit (3).

$$\overset{20}{6\overline{)123.0}} \\ -12 \\ \overline{03.0}$$

6 doesn't go into 3, so place a 0 on top of the 3.

We're not done dividing. 123 is equal to 123.0. Add the decimal point and a 0 in the tenths column. Bring down the 0.

$$\overset{20.5}{6\overline{)123.0}} \\ -12 \\ \overline{030} \\ -30 \\ \overline{0}$$

6 goes into 30 5 times. Place a 5 on top of the 0. Don't forget to put a decimal between the 0 and the 5.

Check Your Skills Answer Key

1.   **181:**
$$\begin{array}{r} \overset{1}{144} \\ +37 \\ \hline 181 \end{array}$$

2.   **–78:** $\begin{array}{r} \overset{9}{\cancel{1}\cancel{0}1} \\ -23 \\ \hline 78 \end{array}$, so $23 - 101 = -78$

3.   **0:** The largest negative integer is –1 and the smallest positive integer is 1. $-1 + 1 = 0$

4.   **5 < 16**   Five is less than sixteen.

5.   **–5 > –16**   Negative five is greater than negative sixteen.

6.   **A positive minus a negative:** (+) – (–) will always be positive, whereas (–) – (+) will always be negative. Any positive number is greater than any negative number.

7.   **42:** $7 \times 6 = 42$

8.   **4:** $52 \div 13 = 4$

9.   **35:** $5 \times (3 + 4) = 5 \times 3 + 5 \times 4 = 15 + 20 = 35$

10. **6(6 – 2):** $36 - 12 = 6 \times 6 - 6 \times 2 = 6(6 - 2) = 24$

11. **–12:** $(3)(-4) = -12$

12. **48:** $-6 \times (-3 + (-5)) = (-6 \times -3) + (-6 \times -5) = 18 + 30 = 48$

13. **Division:** Sometimes an integer divided by an integer equals an integer (ex. $6 \div 2 = 3$) and sometimes it does not (ex. $8 \div 5 = 1.6$)

14. $\mathbf{2 \times \dfrac{1}{7}}$: $2 \div 7 = \dfrac{2}{7} = 2 \times \dfrac{1}{7}$

15. **Multiple:** If 7 is a factor of 21, then 21 is a multiple of 7.

16. **No:** 2,284,623 ends in 3, which means that it is an odd number, and is not divisible by 2.

17. **64:** $2^6 = (2 \times 2) \times (2 \times 2) \times (2 \times 2) = 4 \times 4 \times 4 = 64$

18. **3:** $\sqrt[3]{27} = 3$ because $3^3 = 27$.

1

19.   **11:** If we plug the values of the variables back into the expression we can find the value of the expression.

$$2x - 3y =$$
$$2(4) - 3(-1) = 8 - (-3) = 8 + 3 = 11$$

20. **0:**

$-4 + 12/3 =$	Divide first
$-4 + 4 = 0$	Then add the two numbers

21. **–37:**

$(5 - 8) \times 10 - 7 =$	
$(-3) \times 10 - 7 =$	First, combine what is inside the parentheses
$-30 - 7 =$	Then multiply -3 and 10
$-30 - 7 = -37$	Subtract the two numbers

22. **–74:**

$-3 \times 12 \div 4 \times 8 + (4 - 6)$	
$-3 \times 12 \div 4 \times 8 + (-2)$	First, combine what's in the parentheses
$-36 \div 4 \times 8 + (-2)$	Multiply -3 and 12
$-9 \times 8 - 2$	Divide -36 by 4
$-72 + (-2) = -74$	Multiply -9 by 8 and subtract 2

23. **8:**

$2^4 \times (8 \div 2 - 1) / (9 - 3) =$	
$2^4 \times (4 - 1)/(6) =$	$8/2 = 4$ and $9 - 3 = 6$
$16 \times (3)/(6) =$	$4 - 1 = 3$ and $2^4 = 16$
$48/6 =$	Multiply 16 by 3
$48/6 = 8$	Divide 48 by 6

24. $\mathbf{3.3 + 4\sqrt{2}}$: $(-3 + 6.3) + 4\sqrt{2} = 3.3 + 4\sqrt{2}$

25. $\mathbf{4\pi r^2 - \pi r}$: $4\pi r^2 + (-3\pi r + 2\pi r) = 4\pi r^2 - \pi r$

26. $\mathbf{3ab + 2ab^2 - 2a^2 b}$: $(8ab - 5ab) + (ab^2 + ab^2) + (-2a^2 b) = 3ab + 2ab^2 - 2a^2 b$

27. $\mathbf{3x + x^2}$: $x(3 + x) = x \times 3 + x \times x = 3x + x^2$

28. $\mathbf{2 + \sqrt{2}}$: $4 + \sqrt{2}(1 - \sqrt{2}) = 4 + (\sqrt{2} \times 1) + (\sqrt{2} \times -\sqrt{2}) = 4 + \sqrt{2} - 2 = 2 + \sqrt{2}$

29. $\mathbf{-x(2x^2 - 5x - 3)}$: $-2x^3 \div -x = 2x^2$. $5x^2 \div -x = -5x$. $3x \div -x = -3$.

30. $\mathbf{x(4x + 2y + 6)}$: All the terms contain x. $4x^2 \div x = 4x$. $3xy \div x = 3y$. $-yx \div x = -y$. $6x \div x = 6$. $4x^2 + 3xy - yx + 6x = x(4x + 3y - y + 6)$. $3y - y = 2y$, so $x(4x + 3y - y + 6) = x(4x + 2y + 6)$.

Chapter Review: Drill Sets

Drill 1

Evaluate the following expressions.

1. $39 - (25 - 17) =$
2. $3(4 - 2) \div 2 =$
3. $15 \times 3 \div 9 =$
4. $(9 - 5) - (4 - 2) =$
5. $14 - 3(4 - 6) =$
6. $-5 \times 1 \div 5 =$
7. $(4)(-3)(2)(-1) =$
8. $5 - (4 - (3 - (2 - 1))) =$
9. $-4(5) - 12/(2 + 4) =$
10. $17(6) + 3(6)$

Drill 2

Evaluate the following expressions.

11. $-12 \times 2/(-3) + 5 =$
12. $32/(4 + 6 \times 2) =$
13. $-10 - (-3)^2 =$
14. $-5^2 =$
15. $-2^3/2 =$
16. $5^3 - 5^2 =$
17. $5^{(2+1)} + 25 =$
18. $(-2)^3 - 5^2 + (-4)^3 =$
19. $5(1) + 5(2) + 5(3) + 5(4) =$
20. $3 \times 99 - 2 \times 99 - 1 \times 99$

Drill 3

Combine as many like terms as possible.

21. $\pi r^2 - (2\pi r + \pi r^2)$
22. $1 + 2\sqrt{4} + 2\sqrt{2}$
23. $12xy^2 - 6(xy)^2 + (2xy)^2$
24. $3\pi + x\pi - 2\pi$
25. $\sqrt{2} + x\sqrt{2} - 2\sqrt{2}$

26. $12xy - (6x + 2y)$
27. $3x - (3x + 5 - (2x - 3))$
28. $\pi^2 r^2 - \pi r + 2\pi r^2 + \pi(r^2) + (\pi r)^2 + 2\pi r$
29. $2x^2 - (2x)^2 - 2^2 - x^2$
30. $4x^2 + 2x - (2\sqrt{x})^2$

Drill 4

Distribute the following expressions. Simplify as necessary.

31. $3(5 - y)$
32. $-(a - b)$
33. $(2x + y)z$
34. $\sqrt{3}(\sqrt{2} + \sqrt{3})$
35. $5.2r(2t - 10s)$
36. $(-3.7x + 6.3)10^2$
37. $6k^2l(k - 2l)$
38. $-\sqrt{3}(-n\sqrt{12} + \sqrt{27})$
39. $d(d^2 - 2d + 1)$
40. $xy^2z(x^2z + yz^2 - xy^2)$

Drill Sets Solutions

Drill 1

Evaluate the following expressions.

1. **31:**

    $39 - (25 - 17) =$
    $39 - 8 = 31$

Tip: You could distribute the minus sign
$(39 - 25 + 17)$ if you prefer, but our method is less prone to error.

2. **3:**

    $3 \times (4 - 2) \div 2 =$
    $3 \times (2) \div 2 =$
    $6 \div 2 = 3$

3. **5:**

    $15 \times 3 \div 9 =$
    $45 \div 9 = 5$

4. **2:**

    $(9 - 5) - (4 - 2) =$
    $(4) - (2) = 2$

5. **20:**

    $14 - 3 (4 - 6) =$
    $14 - 3(-2) =$
    $14 + 6 = 20$

6. **−1:**

    $-5 \times 1 \div 5 =$
    $-5 \div 5 = -1$

7. **24:**

    $(4)(-3)(2)(-1) = 24$

Tip: To determine whether a product will be positive or negative, count the number of negative terms being multiplied. An even number of negative terms will give you a positive product; an odd number of negative terms will give you a negative product.

8. **3:**

    $5 - (4 - (3 - (2 - 1))) =$
    $5 - (4 - (3 - 1)) =$

1

$$5 - (4 - 2) =$$
$$5 - (2) = 3$$

Tip: Start with the inner-most parentheses and be careful about the signs!

9. **−22:**

$$-4\,(5) - 12/(2 + 4) =$$
$$-20 - 12/(6) =$$
$$-20 - 2 = -22$$

10. **120:**

$$17(6) + 3(6) =$$
$$102 + 18 = 120$$

Alternatively, you could factor the 6 out of both terms.

$$17(6) + 3(6) =$$
$$6(17 + 3) =$$
$$6(20) = 120$$

Drill 2

Evaluate the following expressions.

11. **13:**

$$-12 \times 2/(-3) + 5 =$$
$$-24/(-3) + 5 =$$
$$8 + 5 = 13$$

12. **2:**

$$32/(4 + 6 \times 2) =$$
$$32/(4 + 12) =$$
$$32/(16) = 2$$

13. **−19:**

$$-10 - (-3)^2 =$$
$$-10 - (9) = -19$$

14. **−25:**

$$-5^2 =$$
$$-(5^2) = -25$$

15. **−4:**

$$-2^3/2 =$$
$$-8/2 = -4$$

16. **100:**

$$5^3 - 5^2 =$$
$$125 - 25 = 100$$

17. **150:**

$$5^{(2+1)} + 25 =$$
$$5^3 + 25 = 125 + 25 = 150$$

18. **−97:**

$$(-2)^3 - 5^2 + (-4)^3 =$$
$$(-8) - 25 + (-64) =$$
$$-33 - 64 = -97$$

19. **50:**

$$5(1) + 5(2) + 5(3) + 5(4) =$$
$$5 + 10 + 15 + 20 = 50$$

Alternatively, you could factor a 5 out of each term.

$$5(1) + 5(2) + 5(3) + 5(4) =$$
$$5(1 + 2 + 3 + 4) =$$
$$5(10) = 50$$

20. **0:**

$$3 \times 99 - 2 \times 99 - 1 \times 99 =$$
$$297 - 198 - 99 =$$
$$99 - 99 = 0$$

Alternatively, you could factor 99 out of each term.

$$3 \times 99 - 2 \times 99 - 1 \times 99 =$$
$$99(3 - 2 - 1) =$$
$$99(0) = 0$$

Drill 3

Combine as many like terms as possible.

21. **−2πr**: We cannot combine the terms in the parentheses so we must start by distributing the negative sign before we can combine:

$\pi r^2 - (2\pi r + \pi r^2) =$
$\pi r^2 - 2\pi r - \pi r^2 =$
$1\pi r^2 - 2\pi r - 1\pi r^2 =$
$0 - 2\pi r = -2\pi r$

22. $\mathbf{5 + 2\sqrt{2}}$: We must deal with the terms with a square root before we can group and combine like terms:

$1 + 2\sqrt{4} + 2\sqrt{2} =$
$1 + 2(2) + 2\sqrt{2} =$
$1 + 4 + 2\sqrt{2} =$
$5 + 2\sqrt{2}$

23. $\mathbf{12xy^2 - 2x^2y^2}$: We must simplify the terms with exponents before we can group and combine like terms:

$12xy^2 - 6(xy)^2 + (2xy)^2 =$
$12xy^2 - 6x^2y^2 + 2^2x^2y^2 =$
$12xy^2 - 6x^2y^2 + 4x^2y^2 =$
$12xy^2 + (-6 + 4)x^2y^2 =$
$12xy^2 + (-2)x^2y^2 =$
$12xy^2 - 2x^2y^2$

24. $\mathbf{(x + 1)\pi}$: We start by grouping like terms and then combine:

$3\pi + x\pi - 2\pi =$
$3\pi - 2\pi + x\pi =$
$(3 - 2)\pi + x\pi =$
$1\pi + x\pi =$
$(1 + x)\pi = (x + 1)\pi$

Remember that it is helpful to add a coefficient of 1 to any terms that do not have an integer coefficient.

25. $\mathbf{(x - 1)\sqrt{2}}$:

$\sqrt{2} + x\sqrt{2} - 2\sqrt{2} =$
$1\sqrt{2} + x\sqrt{2} - 2\sqrt{2} =$
$(1 + x - 2)\sqrt{2} =$
$(-1 + x)\sqrt{2} = (x - 1)\sqrt{2}$

26. $\mathbf{12xy - 6x - 2y}$: We cannot combine the terms in the parentheses so we must distribute the negative sign before grouping and combining like terms:

$12xy - (6x + 2y) =$
$12xy - 6x - 2y$

Note that we cannot actually combine any of the terms.

27. **$2x - 8$:**

$3x - (3x + 5 - (2x - 3)) =$
$3x - (3x + 5 - 2x + 3) =$
$3x - (3x - 2x + 5 + 3) =$
$3x - (1x + 8) =$
$3x - 1x - 8 =$
$2x - 8$

28. **$2\pi^2 r^2 + \pi r + 3\pi r^2$:** We must manipulate the terms with exponents before we can group and combine like terms:

$\pi^2 r^2 - \pi r + 2\pi r^2 + \pi(r^2) + (\pi r)^2 + 2\pi r =$
$\pi^2 r^2 - \pi r + 2\pi r^2 + \pi r^2 + \pi^2 r^2 + 2\pi r =$
$(1\pi^2 r^2 + 1\pi^2 r^2) + (2\pi r - 1\pi r) + (2\pi r^2 + 1\pi r^2) =$
$2\pi^2 r^2 + 1\pi r + 3\pi r^2$

29. **$-3x^2 - 4$:**

$2x^2 - (2x)^2 - 2^2 - x^2 =$
$2x^2 - 2^2 x^2 - 2^2 - 1x^2 =$
$2x^2 - 4x^2 - 1x^2 - 4 =$
$(2 - 4 - 1)x^2 - 4 =$
$(-3)x^2 - 4 =$
$-3x^2 - 4$

30. **$4x^2 - 2x$:**

$4x^2 + 2x - (2\sqrt{x})^2 =$
$4x^2 + 2x - 2^2(\sqrt{x})^2 =$
$4x^2 + 2x - 4x =$
$4x^2 + (2 - 4)x =$
$4x^2 + (-2)x =$
$4x^2 - 2x$

Drill 4

Distribute the following expressions. Simplify as necessary.

31. **$15 - 3y$:**
$\qquad 3(5 - y) = 3 \times 5 + 3 \times (-y) = 15 - 3y$

32. −a + b OR b − a:

The minus sign in front of the left parenthesis should be interpreted as: −1 times the expression $(a − b)$. Because $(−1) \times a = −a$ and $(−1) \times (−b) = b$ we have:

$$-(a - b) = (-1) \times (a - b) = -a + b$$

33. 2xz + yz:

This problem requires us to distribute *from the right*. Ordinarily, we think of the Distributive Property in this form:

$$a(b + c) = ab + ac$$

It is also true that:

$$(b + c)a = ba + ca$$

One way to justify this is to note that $(b + c)a = a(b + c)$ by the Commutative Property of Multiplication, which states that the order in which we multiply numbers does not matter. The GMAT sometimes disguises a possible distribution by presenting it in this alternate form.

In this problem, $(2x + y)z = z(2x + y)$.

$$z(2x + y) = z \times 2x + z \times y = 2xz + yz$$

34. $\sqrt{6} + 3$:

The first step here is to distribute as normal:

$$\sqrt{3}(\sqrt{2} + \sqrt{3}) = \sqrt{3}\sqrt{2} + \sqrt{3}\sqrt{3}$$

However, it is best to then simplify this answer. When multiplying together two square roots we can simply multiply together the two numbers under a single square root sign (more on this later):

$$\sqrt{a}\sqrt{b} = \sqrt{ab}$$

Therefore, $\sqrt{3}\sqrt{2} = \sqrt{3 \times 2} = \sqrt{6}$. The second term $\sqrt{3}\sqrt{3}$ can be dealt with in the same manner, or we can note that it is 3 by definition of the square root. Adding these two terms together gives us the simplified answer.

35. 10.4rt − 52rs:

When distributing more complicated expressions, we should remember to multiply out numbers and combine any copies of the same variable. Here we have:

$$5.2r(2t - 10s) = (5.2r)(2t) - (5.2r)(10s)$$

Because $5.2 \times 2 = 10.4$ and $5.2 \times 10 = 52$, this simplifies to $10.4rt - 52rs$.

36. $-370x + 630$:

In this problem we must both distribute from the right and multiply out the numerical expressions. Multiplying a number by $10^2 = 100$ is the same as moving the decimal point two places to the right. Therefore

$$(-3.7x + 6.3)10^2 = -370x + 630$$

37. $6k^3l - 12k^2l^2$:

The first step in this computation is to distribute normally:

$$6k^2l \times k - 6k^2l \times 2l$$

In the first term, we then multiply together the k^2 and the k to get $6k^3l$, because $k^2 \times k = k^3$. For the second term, we need to multiply together the 6 and 2 as well as the two copies of l, so we have $6k^2l \times 2l = 12k^2l^2$. Putting it all together:

$$6k^2l \times k - 6k^2l \times 2l = 6k^3l - 12k^2l^2$$

38. $6n - 9$:

After distributing, we have:

$$-\sqrt{3}(-n\sqrt{12} + \sqrt{27}) = n\sqrt{3}\sqrt{12} - \sqrt{3}\sqrt{27}$$

We should then simplify the terms $\sqrt{3}\sqrt{12}$ and $\sqrt{3}\sqrt{27}$ using the fact that we can multiply under the square root sign (or more formally, $\sqrt{a}\sqrt{b} = \sqrt{ab}$).

The first term is $\sqrt{3}\sqrt{12} = \sqrt{36} = 6$. The second term involves the multiplication $3 \times 27 = 81$. The square root of 81 is 9.

$$-\sqrt{3}(-n\sqrt{12} + \sqrt{27}) = n\sqrt{3}\sqrt{12} - \sqrt{3}\sqrt{27} = 6n - 9$$

39. $d^3 - 2d^2 + d$:

Even though there are three terms inside the parentheses, distribution works exactly the same. Multiply d by every term in the parentheses.

$$d(d^2 - 2d + 1) = (d \times d^2) - (d \times 2d) + (d \times 1)$$

40. $x^3y^2z^2 + xy^3z^3 - x^2y^4z$:

The term xy^2z on the outside of the parentheses must be multiplied by each of the three terms inside the parentheses. We should then simplify the expression as much as possible.

Taking one term at a time, the first is $xy^2z \times x^2z = x^3y^2z^2$, because there are three factors of x, two factors of y, and two factors of z. Similarly, the second term is $xy^2z \times yz^2 = xy^3z^3$ and the third is $xy^2z \times (-xy^2) = -x^2y^4z$. Adding these three terms together gives us the final answer.

Chapter 2
of
Foundations of GMAT Math

Divisibility

In This Chapter...

Chapter 2:
Divisibility

In This Chapter:

- Divisibility rules
- How to find the factors of a number
- The connection between factors and divisibility
- How to answer questions on the GMAT related to divisibility

Divisibility

Divisibility has to do with **integers**. Recall that integers are the counting numbers (1, 2, 3, etc.), their opposites (−1, −2, −3, etc.), and 0. Integers have no decimals or fractions attached.

Also recall that most integer arithmetic is boring:

integer + integer = always an integer	$4 + 11 = 15$
integer − integer = always an integer	$-5 - 32 = -37$
integer × integer = always an integer	$14 \times 3 = 42$

However, when you divide an integer by another integer, sometimes you get an integer ($18 \div 3 = 6$), and sometimes you don't ($12 \div 8 = 1.5$).

If you get an integer out of the division, then the first number is **divisible** by the second. 18 is divisible by 3 because $18 \div 3 =$ an integer. On the other hand, 12 is *not* divisible by 8, because $12 \div 8$ is not an integer.

Memorize Divisibility Rules for Small Integers

These rules come in very handy. An integer is divisible by:

2 if the integer is even.

Any even number is, by definition, divisible by 2. Even numbers end in 0, 2, 4, 6 or 8.

3 if the sum of the integer's digits is a multiple of 3.

Take the number 147. Its digits are 1, 4 and 7. $1 + 4 + 7 = 12$, which is a multiple of 3. So 147 is divisible by 3.

5 if the integer ends in 0 or 5.

75 and 80 are divisible by 5, but 77 and 84 are not.

9 if the sum of the integer's digits is a multiple of 9.

This rule is very similar to the divisibility rule for 3. Take the number 144. $1 + 4 + 4 = 9$, so 144 is divisible by 9.

10 if the integer ends in 0.

8,730 is divisible by 10, but 8,753 is not.

Check Your Skills

1. Is 123,456,789 divisible by 2?
2. Is 732 divisible by 3?
3. Is 989 divisible by 9?

Answers can be found on page 83.

Factors Are Divisors

What positive integers is 6 divisible by? You only have 6 possibilities: 1, 2, 3, 4, 5, and 6.

$6 \div 1 = 6$ Any number divided by 1 equals itself, so an integer divided by 1 will always be an integer.

$6 \div 2 = 3$
$6 \div 3 = 2$ Note that these form a pair.

$6 \div 4 = 1.5$
$6 \div 5 = 1.2$ Not integers, so 6 is NOT divisible by 4 or by 5.

$6 \div 6 = 1$ Any number divided by itself equals 1, so an integer is always divisible by itself.

6 is divisible by 1, 2, 3 and 6. That means that 1, 2, 3 and 6 are **factors** of 6. Learn all the ways you might see this relationship expressed on the GMAT.

2 is a factor of 6	6 is a multiple of 2
2 is a divisor of 6	6 is divisible by 2
2 divides 6	6 goes into 6 (evenly) (without a remainder)

To find all the factors of a small number, use **factor pairs**. A factor pair of 60 is a pair of integers that multiplies together to 60. For instance, 15 and 4 are a factor pair of 60, because $15 \times 4 = 60$.

Here's an organized way to make a table of factor pairs of 60:

(1) Label 2 columns "Small" and "Large."

(2) Start with 1 in the small column and 60 in the large column. (The first set of factor pairs will always be 1 and the number itself)

(3) The next number after 1 is 2. Since 2 is a factor of 60, then write "2" underneath the "1" in your table. Divide 60 by 2 to find 2's "sibling" in the pair: $60 \div 2 = 30$. Write "30" in the large column.

(4) Repeat this process until the numbers in the small and the large columns run into each other. In this case, you find that 6 and 10 are a factor pair. But 7, 8 and 9 are not factors of 60. The next number after 9 is 10, which appears in the large column, so you can stop.

2

If you…	Then you…	Like this:	
		Small	Large
Want all the factors of 60	Make a table of factor pairs, starting with 1 and 60	1	60
		2	30
		3	20
		4	15
		5	12
		6	10

Check Your Skills

4. Find all the factors of 90.
5. Find all the factors of 72.
6. Find all the factors of 105.
7. Find all the factors of 120.

Answers can be found on pages 83–84.

Prime Number: Only Divisible by 1 and Itself

What is 7 divisible by? The only possibilities are the positive integers less than or equal to 7.

$7 \div 1 = 7$ Every number is divisible by 1—no surprise there!

$7 \div 2 = 3.5$
$7 \div 3 = 2.33\ldots$
$7 \div 4 = 1.75$ 7 is not divisible by *any* integer
$7 \div 5 = 1.4$ besides 1 and itself
$7 \div 6 = 1.16\ldots$

$7 \div 7 = 1$ Every number is divisible by itself—boring!

So 7 only has two factors—1 and itself. Numbers that only have 2 factors are called **prime numbers.** Primes are extremely important in any question about divisibility.

Know the primes less than 20 cold: they are 2, 3, 5, 7, 11, 13, 17 and 19. Note that 1 is not prime. Also, 2 is the only even prime number. Every other even number has another factor besides 1 and itself: namely, 2.

Every positive integer can be placed into one of two categories—prime or not prime.

MANHATTAN
GMAT

Check Your Skills

8. List all the prime numbers between 20 and 50.

Answers can be found on page 84.

Prime Factorization: All the Primes on the Tree

Take another look at the factor pairs of 60. It had 12 factors and 6 factor pairs.

$60 = 1 \times 60$ Always the first factor pair—boring!

and 2×30

and 3×20

and 4×15 5 other factor pairs—interesting!

and 5×12 Let's look at these in a little more detail.

and 6×10

Consider 4×15. One way to think about this pair is that 60 breaks down into 4 and 15. Use a **factor tree** to show this relationship.

Keep going. Neither 4 nor 15 is prime, so they both have factor pairs that you might find interesting. 4 breaks down into 2×2, and 15 breaks down into 3×5:

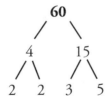

Can you break it down any further? Not with interesting factor pairs. $2 = 2 \times 1$, for instance, but that's nothing new. The numbers you have reached (2, 2, 3 and 5) are all primes.

When you find a prime factor, that branch on the factor tree has reached the end. Circle prime numbers as you go, as if they were fruit on the tree. The factor tree for 60 looks like this:

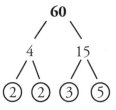

After you break down 60 into 4 and 15, and then break 4 and 15 down further, you end up with
$60 = 2 \times 2 \times 3 \times 5$.

What if you start with a different factor pair of 60? Create a factor tree for 60 in which the first breakdown you make is 6×10.

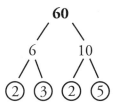

According to this factor tree $60 = 2 \times 3 \times 2 \times 5$. These are the same primes as before (though in a different order). Any way you break down 60, you end up with the same prime factors: two 2's, one 3 and
one 5. $2 \times 2 \times 3 \times 5$ is the **prime factorization** of 60.

Prime factors are the DNA of a number. Every number has a unique prime factorization. 60 is the only
number that can be written as $2 \times 2 \times 3 \times 5$.

Your first instinct on divisibility problems should be to **break numbers down to their prime factors.**
A factor tree is the best way to find a prime factorization.

For large numbers such as 630, generally **start with the smallest prime factors** and work your way up.
Use your divisibility rules!

Start by finding the smallest prime factor of 630. Check 2 first. 630 is even, so it is divisible by 2. 630
divided by 2 is 315, so your first breakdown of 630 is into 2 and 315.

Now you still need to factor 315. It's not even, so it's not divisible by 2. Check 3 by adding up the digits
of 315. $3 + 1 + 5 = 9$, which is a multiple of 3, so 315 is divisible by 3. 315 divided by 3 is 105, so your
factor tree now looks like this:

MANHATTAN
GMAT

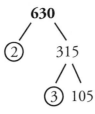

105 might still be divisible by another 3. 1 + 0 + 5 = 6, so 105 is divisible by 3. 105 ÷ 3 = 35, so your tree now looks like this:

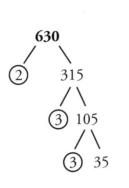

35 is not divisible by 3 (3 + 5 = 8, which is not a multiple of 3), so the next number to try is 5. 35 ends in a 5, so it is divisible by 5. 35 ÷ 5 = 7, so your tree now looks like this:

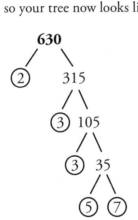

Every number on the tree has now been broken down as far as it can go. The prime factorization of 630 is 2 × 3 × 3 × 5 × 7.

Alternatively, you could have split 630 into 63 and 10, since it's easy to see that 630 is divisible by 10. Then you would proceed from there, breaking 10 into 2 and 5 and breaking 63 into 7 and 9 (which is 3 and 3). As you practice, you'll spot shortcuts.

Either way will get you to the same set of prime factors.

2

If you...	Then you...	Like this:
Want the prime factorization of 96	Break 96 down to primes using a tree	96 / 2 48

Check Your Skills

9. Find the prime factorization of 90.
10. Find the prime factorization of 72.
11. Find the prime factorization of 105.
12. Find the prime factorization of 120.

Answers can be found on pages 84–85.

Every Number is Divisible by the Factors of Its Factors

If *a* is divisible by *b*, and *b* is divisible by *c*, then *a* is divisible by *c* as well. For instance, 12 is divisible by 6, and 6 is divisible by 3. So then 12 is divisible by 3 as well.

This **factor foundation rule** also works in reverse to a certain extent. If *d* is divisible by two different *primes e* and *f*, then *d* is also divisible by *e* × *f*. In other words, if 20 is divisible by 2 and by 5, then 20 is also divisible by 2 × 5 (10).

Divisibility travels up and down the factor tree. Consider the factor tree of 150.

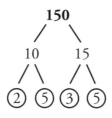

150 is divisible by 10 and by 15, so 150 is also divisible by everything that 10 and 15 are divisible by. For instance, 10 is divisible by 2 and 5, so 150 is also divisible by 2 and 5. Taken all together, the prime factorization of 150 is 2 × 3 × 5 × 5. Represent that information like this:

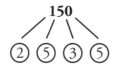

2

Prime factors are building blocks. In the case of 150, you have one 2, one 3 and two 5's at our disposal to build other factors of 150. In the first example, you went down the tree —from 150 down to 10 and 15, and then down again to 2, 5, 3 and 5. But you can also build upwards, starting with our four building blocks. For instance, $2 \times 3 = 6$, and $5 \times 5 = 25$, so your tree could also look like this:

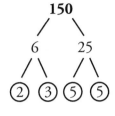

(Even though 5 and 5 are not different primes, 5 appears twice on 150's tree. So you are allowed to multiply those two 5's together to produce another factor of 150, namely 25.)

The tree above isn't even the only other possibility. Here are more:

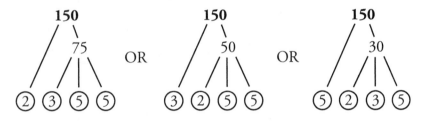

Beginning with four prime factors of 150 (2, 3, 5 and 5), you build different factors by multiplying 2, 3 or even all 4 of those primes together in different combinations. All of the factors of a number (except for 1) can be built with different combinations of its prime factors.

Factors: Built out of Primes

Take one more look at the number 60 and its factors:. Consider the prime factorization of each factor.

	Small	Large	
1	1	60	$2 \times 2 \times 3 \times 5$
2	2	30	$2 \times 3 \times 5$
3	3	20	$2 \times 2 \times 5$
2×2	4	15	3×5
5	5	12	$2 \times 2 \times 3$
2×3	6	10	2×5

All the factors of 60 (except 1) are different combinations of the prime factors of 60. To say this another way, every factor of a number (again, except 1) can be expressed as the product of a set of its prime factors. This relationship between factors and prime factors is true of every number.

To recap what you've learned so far:

1. If a is divisible by b, and b is divisible by c, then a is divisible by c as well. For instance, 100 is divisible by 20, and 20 is divisible by 4, so 100 is divisible by 4 as well.

2. If d has e and f as prime factors, d is also divisible by $e \times f$. For instance, 90 is divisible by 5 and by 3, so 90 is also divisible by $5 \times 3 = 15$. You can let e and f be the same prime, as long as there are at least 2 copies of that prime in d's factor tree.

3. Every factor of a number (except 1) is the product of a different combination of that number's prime factors. For example, $30 = 2 \times 3 \times 5$. The factors of 30 are 1, 2, 3, 5, 6 (2×3), 10 (2×5), 15 (3×5), and 30 ($2 \times 3 \times 5$).

4. To find all the factors of a number in a methodical way, set up a factor pairs table.

5. To find all the prime factors of a number, use a factor tree. With larger numbers, start with the smallest primes and work your way up to larger primes.

If you…	Then you…	Like this:
Want all the factors of 96	Break 96 down to primes, then construct all the factors out of the prime factors of 96	$96 = 2 \times 2 \times 2 \times 2 \times 2 \times 3$ So one factor of 96 is $2 \times 3 = 6$, etc.

Check Your Skills

13. The prime factorization of a number is 3×5. What is the number and what are all its factors?
14. The prime factorization of a number is $2 \times 5 \times 7$. What is the number and what are all its factors?
15. The prime factorization of a number is $2 \times 3 \times 13$. What is the number and what are all its factors?

Answers can be found on pages 85–86.

Factor Tree of A Variable: Contains Unknowns

Say that you are told some unknown positive number x is divisible by 6. You can represent this fact on paper in several different ways. For instance, you could write "x = multiple of 6" or "$x = 6 \times$ an integer."

You could also represent the information with a factor tree. Since the top of the tree is a variable, add in a branch to represent what you *don't* know about the variable. Label this branch with a question mark (?), three dots (...), or something to remind yourself that you have *incomplete* information about x.

2

What *else* do we know about *x*? What can you definitely say about *x* right now?

Take a look at these three statements. For each statement, decide whether it *must* be true, whether it *could* be true, or whether it *cannot* be true.

     I.   *x* is divisible by 3

     II.   *x* is even

     III   *x* is divisible by 12

Begin with statement I—*x* is divisible by 3. Think about the multiples of 6. If *x* is divisible by 6, then *x* is a multiple of 6. List out the first several multiples of 6 to see whether they're divisible by 3.

$$
\begin{array}{l}
\text{\textit{x} is a number} \\
\text{on this list}
\end{array}
\left\{
\begin{array}{ll}
6 & 6 \div 3 = 2 \\
12 & 12 \div 3 = 4 \\
18 & 18 \div 3 = 6 \\
24 & 24 \div 3 = 8 \\
\dots & \dots
\end{array}
\right\}
\begin{array}{l}
\text{All of these numbers are} \\
\text{also divisible by 3.}
\end{array}
$$

At this point, you can be fairly certain that *x* is divisible by 3. In divisibility problems (and elsewhere), isting out possible values of a variable help you wrap your head around a question or a pattern.

But you can easily *prove* that *x* is divisible by 3. Just make one modification to the tree.

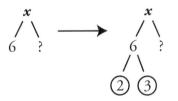

The purpose of the tree is to break integers down into primes, which are the building blocks of larger integers. Now that the factor tree is broken down as far as it will go, apply the factor foundation rule. *x* is divisible by 6, and 6 is divisible by 3, so you can definitively say that *x* is divisible by 3.

Statement II says *x* is even. Must that be true? Return to your factor tree.

2

Again, make use of the factor foundation rule—6 is divisible by 2, so you know that *x* is divisible by 2 as well. Since *x* is divisible by 2, *x* is even.

Statement III says *x* is divisible by 12. Compare the factor tree of *x* with the factor tree of 12.

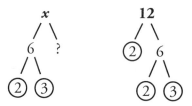

What would you have to know about *x* to guarantee that it is divisible by 12?

12 is 2 × 2 × 3. 12's building blocks are two 2's and a 3. To guarantee that *x* is divisible by 12, you need to know for sure that *x* has two 2's and one 3 among its prime factors. That is, *x* would have to be divisible by everything that 12 is divisible by.

Looking at the factor tree for *x*, you see a 3 but only one 2. So you can't claim that x *must be* divisible by 12. But *could x* be divisible by 12?

Consider the question mark on *x*'s factor tree. That question mark is there to remind you that you *don't* know everything about *x*. After all, *x could* have other prime factors. If one of those unknown factors were another 2, your tree would look like this:

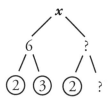

If an unknown factor were a 2, then *x* would indeed be divisible by 12. So *x could* be divisible by 12.

To confirm this thinking, list out a few multiples of 6 and check whether they are divisible by 12.

Some of the possible values of *x* are divisible by 12, and some aren't. *x could* be divisible by 12.

$$\left.\begin{array}{ll}
6 & 6 \div 12 = 0.5 \\
12 & 12 \div 12 = 1 \\
18 & 18 \div 12 = 1.5 \\
24 & 24 \div 12 = 2 \\
\dots & \dots
\end{array}\right\}$$

x is a number on this list

Some, but not all, of these numbers are also divisible by 12.

If you…	Then you…	Like this:
Use a factor tree with a variable on top	Put in a question mark (or something similar) to remind yourself what you *don't* know	$\begin{array}{c} x \\ / \ \backslash \\ 6 \quad ? \end{array}$

Check Your Skills

For each question, the following is true: *x* is divisible by 24. Determine whether each statement below *must* be true, *could* be true, or *cannot* be true.

16. *x* is divisible by 6
17. *x* is divisible by 9
18. *x* is divisible by 8

Answers can be found on pages 86–87.

Factors of X With No Common Primes: Combine

Decide whether each statement *must* be true, *could* be true, or *cannot* be true.

   x is divisible by 3 and by 10.

   I. *x* is divisible by 2

   II. *x* is divisible by 15

   III. *x* is divisible by 45

First, create two factor trees to represent the given information.

Why not write them together at once? "*x* is divisible by 3" is a different fact from "*x* is divisible by 10." **Initially, always write two given facts about a variable separately.** That way, you can think carefully about how to combine those facts.

2

Statement I says that x is divisible by 2. To use the factor foundation rule, finish your trees:

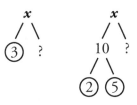

Now you can decide whether statement I is true. x is divisible by 10, and 10 is divisible by 2, so x is definitely divisible by 2. Statement I *must* be true.

Statement II is more difficult. Study the trees. Neither one gives you complete information about x, but you know for certain that x is divisible by 3 and that x is divisible by 2 and by 5. These primes are all different, because the original factors 3 and 10 have no primes in common. **When the primes from two trees are all different, you can put all the primes on one tree:**

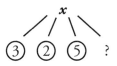

Return to the statement: "x is divisible by 15." Can you guarantee this? If x definitely has all the prime factors that 15 has, then you can guarantee that x is divisible by 15.

The prime factors of 15 are 3 and 5. Being divisible by 15 is the same as being divisible by 3 and by 5.

Look at the combined factor tree. x has both a 3 and a 5, so x is definitely divisible by 15. Statement II *must* be true.

You can look at this issue more visually. Prime factors are building blocks of all other factors (except 1). If you know that x is divisible by 3, 2, and 5, you can combine these primes to form other definite factors of x.

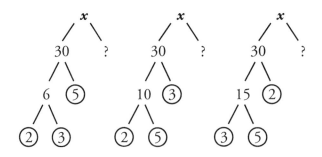

You get 15 on the third tree. Notice what all three trees have in common. No matter how you combine the prime factors, each tree ultimately leads to 30, which is $2 \times 3 \times 5$.

You know that x is divisible by 30. And if x is divisible by 30, it is also divisible by everything 30 is divisible by. 15 is a factor of 30, so x must be divisible by 15. Statement II *must* be true.

On the test, don't draw out the three trees above. Once you get to 2, 3, and 5, realize that you can form other definite factors of x from these primes, such as 15 (from the 3 and the 5).

Statement III says that x is divisible by 45. What do you need to know in order to claim that x is divisible by 45? Build a factor tree of 45:

45 is divisible by 3, 3 and 5. For x to be divisible by 45, you need to know that x has all the same prime factors. Does it?

45 has one 5 and two 3's. You know that x has a 5, but you only *know* that x has one 3. Since you don't know whether x has the second 3 that you want, you can't say for certain whether x is divisible by 45. x *could* be divisible by 45, but you don't know what the question mark contains. If it contains a 3, then x is divisible by 45. If not, then no. Statement III *could* be true.

If you…	Then you…	Like this:
Know two factors of x that have no primes in common	Combine the two trees into one	

Check Your Skills

For each question, the following is true: x is divisible by 28 and by 15. Determine whether each statement below *must* be true, *could* be true, or *cannot* be true.

19. x is divisible by 14.
20. x is divisible by 20.
21. x is divisible by 24.

Answers can be found on pages 87–88.

Factors of X with Primes in Common: Combine to LCM

In the last section, you were told that x was divisible by 3 and by 10, and you figured out the consequences. For instance, you could conclude that x was divisible by 30, the product of 3 and 10.

Now consider a slightly different situation. Let's say that x is divisible by 6 and by 9. Is x divisible by 54, the product of 6 and 9?

Here is the question in tree form:

Given: Question: do we necessarily get this tree?

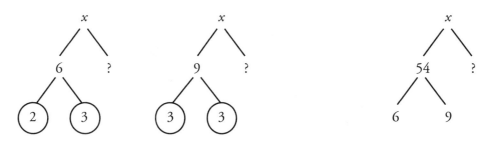

Be very careful. When you were told that x was divisible by 3 and by 10, you had a simpler situation, because 3 and 10 do not share any prime factors. So it was easier to combine the two pieces of information and arrive at conclusions.

Now, however, 6 and 9 share a prime factor: namely, 3. How does this fact change things?

To answer that question, we have to talk about the **least common multiple,** or **LCM.** The least common multiple of two numbers, say *A* and *B*, is the smallest number that is a multiple of both *A* and *B*.

What is the LCM of 3 and 10? Consider the multiples of each number.

Multiples of 3		Multiples of 10
3	18	10
6	21	20
9	24	**30**
12	27	40
15	**30**	50

Notice that the smallest number that appears on both lists is 30. This is the LCM of 3 and 10.

Here's why the LCM is important. **If x is divisible by A and by B, then x is divisible by the LCM of A and B, no matter what.**

For instance, if you are told that x is divisible by 3 and by 10, then you can conclude that x is definitely divisible by the LCM of 3 and 10, which equals 30.

The same principle holds true for the new example, even though 6 and 9 share a common factor. If x is divisible by 6 and 9, then we can conclude that x is definitely divisible by the LCM of 6 and 9.

To find the LCM of 6 and 9, list the multiples of each number and look for the first number on both lists.

Multiples of 6	Multiples of 9
6	9
12	**18**
18	27
24	

The LCM of 6 and 9 is 18. This means that if you know that x is divisible by 6 and by 9, you can conclude that x is divisible by 18.

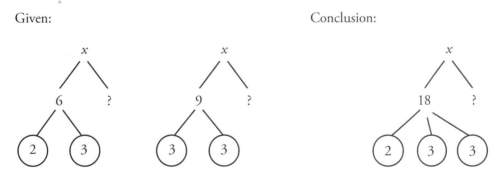

You do *not* know whether x is divisible by 54. It might be. But it doesn't have to be. So the answer to the original question (*is x divisible by 54?*) is "Maybe."

You may have noticed that 6 contains one 3 and that 9 contains two 3's, for a total of three 3's on the left side of the previous picture. Yet 18 contains only *two* 3's. What happened to the extra 3?

What happened is that *x* only needs *two* 3's (as well as a 2) to guarantee divisibility by 6 and by 9. The third 3 is extraneous. **When you combine two factor trees of *x* that contain overlapping primes, drop the overlap.** You're already covered.

Here's another way to think of the situation.

Is a number divisible by 18 also divisible by 6? Sure, because 6 goes into 18.

Is a number divisible by 18 also divisible by 9? Sure, because 9 goes into 18.

So, if you know both facts, all you can guarantee in *x*'s tree is 18, which has just *two* 3's and a 2.

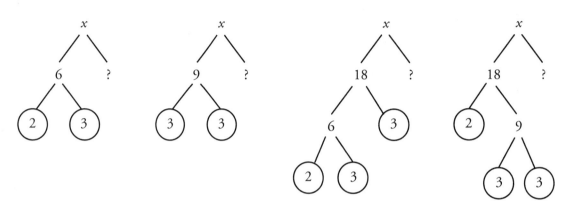

The trees on the left provide information about how many of each kind of prime factors appear in *x*. Those pieces of information can overlap.

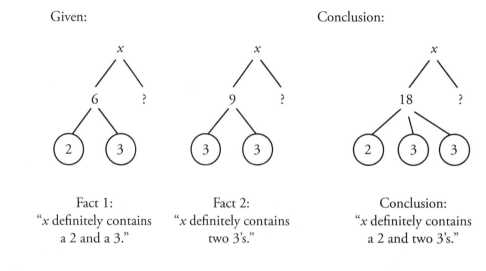

Fact 1:	Fact 2:	Conclusion:
"*x* definitely contains a 2 and a 3."	"*x* definitely contains two 3's."	"*x* definitely contains a 2 and two 3's."

The two given facts are like statements given by two witnesses. The witnesses aren't lying, but they could have seen the same things. **Don't double-count the evidence.** All you can prove about *x* is that it contains a 2 and *two* 3's. The two witnesses could have seen the *same* 3.

2

When two numbers don't share prime factors, their LCM is just their product.

3 and 10 don't share any prime factors, so their LCM = 3 × 10 = 30.

However, **when two numbers share prime factors, their LCM will be *smaller* than their product.**

6 and 9 share prime factors, so their LCM is not 6 × 9 = 54. In fact, their LCM (18) is smaller than 54.

The way we have found the LCM of two numbers is to list the two sets of multiples and find the smallest number on both lists. That method works great for small numbers. A more general way to think of the LCM is this: the LCM of *A* and *B* contains only as many of a prime factor as you see it appear in either *A* or *B* separately.

Consider the LCM of 6 and 9.

How many 2's does the LCM contain? 6 has one 2. 9 has no 2's, so the LCM has to have one 2.

How many 3's does the LCM contain? 6 has one 3. 9 has two 3's, so the LCM has to have two 3's.

Putting all that together, you know that the LCM of 6 and 9 has one 2 and two 3's, so the LCM = 2 × 3 × 3 = 18. That's a long way to find the LCM in this case, but for more complicated situations, it's definitely faster.

Try another question.

If *x* is divisible by 8, 12, and 45, what is the largest number that *x* must be divisible by?

First, draw three separate trees for the given information:

Given:

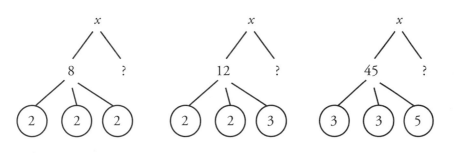

The question is equivalent to this: *what is the LCM of 8, 12, and 45?* You could find this number by listing all the multiples of 8, 12, and 45 and looking for the first number on all 3 lists. That would take some time. Instead, find the LCM by counting up prime factors that you *know* are in *x*.

2

Start with 2. How many 2's are guaranteed to be in *x*? There are three 2's in 8, two 2's in 12, and none in 45. To cover all the bases, there must be at least three 2's in *x*.

Take 3 next. Since 45 has two 3's, the most in any tree above, you know that *x* must contain at least two 3's. Finally, you know that *x* must have at least one 5 because of the 45. So here's the picture:

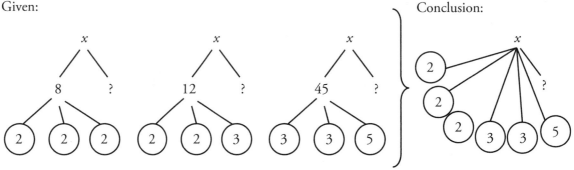

Now calculate the LCM:

$$2 \times 2 \times 2 \times 3 \times 3 \times 5 = 8 \times 45 = 360.$$

360 is the LCM of 8, 12, and 45. It is also the largest number that you know *x* is divisible by.

One final note: if the facts are about *different* variables (*x* and *y*), then the facts don't overlap.

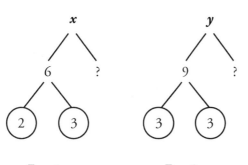 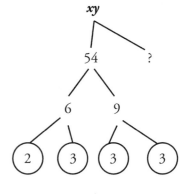

The two witnesses are looking at different crime scenes, so count up everything you see across all the trees.

If you…	Then you…	Like this:
Know two factors of *x* that have primes in common	Combine the two trees into one, eliminating the overlap = Know only that *x* is divisible by the LCM of the factors	*x* is divisible by 6 *x* is divisible by 9 becomes *x* is divisible by 18, the LCM of 6 and 9

Check Your Skills

For each question, the following is true: *x* is divisible by 6 and by 14. Determine whether each statement below *must* be true, *could* be true, or *cannot* be true.

22. *x* is divisible by 42.
23. *x* is divisible by 84.

Answers can be found on page 88.

Check Your Skills Answer Key:

1.   Is 123,456,789 divisible by 2?

        123,456,789 is an odd number, because it ends in 9. So 123,456,789 is not divisible by 2.

2.   Is 732 divisible by 3?

        The digits of 732 add up to a multiple of 3 (7 + 3 + 2 = 12). 732 is divisible by 3.

3.   Is 989 divisible by 9?

        The digits of 989 do not add up to a multiple of 9 (9 + 8 + 9 = 26). 989 is not divisible by 9.

4.   Find all the factors of 90.

Small	Large
1	90
2	45
3	30
5	18
6	15
9	10

5.   Find all the factors of 72.

Small	Large
1	72
2	36
3	24
4	18
6	12
8	9

6.   Find all the factors of 105.

Small	Large
1	105
3	35
5	21
7	15

2

7.   Find all the factors of 120.

Small	Large
1	120
2	60
3	40
4	30
5	24
6	20
8	15
10	12

8.   List all the prime numbers between 20 and 50.

      23, 29, 31, 37, 41, 43, and 47.

9.   Find the prime factorization of 90.

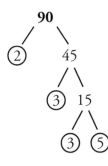

10.   Find the prime factorization of 72.

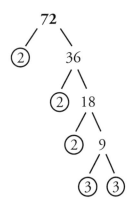

11.   Find the prime factorization of 105.

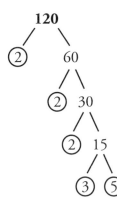

12.   Find the prime factorization of 120.

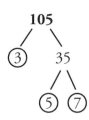

13.   The prime factorization of a number is 3×5. What is the number and what are all its factors?

$3 \times 5 = 15$

Small	Large
1	15
3	5

14.   The prime factorization of a number is $2 \times 5 \times 7$. What is the number and what are all its factors?

$2 \times 5 \times 7 = 70$

	Small	Large	
1	1	70	$2 \times 5 \times 7$
2	2	35	5×7
5	5	14	2×7
7	7	10	2×5

2

15.   The prime factorization of a number is 2 × 3 × 13. What is the number and what are all its factors?

2 × 3 × 13 = 78

	Small	Large	
1	1	78	2 × 3 × 13
2	2	39	3 × 13
3	3	26	2 × 13
2 × 3	6	13	13

For questions 16–18, x is divisible by 24.

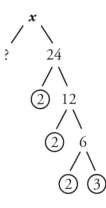

16. x is divisible by 6?

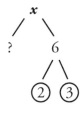

For x to be divisible by 6, we need to know that it contains the same prime factors as 6. 6 contains a 2 and a 3. x also contains a 2 and a 3, therefore x must be divisible by 6.

17. x is divisible by 9?

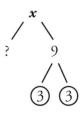

For x to be divisible by 9, we need to know that it contains the same prime factors as 9. 9 contains two 3's. x only contains one 3 that we know of. But the question mark means x may have other prime factors, and may contain another 3. For this reason, x could be divisible by 9.

18. x is divisible by 8?

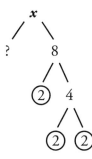

For x to be divisible by 8, we need to know that it contains the same prime factors as 8. 8 contains three 2's. x also contains three 2's, therefore x *must* be divisible by 8.

For questions 19–21, x is divisible by 28 and by 15.

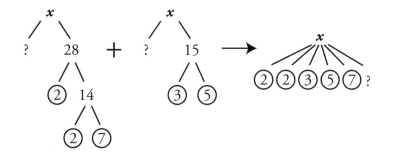

19. x is divisible by 14?

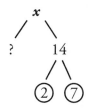

For x to be divisible by 14, we need to know that it contains the same prime factors as 14. 14 contains a 2 and a 7. x also contains a 2 and a 7, therefore x must be divisible by 14.

20. *x* is divisible by 20?

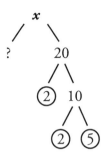

For *x* to be divisible by 20, we need to know that it contains the same prime factors as 20. 20 contains two 2's and a 5. *x* also contains two 2's and a 5, therefore x must be divisible by 20.

21. *x* is divisible by 24?

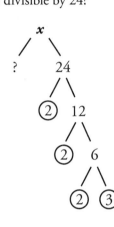

For *x* to be divisible by 24, we need to know that it contains the same prime factors as 24. 24 contains three 2's and a 3. *x* contains a 3, but only two 2's that we know of. But the question mark means *x* may have other prime factors, and may contain another 2. For this reason, *x* could be divisible by 24.

For questions 22–23, *x* is divisible by 6 and by 14.

22. *x* is divisible by 42?

The LCM of 6 and 14 is 42. We can guarantee that *x* is divisible by the LCM. x must be divisible by 42.

23. *x* is divisible by 84?

6 and 14 have an overlapping prime factor (2). Thus, we cannot simply combine 6 and 14 to get 84. *x* could be divisible by 84, but does not have to be.

Chapter Review: Drill Sets

Drill 1

Drill 1

1. Is 4,005 divisible by 5?
2. Does 51 have any factors besides 1 and itself?
3. $x = 20$
The prime factors of x are:
The factors of x are:
4. If 33 is a factor of 594, is 11 a factor of 594?
5. Will 15 divide 4,725?

Drill 2

6. Is 123 divisible by 3?
7. Does 23 have any factors besides 1 and itself?
8. $x = 100$
The prime factors of x are:
The factors of x are:
9. If 2,499 is divisible by 147, is 2,499 divisible by 49?
10. Name three positive multiples of 12 that are less than 50.

Drill 3

11. Is 285,284,901 divisible by 10?
12. Is 539,105 prime?
13. $x = 42$
The prime factors of x are:
The factors of x are:
14. Find four even divisors of 84.
15. What are the prime factors of 30×49?

Drill 4

16. Is 9,108 divisible by 9 and/or by 2?
17. Is 937,184 prime?
18. $x = 39$
The prime factors of x are:
The factors of x are:

19. How many more prime factors does the product of 28×75 have than the product of 14×25?

Drill 5

20. Is 43,360 divisible by 5 and/or by 3?
21. Is 81,063 prime?
22. $x = 37$
The prime factors of x are:
The factors of x are:
23. What are the two largest odd factors of 90?

Drill 6

24. Determine which of the following numbers are prime numbers. Remember, you only need to find one factor other than the number itself to prove that the number is not prime.

2	3	5	6
7	9	10	15
17	21	27	29
31	33	258	303
655	786	1,023	1,325

Drill 7

25. If x is divisible by 33, what other numbers is x divisible by?
26. The prime factorization of a number is $3 \times 3 \times 7$. What is the number and what are all its factors?
27. If x is divisible by 8 and by 3, is x also divisible by 12?
28. If $7x$ is a multiple of 210, must x be a multiple of 12?
29. If integer a is not a multiple of 30, but ab is, what is the smallest possible value of integer b?

Drill 8

30. If 40 is a factor of x, what other numbers are factors of x?
31. The only prime factors of a number are 5 and 17. What is the number and what are all its factors?

2

32. 5 and 6 are factors of x. Is x divisible by 15?

33. If q is divisible by 2, 6, 9, 12, 15, & 30, is q divisible by 8?

34. If p is a prime number, and q is a non-prime integer, what are the minimum and maximum numbers of factors they can have in common?

Drill 9

35. If 64 divides n, what other divisors does n have?

36. The prime factorization of a number is $2 \times 2 \times 3 \times 11$. What is the number and what are all its factors?

37. 14 and 3 divide n. Is 12 a factor of n?

38. Positive integers a and b both have exactly four factors. If a is a one-digit number and $b = a + 9$, $a =$

39. If n is the product of 2, 3, and a two-digit prime number, how many of its factors are greater than 6?

Drill 10

40. If n is a multiple of both 21 and 10, is 30 a divisor of n?

41. 4, 21, and 55 are factors of n. Does 154 divide n?

42. If n is divisible by 196 and by 15, is 270 a factor of n?

Drill Sets Solutions

Drill 1

1. **Yes:** 4,005 ends in 5, so it is divisible by 5.
2. **Yes:** The digits of 51 add up to a multiple of 3 (5 + 1 = 6), so 3 is a factor of 51.
3. **Prime factors: 2, 2, 5.**
Factors: 1, 2, 4, 5, 10, 20
The prime factors of *x* are:

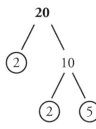

The factors of *x* are:

Small	Large
1	20
2	10
4	5

4. **Yes:** We could divide 594 by 11 to determine divisibility, but it is faster to use the Factor Foundation rule. The Factor Foundation rule states that if 594 is divisible by 33, 594 will also be divisible by all of the factors of 33. 11 is a factor of 33 (33 = 11 × 3); therefore, 594 is also divisible by 11.
5. **Yes:** In order to be divisible by 15, a number must be divisible by both 3 and 5, the prime factors that make up 15. Based on the rules of divisibility, because 4,725 ends in a 5, it is divisible by 5. The digits of 4,725 add to 18 (4 + 7 + 2 + 5 = 18), and 18 is divisible by 3—so 4,725 is divisible by 3. Because 4,725 is divisible by 3 and 5, it is also divisible by 15.

Drill 2

6. **Yes:** The digits of 123 add up to a multiple of 3 (1 + 2 + 3 = 6), so 123 is divisible by 3.
7. **No:** 23 is a prime number. It has no factors besides 1 and itself.

8. **Prime factors: 2, 2, 5, 5**
Factors: 1, 2, 4, 5, 10, 20, 25, 50, 100
The prime factors of *x* are: **100**

The factors of *x* are:

Small	Large
1	100
2	50
4	25
5	20
10	10

9. **Yes:** The Factor Foundation rule is helpful in this question. The problem states that 2,499 is divisible by 147. The Factor Foundation rule states that if 2,499 is divisible by 147, 2,499 will also be divisible by all of the factors of 147. 147 is divisible by 49 (147/49 = 3). Since 49 is a factor of 147, 2,499 is also divisible by 49.

10. **12, 24, 36, and 48:** In order to generate multiples of 12 that are less than 50, we can multiply 12 by small integers.

$12 \times 1 = 12$
$12 \times 2 = 24$
$12 \times 3 = 36$
$12 \times 4 = 48$

All other positive multiples of 12 are larger than 50.

Drill 3

11. **No:** 285,284,901 ends in a 1, not a 0. It is not divisible by 10.
12. **No:** 539,105 ends in a 5, so 5 is a factor of 539,105. So are 1 and 539,105. Prime numbers have only two factors, so 539,105 is not prime.

13. **Prime factors: 2, 3, 7**
Factors: 1, 2, 3, 6, 7, 14, 21, 42

The prime factors of *x* are:

The factors of x are:

Small	Large
1	42
2	21
3	14
6	7

14. **2, 4, 6, 12, 14, 28, 42, and 84:** The first step in identifying the divisors, or factors, is breaking 84 down into its prime factors. The prime factors of 84 are 2, 2, 3, and 7. In other words, $2 \times 2 \times 3 \times 7 = 84$. The prime factors can be used to build all of the factors of 84. Because the question asks for even factors, only factors that are built with at least one 2 will be correct.

Even divisors can be built using one 2.

$2; 2 \times 3 = 6; 2 \times 7 = 14; 2 \times 3 \times 7 = 42$

Even divisors can also be built using both the twos that are prime factors of 84.

$2 \times 2 = 4; 2 \times 2 \times 3 = 12; 2 \times 2 \times 7 = 28; 2 \times 2 \times 3 \times 7 = 84$

The even divisors of 84 are 2, 4, 6, 12, 14, 28, 42, and 84.

Alternatively, you could make a factor pair table to see which factors are even:

Small	Large
1	84
2	42
3	28
4	21
6	14
7	12

15. **2, 3, 5, 7, and 7:** While we could multiply the numbers together to find the prime factors, there is a faster way. The prime factors of the product of 30 and 49 will consist of the prime factors of 30 and the prime factors of 49. The prime factors of 30 are 2, 3, and 5. The prime factors of 49 are 7 and 7. Therefore, the prime factors of 30×49 are 2, 3, 5, 7, and 7.

Drill 4

16. **9,108 is divisible by 9 AND by 2:** The digits of 9,108 add up to a multiple of 9 ($9 + 1 + 0 + 8 = 18$), so it is a multiple of 9. 9,108 ends in 8, so it is even, which means it is divisible by 2.
17. **No:** 937,184 ends in 4, which means it's even. Therefore, it's divisible by 2. It's also divisible by 1 and itself. Prime numbers have only two factors, so 937,184 is not prime.

2

18. **Primer factors: 3, 13**
Factors: 1, 3, 13, 39

The prime factors of x are:

39

③   ⑬

The factors of x are:

Small	Large
1	39
3	13

19. **Two:** We could multiply these products out or identify all of the prime factors of each number, but there is a more efficient way. Because the question is asking us to make a comparison, we can just focus on the *differences* between the two products we are comparing.

$28 = 14 \times 2$ (that is, 28 contains everything that 14 contains, and 28 also has one additional factor of 2)

$75 = 25 \times 3$ (that is, 75 contains everything that 25 contains, and 75 also has one additional factor of 3)

Therefore, the only additional prime factors in 28×75 are the 2 in 28 and the 3 in 75. Thus, the first product has two more prime factors than the second product.

Drill 5

20. **43,360 is divisible by 5 but is NOT divisible by 3:** 43,360 ends in 0, so it is divisible by 5. The digits of 43,360 do not add up to a multiple of 3 ($4 + 3 + 3 + 6 + 0 = 16$) so it is not divisible by 3.

21. **No:** The digits of 81,063 add up to a multiple of 3 ($8 + 1 + 0 + 6 + 3 = 18$), so 3 is a factor of 81,063. 1 and 81,063 are also factors of 81,063. Prime numbers have only two factors, so 81,063 is not prime.

22. **Prime factors: 37**
Factors: 1, 37

Small	Large
1	37

23. **45, 15:** We can break 90 down into its factor pairs.

Small	Large
1	90
2	**45**
3	30
5	18
6	**15**
9	10

Looking at the table, we can see that 45 and 15 are the two largest odd factors of 90.

Drill 6

24. **Prime numbers: 2, 3, 5, 7, 17, 29, 31**

The numbers in bold below are prime numbers.

2	**3**	**5**	6
7	9	10	15
17	21	27	**29**
31	33	258	303
655	786	1,023	1,325

Not prime: All of the even numbers other than 2 (6, 10, 258, 786), since they are divisible by 2.

All of the remaining multiples of 5 (15, 655, 1,325)

All of the remaining numbers whose digits add up to a multiple of 3, since they are divisible by 3, by definition: 9, 21 (digits add to 3), 27 (digits add to 9), 33 (digits add to 6), 303 (digits add to 6), and 1,023 (digits add to 6). All of these numbers are divisible by 3.

Drill 7

25. **1, 3, 11, 33:** If x is divisible by 33, then x is also divisible by everything 33 is divisible by. The factors of 33 are:

Small	Large
1	33
3	11

2

26. **63: The factors are 1, 3, 7, 9, 21, and 63.** $3 \times 3 \times 7 = 63$

Small	Large
1	63
3	21
7	9

27. **Yes:**

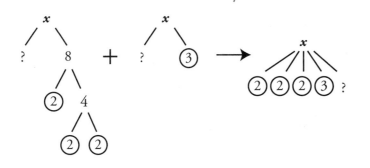

For x to be divisible by 12, we need to know that it contains all of the prime factors of 12. $12 = 2 \times 2 \times 3$. Therefore 12 contains two 2's and a 3. x also contains two 2's and a 3, therefore x is divisible by 12.

28. **No:** For x to be a multiple of 12, it would need to contain all of the prime factors of 12: 2, 2, and 3. If $7x$ is a multiple of 210, it contains the prime factors 2, 3, 5, and 7. However, we want to know about x, not $7x$, so we need to divide out the 7. Therefore, x must contain the remaining primes: 2, 3, and 5. Comparing this to the prime factorization of 12, we see that x does have a 2 and a 3, but we don't know whether it has *two* 2's. Therefore, we can't say that x must be a multiple of 12; it could be, but it doesn't have to be.

Alternatively, we could start by dividing out the 7. If $7x$ is divisible by 210, x is divisible by 30. We therefore know that x contains the prime factors 2, 3, and 5, and we can follow the remaining reasoning from above.

29. $b = 2$: For integer a to be a multiple of 30, it would need to contain all of the prime factors of 30: 2, 3, and 5. Since a is not a multiple of 30, it must be missing at least one of these prime factors. So if ab is a multiple of 30, b must supply that missing prime factor. The smallest possible missing prime is 2. If $b = 2$ and $a = 15$ (or any multiple of 15), both of the initial constraints are met.

Drill 8

30. **1, 2, 4, 5, 8, 10, 20, and 40:** If 40 is a factor of *x*, then any factor of 40 is also a factor of *x*.

Small	Large
1	40
2	20
4	10
5	8

31. **The number is 85 and the factors are 1, 5, 17, and 85.** If 5 and 17 are the only prime factors of the number, then the number = 5 × 17, which means the number is 85.

Small	Large
1	85
5	17

32. **Yes:**

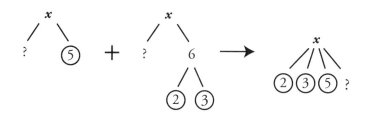

For *x* to be divisible by 15, we need to know that it contains all of the prime factors of 15. 15 = 3 × 5. Therefore 15 contains a 3 and a 5. *x* also contains a 3 and a 5, therefore *x* is divisible by 15.

33. **Maybe:** To be divisible by 8, *q* needs three 2's in its prime factorization. Rather than combine all of the listed factors (too hard!), we can just look through and see how many 2's we have.

We can't simply count all of the numbers that contain 2, because we might have some overlapping factors. For instance, 6 is a multiple of 2 and 3, so the fact that *q* is divisible by both 2 and 6 tells us only that we have at least one 2 (and at least one 3); we don't necessarily have two factors of 2.

Instead, we need to look for the largest number of 2's we see *in one factor*. 12 contains two 2's, so we know that *q* must be a multiple of 4, but we do not know whether *q* contains three 2's. It might or it might not.

Alternately, we could run through our list of factors, adding to the list when *new* factors appear.

2: *q* must be divisible by 2.
6: The 3 is new. *q* must be divisible by 2 and 3.
9: The second 3 is new. *q* must be divisible by 2, 3, and 3.

2

12: The second 2 is new. q must be divisible by 2, 2, 3, and 3.

15: The 5 is new. q must be divisible by 2, 2, 3, 3, and 5.

30: Nothing new. q must be divisible by 2, 2, 3, 3, and 5.

Again, we see that we only have two 2's for certain. Therefore q must be a multiple of 180 (that is, $2 \times 2 \times 3 \times 3 \times 5$), but it does not absolutely have to be a multiple of 8.

34. **minimum = 1; maximum = 2:** Let's start with our more constrained variable: p. Because it is prime, we know that it has exactly 2 factors—itself and 1. Therefore, our maximum number of "factors in common" cannot be more than 2. Can p and q have exactly 2 factors in common? Certainly; q can be a multiple of p. (For instance, if $p = 3$ and $q = 12$, the common factors are 1 and 3.)

What about the minimum? Can p and q have absolutely no factors in common? Try some numbers. If we choose p = 3 and q = 10, then the two numbers don't have any prime factors in common, but notice that they are both divisible by 1. Any number is always divisible by 1. Therefore, our minimum possible number of factors is 1 (the number one itself) and our maximum is 2 (the two factors of prime number p).

Drill 9

35. **1, 2, 4, 8, 16, 32, and 64:** If 64 divides n, then any divisors of 64 will also be divisors of n.

Small	Large
1	64
2	32
4	16
8	8

36. **The number is 132 and the factors are 1, 2, 3, 4, 6, 11, 12, 22, 33, 44, 66, and 132:** $2 \times 2 \times 3 \times 11 = 132$

Small	Large
1	132
2	66
3	44
4	33
6	22
11	12

37. **Maybe:**

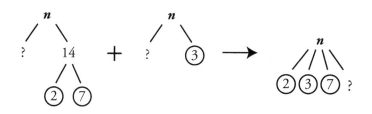

2

For 12 to be a factor of *n*, *n* must contain all of the prime factors of 12. $12 = 2 \times 2 \times 3$, so 12 contains two 2s and a 3. *n* also contains a 3 but only contains one 2 that we know of, so we don't know whether 12 is a factor of *n*.

38. ***a* = 6:** We have a bit of a puzzle here. What kind of number has exactly four factors? Let's start by looking at our most constrained variable—*a*. It is a positive one-digit number, so something between 1 and 9, inclusive, and it has four factors. We know that prime numbers have exactly two factors: themselves and one, so we only need to look at non-prime one-digit positive integers. That's a small enough field that we can list them out:

1—just one factor!
4—3 factors: 1, 2, and 4
6—4 factors: 1, 2, 3, and 6
8—4 factors: 1, 2, 4, and 8
9—3 factors: 1, 3, and 9

So our two possibilities for *a* are 6 and 8. We now have to apply our two constraints for *b*. It is 9 greater than *a*, and it has exactly four factors. Here are our possibilities:

If *a* = 6, then *b* = 15. 15 has 4 factors: 1, 3, 5, and 15.
If *a* = 8, then *b* = 17. 17 is prime, so it has only has 2 factors: 1 and 17.
Only *b* = 15 works, so *a* must be 6.

39. **4:** Because we have been asked for a concrete answer, we can infer that the answer will be the same regardless of which 2-digit prime we pick. So for simplicity's sake, let's pick the smallest and most familiar one: 11.

If *n* is the product of 2, 3, and 11, its factors are:

Small	Large
1	66
2	33
3	22
6	11

In this case, we can simply use the right-hand portion of our chart. We have four factors larger than 6: 11, 22, 33, and 66.

Notice that because the other given prime factors of *n* (2 and 3) multiply to get exactly 6, we can only get a number greater than 6 by multiplying by the third factor, the "two-digit prime number." The right hand column represents that third factor multiplied by all of the other factors: 11×6, 11×3, 11×2, and 11×1. If we replace 11 with another two-digit prime, we will get the same result. (If you're not sure, try it!)

Drill 10

40. **Yes:**

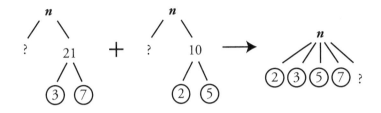

For 30 to be a divisor of *n*, *n* has to contain all of the prime factors of 30. $30 = 2 \times 3 \times 5$, so 30 contains 2, 3, and 5. *n* also contains 2, 3 and 5, so 30 is a divisor of *n*.

41. **Yes:**

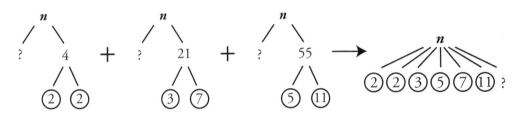

For 154 to divide *n*, *n* has to contain all the same prime factors as 154. $154 = 2 \times 7 \times 11$, so 154 contains 2, 7, and 11. *n* also contains 2, 7 and 11, so 154 divides *n*.

42. **Maybe:**

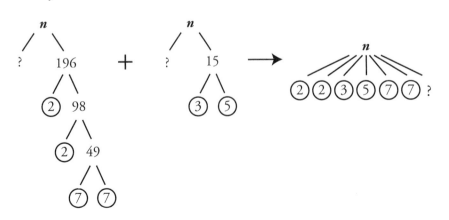

For 270 to be a factor of *n*, *n* must contain all the same prime factors as 270. $270 = 2 \times 3 \times 3 \times 3 \times 5$, so 270 contains a 2, three 3's, and a 5. *n* contains a 2 and a 5, but only one 3. Therefore, 270 is not definitely a factor of *n*.

Chapter 3
of
Foundations of GMAT Math

Exponents & Roots

In This Chapter...

Chapter 3:
Exponents & Roots

In This Chapter:

- Rules of exponents
- Rules of roots

Basics of Exponents

To review, exponents represent repeated multiplication. The **exponent**, or power, tells you how many **bases** to multiply together.

5^3	=	$5 \times 5 \times 5$	=	125
Five cubed	equals	three fives multiplied together, or five times five times five,	which equals	one hundred twenty-five.

An **exponential expression** or term simply has an exponent in it. Exponential expressions can contain variables as well. The variable can be the base, the exponent, or even both.

a^4	=	$a \times a \times a \times a$
a to the fourth	equals	four a's multiplied together, or a times a times a times a.

3^x	=	$3 \times 3 \times \ldots \times 3$
Three to the xth power	equals	three times three times dot dot dot times three. There are x three's in the product, whatever x is.

Any base to the first power is just that base.

$$7^1 \qquad = \qquad 7$$

Seven to the first   equals   seven.

Memorize the following powers of positive integers.

Squares
$1^2 = 1$
$2^2 = 4$
$3^2 = 9$
$4^2 = 16$
$5^2 = 25$
$6^2 = 36$
$7^2 = 49$
$8^2 = 64$
$9^2 = 81$
$10^2 = 100$
$11^2 = 121$
$12^2 = 144$
$13^2 = 169$
$14^2 = 196$
$15^2 = 225$
$20^2 = 400$
$30^2 = 900$

Cubes
$1^3 = 1$
$2^3 = 8$
$3^3 = 27$
$4^3 = 64$
$5^3 = 125$
$10^3 = 1,000$

Powers of 2
$2^1 = 2$
$2^2 = 4$
$2^3 = 8$
$2^4 = 16$
$2^5 = 32$
$2^6 = 64$
$2^7 = 128$
$2^8 = 256$
$2^9 = 512$
$2^{10} = 1,024$

Powers of 3
$3^1 = 3$
$3^2 = 9$
$3^3 = 27$
$3^4 = 81$

Powers of 4
$4^1 = 4$
$4^2 = 16$
$4^3 = 64$

Powers of 5
$5^1 = 5$
$5^2 = 25$
$5^3 = 125$

Powers of 10
$10^1 = 10$
$10^2 = 100$
$10^3 = 1,000$

Remember PEMDAS? Exponents come before everything else, except Parentheses. That includes negative signs.

$$-3^2 \qquad = \qquad -(3^2) \qquad = \qquad -9$$

| The negative of | equals | the negative of the | which | negative |
| three squared | | quantity three squared, | equals | nine. |

To calculate -3^2, square the 3 **before** you multiply by negative one (-1). If you want to square the negative sign, throw parentheses around -3.

$$(-3)^2 \quad = \quad 9$$

The square of   equals   nine.
negative three

In $(-3)^2$, the negative sign and the three are both inside the parentheses, so they both get squared. If you say "negative three squared," you probably mean $(-3)^2$, but someone listening might write down -3^2, so say "the square of negative three" instead.

The powers of -1 alternate between 1 and -1. Even powers of -1 are always 1, while odd powers of -1 are always -1.

$(-1)^1$	$= -1$	$= -1$
$(-1)^2$	$= -1 \times -1$	$= 1$
$(-1)^3$	$= -1 \times -1 \times -1$	$= -1$
$(-1)^4$	$= -1 \times -1 \times -1 \times -1$	$= 1$

Negative numbers raised to an even power are always positive. Negative numbers raised to an odd number are always negative.

(Negative)^even = Positive   **(Negative)^odd = Negative**

A positive base raised to any power is always positive, because positive times positive is positive—no matter how many times you multiply.

Since an even exponent gives you a positive result for both a positive and a negative base, **an even exponent can hide the sign of the base.** Consider this equation:

$$x^2 = 16$$

In Chapter 6, "Equations," we will cover in more depth how to solve an equation such as this one. For now, notice that *two* numbers for x would make the equation true:

$$4^2 = 16 \qquad\qquad (-4)^2 = 16$$

The value of x could be either 4 or -4. **Always be careful when dealing with even exponents in equations.** Look for more than one possible solution.

Check Your Skills

1. Which is greater, -5^8 or $(-5)^8$?

Answers can be found on page 131.

Multiply Terms with Same Base: Add the Exponents

Imagine that you multiply together a string of five a's. Now multiply a second string of three a's together. Finally, because you love multiplication, go ahead and multiply the two strings together. How many a's do you end up with?

Write it all out longhand:

$$(a \times a \times a \times a \times a) \times (a \times a \times a) = a \times a \times a \times a \times a \times a \times a \times a$$

Now use exponential notation:

$$a^5 \qquad \times \qquad a^3 \qquad = \qquad a^8$$

a to the **fifth**   times   a to the **third**   equals   a to the **eighth**.

What happens to the exponents 5 and 3? They add up: $5 + 3 = 8$. This works because we only have a's in the equation. The two terms on the left (a^5 and a^3) have the same base (a), so we have eight a's on each side of the equation.

When you multiply exponential terms that have the same base, add the exponents.

Treat any term without an exponent as if it had an exponent of 1.

$$y(y^6) = y \times y^6 = y^1 \times y^6 = y^{1+6} = y^7$$

Adding exponents works with numbers in the base, even weird numbers such as π. You just have to make sure that the bases are the same.

$$5^3 \times 5^6 = 5^9 \qquad\qquad \pi \times \pi^2 = \pi^3$$

The rule also works with variables in the exponent.

$$2^3 \times 2^z = 2^{3+z} \qquad\qquad 6(6^x) = 6^1 \times 6^x = 6^{1+x} = 6^{x+1}$$

Check Your Skills

Simplify the following expressions.

2. $b^5 \times b^7 =$
3. $(x^3)(x^4) =$

Answers can be found on page 131.

Divide Terms with Same Base: Subtract the Exponents

Now divide a string of five a's by a string of three a's. Again, these are strings of *multiplied* a's. What is the result?

$$\frac{a \times a \times a \times a \times a}{a \times a \times a} = \frac{a \times \cancel{a} \times \cancel{a} \times \cancel{a} \times a}{\cancel{a} \times \cancel{a} \times \cancel{a}} = a \times a$$

In exponential notation, you have this: $\dfrac{a^5}{a^3} = a^2$

What happens to the exponents? You subtract the bottom exponent from the top exponent. $5 - 3 = 2$.

When you divide exponential terms that have the same base, subtract the exponents.

This rule works the same for numbers as for variables, either in the base or in the exponent.

$$\frac{2^{16}}{2^{13}} = 2^{16-13} = 2^3 = 8 \qquad\qquad \frac{x^y}{x^2} = x^{y-2}$$

Again, treat any term without an exponent as if it had an exponent of 1.

$$\frac{f^9}{f} = \frac{f^9}{f^1} = f^8$$

Just always make sure that the bases are the same.

Here's the rule book so far.

If you...	Then you...	Like this:
Multiply exponential terms that have the same base	Add the exponents	$a^2 \times a^3 = a^5$
Divide exponential terms that have the same base	Subtract the exponents	$\dfrac{a^5}{a^3} = a^2$

Check Your Skills
Simplify the following expressions.

4. $\dfrac{y^5}{y^2}$

5. $\dfrac{d^8}{d^7}$ *Answers can be found on page 131.*

Pretty Much Anything to the Zeroth Power: One

Divide a string of five a's by a string of five a's. As before, each string is internally multiplied. What do you get?

Using longhand, you get 1.

$$\frac{a \times a \times a \times a \times a}{a \times a \times a \times a \times a} = \frac{\cancel{a} \times \cancel{a} \times \cancel{a} \times \cancel{a} \times \cancel{a}}{\cancel{a} \times \cancel{a} \times \cancel{a} \times \cancel{a} \times \cancel{a}} = 1$$

Using the exponent subtraction rule, you get a^0.

$$\frac{a^5}{a^5} = a^{5-5} = a^0$$

So a^0 must equal 1. That's true for practically any value of a.

$$1^0 = 1 \qquad 6.2^0 = 1 \qquad (-4)^0 = 1 \qquad \left(\frac{3}{4}\right)^0 = 1 \qquad \left(\sqrt{2}\right)^0 = 1$$

The *only* value of a that doesn't work is 0 itself. The expression 0^0 is **undefined**. Notice that the argument above required us to divide by a. Since you can't divide by 0, you can't raise 0 to the 0th power either. The GMAT will never ask you to do so.

For any nonzero value of a, we can say that $a^0 = 1$.

Now we can extend the powers of 2 to include 2^0.

Powers of 2
$2^0 = 1$
$2^1 = 2$
$2^2 = 4$
$2^3 = 8$
$2^4 = 16$

The pattern should make sense. Each power of 2 is 2 times the previous power of 2.

Negative Power: One Over a Positive Power

What happens if you divide a string of three a's by a string of five a's?

Using longhand, you get a leftover a^2 in the denominator of the fraction.

$$\frac{a \times a \times a}{a \times a \times a \times a \times a} = \frac{\cancel{a} \times \cancel{a} \times \cancel{a}}{a \times a \times \cancel{a} \times \cancel{a} \times \cancel{a}} = \frac{1}{a \times a} = \frac{1}{a^2}$$

Using the exponent subtraction rule, you get a^{-2}.

$$\frac{a^3}{a^5} = a^{3-5} = a^{-2}$$

So those two results must be equal. **Something with a negative exponent is just "one over" that same thing with a positive exponent.**

$$a^{-2} \qquad = \qquad \frac{1}{a^2}$$

a to the negative two   equals   one over a squared

In other words, a^{-2} is the **reciprocal** of a^2. The reciprocal of 5 is "one over" 5, or $\frac{1}{5}$. You can also think of reciprocals this way: something times its reciprocal always equals 1.

$$5 \times \frac{1}{5} = 1 \qquad\qquad a^2 \times \frac{1}{a^2} = 1 \qquad\qquad a^2 \times a^{-2} = a^{2-2} = a^0 = 1$$

Now we can extend the powers of 2 to include negative exponents.

Powers of 2

$$2^{-3} = \frac{1}{2^3} = \frac{1}{8} = 0.125$$

$$2^{-2} = \frac{1}{2^2} = \frac{1}{4} = 0.25$$

$$2^{-1} = \frac{1}{2} = 0.5$$

$$2^0 = 1$$
$$2^1 = 2$$
$$2^2 = 4$$
$$2^3 = 8$$
$$2^4 = 16$$

The pattern should still make sense. Each power of 2 is 2 times the previous power of 2.

The rules we've seen so far work the same for negative exponents.

$$5^{-3} \times 5^{-6} = 5^{-3+(-6)} = 5^{-9}$$

$$\frac{x^3}{x^{-5}} = x^{3-(-5)} = x^8$$

Negative exponents are tricky, so it can be useful to rewrite them using positive exponents. A negative exponent in a term on top of a fraction becomes positive when you move the term to the bottom.

3

$$\frac{5x^{-2}}{y^3} = \frac{5}{x^2 y^3}$$

Here, we moved x^{-2} from the numerator to the denominator and switched the sign of the exponent from −2 to 2. Everything else stays the same.

Likewise, a negative exponent in the bottom of a fraction becomes positive when the term moves to the top.

$$\frac{3}{z^{-4} w^2} = \frac{3z^4}{w^2}$$

Here, we moved z^{-4} from the denominator to the numerator and switched the sign of the exponent from −4 to 4.

If you move the entire denominator, leave a 1 behind.

$$\frac{1}{z^{-4}} = \frac{1 \times z^4}{1} = z^4$$

The same is true for a numerator.

$$\frac{w^{-5}}{2} = \frac{1}{2w^5}$$

Don't confuse the sign of the base with the sign of the exponent. A positive base raised to a negative exponent stays positive.

$$3^{-3} = \frac{1}{3^3} = \frac{1}{27}$$

A negative base follows the same rules as before. Odd powers of a negative base produce negative numbers.

$$(-4)^{-3} = \frac{1}{(-4)^3} = \frac{1}{-64} = -\frac{1}{64}$$

Even powers of a negative base produce positive numbers.

$$\frac{1}{(-6)^{-2}} = (-6)^2 = 36$$

Here are additional rules for the rule book.

If you...	Then you...	Like this:
Raise anything to the zeroth power (besides zero itself)	Get one	$a^0 = 1$
Raise anything to a negative power	Get one over that same thing to the corresponding positive power	$a^{-2} = \dfrac{1}{a^2}$
Move a term from top to bottom of a fraction (or vice versa)	Switch the sign of the exponent	$\dfrac{2a^{-2}}{3} = \dfrac{2}{3a^2}$

Check Your Skills

Simplify the following expressions.

6. 2^{-3}

7. $\dfrac{1}{3^{-3}}$

Answers can be found on page 131.

Apply Two Exponents: Multiply the Exponents

How do you simplify this expression?

$(a^2)^4$

Use the definition of exponents. First you square a. Then you multiply four separate a^2 terms together. In longhand:

$(a^2)^4 = a^2 \times a^2 \times a^2 \times a^2 = a^{2+2+2+2} = a^8$

What happens to the exponents 2 and 4? You multiply them: $2 \times 4 = 8$. On each side, you have eight a's multiplied together.

When you raise something that already has an exponent to another power, multiply the two exponents together.

Always keep these two cases straight.

Addition rule: $a^2 \times a^4 = a^{2+4} = a^6$

Multiplication rule: $(a^2)^4 = a^{2 \times 4} = a^8$

To add exponents, you should see *two* bases, as in $a^2 \times a^4$. To multiply exponents, you should be applying two exponents, one after the other, to just *one* base: $(a^2)^4$.

The "apply two exponents" rule works perfectly with negative exponents as well.

$$(x^{-3})^5 = x^{-3 \times 5} = x^{-15}$$

$$(4^{-2})^{-3} = 4^{-2 \times -3} = 4^6$$

If you...	Then you...	Like this:
Raise something to two successive powers	Multiply the powers	$(a^2)^4 = a^8$

Put it all together. Now you can handle this expression:

$$\frac{x^{-3}\left(x^2\right)^4}{x^5}$$

First, simplify $(x^2)^4$.

$$(x^2)^4 = x^{2 \times 4} = x^8$$

The fraction now reads:

$$\frac{x^{-3}x^8}{x^5}$$

Now follow the rules for multiplying and dividing terms that have the same base. That is, you add and subtract the exponents:

$$\frac{x^{-3}x^8}{x^5} = x^{-3+8-5} = x^0 = 1$$

If you have *different* bases that are numbers, try breaking the bases down to prime factors. You might discover that you can express everything in terms of one base.

$$2^2 \times 4^3 \times 16 =$$

    (A) 2^6
    (B) 2^{12}
    (C) 2^{18}

The efficient way to attack this problem is to break down 4 and 16 into prime factors. Both 4 and 16 are powers of 2, so we have:

$$4 = 2^2 \text{ and } 16 = 2^4$$

Everything can now be expressed with 2 as the base.

$$
\begin{aligned}
2^2 \times 4^3 \times 16 \quad &= 2^2 \times (2^2)^3 \times 2^4 \\
&= 2^2 \times 2^6 \times 2^4 \\
&= 2^{2+6+4} \\
&= 2^{12}
\end{aligned}
$$

The correct answer is (B).

Check Your Skills

Simplify the following expressions:

8. $(x^3)^4$

9. $\dfrac{a^{15}}{a^0 \left(a^3\right)^3}$

Answers can be found on page 131.

Apply an Exponent to a Product: Apply the Exponent to Each Factor

Consider this expression:

$$(xy)^3$$

How can you rewrite this? Use the definition of exponents. You multiply three xy terms together.

$$(xy)^3 = xy \times xy \times xy$$

So you have three x's multiplied together and three y's multiplied together. You can group these up separately, because everything's multiplied.

$$(xy)^3 = xy \times xy \times xy = x^3 y^3$$

When you apply an exponent to a product, apply the exponent to each factor.

This rule works with every kind of base and exponent we've seen so far.

$$(3x)^4 = 3^4 x^4 = 81 x^4$$
$$(wz^3)^x = w^x z^{3x}$$

$$(2^{-2}y^2)^{-3} = 2^{-2\times-3}y^{2\times-3} = 2^6y^{-6} = 64y^{-6} = \frac{64}{y^6}$$

You do the same thing with division. In particular, if you raise an entire fraction to a power, you separately apply the exponent to the numerator and to the denominator.

$$\left(\frac{3}{4}\right)^{-2} = \frac{3^{-2}}{4^{-2}} = \frac{4^2}{3^2} = \frac{16}{9}$$

Notice that the following case is different.

$$\frac{3^{-2}}{4} = \frac{1}{4\times3^2} = \frac{1}{36}$$

In $\frac{3^{-2}}{4}$, the exponent applies only to the numerator (3). Respect PEMDAS, as always. Here's more for the rule book.

If you...	Then you...	Like this:
Apply an exponent to a product	Apply the exponent to each factor	$(ab)^3 = a^3b^3$
Apply an exponent to an entire fraction	Apply the exponent separately to top and bottom	$\left(\frac{a}{b}\right)^4 = \frac{a^4}{b^4}$

You can use this principle to write the prime factorization of big numbers without computing those numbers directly.

What is the prime factorization of 18^3?

Don't multiply out $18 \times 18 \times 18$. Just figure out the prime factorization of 18 itself, then apply the rule above.

$$18 = 2 \times 9 = 2 \times 3^2$$

$$18^3 = (2 \times 3^2)^3 = 2^3 \times 3^6 = 2^33^6$$

Now simplify this harder example.

$$\frac{12^2 \times 8}{18} =$$

First, break each base into its prime factors and substitute.

$$12 = 2^2 \times 3 \qquad\qquad 8 = 2^3 \qquad\qquad 18 = 2 \times 3^2$$

$$\frac{12^2 \times 8}{18} = \frac{\left(2^2 \times 3\right)^2 \times 2^3}{2 \times 3^2}$$

Now apply the exponent on the parentheses.

$$\frac{\left(2^2 \times 3\right)^2 \times 2^3}{2 \times 3^2} = \frac{2^4 \times 3^2 \times 2^3}{2 \times 3^2}$$

Finally, combine the terms with 2 as their base. Remember that a 2 without a written exponent really has an exponent of 1. Separately, combine the terms with 3 as their base.

$$\frac{2^4 \times 3^2 \times 2^3}{2 \times 3^2} = 2^{4+3-1} \times 3^{2-2} = 2^6 \times 3^0 = 2^6 \times 1 = 2^6 = 64$$

Occasionally, it's faster *not* to break down all the way to primes. If you spot a larger common base, feel free to use it. Try this example:

$$\frac{36^3}{6^4} =$$

You can simplify this expression by breaking 36 and 6 down to primes. But if you recognize that $36 = 6^2$, then you can go much faster:

$$\frac{36^3}{6^4} = \frac{\left(6^2\right)^3}{6^4} = \frac{6^6}{6^4} = 6^2 = 36$$

One last point: be ready to rewrite $a^3 b^3$ as $(ab)^3$.

Consider $2^4 \times 3^4$. Here's a way to see that $2^4 \times 3^4$ equals $(2 \times 3)^4$, or 6^4:

$$2^4 \times 3^4 = (2 \times 2 \times 2 \times 2) \times (3 \times 3 \times 3 \times 3)$$

$$= (2 \times 3) \times (2 \times 3) \times (2 \times 3) \times (2 \times 3) \qquad\qquad \text{by regrouping}$$

$$= (2 \times 3)^4 = 6^4$$

More often you need to change $(ab)^3$ into $a^3 b^3$, but occasionally it's handy to go in reverse.

If you...	Then you...	Like this:
See two factors with the same exponent	Might regroup the factors as a product	$a^3 b^3 = (ab)^3$

Check Your Skills

Simplify the following expressions.

10. $\left(\dfrac{x^2 y}{z^{-3}} \right)^2$

11. $\dfrac{75^3 \times 45^3}{15^8}$

Answers can be found on page 131.

Add or Subtract Terms with the Same Base: Pull Out a Common Factor

Every case so far in this chapter has involved *only* multiplication and division. What if you are adding or subtracting exponential terms?

Consider this example:

$$13^5 + 13^3 =$$

Do not be tempted to add the exponents and get 13^8. That is the answer to a similar but different question (namely, what is $13^5 \times 13^3$?). The right answer to a different question is always wrong.

Instead, **look for a common factor and pull it out**. Both 13^5 and 13^3 are divisible by 13^3, so that's your common factor. If necessary, rewrite 13^5 as $13^3 13^2$ first.

$$13^5 + 13^3 = 13^3 \times 13^2 + 13^3 = 13^3(13^2 + 1)$$

You could go further and rewrite 13^2 as 169. The right answer choice would possibly look like this: $13^3(170)$.

If we had x's instead of 13's as bases, the factoring would work the same way.

$$x^5 + x^3 = x^3 \times x^2 + x^3 = x^3(x^2 + 1)$$

Try this example:

$$3^8 - 3^7 - 3^6 =$$

(A) $3^6(5)$
(B) 3^6
(C) 3^{-5}

All three terms (3^8, 3^7, and 3^6) are divisible by 3^6, so pull 3^6 out of the expression:

$$3^8 - 3^7 - 3^6 = 3^6(3^2 - 3^1 - 3^0) = 3^6(9 - 3 - 1) = 3^6(5)$$

The correct answer is (A).

Now try to simplify this fraction:

$$\frac{3^4 + 3^5 + 3^6}{13} =$$

Ignore the 13 on the bottom of the fraction for the moment. On the top, each term is divisible by 3^4.

$$\frac{3^4 + 3^5 + 3^6}{13} = \frac{3^4\left(3^0 + 3^1 + 3^2\right)}{13}$$

Continue to simplify the small powers of 3 in the parentheses:

$$\frac{3^4 + 3^5 + 3^6}{13} = \frac{3^4\left(3^0 + 3^1 + 3^2\right)}{13} = \frac{3^4\left(1 + 3 + 9\right)}{13} = \frac{3^4\left(13\right)}{13}$$

Now we can cancel the 13's on the top and bottom of the fraction.

$$\frac{3^4 + 3^5 + 3^6}{13} = \frac{3^4\left(3^0 + 3^1 + 3^2\right)}{13} = \frac{3^4\left(1 + 3 + 9\right)}{13} = \frac{3^4\left(13\right)}{13} = 3^4$$

If you *don't* have the same bases in what you're adding or subtracting, you can't immediately factor. If the bases are numbers, break them down to smaller factors and see whether you now have anything in common.

$$4^6 + 20^6 =$$

Again, don't answer the wrong question. $4^6 \times 20^6 = (4 \times 20)^6 = 80^6$, but that doesn't answer this question. We need to add 4^6 and 20^6, **not** multiply them.

Since 4 is a factor of 20, rewrite 20 as 4×5 and apply the exponent to that product.

$$4^6 + 20^6 = 4^6 + (4 \times 5)^6 = 4^6 + 4^6 \times 5^6$$

Now pull out the common factor of 4^6.

$$4^6 + 20^6 = 4^6 + (4 \times 5)^6 = 4^6 + 4^6 \times 5^6 = (1 + 5^6)4^6.$$

That's as far as you'd reasonably go, given the size of 4^6 and 5^6. Finally, try this one:

$$4^5 + 20^3 =$$

Start it the same way as before. Rewrite 20 as 4×5 and apply the exponent.

$$4^5 + 20^3 = 4^5 + (4 \times 5)^3 = 4^5 + 4^3 \times 5^3$$

Now, the common factor is only 4^3.

$$4^5 + 20^3 = 4^5 + (4 \times 5)^3 = 4^5 + 4^3 \times 5^3 = 4^3 \times 4^2 + 4^3 \times 5^3 = 4^3(4^2 + 5^3)$$

The result isn't especially pretty, but it's legitimate. Here's the rule book:

If you...	Then you...	Like this:
Add or subtract terms with the same base	Pull out the common factor	$2^3 + 2^5$ $= 2^3(1 + 2^2)$
Add or subtract terms with different bases	Break down the bases and pull out the common factor	$2^3 + 6^3$ $= 2^3(1 + 3^3)$

Check Your Skills

Simplify the following expression by factoring out a common term:

12. $5^5 + 5^4 - 5^3$

Answers can be found on page 131.

Roots: Opposite of Exponents

Squaring a number means raising it to the 2nd power (or multiplying it by itself). Square-rooting a number undoes that process.

$$3^2 \quad = \quad 9 \quad \text{and} \quad \sqrt{9} \quad = \quad 3$$

Three   is   nine,   and   the square   is   three.
squared   root of nine

If you square-root first, then square, you get back to the original number.

$$\left(\sqrt{16}\right)^2 \quad = \quad \sqrt{16} \times \sqrt{16} \quad = \quad 16$$

The square of the   equals   the square root of   which   sixteen.
square root of sixteen   sixteen times the   equals
                                           square root of sixteen,

If you square first, then square-root, you get back to the original number if the original number is positive.

$$\sqrt{5^2} \qquad = \qquad \sqrt{5\times5} \qquad = \qquad 5$$

| The square root of | equals | the square root of | which | five. |
| five squared | | five times five, | equals | |

If the original number is negative, you just flip the sign, so you end up with a positive.

$$\sqrt{(-5)^2} \qquad = \qquad \sqrt{25} \qquad = \qquad 5$$

| The square root of the | equals | the square root of | which | five. |
| square of negative five | | twenty-five, | equals | |

In fact, square-rooting the square of something is just like taking the absolute value of that thing (see Chapter 8).

If you...	Then you...	Like this:
Square a square root	Get the original number	$\left(\sqrt{10}\right)^2 = 10$
Square-root a square	Get the absolute value of the original number	$\sqrt{10^2} = 10$ $\sqrt{(-10)^2} = 10$

Because 9 is the square of an integer ($9 = 3^2$), 9 is a perfect square and has a nice integer square root. In contrast, 2 is not the square of an integer, so its square root is an ugly decimal, as we saw in Chapter 1.

Memorize the perfect squares on page 106 so you can take their square roots easily. Also memorize these approximations:

$$\sqrt{2} \approx 1.4 \qquad \sqrt{3} \approx 1.7$$

You can approximate the square root of a non-perfect square by looking at nearby perfect squares. The square root of a bigger number is always bigger than the square root of a smaller number. Try this example:

$$\sqrt{70} \text{ is between what two integers?}$$

Two nearby perfect squares are 64 and 81. $\sqrt{64} = 8$ and $\sqrt{81} = 9$, so $\sqrt{70}$ must be between 8 and 9. It's closer to 8, in fact, but you won't have to approximate the decimal part.

The square root of a number bigger than 1 is smaller than the original number.

$$\sqrt{2} < 2 \qquad \sqrt{21} < 21 \qquad \sqrt{1.3} < 1.3$$

However, the square root of a number between 1 and 0 is *bigger* than the original number.

$$\sqrt{0.5} > 0.5 \qquad \left(\sqrt{0.5} \approx 0.7\right) \qquad \sqrt{\frac{2}{3}} > \frac{2}{3}$$

In either case, the square root of a number is **closer to 1** than the original number.

The square root of 1 is 1, since $1^2 = 1$. Likewise, the square root of 0 is 0, since $0^2 = 0$.

$$\sqrt{1} = 1 \qquad \sqrt{0} = 0$$

You cannot take the square root of a negative number in GMAT world. What is inside the radical sign must never be negative.

Likewise, the square root symbol never gives a negative result. This may seem strange. After all, both 5^2 and $(-5)^2$ equal 25, so shouldn't the square root of 25 be either 5 or -5? No. Mathematicians like to have symbols mean one thing.

$$\sqrt{25} = 5 \text{ and that's that.}$$

When you see the square root symbol on the GMAT, **only consider the positive root**.

In contrast, when *you* take the square root of both sides of an equation, you have to consider both positive and negative roots.

$$x = \sqrt{25} \qquad \text{solution: } x = 5$$

$$x^2 = 25 \qquad \text{solutions: } x = 5 \text{ OR } x = -5$$

Be careful with square roots of variable expressions. The expression must not be negative, or the square root is illegal.

Check Your Skills

13. $\sqrt{27} \times \sqrt{27} =$

Answers can be found on page 131.

Square Root: Power of One Half

Consider this equation:

$$\left(9^x\right)^2 = 9$$

What is x? We can find x using tools we already have.

$$\left(9^x\right)^2 = 9$$
$$9^{2x} = 9^1$$

The exponents must be equal. So $2x = 1$, or $x = \dfrac{1}{2}$.

Now we know that $\left(9^{\frac{1}{2}}\right)^2 = 9$. We also know that $\left(\sqrt{9}\right)^2 = 9$. So we can conclude that $\sqrt{9} = 9^{\frac{1}{2}}$.

For expressions with positive bases, **a square root is equivalent to an exponent of $\dfrac{1}{2}$.**

Try to simplify this example:

$$\sqrt{7^{22}} =$$

You can approach the problem in either of two ways.

1. Rewrite the square root as an exponent of $\dfrac{1}{2}$, then apply the two-exponent rule (multiply exponents).

$$\sqrt{7^{22}} = \left(7^{22}\right)^{\frac{1}{2}} = 7^{\frac{22}{2}} = 7^{11}$$

2. Rewrite what's inside the square root as a product of two equal factors. The square root is therefore one of those factors.

$$7^{22} = 7^{11} \times 7^{11}$$

$$\sqrt{7^{22}} = \sqrt{7^{11} \times 7^{11}} = 7^{11}$$

Notice that you get an exponent that is exactly *half* of the exponent inside the square root. This tells you that a number such as 7^{22} is a perfect square: $7^{22} = (7^{11})^2$. An integer raised to a positive even power is always a perfect square.

Here's the rule book:

If you...	Then you...	Like this:
Take a square root of a positive number raised to a power	Rewrite the square root as an exponent of $\frac{1}{2}$, then multiply exponents	$\sqrt{5^{12}} = \left(5^{12}\right)^{\frac{1}{2}}$ $= 5^6$
	OR Rewrite what's inside the root as a product of two equal factors	$\sqrt{5^{12}} = \sqrt{5^6 \times 5^6}$ $= 5^6$

Avoid changing the square root to an exponent of $\frac{1}{2}$ when you have variable expressions inside the radical, since the output depends on the sign of the variables.

Check Your Skills

14. If x is positive, $\sqrt{x^6} =$

Answers can be found on page 131.

Cube Roots Undo Cubing

Cubing a number means raising it to the 3rd power. Cube-rooting a number undoes that process.

$$4^3 \quad = \quad 64 \quad \text{and} \quad \sqrt[3]{64} \quad = \quad 4$$

Four   is   sixty-four,   and   the cube   is   four.
cubed   root of
                                           sixty-four

Many of the properties of square roots carry over to cube roots. You can approximate cube roots the same way.

$\sqrt[3]{66}$ is a little more than 4, but less than 5, because $\sqrt[3]{64} = 4$ and $\sqrt[3]{125} = 5$.

Like square-rooting, cube-rooting a positive number pushes it toward 1.

$$\sqrt[3]{17} < 17 \qquad \text{but} \qquad \sqrt[3]{0.17} > 0.17$$

The main difference in behavior between square roots and cube roots is that you *can* take the cube root of a negative number. You wind up with a negative number.

$$\sqrt[3]{-64} = -4 \qquad \text{because } (-4)^3 = -64$$

As a fractional exponent, cube roots are equivalent to exponents of $\frac{1}{3}$, just as square roots are equivalent to exponents of $\frac{1}{2}$. Going further, fourth roots are equivalent to exponents of $\frac{1}{4}$, and so on.

We now can deal with **fractional exponents**. Consider this example:

$$8^{\frac{2}{3}} =$$

Rewrite $\frac{2}{3}$ as $2 \times \frac{1}{3}$, making two successive exponents. This is the same as squaring first, then cube-rooting.

$$8^{\frac{2}{3}} = 8^{2 \times \frac{1}{3}} = \left(8^2\right)^{\frac{1}{3}} = \sqrt[3]{8^2} = \sqrt[3]{64} = 4$$

Since you can rewrite $\frac{2}{3}$ as $\frac{1}{3} \times 2$ instead, you can take the cube root first and then square the result, if you like.

$$8^{\frac{2}{3}} = 8^{\frac{1}{3} \times 2} = \left(8^{\frac{1}{3}}\right)^2 = \left(\sqrt[3]{8}\right)^2 = 2^2 = 4$$

If you...	Then you...	Like this:
Raise a number to a fractional power	Apply two exponents—the numerator as is and the denominator as a root, in either order	$125^{\frac{2}{3}} = \left(\sqrt[3]{125}\right)^2$ $= 5^2 = 25$

Check Your Skills

15. $64^{2/3} =$

Answers can be found on page 131.

Multiply Square Roots: Multiply the Insides

Consider this example:

$$\sqrt{8} \times \sqrt{2} =$$

We saw before that $8^a 2^a = (8 \times 2)^a$. This principle holds true for fractional exponents as well.

$$\sqrt{8} \times \sqrt{2} = 8^{\frac{1}{2}} \times 2^{\frac{1}{2}} = (8 \times 2)^{\frac{1}{2}} = \sqrt{8 \times 2}$$

3

In practice, we can usually skip the fractional exponents. **When you multiply square roots, multiply the insides.**

$$\sqrt{8} \times \sqrt{2} = \sqrt{8 \times 2} = \sqrt{16} = 4$$

This shortcut works for division too. **When you divide square roots, divide the insides.**

$$\frac{\sqrt{27}}{\sqrt{3}} = \sqrt{\frac{27}{3}} = \sqrt{9} = 3$$

As long as you're only multiplying and dividing, you can deal with more complicated expressions.

$$\frac{\sqrt{15} \times \sqrt{12}}{\sqrt{5}} = \sqrt{\frac{15 \times 12}{5}} = \sqrt{36} = 6$$

If you...	Then you...	Like this:
Multiply square roots	Multiply the insides, then square-root	$\sqrt{a} \times \sqrt{b} = \sqrt{ab}$
Divide square roots	Divide the insides, then square-root	$\dfrac{\sqrt{a}}{\sqrt{b}} = \sqrt{\dfrac{a}{b}}$

Check Your Skills

Simplify the following expressions.

16. $\sqrt{20} \times \sqrt{5}$

17. $\dfrac{\sqrt{384}}{\sqrt{2} \times \sqrt{3}}$

Answers can be found on page 131.

Simplify Square Roots: Factor Out Squares

What does this product equal?

$$\sqrt{6} \times \sqrt{2} =$$

First, you multiply the insides:

$$\sqrt{6} \times \sqrt{2} = \sqrt{12}$$

You might think that you're done—after all, 12 is not a perfect square, so you won't get an integer out of $\sqrt{12}$. $\sqrt{12}$ is mathematically correct, but it will never be a correct answer on the GMAT, because it can be simplified. That is, $\sqrt{12}$ can be written in terms of smaller roots.

Here's how. 12 has a perfect square as a factor. Namely, $12 = 4 \times 3$. So plug in this product and separate the result into two roots.

$$\sqrt{12} = \sqrt{4 \times 3} = \sqrt{4} \times \sqrt{3}$$

The point of this exercise is that $\sqrt{4}$ is nice and tidy: $\sqrt{4} = 2$. So finish up:

$$\sqrt{12} = \sqrt{4 \times 3} = \sqrt{4} \times \sqrt{3} = 2\sqrt{3}$$

If the GMAT asks you for the value of $\sqrt{6} \times \sqrt{2}$, then $2\sqrt{3}$ will be the answer.

To simplify square roots, factor out squares.

If you…	Then you…	Like this:
Have the square root of a large number (or a root that doesn't match any answer choices)	Pull square factors out of the number under the radical sign	$\sqrt{50} = \sqrt{25 \times 2}$ $= \sqrt{25} \times \sqrt{2}$ $= 5\sqrt{2}$

Sometimes you can spot the square factor, if you know your perfect squares.

$$\sqrt{360} =$$

360 should remind you of 36, which is a perfect square. $360 = 36 \times 10$.

$$\sqrt{360} = \sqrt{36 \times 10} = \sqrt{36} \times \sqrt{10} = 6\sqrt{10}$$

What if you don't spot a perfect square? You can always **break the number down to primes.** This method is longer but guaranteed.

Consider $\sqrt{12}$ again. The prime factorization of 12 is $2 \times 2 \times 3$, or $2^2 \times 3$.

$$\sqrt{12} = \sqrt{2^2 \times 3} = \sqrt{2^2} \times \sqrt{3} = 2\sqrt{3}$$

Each pair of prime factors under the radical (2×2, or 2^2) turns into a single copy as it emerges (becoming the 2 in $2\sqrt{3}$). In this exercise, it can be useful to write out the prime factorization without exponents, so that you can spot the prime pairs quickly.

3

Take $\sqrt{360}$ again. Say you don't spot the perfect square factor (36). Write out the prime factorization of 360.

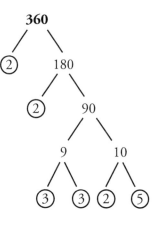

$$360 = 2 \times 2 \times 2 \times 3 \times 3 \times 5$$

Now pair off two 2's and two 3's, leaving an extra 2 and 5 under the radical.

$$\sqrt{360} = \sqrt{2 \times 2 \times 2 \times 3 \times 3 \times 5} = \sqrt{2 \times 2} \times \sqrt{3 \times 3} \times \sqrt{2 \times 5} = 2 \times 3 \times \sqrt{2 \times 5} = 6\sqrt{10}$$

Check Your Skills

Simplify the following roots.

18. $\sqrt{96}$

19. $\sqrt{441}$

Answers can be found on page 131.

Add or Subtract Inside the Root: Pull Out Common Square Factors

Consider this example:

$$\sqrt{3^2 + 4^2} =$$

Don't be fooled. **You cannot break this root** into $\sqrt{3^2} + \sqrt{4^2}$. You can only break up *products*, not sums, inside the square root. For instance, this is correct:

$$\sqrt{3^2 \times 4^2} = \sqrt{3^2} \times \sqrt{4^2} = 3 \times 4 = 12$$

To evaluate $\sqrt{3^2 + 4^2}$, follow PEMDAS under the radical, then take the square root.

$$\sqrt{3^2 + 4^2} = \sqrt{9 + 16} = \sqrt{25} = 5$$

The same goes for subtraction.

$$\sqrt{13^2 - 5^2} = \sqrt{169 - 25} = \sqrt{144} = 12$$

Often you have to just crunch the numbers if they're small. However, when the numbers get large, the GMAT will give you a necessary shortcut: factoring out squares.

You'll need to find a square factor that is common to both terms under the radical. This square term will probably have an exponent in it.

$$\sqrt{3^{10} + 3^{11}} =$$

First, consider $3^{10} + 3^{11}$ by itself. What is the largest factor that the two terms in the sum have in common? 3^{10}. Note that $3^{11} = 3^{10} \times 3$.

$$3^{10} + 3^{11} = 3^{10}(1 + 3) = 3^{10}(4)$$

After you've factored, the addition becomes simply $1 + 3$. Now plug back into the square root.

$$\sqrt{3^{10} + 3^{11}} = \sqrt{3^{10}(1 + 3)} = \sqrt{3^{10}(4)} = \sqrt{3^{10}} \times \sqrt{4}$$

Since $3^{10} = (3^5)^2$, $\sqrt{3^{10}} = 3^5$. Alternatively, you can apply the square root as an exponent of $\dfrac{1}{2}$: $\sqrt{3^{10}} = \left(3^{10}\right)^{\frac{1}{2}} = 3^{\frac{10}{2}} = 3^5$. And, of course, $\sqrt{4} = 2$.

$$\sqrt{3^{10} + 3^{11}} = \sqrt{3^{10}(1 + 3)} = \sqrt{3^{10}(4)} = \sqrt{3^{10}} \times \sqrt{4} = 3^5 \times 2$$

The answer might be in the form $3^5(2)$.

If you…	Then you…	Like this:
Add or subtract underneath the square root symbol	Factor out a square factor from the sum or difference	$\sqrt{4^{14} + 4^{16}} = \sqrt{4^{14}\left(1 + 4^2\right)}$ $= \sqrt{4^{14}} \times \sqrt{1 + 16}$ $= 4^7\sqrt{17}$
	OR Go ahead and crunch the numbers as written, *if they're small*	$\sqrt{6^2 + 8^2} = \sqrt{36 + 64}$ $= \sqrt{100} = 10$

Check Your Skills

20. $\sqrt{10^5 - 10^4} =$

Answers can be found on page 131.

Check Your Skills Answer Key:

1. $(-5)^8$: $-5^8 = -1 \times 5^8$, and is thus negative. $(-5)^8$ will be positive.

2. $b^5 \times b^7 = b^{(5+7)} = \boldsymbol{b^{12}}$

3. $(x^3)(x^4) = x^{(3+4)} = \boldsymbol{x^7}$

4. $\dfrac{y^5}{y^2} = y^{(5-2)} = \boldsymbol{y^3}$

5. $\dfrac{d^8}{d^7} = d^{(8-7)} = \boldsymbol{d}$

6. $2^{-3} = \dfrac{\mathbf{1}}{\mathbf{8}}$

7. $\dfrac{1}{3^{-3}} = 3^3 = \mathbf{27}$

8. $(x^3)^4 = x^{3 \times 4} = \boldsymbol{x^{12}}$

9. $\dfrac{a^{15}}{a^0 \left(a^3\right)^3} = a^{15-0-9} = \boldsymbol{a^6}$

10. $\left(\dfrac{x^2 y}{z^{-3}}\right)^2 = \dfrac{x^{2 \times 2} y^{1 \times 2}}{z^{-3 \times 2}} = \dfrac{x^4 y^2}{z^{-6}} = \boldsymbol{x^4 y^2 z^6}$

11. $\dfrac{75^3 \times 45^3}{15^8} = \dfrac{(3 \times 5^2)^3 \times (3^2 \times 5)^3}{(3 \times 5)^8} = \dfrac{(3^3 \times 5^6) \times (3^6 \times 5^3)}{(3^8 \times 5^8)} = \dfrac{3^9 \times 5^9}{3^8 \times 5^8} = 3 \times 5 = \mathbf{15}$

12. $\mathbf{5^3(5^2 + 5 - 1)}$

13. **27:** any square root times itself equals the number inside.

14. $\sqrt{x^6} = \sqrt{x^3 \times x^3} = \boldsymbol{x^3}$. Since x is positive, x^3 is positive too.

15. $64^{2/3} = (\sqrt[3]{64})^2 = (4)^2 = \mathbf{16}$

16. $\sqrt{20} \times \sqrt{5} = \sqrt{20 \times 5} = \sqrt{100} = \mathbf{10}$

17. $\dfrac{\sqrt{384}}{\sqrt{2} \times \sqrt{3}} = \sqrt{\dfrac{384}{2 \times 3}} = \sqrt{\dfrac{384}{6}} = \sqrt{64} = \mathbf{8}$

18. $\sqrt{96} = \sqrt{3 \times 2 \times 2 \times 2 \times 2 \times 2} = \sqrt{16} \times \sqrt{3 \times 2} = \mathbf{4\sqrt{6}}$

19. $\sqrt{441} \rightarrow \sqrt{3 \times 3 \times 7 \times 7} = \sqrt{3 \times 3} \times \sqrt{7 \times 7} = 3 \times 7 = \mathbf{21}$

20. $\sqrt{10^5 - 10^4} = \sqrt{10^4(10-1)} = 10^2 \sqrt{9} = 100 \times 3 = \mathbf{300}$

Chapter Review: Drill Sets

Drill 1

Simplify the following expressions by combining like terms. If the base is a number, leave the answer in exponential form (i.e. 2^3, not 8).

1. $x^5 \times x^3 =$ $\quad x^8$
2. $7^6 \times 7^9 =$ $\quad 7^{15}$
3. $\dfrac{5^5}{5^3} =$ $\quad 5^2$
4. $(a^3)^2 =$ $\quad a^6$
5. $4^{-2} \times 4^5 =$ $\quad 4^3$
6. $\dfrac{(-3)^a}{(-3)^2} =$ $\quad -3^{a-2}$
7. $(3^2)^{-3} =$ $\quad 3^{-6} = \dfrac{1}{3^6}$
8. $\dfrac{11^4}{11^x} =$ $\quad 11^{4-x}$
9. $x^2 \times x^3 \times x^5 =$ $\quad x^{10}$
10. $(5^2)^x =$

Drill 2

Simplify the following expressions by combining like terms. If the base is a number, leave the answer in exponential form (i.e. 2^3, not 8).

11. $3^4 \times 3^2 \times 3^1 =$ $\quad 3^7$
12. $\dfrac{x^5 \times x^6}{x^2} =$ $\quad \dfrac{x^{11}}{x^2} = x^9$
13. $\dfrac{5^6 \times 5^{4x}}{5^4} =$ $\quad 5^{(6-4+4x)}$
14. $y^7 \times y^8 \times y^{-6} =$ $\quad y^9$
15. $\dfrac{x^4}{x^{-3}} =$ $\quad \boxed{x^7}$ $4+\cancel{}3$
16. $\dfrac{z^5 \times z^{-3}}{z^{-8}} =$ $\quad z^{5-3+8}$ $\boxed{z^{10}}$
17. $\dfrac{3^{2x} \times 3^{6x}}{3^{-3y}} =$ $\quad 3^{(2x-6x+3y)}$ 3^{-4x+3y}
18. $(x^2)^6 \times x^3 =$ $\quad x^{12+3} = x^{15}$
19. $(z^6)^x \times z^{3x} =$ $\quad z^{9x}$
20. $\dfrac{5^3 \times (5^4)^y}{(5^y)^3} =$ $\quad \dfrac{5^{(3+4y+3y)}}{25}$

Drill 3

handwritten: 9 3^3

Follow the directions for each question.

21. Compute the sum. $27^{\frac{1}{3}} + 9^{\frac{1}{2}} + \frac{3}{9^0} = ?$ *handwritten:* $3 + 3 + 3 = 9$

22. Which of the following has the lowest value?

    (A) $(-3)^4$

    (B) -3^3 *handwritten:* -27

    (C) $(-3)^{-3}$ *handwritten:* $= -8$ $\frac{1}{-3^{-3}}$

    (D) $(-2)^3$

    (E) 2^{-6} *handwritten:* $\frac{1}{2^6}$ positive

    handwritten: negative exponent you put in reciprocal

    handwritten: $-3^3 =$ $-3 \times -3 \times -3$

    handwritten: $\frac{1}{-3^3}$

23. Compute the sum. $6^{-3} - \left(\frac{1}{6}\right)^3 + 8^{\frac{2}{3}} = ?$

24. Which of the following is equal to $\left(\frac{2}{5}\right)^{-3}$?

    (A) $-\left(\frac{2}{5}\right)^3$

    (B) $\left(\frac{2}{5}\right)^{\frac{1}{3}}$ *handwritten:* $\frac{1}{\frac{2}{5}^3}$

    (C) $\left(-\frac{2}{5}\right)^3$ *handwritten:* $6^{-3} - \left(\frac{1}{6}\right)^3$

    (D) $\left(\frac{5}{2}\right)^{\frac{1}{3}}$

    (E) $\left(\frac{5}{2}\right)^3$

25. Which of the following has a value less than 1? (Select all that apply)

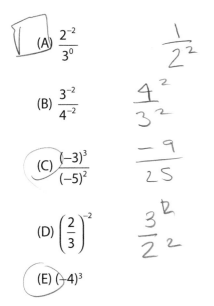

(A) $\dfrac{2^{-2}}{3^0}$ $\dfrac{1}{2^2}$

(B) $\dfrac{3^{-2}}{4^{-2}}$ $\dfrac{4^2}{3^2}$

(C) $\dfrac{(-3)^3}{(-5)^2}$ $\dfrac{-9}{25}$

(D) $\left(\dfrac{2}{3}\right)^{-2}$ $\dfrac{3^2}{2^2}$

(E) $(-4)^3$

Drill 4

Simplify the following expressions by <u>finding common bases</u>.

26. $8^3 \times 2^6$ $(2^3)^3 \times 2^6$ 2^{15}
27. $49^2 \times 7^7$ $(7^2)^2 \times 7^7 = 7^{11}$
28. $25^4 \times 125^3$ $25^4 \times 25$
29. $9^{-2} \times 27^2$ 9^3
30. $2^{-7} \times 8^2$ $(5^2)^4 5^3$ ^{3} $5 \times 5 \times 5$

Drill 5

Simplify the following expressions by pulling out as many common factors as possible.

31. $6^3 + 3^3 =$ $2(3 \times 2)^3$

(A) 3^5 (B) 3^9 (C) $2(3^3)$ $(3^3)(2)$

32. $81^3 + 27^4 =$ $(3^4)^3 + 3^{3(4)}$ $3^{12} + 3^{12}$

(A) $3^7(2)$ (B) $3^{12}(2)$ (C) 3^{14}

33. $15^2 - 5^2 =$ $(5 \times 3)^2 - 5^2$ 3^{12}

(A) $5^2(2)$ (B) $5^2 2^3$ (C) $5^2 3^2$

34. $4^3 + 4^3 + 4^3 + 4^3 + 3^2 + 3^2 + 3^2 =$

(A) $4^4 + 3^3$ (B) $4^{12} + 3^6$ (C) $4^3(3^2)$

35. $\dfrac{4^8 - 8^4}{2^4 + 4^2} =$

(handwritten) $\left(2^2\right)^8 - \left(2^3\right)^4$ $\quad$ $2^{16} \cdot 2^{12} = 2^A$

(A) $\dfrac{1}{2^5}$ $\qquad$ (B) $2^2(7)$ $\qquad$ (C) $2^7(15)$

(handwritten) $\dfrac{}{2^4 + \left(2^2\right)^2}$

$2^8 \quad 2^{14-8} = 2^6$

Drill 6

Simplify the following expressions. All final answers should be integers.

36. $\sqrt{3} \times \sqrt{27}$ $\quad$ *(handwritten)* $\sqrt{3} \times \sqrt{9} \times \sqrt{3} = 9$

37. $\sqrt{2} \times \sqrt{18}$ $\quad$ *(handwritten)* $\sqrt{2} \times \sqrt{9} \times \sqrt{2} = 6$

38. $\dfrac{\sqrt{48}}{\sqrt{3}}$ $\quad$ *(handwritten)* $\dfrac{\sqrt{4} \ \sqrt{12}}{\sqrt{3}}$ $\quad 2 \cdot 2\sqrt{3}$

$= 15\sqrt{3}$

39. $\sqrt{5} \times \sqrt{45}$ $\quad$ *(handwritten)* $\sqrt{5} \times \sqrt{5} \times \sqrt{9}$ $\quad 4\sqrt{3}$

40. $\dfrac{\sqrt{5,000}}{\sqrt{50}}$ $\quad$ *(handwritten)* $\dfrac{\sqrt{100} \ \sqrt{5}}{\sqrt{5}} = 10 \quad \dfrac{4\sqrt{3}}{\sqrt{3}}$

41. $\sqrt{36} \times \sqrt{4}$ $\quad$ *(handwritten)* $\sqrt{9} \times \sqrt{4} \times \sqrt{9} \quad 3 \times 2 \times 2 = 12$

42. $\dfrac{\sqrt{128}}{\sqrt{2}}$ $\quad$ *(handwritten)* $= \sqrt{\dfrac{128}{2}} = \sqrt{64} = 8 \qquad 3 = 9$

43. $\dfrac{\sqrt{54} \times \sqrt{3}}{\sqrt{2}}$ $\quad$ *(handwritten)* $\sqrt{9}\sqrt{6}\sqrt{3} \quad 3 \times \sqrt{3} \times \sqrt{3} \times \sqrt{2} \quad \dfrac{54 \times 3}{2} \ \sqrt{81} = 9$

44. $\dfrac{\sqrt{640}}{\sqrt{2} \times \sqrt{5}}$ $\quad$ *(handwritten)* $\sqrt{\dfrac{640}{10}} \quad \sqrt{64}$

45. $\dfrac{\sqrt{30} \times \sqrt{12}}{\sqrt{10}}$ $\quad$ *(handwritten)* $4\sqrt{\dfrac{36}{1}} = 3^6$

Drill 7

Simplify the following roots. Not every answer will be an integer.

46. $\sqrt{32}$ $\quad$ *(handwritten)* $\sqrt{4}\sqrt{8} \quad \sqrt{4}\sqrt{4}\sqrt{2} \quad 4\sqrt{2}$

47. $\sqrt{24}$ $\quad$ *(handwritten)* $\sqrt{2 \times 2 \times 2 \times 2 \times 3} \quad \sqrt{2}\sqrt{12}\sqrt{1}$

48. $\sqrt{180}$ $\quad$ *(handwritten)* $\sqrt{9}\sqrt{2}\sqrt{10} \quad 3\sqrt{20} \quad 3\sqrt{5} \times 2$

49. $\sqrt{490}$ $\quad$ *(handwritten)* $\sqrt{9}\sqrt{7}\sqrt{10} \quad 3\sqrt{70}$

50. $\sqrt{450}$

51. $\sqrt{135}$ $\quad$ *(handwritten)* $\sqrt{9}\sqrt{15} \quad 3\sqrt{5}\sqrt{3}$

52. $\sqrt{224}$ $\quad$ *(handwritten)* $\sqrt{12}\sqrt{12} \quad \sqrt{4}\sqrt{3} \quad 2\sqrt{3} \times 2\sqrt{5} \quad 4 \times 3 \quad \sqrt{16}\sqrt{14}$

53. $\sqrt{343}$

54. $\sqrt{208}$

55. $\sqrt{432}$

Drill 8

Simplify the following roots. You will be able to completely eliminate the root in every question. Express answers as integers.

3

56. $\sqrt{36^2 + 15^2}$

57. $\sqrt{35^2 - 21^2}$

58. $\sqrt{6(5^6 + 5^7)}$

59. $\sqrt{8^4 + 8^5}$

60. $\sqrt{2^{15} + 2^{13} - 2^{12}}$

61. $\sqrt{50^3 - 50^2}$

62. $\sqrt{\dfrac{11^4 - 11^2}{30}}$

63. $\sqrt{5^7 - 5^5 + 5^4}$

$\sqrt{7^2(5^2 - 3^2)}$ $\sqrt{7^2 \times 2^2} = 7 \times 2 = 14$

$7^2(25 - 9) = 16$ $\sqrt{7^2 \times 16}$ $\sqrt{7^2 \times 4^2}$

$\sqrt{8^4(1 + 8)}$ $\sqrt{8^4 \times 9}$ $\sqrt{8^4 + 3^2} = 8^2 + 3$

$\dfrac{11^2(11^2 - 1)}{30}$ $\dfrac{121 - 1}{120/30 = 90}$

$\sqrt{11^2 \times 4 \cdot 2^2}$ 11×2

$\sqrt{6 \times 5^6(1 + 5)}$
$\phantom{\sqrt{6 \times 5^6(}}6$

$\sqrt{6^2 \times 5^6} = 6 \times 5^3$

ι

Drill Sets Solutions

Drill 1

Simplify the following expressions by combining like terms. If the base is a number, leave the answer in exponential form (i.e. 2^3, not 8).

1. $x^5 \times x^3 = x^{(5+3)} = x^8$

2. $7^6 \times 7^9 = 7^{(6+9)} = 7^{15}$

3. $\dfrac{5^5}{5^3} = 5^{(5-3)} = 5^2$

4. $(a^3)^2 = a^{(3 \times 2)} = a^6$

5. $4^{-2} \times 4^5 = 4^{(-2+5)} = 4^3$

6. $\dfrac{(-3)^a}{(-3)^2} = (-3)^{(a-2)}$

7. $(3^2)^{-3} = 3^{(2 \times -3)} = 3^{-6}$

8. $\dfrac{11^4}{11^x} = 11^{(4-x)}$

9. $x^2 \times x^3 \times x^5 = x^{(2+3+5)} = x^{10}$

10. $(5^2)^x = 5^{(2 \times x)} = 5^{2x}$

Drill 2

Simplify the following expressions by combining like terms. If the base is a number, leave the answer in exponential form (i.e. 2^3, not 8).

11. $3^4 \times 3^2 \times 3 = 3^{(4+2+1)} = 3^7$

12. $\dfrac{x^5 \times x^6}{x^2} = x^{(5+6-2)} = x^9$

13. $\dfrac{5^6 \times 5^{4x}}{5^4} = 5^{(6+4x-4)} = 5^{4x+2}$

14. $y^7 \times y^8 \times y^{-6} = y^{(7+8+(-6))} = y^9$

3

15. $\dfrac{x^4}{x^{-3}} = x^{(4-(-3))} = x^7$

16. $\dfrac{z^5 \times z^{-3}}{z^{-8}} = z^{(5+(-3)-(-8))} = z^{10}$

17. $\dfrac{3^{2x} \times 3^{6x}}{3^{-3y}} = 3^{(2x+6x-(-3y))} = 3^{8x+3y}$

18. $(x^2)^6 \times x^3 = x^{(2\times 6+3)} = x^{(12+3)} = x^{15}$

19. $(z^6)^x \times z^{3x} = z^{(6\times x+3x)} = z^{(6x+3x)} = z^{9x}$

20. $\dfrac{5^3 \times (5^4)^y}{(5^y)^3} = 5^{(3+(4\times y)-(y\times 3))} = 5^{(3+4y-3y)} = 5^{y+3}$

Drill 3

Follow the directions for each question.

21. $27^{\frac{1}{3}} + 9^{\frac{1}{2}} + \dfrac{3}{9^0} = \sqrt[3]{27} + \sqrt{9} + \dfrac{3}{1} = 3+3+3 = 9$

22. We are looking for the answer with the lowest value, so we can focus only on answers that are negative as these answers have lower values than any positive answers.

(A) $(-3)^4$ will result in a positive number because 4 is an even power.

(B) $-3^3 = -(3^3) = -27$

The exponent is done before multiplication (by –1) because of the order of operations.

(C) $(-3)^{-3} = \dfrac{1}{(-3)^3} = \dfrac{1}{-27} = -\dfrac{1}{27}$

(D) $(-2)^3 = -8$

(E) $2^{-6} = \dfrac{1}{2^6}$ The value of this expression is positive.

–27 has the lowest value of the three answer choices that result in negative numbers. The correct answer is (B).

23. $6^{-3} - \left(\dfrac{1}{6}\right)^3 + 8^{\frac{2}{3}} = \dfrac{1}{6^3} - \dfrac{1^3}{6^3} + \sqrt[3]{8^2} = \dfrac{1}{6^3} - \dfrac{1}{6^3} + \sqrt[3]{64} = \sqrt[3]{64} = 4$

The first two terms in the expression are in fact the same. Because these terms are equal, when the second is subtracted from the first they cancel out leaving only the third term.

MANHATTAN
GMAT

24. $\left(\dfrac{2}{5}\right)^{-3} = \dfrac{2^{-3}}{5^{-3}} = \dfrac{5^3}{2^3} = \left(\dfrac{5}{2}\right)^3$

The correct answer is (E).

Note: when a problem asks you to find a different or more simplified version of the same thing, check your work against the answer choices frequently to ensure that you don't simplify or manipulate too far!

25. We are looking for values less than 1 so any expressions with negative values, zero itself, or values between 0 and 1 will work.

(A) $\dfrac{2^{-2}}{3^0} = \dfrac{1}{3^0 \times 2^2} = \dfrac{1}{1 \times 4} = \dfrac{1}{4}$

Dividing a smaller positive number by a larger positive number will result in a number less than 1.

(B) $\dfrac{3^{-2}}{4^{-2}} = \dfrac{4^2}{3^2} = \dfrac{16}{9}$

Dividing a larger positive number by a smaller positive number will result in a number greater than 1.

(C) $\dfrac{(-3)^3}{(-5)^2} = \dfrac{-27}{25} = -\dfrac{27}{25}$

This answer is negative; therefore, it is less than 1.

(D) $\left(\dfrac{2}{3}\right)^{-2} = \dfrac{2^{-2}}{3^{-2}} = \dfrac{3^2}{2^2} = \dfrac{9}{4}$

Dividing a larger positive number by a smaller positive number will result in a number greater than 1.

(E) $(-4)^3 = -64$

This answer is negative; therefore, it is less than 1.

Drill 4

Simplify the following expressions by finding common bases.

26. $8^3 \times 2^6 = (2^3)^3 \times 2^6 = 2^9 \times 2^6 = 2^{15}$

27. $49^2 \times 7^7 = (7^2)^2 \times 7^7 = 7^4 \times 7^7 = 7^{11}$

28. $25^4 \times 125^3 = (5^2)^4 \times (5^3)^3 = 5^8 \times 5^9 = 5^{17}$

29. $9^{-2} \times 27^2 = (3^2)^{-2} \times (3^3)^2 = 3^{-4} \times 3^6 = 3^2$

30. $2^{-7} \times 8^2 = 2^{-7} \times (2^3)^2 = 2^{-7} \times 2^6 = 2^{-1}$

Drill 5

Simplify the following expressions by pulling out as many common factors as possible.

31. Begin by breaking 6 down into its prime factors.

$$6^3 + 3^3 =$$
$$(2 \times 3)^3 + 3^3 =$$
$$(2^3)(3^3) + 3^3$$

Now each term contains (3^3). Factor it out.

$$(2^3)(3^3) + 3^3 =$$
$$3^3(2^3 + 1) =$$
$$3^3(9) =$$
$$3^3(3^2) = 3^5$$

We have a match. The answer is A.

32. Both bases are powers of 3. Rewrite the bases and combine.

$$81^3 + 27^4 =$$
$$(3^4)^3 + (3^3)^4 =$$
$$3^{12} + 3^{12} =$$
$$3^{12}(1 + 1) =$$
$$3^{12}(2)$$

We have a match. The answer is B.

33. Begin by breaking 15 down into its prime factors.

$$15^2 - 5^2 =$$
$$(3 \times 5)^2 - 5^2 =$$
$$(3^2)(5^2) - 5^2 \qquad 5^2(3^2 - 1)$$

Now both terms contain 5^2. Factor it out.

$$(3^2)(5^2) - 5^2 = \qquad 5^2(9 - 2)$$
$$5^2(3^2 - 1) =$$
$$5^2(9 - 1) =$$
$$5^2(8)$$

We still don't have a match, but we can break 8 down into its prime factors.

$$5^2(8) =$$

$$5^2(2^3)$$

We have a match. The answer is B.

34. Factor 4^3 out of the first four terms and factor 3^2 out of the last three terms.

$$4^3 + 4^3 + 4^3 + 4^3 + 3^2 + 3^2 + 3^2 =$$
$$4^3(1 + 1 + 1 + 1) + 3^2(1 + 1 + 1) =$$
$$4^3(4) + 3^2(3) =$$
$$4^4 + 3^3$$

We have a match. The answer is A.

35. Every base in the fraction is a power of 2. Begin by rewriting every base.

$$\frac{4^8 - 8^4}{2^4 + 4^2} = \frac{(2^2)^8 - (2^3)^4}{2^4 + (2^2)^2} = \frac{2^{16} - 2^{12}}{2^4 + 2^4}$$

The terms in the numerator both contain 2^{12}, and the terms in the denominator both contain 2^4. Factor the numerator and denominator.

$$\frac{2^{16} - 2^{12}}{2^4 + 2^4} = \frac{2^{12}(2^4 - 1)}{2^4(1 + 1)} = \frac{2^{12}(16 - 1)}{2^4(2)} = \frac{2^{12}(15)}{2^5}$$

At this point, we can combine the 2's in the numerator and the denominator.

$$\frac{2^{12}(15)}{2^5} = 2^7(15)$$

We have a match. The answer is C.

Drill 6

Simplify the following expressions. All final answers should be integers.

36. $\sqrt{3} \times \sqrt{27} = \sqrt{3 \times 27} = \sqrt{81} = 9$

37. $\sqrt{2} \times \sqrt{18} = \sqrt{2 \times 18} = \sqrt{36} = 6$

38. $\dfrac{\sqrt{48}}{\sqrt{3}} = \sqrt{\dfrac{48}{3}} = \sqrt{16} = 4$

39. $\sqrt{5} \times \sqrt{45} = \sqrt{5 \times 45} = \sqrt{225} = 15$

40. $\dfrac{\sqrt{5{,}000}}{\sqrt{50}} = \sqrt{\dfrac{5{,}000}{50}} = \sqrt{100} = 10$

3

41. $\sqrt{36} \times \sqrt{4} = \sqrt{36 \times 4} = \sqrt{144} = 12$ OR

$\sqrt{36} \times \sqrt{4} = 6 \times 2 = 12$

42. $\dfrac{\sqrt{128}}{\sqrt{2}} = \sqrt{\dfrac{128}{2}} = \sqrt{64} = 8$

43. $\dfrac{\sqrt{54} \times \sqrt{3}}{\sqrt{2}} = \sqrt{\dfrac{54 \times 3}{2}} = \sqrt{81} = 9$

44. $\dfrac{\sqrt{640}}{\sqrt{2} \times \sqrt{5}} = \sqrt{\dfrac{640}{2 \times 5}} = \sqrt{\dfrac{640}{10}} = \sqrt{64} = 8$

45. $\dfrac{\sqrt{30} \times \sqrt{12}}{\sqrt{10}} = \sqrt{\dfrac{30 \times 12}{10}} = \sqrt{36} = 6$

Drill 7

Simplify the following roots. Not every answer will be an integer.

46. $\sqrt{32} = \sqrt{2 \times 2 \times 2 \times 2 \times 2} = \sqrt{2 \times 2} \times \sqrt{2 \times 2} \times \sqrt{2} = 2 \times 2 \times \sqrt{2} = 4\sqrt{2}$

47. $\sqrt{24} = \sqrt{2 \times 2 \times 2 \times 3} = \sqrt{2 \times 2} \times \sqrt{2 \times 3} = 2\sqrt{6}$

48. $\sqrt{180} = \sqrt{2 \times 2 \times 3 \times 3 \times 5} = \sqrt{2 \times 2} \times \sqrt{3 \times 3} \times \sqrt{5} = 2 \times 3 \times \sqrt{5} = 6\sqrt{5}$

49. $\sqrt{490} = \sqrt{2 \times 5 \times 7 \times 7} = \sqrt{7 \times 7} \times \sqrt{2 \times 5} = 7\sqrt{10}$

50. $\sqrt{450} = \sqrt{2 \times 3 \times 3 \times 5 \times 5} = \sqrt{3 \times 3} \times \sqrt{5 \times 5} \times \sqrt{2} = 3 \times 5 \times \sqrt{2} = 15\sqrt{2}$

51. $\sqrt{135} = \sqrt{3 \times 3 \times 3 \times 5} = \sqrt{3 \times 3} \times \sqrt{3 \times 5} = 3\sqrt{15}$

52. $\sqrt{224} = \sqrt{2 \times 2 \times 2 \times 2 \times 2 \times 7} = \sqrt{2 \times 2} \times \sqrt{2 \times 2} \times \sqrt{2 \times 7} = 2 \times 2 \times \sqrt{14} = 4\sqrt{14}$

53. $\sqrt{343} = \sqrt{7 \times 7 \times 7} = \sqrt{7 \times 7} \times \sqrt{7} = 7\sqrt{7}$

54. $\sqrt{208} = \sqrt{2 \times 2 \times 2 \times 2 \times 13} = \sqrt{2 \times 2} \times \sqrt{2 \times 2} \times \sqrt{13} = 2 \times 2 \times \sqrt{13} = 4\sqrt{13}$

55. $\sqrt{432} = \sqrt{2 \times 2 \times 2 \times 2 \times 3 \times 3 \times 3} = \sqrt{2 \times 2} \times \sqrt{2 \times 2} \times \sqrt{3 \times 3} \times \sqrt{3} = 2 \times 2 \times 3 \times \sqrt{3} = 12\sqrt{3}$

Drill 8

Simplify the following roots. You will be able to completely eliminate the root in every question. Express answers as integers.

56. Pull out the greatest common factor of 36^2 and 15^2, namely 3^2, to give

$\sqrt{3^2(12^2 + 5^2)} = \sqrt{3^2(144 + 25)} = \sqrt{3^2(169)}$. Both 3^2 and 169 are perfect squares ($169 = 13^2$), so

$\sqrt{3^2(169)} = \sqrt{3^2(13^2)} = 3 \times 13 = 39$.

57. Pull out the greatest common factor of 35^2 and 21^2, namely 7^2, to give

$\sqrt{7^2(5^2 - 3^2)} = \sqrt{7^2(25 - 9)} = \sqrt{7^2(16)}$. Both 7^2 and 16 are perfect squares ($16 = 4^2$), so

$\sqrt{7^2(16)} = \sqrt{7^2(4^2)} = 7 \times 4 = 28$.

58. Pull out the greatest common factor of 5^6 and 5^7, namely 5^6, to give

$\sqrt{6(5^6(1+5))} = \sqrt{6(5^6(6))} = \sqrt{6^2(5^6)}$. Both 6^2 and 5^6 are perfect squares ($5^6 = 5^3 \times 5^3$), so

$\sqrt{6^2(5^6)} = 6 \times 5^3 = 6 \times 125 = 750$.

59. Pull out the greatest common factor of 8^4 and 8^5, namely 8^4, to give $\sqrt{8^4(1+8)} = \sqrt{8^4(9)} = \sqrt{8^4(3^2)}$.

Both 8^4 and 3^2 are perfect squares ($8^4 = 8^2 \times 8^2$), so $\sqrt{8^4(3^2)} = 8^2 \times 3 = 64 \times 3 = 192$.

60. Pull out the greatest common factor of 2^{15}, 2^{13}, and 2^{12}, namely 2^{12}, to give

$\sqrt{2^{12}(2^3 + 2 - 1)} = \sqrt{2^{12}(8 + 2 - 1)} = \sqrt{2^{12}(9)} = \sqrt{2^{12}(3^2)}$. Both 2^{12} and 3^2 are perfect squares ($2^{12} = 2^6 \times$

2^6), so $\sqrt{2^{12}(3^2)} = 2^6 \times 3 = 64 \times 3 = 192$.

61. Pull out the greatest common factor of 50^3 and 50^2, namely 50^2, to give

$\sqrt{50^2(50 - 1)} = \sqrt{50^2(49)} = \sqrt{50^2(7^2)}$. Both 50^2 and 7^2 are perfect squares, so $\sqrt{50^2(7^2)} = 50 \times 7 = 350$.

62. First focus on the numerator of the fraction under the radical and pull out the greatest common

factor of 11^4 and 11^2, namely 11^2, to give $\sqrt{\dfrac{11^2(11^2 - 1)}{30}} = \sqrt{\dfrac{11^2(121 - 1)}{30}} = \sqrt{\dfrac{11^2(120)}{30}}$. The denominator

(30) divides evenly into 120: $\sqrt{\dfrac{11^2(120)}{30}} = \sqrt{11^2(4)} = \sqrt{11^2(2^2)}$. Both 11^2 and 2^2 are perfect squares, so

$\sqrt{11^2(2^2)} = 11 \times 2 = 22$.

63. Pull out the greatest common factor of 5^7, 5^5, and 5^4, namely 5^4, to give

$\sqrt{5^4(5^3 - 5 + 1)} = \sqrt{5^4(125 - 5 + 1)} = \sqrt{5^4(121)} = \sqrt{5^4(11^2)}$. Both 5^4 and 11^2 are perfect squares ($5^4 = 5^2 \times$

5^2), so $\sqrt{5^4(11^2)} = 5^2 \times 11 = 25 \times 11 = 275$.

Chapter 4
of
Foundations of GMAT Math

Fractions

In This Chapter...

Chapter 4:
Fractions

In This Chapter:

• Rules for manipulating fractions

Basics of Fractions

To review, a fraction expresses division.

The **numerator** on top is divided by the **denominator** on bottom.

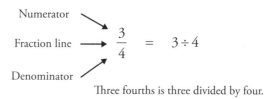

Three fourths is three divided by four.

The result of the division is a number. If you punch "3 ÷ 4 =" into a calculator, you get the decimal 0.75. But you can also think of 0.75 as $\frac{3}{4}$, because $\frac{3}{4}$ and 0.75 are two different names for the same number. (We'll deal with decimals in the next chapter.)

Fractions express a part-to-whole relationship.

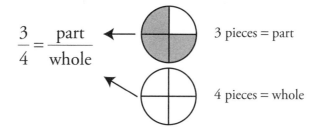

In this picture, a circle represents a whole unit—a full pizza. Each pizza has been divided into 4 equal parts, or fourths, because the denominator of the fraction is 4. In any fraction, the denominator tells you how many equal slices a pizza has been broken into. In other words, the denominator tells you the size of a slice.

The numerator of the fraction is 3. This means that we actually have 3 slices of the pizza. In any fraction, the numerator tells you how many slices you have.

Together, we have three fourths: three slices that are each a fourth of a whole pizza.

Since fractions express division, all the arithmetic rules of division apply. For instance, a negative divided by a positive gives you a negative, and so on.

$$\frac{-3}{4} = -3 \div 4 = -0.75 \qquad\qquad \frac{3}{-4} = 3 \div (-4) = -0.75$$

So $\frac{-3}{4}$ and $\frac{3}{-4}$ represent the same number. We can even write that number as $-\frac{3}{4}$. Just don't mix up the negative sign with the fraction bar.

PEMDAS also applies. The fraction bar means that you always **divide the entire numerator by the entire denominator**.

$$\frac{3x^2 + y}{2y^2 - z} = \left(3x^2 + y\right) \div \left(2y^2 - z\right)$$

The entire quantity $3x^2 + y$ is being divided by the entire quantity $2y^2 - z$.

If you rewrite a fraction, be ready to put parentheses around the numerator or denominator to preserve the correct order of operations.

Finally, remember that you can't divide by 0. So **a denominator can never equal zero.** If you have a variable expression in the denominator, that expression cannot equal zero. If a problem contains the fraction $\frac{3x^2 + y}{2y^2 - z}$, then we know that $2y^2 - z$ cannot equal zero. In other words, we know

$$2y^2 - z \neq 0 \qquad \text{or} \qquad 2y^2 \neq z$$

If the GMAT tells you that something does *not* equal something else (using the $\neq$ sign), the purpose is often to rule out dividing by 0 somewhere in the problem.

To compare fractions with the same denominator, compare the numerators. The numerator tells you how many pieces you have. **The larger the numerator, the larger the fraction** (assuming positive numbers everywhere). You have more slices of pie.

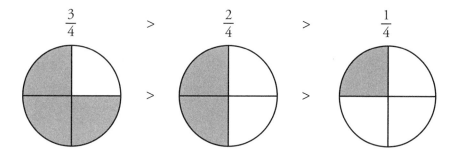

To compare fractions with the same numerator, compare the denominators. Again assume positive numbers everywhere. **The larger the denominator, the *smaller* the fraction.** Each slice of pie is smaller. So the same number of smaller slices is smaller.

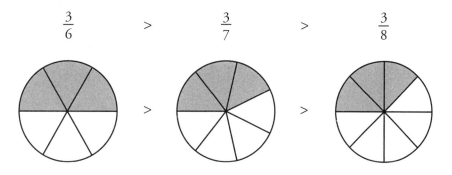

If the numerator and denominator are the same, then the fraction equals 1.

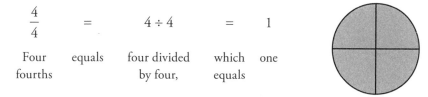

$$\frac{4}{4} \quad = \quad 4 \div 4 \quad = \quad 1$$

Four   equals   four divided   which   one
fourths   by four,   equals

If the numerator is larger than the denominator (again, assume positive numbers), then you have more than one pizza.

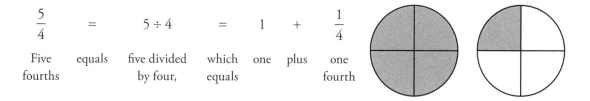

$$\frac{5}{4} \quad = \quad 5 \div 4 \quad = \quad 1 \quad + \quad \frac{1}{4}$$

Five   equals   five divided   which   one   plus   one
fourths   by four,   equals   fourth

Another way to write $1+\frac{1}{4}$ is $1\frac{1}{4}$ ("one and one fourth"). This is the only time in GMAT math when we put two things next to each other (1 and $\frac{1}{4}$) in order to *add* them. In all other circumstances, we mean *multiplication* when we put two things next to each other.

A **mixed number** such as $1\frac{1}{4}$ contains both an integer part (1) and a fractional part $\frac{1}{4}$. You can always rewrite a mixed number as a sum of the integer part and the fractional part.

$$3\frac{3}{8} = 3 + \frac{3}{8}$$

In an **improper fraction** such as $\frac{5}{4}$, the numerator is larger than the denominator. Improper fractions and mixed numbers express the same thing. Later we'll discuss how to convert between them.

A **proper fraction** such as $\frac{3}{4}$ has a value between 0 and 1. In a proper fraction, the numerator is smaller than the denominator.

Add Fractions with the Same Denominator: Add the Numerators

The numerator of a fraction tells you how many slices of the pizza you have. So when you add fractions, you add the numerators. You just have to make sure that the slices are the same size—in other words, that the denominators are equal. Otherwise you aren't adding apples to apples.

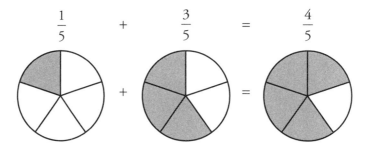

In words, one fifth plus three fifths equals four fifths. The "fifth" is the size of the slice, so the denominator (5) doesn't change.

Since 4 = 1 + 3, you can write the fraction with 1 + 3 in the numerator.

$$\frac{1}{5} + \frac{3}{5} = \frac{1+3}{5} = \frac{4}{5}$$

The same process applies with subtraction. Subtract the numerators and leave the denominator the same.

$$\frac{9}{14} - \frac{4}{14} = \frac{9-4}{14} = \frac{5}{14}$$

If variables are involved, add or subtract the same way. Just make sure that the denominators in the original fractions are equal. It doesn't matter how complicated they are.

$$\frac{3a}{b} + \frac{4a}{b} = \frac{3a + 4a}{b} = \frac{7a}{b} \qquad\qquad \frac{5x^2}{z+w} - \frac{2x^2}{z+w} = \frac{5x^2 - 2x^2}{z+w} = \frac{3x^2}{z+w}$$

If you can't simplify the numerator, leave it as a sum or a difference. Remember that the denominator stays the same: it just tells you the *size* of the slices you're adding or subtracting.

$$\frac{x}{y} + \frac{z}{y} = \frac{x+z}{y} \qquad\qquad \frac{3n}{2w^3} - \frac{5m}{2w^3} = \frac{3n - 5m}{2w^3}$$

If you…	Then you…	Like this:
Add or subtract fractions that have the same denominator	Add or subtract the numerators, leaving the denominator alone	$\frac{2}{7} + \frac{3}{7} = \frac{2+3}{7}$ $= \frac{5}{7}$

Check Your Skills

1. $\dfrac{3x}{yz^2} + \dfrac{7x}{yz^2} =$

Answers can be found on page 179.

Add Fractions with Different Denominators: Find a Common Denominator First

Consider this example:

$$\frac{1}{4} + \frac{3}{8} =$$

The denominators (the sizes of the slices) aren't the same, so you can't just add the numerators and call it a day.

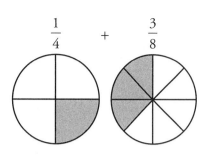

To add these fractions correctly, we need to re-express one or both of the fractions so that the slices are the same size. In other words, we need the fractions to have a **common denominator**—that is, the *same* denominator. Once they have the same denominator, we can add the numerators and be finished.

Since a fourth of a pizza is twice as big as an eighth, we can take the fourth in the first circle and cut it in two.

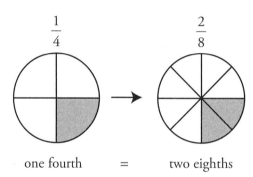

one fourth   =   two eighths

We have the same amount of pizza—the shaded area hasn't changed in size. So one fourth $\left(\dfrac{1}{4}\right)$ must equal two eighths $\left(\dfrac{2}{8}\right)$.

When we cut the fourth in two, we have twice as many slices. So the numerator is doubled. But we're breaking the whole circle into twice as many pieces, so the denominator is doubled as well. If you double both the numerator and the denominator, the fraction's value stays the same.

$$\frac{1}{4} = \frac{1 \times 2}{4 \times 2} = \frac{2}{8}$$

Without changing the value of $\dfrac{1}{4}$, we have renamed it $\dfrac{2}{8}$. Now we can add it to $\dfrac{3}{8}$.

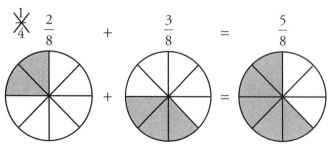

All in one line:

$$\frac{1}{4}+\frac{3}{8}=\frac{1\times2}{4\times2}+\frac{3}{8}=\frac{2}{8}+\frac{3}{8}=\frac{5}{8}$$

To add fractions with different denominators, find a common denominator first. That is, rename the fractions so that they have the same denominator. Then add the new numerators. The same holds true for subtraction.

How do you rename a fraction without changing its value? Multiply the top and bottom by the same number.

$$\frac{1}{4}=\frac{1\times2}{4\times2}=\frac{2}{8} \qquad \frac{3}{4}=\frac{3\times25}{4\times25}=\frac{75}{100} \qquad \frac{5}{12}=\frac{5\times7}{12\times7}=\frac{35}{84}$$

Here's why this works. Doubling the top and doubling the bottom of a fraction is the same as multiplying the fraction by $\frac{2}{2}$. (More on fraction multiplication later.)

Moreover, $\frac{2}{2}$ is equal to 1. And multiplying a number by 1 leaves the number the same. So if we multiply by $\frac{2}{2}$, we aren't really changing the number. We're just changing its look.

$$\frac{1}{4}=\frac{1}{4}\times\frac{2}{2}=\frac{1\times2}{4\times2}=\frac{2}{8}$$

You can rename fractions that have variables in them, too. You can even multiply top and bottom by the same variable.

$$\frac{x}{y}=\frac{x}{y}\times\frac{2}{2}=\frac{x\times2}{y\times2}=\frac{2x}{2y} \qquad \frac{a}{2}=\frac{a}{2}\times\frac{b}{b}=\frac{a\times b}{2\times b}=\frac{ab}{2b}$$

Just make sure the expression on the bottom can never equal zero, of course.

If you...	Then you...	Like this:
Want to give a fraction a different denominator but keep the value the same	Multiply top and bottom of the fraction by the same number	$\frac{1}{4}=\frac{1\times2}{4\times2}=\frac{2}{8}$

Say you have this problem:

$$\frac{1}{4}+\frac{1}{3}=$$

What should the common denominator of these fractions be? It should be both a multiple of 4 and a multiple of 3. That is, it should be a multiple that 3 and 4 have in common. The easiest multiple to pick is usually the **least common multiple** (LCM) of 3 and 4. Least common multiples were discussed on page 77.

The least common multiple of 4 and 3 is 12. So we should rename our two fractions so that they each have a denominator of 12.

$$\frac{1}{4} = \frac{1 \times 3}{4 \times 3} = \frac{3}{12} \qquad\qquad \frac{1}{3} = \frac{1 \times 4}{3 \times 4} = \frac{4}{12}$$

Once you have a common denominator, add the numerators:

$$\frac{1}{4} + \frac{1}{3} = \frac{1 \times 3}{4 \times 3} + \frac{1 \times 4}{3 \times 4} = \frac{3}{12} + \frac{4}{12} = \frac{7}{12}$$

The process works the same if we subtract fractions or even have more than two fractions. Try this example:

$$\frac{5}{6} + \frac{2}{9} - \frac{3}{4} =$$

First, find the common denominator by finding the least common multiple. All three denominators (6, 9, and 4) are composed of 2's and 3's.

$$6 = 2 \times 3 \qquad\qquad 9 = 3 \times 3 \qquad\qquad 4 = 2 \times 2$$

The LCM will contain two 2's (because there are two 2's in 4) and two 3's (because there are two 3's in 9).

$$2 \times 2 \times 3 \times 3 = 36$$

To make each of the denominators equal 36, multiply the fractions by $\frac{6}{6}$, $\frac{4}{4}$, and $\frac{9}{9}$, respectively.

$$\frac{5}{6} = \frac{5 \times 6}{6 \times 6} = \frac{30}{36} \qquad\qquad \frac{2}{9} = \frac{2 \times 4}{9 \times 4} = \frac{8}{36} \qquad\qquad \frac{3}{4} = \frac{3 \times 9}{4 \times 9} = \frac{27}{36}$$

Now that the denominators are all the same, we can add and subtract normally.

$$\frac{5}{6} + \frac{2}{9} - \frac{3}{4} = \frac{30}{36} + \frac{8}{36} - \frac{27}{36} = \frac{30 + 8 - 27}{36} = \frac{11}{36}$$

The process works even if we have variables. Try adding these two fractions:

$$\frac{2}{x} + \frac{3}{2x} =$$

First, find the common denominator by finding the least common multiple of x and $2x$. The LCM is $2x$, since you can just multiply the x by 2. So give the first fraction a denominator of $2x$, then add:

$$\frac{2}{x} + \frac{3}{2x} = \frac{2 \times 2}{x \times 2} + \frac{3}{2x} = \frac{4}{2x} + \frac{3}{2x} = \frac{4+3}{2x} = \frac{7}{2x}$$

If you…	Then you…	Like this:
Add or subtract fractions with different denominators	Put the fractions in terms of a common denominator, then add or subtract	$\dfrac{1}{3} + \dfrac{1}{5} = \dfrac{1 \times 5}{3 \times 5} + \dfrac{1 \times 3}{5 \times 3}$ $= \dfrac{5}{15} + \dfrac{3}{15} = \dfrac{8}{15}$

Check Your Skills

2. $\dfrac{1}{2} + \dfrac{3}{4} =$

3. $\dfrac{2}{3} - \dfrac{3}{8} =$

Answers can be found on page 179.

Compare Fractions: Find a Common Denominator (or Cross-Multiply)

Earlier in the chapter, we talked a little about comparing fractions. If two fractions have the same denominator, then you compare the numerators.

Now you can compare *any* two fractions. Just give them the same denominator first.

Which is larger, $\dfrac{4}{7}$ or $\dfrac{3}{5}$?

First, find a common denominator and re-express the fractions in terms of that denominator. The least common multiple of 7 and 5 is 35, so convert the fractions appropriately:

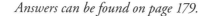

$$\frac{4}{7} = \frac{4 \times 5}{7 \times 5} = \frac{20}{35} \qquad\qquad \frac{3}{5} = \frac{3 \times 7}{5 \times 7} = \frac{21}{35}$$

Now you can tell at a glance which fraction is larger. Since 21 is greater than 20, you know that $\dfrac{3}{5}$ is greater than $\dfrac{4}{7}$.

A good shortcut is to **cross-multiply** the fractions. Here's how:

(1)   Set them up near each other.

(2)   Multiply "up" the arrows as shown.

Be sure to put the results at the top.

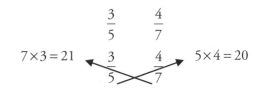

(3)   Now compare the numbers you get. The side with the bigger number is bigger.

$21 > 20$, so $\dfrac{3}{5}$ is greater than $\dfrac{4}{7}$.

This process generates the numerators we saw before (21 and 20). You don't really care about the common denominator itself (35) so cross-multiplying can be fast.

If you...	Then you...	Like this:
Want to compare fractions	Put them in terms of a common denominator, or just cross-multiply	㉘ $\dfrac{4}{9}$ $\dfrac{3}{7}$ 27

Check Your Skills

For each of the following pairs of fractions, decide which fraction is greater.

4. $\dfrac{5}{7}, \dfrac{3}{7}$

5. $\dfrac{3}{10}, \dfrac{3}{13}$

Answers can be found on page 179.

Change an Improper Fraction To a Mixed Number: Actually Divide

What is $\dfrac{13}{4}$ as a mixed number? Note that $\dfrac{13}{4}$ is an improper fraction, because $13 > 4$.

Since the fraction bar represents division, go ahead and divide 13 by 4. Try doing this by long division:

$$
\begin{array}{r}
3 \\
4{\overline{\smash{)}13}} \\
\underline{12} \\
1
\end{array}
$$

4 goes into 13 three times, with 1 left over. 3 is the **quotient**, representing how many whole times the denominator (4) goes into the numerator (13).

Meanwhile, 1 is the **remainder**.

So $\dfrac{13}{4}$ equals 3, plus a remainder of 1. This remainder of 1 is literally "left over" the 4, so we can write the whole thing out:

$$\frac{13}{4} = 3 + \frac{1}{4}$$

As a mixed number, then, $\dfrac{13}{4}$ equals $3\dfrac{1}{4}$.

To convert an improper fraction to a mixed number, actually divide the numerator by the denominator. The quotient becomes the integer part of the mixed number. The remainder over the denominator becomes the left-over fractional part of the mixed number.

To do the division, look for the largest multiple of the denominator that is less than or equal to the numerator. In the case of $\dfrac{13}{4}$, we should see that 12 is the largest multiple of 4 less than 13. $12 = 4 \times 3$, so 3 is the quotient. $13 - 12 = 1$, so 1 is the remainder.

Here's another way to understand this process. Fraction addition can go forward and in reverse.

$$\text{Forward:} \quad \frac{2}{7} + \frac{4}{7} = \frac{2+4}{7} = \frac{6}{7} \qquad \text{Reverse:} \quad \frac{6}{7} = \frac{2+4}{7} = \frac{2}{7} + \frac{4}{7}$$

In other words, you can **rewrite a numerator as a sum, then split the fraction.** Try this with $\dfrac{13}{4}$.

Rewrite 13 as 12 + 1, then split the fraction:

$$\frac{13}{4} = \frac{12+1}{4} = \frac{12}{4} + \frac{1}{4}$$

Since $\dfrac{12}{4} = 12 \div 4 = 3$, we have $\dfrac{13}{4} = \dfrac{12}{4} + \dfrac{1}{4} = 3 + \dfrac{1}{4} = 3\dfrac{1}{4}$.

You still need to find the largest multiple of 4 that's less than 13, so that you can write 13 as 12 + 1.

If you…	Then you…	Like this:
Want to convert an improper fraction to a mixed number	Actually divide the numerator by the denominator	$\dfrac{13}{4} = 13 \div 4$ $= 3 \text{ remainder } 1$ $= 3\dfrac{1}{4}$
	OR Rewrite the numerator as a sum, then split the fraction	$\dfrac{13}{4} = \dfrac{12+1}{4}$ $= \dfrac{12}{4} + \dfrac{1}{4}$ $= 3\dfrac{1}{4}$

Check Your Skills

Change the following improper fractions to mixed numbers.

6. $\dfrac{11}{6}$

7. $\dfrac{100}{11}$

Answers can be found on page 179.

Change a Mixed Number To an Improper Fraction: Actually Add

What is $5\dfrac{2}{3}$ as an improper fraction?

First, rewrite the mixed number as a sum. $5\dfrac{2}{3} = 5 + \dfrac{2}{3}$.

Now, let's actually add these two numbers together by rewriting 5 as a fraction. You can always write any integer as a fraction by just putting it over 1:

$$5 = \dfrac{5}{1} \qquad \text{This is true because } 5 \div 1 = 5.$$

So $5\dfrac{2}{3} = 5 + \dfrac{2}{3} = \dfrac{5}{1} + \dfrac{2}{3}$. At this point, you're adding fractions with different denominators, so find a common denominator.

The least common multiple of 1 and 3 is simply 3, so convert $\frac{5}{1}$ to a fraction with a 3 in its denominator:

$$\frac{5}{1} = \frac{5 \times 3}{1 \times 3} = \frac{15}{3}$$

Finally, complete the addition:

$$5\frac{2}{3} = 5 + \frac{2}{3} = \frac{5}{1} + \frac{2}{3} = \frac{15}{3} + \frac{2}{3} = \frac{15+2}{3} = \frac{17}{3}$$

The quick shortcut is that the new numerator is $5 \times 3 + 2 = 17$. That's the integer times the denominator of the fractional part, plus the numerator of that part (the remainder).

But don't just memorize a recipe. Make sure that you see how this shortcut is equivalent to the addition process above. 5×3 gives you 15, the numerator of the fraction that the integer 5 becomes. Then you add 15 to 2 to get 17.

If you…	Then you…	Like this:
Want to convert a mixed number to an improper fraction	Convert the integer to a fraction over 1, then add it to the fractional part	$7\frac{3}{8} = \frac{7}{1} + \frac{3}{8}$ $= \frac{56}{8} + \frac{3}{8}$ $= \frac{59}{8}$

Check Your Skills

Change the following mixed numbers to improper fractions.

8. $3\frac{3}{4}$
9. $5\frac{2}{3}$

Answers can be found on page 179.

Simplify a Fraction: Cancel Common Factors on Top and Bottom

Consider this problem:

$$\frac{5}{9}+\frac{1}{9}=$$

(A) $\frac{4}{9}$ (B) $\frac{6}{18}$ (C) $\frac{2}{3}$

You know how to add fractions with the same denominator: $\frac{5}{9}+\frac{1}{9}=\frac{5+1}{9}=\frac{6}{9}$. This is mathematically

correct so far. But $\frac{6}{9}$ is not an answer choice, because it isn't **simplified** or **reduced** to lowest terms.

To simplify a fraction, cancel out common factors from the numerator and denominator.

$$\frac{6}{9}=\frac{2\times3}{3\times3}$$ Since 3 is a common factor on top and bottom, cancel it.

$$\frac{6}{9}=\frac{2\times\cancel{3}}{3\times\cancel{3}}=\frac{2}{3}$$

Before, we saw that we can multiply top and bottom of a fraction by the same number without changing the value of the fraction. The fraction stays the same because we are actually multiplying the whole fraction by 1.

$$\frac{2}{3}=\frac{2\times3}{3\times3}=\frac{6}{9}$$

Now we're just dividing the fraction by 1, which also leaves the value unchanged. As we divide away the $\frac{3}{3}$ (which equals 1), the look of the fraction changes from $\frac{6}{9}$ to $\frac{2}{3}$, but the value of the fraction is the same.

This process works with both numbers and variables. Try reducing the following fraction:

$$\frac{18x^2}{60x}=$$

Start cancelling common factors on top and bottom. You can do so in any order. If you want, you can even break all the way down to primes, then cancel. (We'll use the × symbol to be very explicit about all the multiplication.)

$$\frac{18x^2}{60x}=\frac{2\times3\times3\times x\times x}{2\times2\times3\times5\times x}$$

The top and the bottom each contain a 2, a 3, and an x. These are the common factors to cancel, either one at a time or in groups.

$$\frac{18x^{\cancel{2}}}{60\cancel{x}} = \frac{18x}{60} = \frac{\cancel{2} \times 9x}{\cancel{2} \times 30} = \frac{9x}{30} = \frac{\cancel{3} \times 3x}{\cancel{3} \times 10} = \frac{3x}{10}$$

$$\frac{18x^2}{60x} = \frac{\cancel{6x} \times 3x}{\cancel{6x} \times 10} = \frac{3x}{10}$$

If you…	Then you…	Like this:
Want to simplify a fraction	Cancel out common factors from top and bottom	$\frac{14}{35} = \frac{2 \times \cancel{7}}{5 \times \cancel{7}} = \frac{2}{5}$

Check Your Skills

Simplify the following fractions.

10. $\dfrac{25}{40}$

11. $\dfrac{16}{24}$

Answers can be found on page 179.

Multiply Fractions: Multiply Tops and Multiply Bottoms (But Cancel First)

What is $\dfrac{1}{2}$ of 6?

One half of 6 is 3. When you take $\dfrac{1}{2}$ of 6, you divide 6 into 2 equal parts (since the denominator of $\dfrac{1}{2}$ is 2). Then you keep 1 part (since the numerator of $\dfrac{1}{2}$ is 1). That part equals 3.

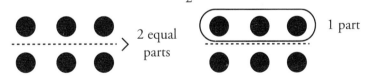

One half *of* 6 is the same thing as one half *times* 6. It's also the same thing as 6 divided by 2. Either way, you get 3.

$$\frac{1}{2} \times 6 = 3 \qquad\qquad \frac{6}{2} = 6 \div 2 = 3$$

Now consider this problem:

What is $\dfrac{1}{2}$ of $\dfrac{3}{4}$?

In other words, $\dfrac{1}{2} \times \dfrac{3}{4} =$

To multiply two fractions, multiply the tops together and multiply the bottoms together.

$$\frac{1}{2} \times \frac{3}{4} = \frac{1 \times 3}{2 \times 4} = \frac{3}{8}$$

That's not so hard mechanically. Why is it true conceptually? Again, to take half of something, you cut it into 2 equal parts, then you keep 1 part. So to take $\dfrac{1}{2}$ of $\dfrac{3}{4}$, cut $\dfrac{3}{4}$ into 2 equal parts. Since $\dfrac{3}{4}$ is three fourths, or three pizza slices of a certain size, you can cut each slice in half. That gives you six smaller slices.

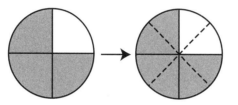

Cut each slice in half

Now keep just 1 out of every 2 of those slices.

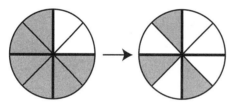

Keep 1 out of 2 smaller slices.

You wind up with 3 slices. So your numerator is 3. The slices are now "eighths" of a whole pizza, so the denominator is 8. Thus, $\dfrac{1}{2}$ of $\dfrac{3}{4}$ is $\dfrac{3}{8}$.

In practice, don't try to think through that logic very often. It's much tougher than the mechanical rule: multiply tops and multiply bottoms. The rule works for integers too. Just put the integer over 1.

$$\frac{3}{4} \times \frac{5}{7} = \frac{3 \times 5}{4 \times 7} = \frac{15}{28} \qquad\qquad \frac{1}{2} \times 6 = \frac{1}{2} \times \frac{6}{1} = \frac{6}{2} = 3$$

To avoid unnecessary computations, **always try to cancel factors before you multiply out.**

$$\frac{33}{7} \times \frac{14}{3} =$$

The terribly long way to do this multiplication is to multiply the tops, then multiply the bottoms, then reduce the numerator and denominator.

Long way: $33 \times 14 =$

$$
\begin{array}{r}
33 \\
\times\ 14 \\
\hline
132 \\
330 \\
\hline
462
\end{array}
$$

$7 \times 3 = 21$

You wind up with $\dfrac{462}{21}$.

$$
\begin{array}{r}
22 \\
21\overline{)462} \\
-42 \\
\hline
42 \\
-42
\end{array}
$$

4

The final answer is 22. However, we can get there much faster and more safely by cancelling factors *before* multiplying. Break the numerators into smaller factors.

$33 = 3 \times 11$ This 3 cancels with the 3 on the bottom of fraction #2.

$14 = 2 \times 7$ This 7 cancels with the 7 on the bottom of fraction #1.

You can cancel across the multiplication sign (×). In other words, a factor on top of fraction #1 can cancel with a factor on the bottom of fraction #2.

As you cancel, leave behind the factors that don't cancel (the 11 and the 2). Write those factors nearby.

$$
\frac{33}{7} \times \frac{14}{3} = \frac{\overset{11}{\cancel{33}}}{7} \times \frac{14}{\cancel{3}} = \frac{\overset{11}{\cancel{33}}}{\cancel{7}} \times \frac{\overset{2}{\cancel{14}}}{\cancel{3}}
$$

If it seems that no factors are left behind in a position, then the remaining factor is 1 and doesn't matter. In the case above, we only have 1's left over on the bottom.

So we are left with 11×2 on top and nothing but 1's on the bottom, giving us 22.

$$
\frac{33}{7} \times \frac{14}{3} = \frac{\overset{11}{\cancel{33}}}{7} \times \frac{14}{\cancel{3}} = \frac{\overset{11}{\cancel{33}}}{\cancel{7}} \times \frac{\overset{2}{\cancel{14}}}{\cancel{3}} = 11 \times 2 = 22
$$

Negative signs make fraction multiplication trickier. Again, a negative sign can appear anywhere in a fraction:

$$
-\frac{2}{3} = \frac{-2}{3} = \frac{2}{-3}
$$

When you multiply a fraction by −1, you add a negative sign to the fraction. Where you put it is up to you.

$$-1 \times \frac{3}{5} = -\frac{3}{5} = \frac{-3}{5} = \frac{3}{-5}$$

In general, you are multiplying *either* the numerator *or* the denominator by −1. If the fraction already contains a negative sign, then cancel out both negatives, because −1 × −1 = 1.

$$-1 \times -\frac{8}{7} = -1 \times -1 \times \frac{8}{7} = \frac{8}{7}$$

$$-1 \times \frac{-8}{7} = \frac{-1 \times (-8)}{7} = \frac{8}{7}$$

$$-1 \times \frac{8}{-7} = \frac{8}{-1 \times (-7)} = \frac{8}{7}$$

If you…	Then you…	Like this:
Multiply two fractions	Multiply tops and multiply bottoms, cancelling common factors first	$\frac{20}{9} \times \frac{6}{5} = \frac{\overset{4}{\cancel{20}}}{\underset{3}{\cancel{9}}} \times \frac{\overset{2}{\cancel{6}}}{\cancel{5}}$ $= \frac{4 \times 2}{3} = \frac{8}{3}$

Check Your Skills

Evaluate the following expressions. Simplify all fractions.

12. $\dfrac{3}{7} \times \dfrac{6}{10} =$

13. $\dfrac{5}{14} \times \dfrac{7}{20} =$

Answers can be found on page 179.

Square a Proper Fraction: It Gets Smaller

What is $\left(\dfrac{1}{2}\right)^2$?

Now that you can multiply fractions, you can apply exponents.

$$\left(\frac{1}{2}\right)^2 = \frac{1}{2} \times \frac{1}{2} = \frac{1}{4}$$

Notice that $\frac{1}{4}$ is *less* than $\frac{1}{2}$. When you square numbers larger than 1, they get bigger. But when you square proper fractions (between 0 and 1), they get *smaller*. The same is true for larger powers (cubes, etc.).

If you multiply any positive number by a proper fraction, the result is smaller than the original number. You are taking a "fraction" of that number.

If you...	Then you...	Like this:
Square a proper fraction (between 0 and 1)	Get a smaller number	$\left(\dfrac{1}{3}\right)^2 = \dfrac{1}{9}$ $\dfrac{1}{9} < \dfrac{1}{3}$

Take a Reciprocal: Flip the Fraction

The **reciprocal** of a number is "one over" that number. The reciprocal of 5 is $\frac{1}{5}$. Any number times its reciprocal equals 1.

$$5 \times \frac{1}{5} = \frac{5}{1} \times \frac{1}{5} = \frac{5}{5} = 1 \qquad \text{(You could also cancel all the factors as you multiply.)}$$

What is the reciprocal of $\frac{2}{3}$?

Just **flip the fraction**. The reciprocal of $\frac{2}{3}$ is $\frac{3}{2}$, since the product of $\frac{2}{3}$ and $\frac{3}{2}$ is 1:

$$\frac{2}{3} \times \frac{3}{2} = \frac{6}{6} = 1$$

If you write an integer as a fraction over 1, then the flipping rule works for integers as well. The integer 9 is $\frac{9}{1}$, and the reciprocal of 9 is $\frac{1}{9}$.

Keep track of negative signs. The reciprocal of a negative fraction will also be negative.

$$\frac{-5}{6} \times \frac{6}{-5} = \frac{-30}{-30} = 1$$

The reciprocal of $\frac{-5}{6}$ is $\frac{6}{-5}$, more commonly written as $\frac{-6}{5}$ or $-\frac{6}{5}$.

If you…	Then you…	Like this:
Want the reciprocal of a fraction	Flip the fraction	Fraction Reciprocal $\dfrac{4}{7} \rightarrow \dfrac{7}{4}$ $\dfrac{4}{7} \times \dfrac{7}{4} = 1$

Divide by a Fraction: Multiply by the Reciprocal

What is $6 \div 2$?

Stunningly, the answer is 3. We saw this example before in the discussion of fraction multiplication. $6 \div 2$ gives the same result as $6 \times \dfrac{1}{2}$.

$$6 \div 2 = 6 \times \frac{1}{2} = 3 \qquad \text{Dividing by 2 is the same as multiplying by } \frac{1}{2}.$$

2 and $\dfrac{1}{2}$ are reciprocals of each other. This pattern generalizes. **Dividing by a number is the same as multiplying by its reciprocal.** Try this example:

$$\frac{5}{6} \div \frac{4}{7} =$$

First, find the reciprocal of the second fraction (the one you're dividing *by*). Then multiply the first fraction by that reciprocal.

$$\frac{5}{6} \div \frac{4}{7} = \frac{5}{6} \times \frac{7}{4} = \frac{35}{24}$$

Sometimes you see a "double-decker" fraction. It's just one fraction divided by another. The longer fraction bar is the primary division.

$$\frac{\dfrac{5}{6}}{\dfrac{4}{7}} = \frac{5}{6} \div \frac{4}{7} = \frac{5}{6} \times \frac{7}{4} = \frac{35}{24}$$

This works with variables as well. Flip the bottom fraction and multiply.

$$\frac{\frac{3}{x}}{\frac{5}{x}} = \frac{3}{x} \times \frac{x}{5} = \frac{3}{\cancel{x}} \times \frac{\cancel{x}}{5} = \frac{3}{5}$$

As always, dividing by 0 is forbidden, so x cannot equal 0 in this case.

If you…	Then you…	Like this:
Divide something by a fraction	Multiply by that fraction's reciprocal	$\frac{3}{2} \div \frac{7}{11} = \frac{3}{2} \times \frac{11}{7}$

4

Check Your Skills

14. $\dfrac{1}{6} \div \dfrac{1}{11} =$

15. $\dfrac{8}{5} \div \dfrac{4}{15} =$

Answers can be found on page 179.

Addition in the Numerator: Pull Out a Common Factor

Up to now, the numerators and denominators were each one product. But if there is addition (or subtraction) in the numerator or denominator, tread carefully.

The fraction bar always tells you to **divide the entire numerator by the entire denominator**. To respect PEMDAS, think of the fraction bar as a grouping symbol, like parentheses.

$$\frac{3x^2 + y}{2y^2 - z} = (3x^2 + y) \div (2y^2 - z)$$

Consider a nicer example, one with simple terms and one subtraction in the numerator:

$$\frac{9x - 6}{3x}$$

The entire quantity $9x - 6$ is divided by $3x$. In other words, you have $(9x - 6) \div 3x$.

To simplify $\dfrac{9x - 6}{3x}$, you need to **find a common factor of the entire numerator and the entire denominator.** That is, you need a common factor of the *entire quantity* $9x - 6$ and of $3x$.

So you need to be able to pull that common factor out of $9x - 6$.

What factor does $3x$ have in common with the quantity $9x - 6$? The answer is 3. Notice that x is not a common factor, because you can't pull it out of the *entire* numerator. But you can pull a 3 out.

$$9x - 6 = \mathbf{3} \times (3x - 2), \text{ or } 3(3x - 2)$$

$$3x = \mathbf{3} \times x$$

$$\frac{9x - 6}{3x} = \frac{3(3x - 2)}{3x}$$

Now you can **cancel out the common factor on top and bottom.**

$$\frac{9x - 6}{3x} = \frac{\cancel{3}(3x - 2)}{\cancel{3}x} = \frac{3x - 2}{x}$$

The common factor could include a variable.

$$\frac{9y^2 - 6y}{12y} = \frac{\cancel{3y}(3y - 2)}{\cancel{3y}(4)} = \frac{3y - 2}{4}$$

If you…	Then you…	Like this:
Have addition or subtraction in the numerator	Pull out a factor from the entire numerator and cancel that factor with one in the denominator	$\dfrac{5x + 10y}{25y} = \dfrac{\cancel{5}(x + 2y)}{\cancel{5}(5y)}$ $= \dfrac{x + 2y}{5y}$

Check Your Skills

16. $\dfrac{4x^2 + 20xy}{12x}$

Answers can be found on page 179.

Addition in the Numerator: Split into Two Fractions (Maybe)

After you've cancelled common factors, you still might not see your answer. In that case, you can try one more thing. Remember this?

$$\frac{13}{4} = \frac{12+1}{4} = \frac{12}{4} + \frac{1}{4}$$

If you have a sum in the numerator, you can rewrite the fraction as the sum of two fractions. The same is true if you have a difference.

Consider this example again.

$$\frac{9x-6}{3x} =$$

The first step is to cancel common factors from the numerator and denominator.

$$\frac{9x-6}{3x} = \frac{\cancel{3}(3x-2)}{\cancel{3}x} = \frac{3x-2}{x}$$

It's often fine to stop there. But since you have a difference on top, you can go further by splitting the fraction into two fractions:

$$\frac{9x-6}{3x} = \frac{\cancel{3}(3x-2)}{\cancel{3}x} = \frac{3x-2}{x} = \frac{3x}{x} - \frac{2}{x}$$

Now you can simplify the first fraction further by cancelling the common factor of x on top and bottom.

$$\frac{9x-6}{3x} = \frac{\cancel{3}(3x-2)}{\cancel{3}x} = \frac{3x-2}{x} = \frac{3\cancel{x}}{\cancel{x}} - \frac{2}{x} = 3 - \frac{2}{x}$$

That's as far as we can possibly go. Is $3 - \frac{2}{x}$ simpler than $\frac{3x-2}{x}$? In a technical sense, no. But you still might have to split the fraction, depending on the available answer choices. In fact, one of the main reasons we simplify is to make an expression or equation look like the answer choices. The answer choice that the simplified expression or equation matches is the correct answer.

Consider this problem involving square roots:

$$\frac{10\sqrt{2} + \sqrt{6}}{2\sqrt{2}} =$$

(A) $\dfrac{5+\sqrt{6}}{2}$ (B) $5 + \dfrac{\sqrt{6}}{2}$ (C) $5 + \dfrac{\sqrt{3}}{2}$

It's hard to spot a common factor in the numerator that will cancel with one in the denominator. So a good first step here is to split the fraction in two.

$$\frac{10\sqrt{2}+\sqrt{6}}{2\sqrt{2}}=\frac{10\sqrt{2}}{2\sqrt{2}}+\frac{\sqrt{6}}{2\sqrt{2}}$$

Now deal with the two fractions separately. Cancel a $\sqrt{2}$ out of top and bottom of the first fraction.

$$\frac{10\cancel{\sqrt{2}}}{2\cancel{\sqrt{2}}}=\frac{10}{2}=5$$

The second fraction is trickier. A rule from the Exponents & Roots chapter is that when you divide roots, you divide what's inside. $\frac{\sqrt{6}}{\sqrt{2}}=\sqrt{\frac{6}{2}}=\sqrt{3}$. That's not exactly the second fraction, but it's close. Just keep the extra 2 on the bottom, separated out. Introduce a factor of 1 on top as a temporary place-holder.

$$\frac{\sqrt{6}}{2\sqrt{2}}=\frac{1\times\sqrt{6}}{2\times\sqrt{2}}=\frac{1}{2}\times\sqrt{\frac{6}{2}}=\frac{1}{2}\times\sqrt{3}=\frac{\sqrt{3}}{2}$$

Putting it all together, you have $5+\frac{\sqrt{3}}{2}$. The answer is (C).

If you…	Then you…	Like this:
Have addition or subtraction in the numerator	Might split the fraction into two fractions	$\frac{a+b}{c}=\frac{a}{c}+\frac{b}{c}$

Check Your Skills

17. $\dfrac{x+y}{xy}=$

(A) $\dfrac{1}{x}+\dfrac{1}{y}$ (B) $\dfrac{1+y}{y}$ (C) $\dfrac{x+1}{x}$

Answers can be found on page 179.

Addition in the Denominator: Pull Out a Common Factor But Never Split

To simplify a fraction with addition (or subtraction) in the *denominator*, you can do one of the same things as before. You can **pull out a common factor from the denominator and cancel with a factor in the numerator.**

Consider this example:

$$\frac{4x}{8x-12} =$$

You can factor a 4 out of $8x - 12$ and cancel it with the 4 in the numerator.

$$\frac{4x}{8x-12} = \frac{4x}{4(2x-3)} = \frac{\cancel{4}x}{\cancel{4}(2x-3)} = \frac{x}{2x-3}$$

That's all legal so far. But you cannot go any further. **Never split a fraction in two because of addition or subtraction in the _denominator_.**

Is $\dfrac{1}{3+4}$ equal to $\dfrac{1}{3} + \dfrac{1}{4}$? **No.** $\dfrac{1}{3+4} = \dfrac{1}{7}$, while $\dfrac{1}{3} + \dfrac{1}{4} = \dfrac{7}{12}$.

Do not be tempted to split $\dfrac{x}{2x-3}$ into anything else. That's as far as you can go.

If you…	Then you…	Like this:
Have addition or subtraction in the denominator	Pull out a factor from the entire denominator and cancel that factor with one in the numerator… but **never** split the fraction in two!	$\dfrac{3y}{y^2 + xy} = \dfrac{\cancel{y} \times 3}{\cancel{y}(y+x)}$ $= \dfrac{3}{y+x}$

Check Your Skills

18. $\dfrac{5a^3}{15ab^2 - 5a^3}$

(A) $\dfrac{a^2}{3b^2} - 1$ (B) $\dfrac{a^2}{3b^2 - a^2}$ (C) $\dfrac{1}{15ab^2}$

Answers can be found on page 180.

Add, Subtract, Multiply, Divide Nasty Fractions: Put Parentheses On

"Nasty," complicated fractions with addition and subtraction on the inside, such as $\dfrac{4x}{8x-12}$, are more of a headache than plain vanilla fractions. But they follow the same rules of addition, subtraction, multiplication, and division as all other fractions do.

Addition: Find a common denominator, then add numerators.
Subtraction: Find a common denominator, then subtract numerators.
Multiplication: Multiply tops and multiply bottoms, cancelling common factors.
Division: Flip, then multiply.

With nasty fractions, the most important point to remember is this. **Whenever necessary, treat the numerators and denominators as if they have parentheses around them.** This preserves PEMDAS order of operations.

Consider this sum:

$$\frac{1}{y+1} + \frac{2}{y} =$$

The same principle of addition holds. Do these fractions have the same denominator? No. So find a common denominator. We need a common multiple of y and $(y + 1)$. We can just multiply these two expressions together to get a common multiple:

$$(y) \times (y + 1) = (y)(y + 1)$$

Don't distribute yet. Simply convert each fraction so that it has $(y)(y + 1)$ in the denominator. Throw parentheses around $y + 1$ as needed.

$$\frac{1}{y+1} \times \frac{y}{y} = \frac{1 \times y}{(y+1) \times y} = \frac{y}{y(y+1)}$$

$$\frac{2}{y} \times \frac{y+1}{y+1} = \frac{2 \times (y+1)}{y \times (y+1)} = \frac{2y+2}{y(y+1)}$$

Now add.

$$\frac{1}{y+1} + \frac{2}{y} = \frac{y}{y(y+1)} + \frac{2y+2}{y(y+1)} = \frac{3y+2}{y(y+1)}$$

You could also write the answer as $\dfrac{3y+2}{y^2+y}$.

Consider this product:

$$\left(\frac{2w+4}{z^3+z}\right)\left(\frac{z}{2}\right) =$$

You could just multiply the tops and multiply the bottoms, but don't forget to cancel common factors as best you can *before* you multiply. So pull out factors from the nasty fraction on the left.

$$\frac{2w+4}{z^3+z} = \frac{2(w+2)}{z(z^2+1)}$$

Now plug that back into the product and cancel common factors.

$$\left(\frac{2w+4}{z^3+z}\right)\left(\frac{z}{2}\right) = \left(\frac{2(w+2)}{z(z^2+1)}\right)\left(\frac{z}{2}\right) = \left(\frac{2(w+2)}{z(z^2+1)}\right)\left(\frac{z}{2}\right) = \frac{w+2}{z^2+1}$$

If you...	Then you...	Like this:
Add, subtract, multiply or divide "nasty" fractions with complicated numerators and/or denominators	Throw parentheses around those numerators and/or denominators, then proceed normally— find common denominators, etc.	$\dfrac{1}{y+1} + \dfrac{2}{y} = \dfrac{y}{y(y+1)} + \dfrac{2(y+1)}{y(y+1)}$ $= \dfrac{3y+2}{y(y+1)}$

Check Your Skills

19. $\dfrac{x+1}{x-1} - \dfrac{4}{3} =$

Answers can be found on page 180.

Fractions Within Fractions: Work Your Way Out

Remember "double-decker" fractions in fraction division?

$$\frac{\frac{5}{6}}{\frac{4}{7}} = \frac{5}{6} \times \frac{7}{4} = \frac{35}{24}$$

The GMAT likes to put fractions within fractions, as in the movie "Inception." Just as in that movie, you have to **work your way out from the deepest level inside**. Try this example:

$$\frac{1}{1+\frac{1}{3}} =$$

Forget about the whole thing. Just focus on the deepest level: $1+\dfrac{1}{3}$. This you can solve by finding a common denominator: $1+\dfrac{1}{3} = \dfrac{3}{3} + \dfrac{1}{3} = \dfrac{4}{3}$

Now move up a level:

$$\frac{1}{1+\dfrac{1}{3}} = \frac{1}{\dfrac{4}{3}}$$

You are dividing 1 by the fraction $\dfrac{4}{3}$. You can do that too. Just turn 1 into a fraction $\left(\dfrac{1}{1}\right)$.

$$\frac{1}{1+\dfrac{1}{3}} = \frac{1}{\dfrac{4}{3}} = \frac{1}{1} \times \frac{3}{4} = \frac{3}{4}$$

That's the answer. Try this three-level problem:

$$\frac{1}{2+\dfrac{1}{3+\dfrac{1}{x}}} =$$

Again, start at the deepest level: $3+\dfrac{1}{x}$. Find a common denominator: $3+\dfrac{1}{x} = \dfrac{3x}{x} + \dfrac{1}{x} = \dfrac{3x+1}{x}$. Now move up a level:

$$\frac{1}{2+\dfrac{1}{3+\dfrac{1}{x}}} = \frac{1}{2+\dfrac{1}{\dfrac{3x+1}{x}}}$$

"One over" $\dfrac{3x+1}{x}$ means take the reciprocal, or flip the fraction: $\dfrac{x}{3x+1}$. Move up another level:

$$\frac{1}{2+\dfrac{1}{3+\dfrac{1}{x}}} = \frac{1}{2+\dfrac{1}{\dfrac{3x+1}{x}}} = \frac{1}{2+\dfrac{x}{3x+1}}$$

To add 2 and the new part, find a common denominator:

$$2+\frac{x}{3x+1} = \frac{2(3x+1)}{3x+1} + \frac{x}{3x+1} = \frac{6x+2}{3x+1} + \frac{x}{3x+1} = \frac{7x+2}{3x+1}$$

Now replace that in the master fraction. You've almost reached the surface:

$$\cfrac{1}{2+\cfrac{1}{3+\cfrac{1}{x}}} = \cfrac{1}{2+\cfrac{1}{\cfrac{3x+1}{x}}} = \cfrac{1}{2+\cfrac{x}{3x+1}} = \cfrac{1}{\cfrac{7x+2}{3x+1}}$$

Finally, we have another reciprocal. Do one more flip:

$$\cfrac{1}{2+\cfrac{1}{3+\cfrac{1}{x}}} = \cfrac{1}{2+\cfrac{1}{\cfrac{3x+1}{x}}} = \cfrac{1}{2+\cfrac{x}{3x+1}} = \cfrac{1}{\cfrac{7x+2}{3x+1}} = \cfrac{3x+1}{7x+2}$$

That was a lot of steps, but each one should make sense.

If you…	Then you…	Like this:
Encounter a fraction within a fraction	Work your way out from the deepest level inside	$$\cfrac{1}{y+\cfrac{1}{\boxed{2-\cfrac{3}{y}}}}$$ Focus here

Check Your Skills

20. $\dfrac{1+\dfrac{3}{4}}{2}$

Answers can be found on page 180.

Check Your Skills Answer Key:

1. $\dfrac{3x}{yz^2} + \dfrac{7x}{yz^2} = \dfrac{3x+7x}{yz^2} = \dfrac{10x}{yz^2}$

2. $\dfrac{1}{2} + \dfrac{3}{4} = \dfrac{1}{2} \times \dfrac{2}{2} + \dfrac{3}{4} = \dfrac{2}{4} + \dfrac{3}{4} = \dfrac{2+3}{4} = \dfrac{5}{4}$ (you have five quarters of a pie)

3. $\dfrac{2}{3} - \dfrac{3}{8} = \dfrac{2}{3} \times \dfrac{8}{8} - \dfrac{3}{8} \times \dfrac{3}{3} = \dfrac{16}{24} - \dfrac{9}{24} = \dfrac{16-9}{24} = \dfrac{7}{24}$

4. The denominators of the two fractions are the same, but the numerator of $\dfrac{5}{7}$ is bigger, so $\dfrac{5}{7} > \dfrac{3}{7}$.

5. The numerators of the two fractions are the same, but the denominator of $\dfrac{3}{10}$ is smaller, so $\dfrac{3}{10} > \dfrac{3}{13}$.

6. $\dfrac{11}{6} = \dfrac{6+5}{6} = \dfrac{6}{6} + \dfrac{5}{6} = 1 + \dfrac{5}{6} = 1\tfrac{5}{6}$

7. $\dfrac{100}{11} = \dfrac{99+1}{11} = \dfrac{99}{11} + \dfrac{1}{11} = 9 + \dfrac{1}{11} = 9\tfrac{1}{11}$

8. $3\tfrac{3}{4} = 3 + \dfrac{3}{4} = \dfrac{3}{1} \times \dfrac{4}{4} + \dfrac{3}{4} = \dfrac{12}{4} + \dfrac{3}{4} = \dfrac{15}{4}$

9. $5\tfrac{2}{3} = 5 + \dfrac{2}{3} = \dfrac{5}{1} \times \dfrac{3}{3} + \dfrac{2}{3} = \dfrac{15}{3} + \dfrac{2}{3} = \dfrac{17}{3}$

10. $\dfrac{25}{40} = \dfrac{5\times5}{8\times5} = \dfrac{5\times\cancel{5}}{8\times\cancel{5}} = \dfrac{5}{8}$

11. $\dfrac{16}{24} = \dfrac{2\times8}{3\times8} = \dfrac{2\times\cancel{8}}{3\times\cancel{8}} = \dfrac{2}{3}$

12. $\dfrac{3}{7} \times \dfrac{6}{10} = \dfrac{3\times3}{7\times5} = \dfrac{9}{35}$

13. $\dfrac{5}{14} \times \dfrac{7}{20} = \dfrac{5}{2\times7} \times \dfrac{7}{4\times5} = \dfrac{\cancel{5}}{2\times\cancel{7}} \times \dfrac{\cancel{7}}{4\times\cancel{5}} = \dfrac{1}{8}$

14. $\dfrac{1}{6} \div \dfrac{1}{11} = \dfrac{1}{6} \times \dfrac{11}{1} = \dfrac{11}{6}$

15. $\dfrac{8}{5} \div \dfrac{4}{15} = \dfrac{8}{5} \times \dfrac{15}{4} = \dfrac{2\times4}{5} \times \dfrac{3\times5}{4} = \dfrac{2\times\cancel{4}}{\cancel{5}} \times \dfrac{3\times\cancel{5}}{\cancel{4}} = \dfrac{6}{1} = 6$

16. $\dfrac{4x^2 + 20xy}{12x} = \dfrac{\cancel{4x}(x+5y)}{\cancel{4x}(3)} = \dfrac{x+5y}{3}$

17. $\dfrac{x+y}{xy} = \dfrac{\cancel{x}}{\cancel{x}\,y} + \dfrac{\cancel{y}}{x\,\cancel{y}} = \dfrac{1}{y} + \dfrac{1}{x}$. The answer is (A).

18. $\dfrac{5a^3}{15ab^2 - 5a^3} = \dfrac{\cancel{5a}(a^2)}{\cancel{5a}(3b^2 - a^2)} = \dfrac{a^2}{3b^2 - a^2}$. Remember that you can't split the denominator. This fraction is simplified as much as it can be. The answer is (B).

19. $\dfrac{x+1}{x-1} - \dfrac{4}{3} = \dfrac{3}{3}\left(\dfrac{x+1}{x-1}\right) - \dfrac{x-1}{x-1}\left(\dfrac{4}{3}\right) = \dfrac{3x+3}{3x-3} - \dfrac{4x-4}{3x-3}$

$\dfrac{3x+3}{3x-3} - \dfrac{4x-4}{3x-3} = \dfrac{(3x+3)-(4x-4)}{3x-3} = \dfrac{3x+3-4x+4}{3x-3} = \dfrac{-x+7}{3x-3}$

20. $\dfrac{1+\dfrac{3}{4}}{2} = \dfrac{\dfrac{4}{4}+\dfrac{3}{4}}{2} = \dfrac{\dfrac{7}{4}}{2} = \dfrac{7}{4} \times \dfrac{1}{2} = \dfrac{7}{8}$

4

Chapter Review: Drill Sets

Drill 1

For each of the following pairs of fractions, decide which fraction is larger.

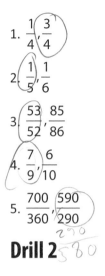

1. $\dfrac{1}{4}$, $\dfrac{3}{4}$

2. $\dfrac{1}{5}$, $\dfrac{1}{6}$

3. $\dfrac{53}{52}$, $\dfrac{85}{86}$

4. $\dfrac{7}{9}$, $\dfrac{6}{10}$

5. $\dfrac{700}{360}$, $\dfrac{590}{290}$

Drill 2

Add or subtract the following fractions. Fractions should be in their most simplified form.

6. $\dfrac{7}{9} - \dfrac{2}{9} =$

7. $\dfrac{2}{3} + \dfrac{5}{9}$

8. $\dfrac{4}{9} + \dfrac{8}{11}$

9. $\dfrac{20}{12} - \dfrac{5}{3}$

10. $\dfrac{52}{11x} + \dfrac{25}{11x} =$

11. $\dfrac{a}{12} - \dfrac{b}{6} - \dfrac{b}{4} =$

12. $\dfrac{u}{v} + 1 =$

13. $\sqrt{\dfrac{3}{2}} - \sqrt{\dfrac{2}{3}} =$

(A) $\dfrac{\sqrt{3}}{3}$ (B) $\dfrac{1}{\sqrt{6}}$ (C) $\sqrt{6}$

14. $\dfrac{ab}{cb} + \dfrac{a}{c} - \dfrac{a^2 b^3}{abc} =$

A) $\dfrac{a-b^2}{c}$ B) $\dfrac{a(2-b^2)}{c}$ C) $\dfrac{a^2 b(2-b^2)}{c}$

15. $\dfrac{24}{3\sqrt{2}} - \dfrac{4}{\sqrt{2}} =$

A) $2\sqrt{2}$ B) 4   C) $8\sqrt{2}$

Drill 3

Convert the following improper fractions to mixed numbers.

16. $\dfrac{9}{4}$

17. $\dfrac{31}{7}$

18. $\dfrac{47}{15}$

19. $\dfrac{70}{20}$

20. $\dfrac{91}{13}$

Drill 4

Convert the following mixed numbers to improper fractions.

21. $3\frac{2}{3}$

22. $2\frac{1}{6}$

23. $6\frac{3}{7}$

24. $4\frac{5}{9}$

25. $12\frac{5}{12}$

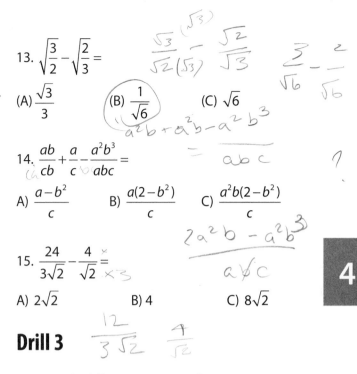

Drill 5

Simplify the following expressions.

26. $\dfrac{5}{8} - \dfrac{4}{8} =$ $\dfrac{8}{8}$

27. $\dfrac{7}{9} - \dfrac{2}{9} =$ $\dfrac{5}{9}$

28. $\dfrac{9}{11} + \dfrac{20}{11} =$ $\dfrac{29}{11}$

29. $\dfrac{3}{4} - \dfrac{10}{4} =$ $\dfrac{-7}{4}$

30. $\dfrac{2\sqrt{18}}{15}$ $\dfrac{2\sqrt{9}\sqrt{2}}{15}$ $\dfrac{2 \times 3\sqrt{2}}{15}$

31. $\dfrac{17^2 \times 22}{11 \times 34}$ $\dfrac{17^2 \times 2}{34 \cdot 2}$ $\dfrac{6\sqrt{2}}{15} \cdot \dfrac{15}{3 \times 2\sqrt{2}}{3 \times 5}$

$\dfrac{17}{9}$

32. $\dfrac{14x^2 y}{42x}$

33. $\dfrac{2r\sqrt{54}}{r^2 s\sqrt{12}}$

34. $\dfrac{6x^8 yz^5}{46x^6 y^2 z^3}$

35. $\dfrac{3ab^2\sqrt{50}}{\sqrt{18a^2}}$ if $a > 0$

Drill 6

Multiply or divide the following fractions. Fractions should be in their most simplified form.

36. $\dfrac{14}{20} \times \dfrac{15}{21}$

37. $\dfrac{6}{25} \div \dfrac{9}{10}$

38. $\dfrac{3}{11} \div \dfrac{3}{11}$

39. $\dfrac{a^2 b}{cd^2} \times \dfrac{d^3}{abc}$

40. $\dfrac{3^2}{4^2} \times \dfrac{2^2}{5^2} \times \dfrac{10}{3}$

41. $\dfrac{\sqrt{25}}{\sqrt{10}} \times \dfrac{\sqrt{8}}{\sqrt{15}}$

42. $\dfrac{\sqrt{12}}{5} \times \dfrac{\sqrt{60}}{2^4} \times \dfrac{\sqrt{45}}{3^2}$

43. $\dfrac{\sqrt{10}}{\sqrt{8}} \div \dfrac{\sqrt{9}}{\sqrt{10}}$

44. $\dfrac{xy^3 z^4}{x^3 y^4 z^2} \div \dfrac{x^6 y^2 z}{x^3 y^5 z^2}$

45. $\dfrac{39^2}{2^4} \div \dfrac{13^3}{4^2}$

Drill 7

Simplify the following fractions.

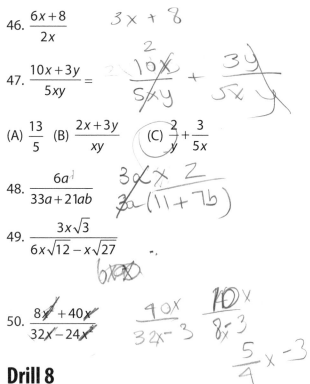

46. $\dfrac{6x+8}{2x}$ $3x + 8$

47. $\dfrac{10x+3y}{5xy} =$ $\dfrac{\overset{2}{10x}}{5xy} + \dfrac{3y}{5x}$

(A) $\dfrac{13}{5}$ (B) $\dfrac{2x+3y}{xy}$ (C) $\dfrac{2}{y} + \dfrac{3}{5x}$

48. $\dfrac{6a}{33a+21ab}$ $\dfrac{3a \cdot x \cdot 2}{3a(11+7b)}$

49. $\dfrac{3x\sqrt{3}}{6x\sqrt{12} - x\sqrt{27}}$

$6\sqrt{x}$

50. $\dfrac{8x + 40x}{32x - 24x}$ $\dfrac{40x}{32x-3}$ $\dfrac{10x}{8-3}$ $\dfrac{5}{4}x - 3$

Drill 8

Simplify the following expressions. Final answers should be in their most simplified forms.

51. $\dfrac{3+4}{1+2} - \dfrac{1+2}{3+4}$

52. $\dfrac{3}{x+2} \times \dfrac{1}{5}$ $\dfrac{3}{5x+10}$

MANHATTAN
GMAT

53. $\dfrac{7}{n+3} \times \dfrac{n+1}{2}$

54. $\dfrac{x+2}{4} + \dfrac{x+3}{4}$

55. $\dfrac{-t+1}{t-2} \times \dfrac{-t}{2}$

56. $\dfrac{b+6}{6} - \dfrac{3+b}{6}$

57. $\dfrac{x(3+\sqrt{3})}{9} - \dfrac{x}{3}$

58. $\dfrac{3x^2+3y}{40} + \dfrac{x^2+y}{8}$

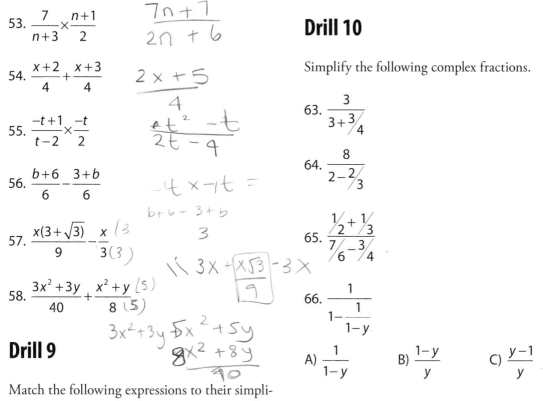

Drill 9

Match the following expressions to their simplified forms.

59. $\dfrac{4t}{6} \times \dfrac{-3}{t-3} =$

(A) $\dfrac{-2t}{t-3}$ (B) $\dfrac{4t-3}{6t-18}$ (C) $\dfrac{2}{3}$

60. $\dfrac{j-2}{8} \times \dfrac{12}{j-2} =$

(A) $\dfrac{3}{2}$ (B) $\dfrac{4j-2}{3j-2}$ (C) $4j-8$

61. $\dfrac{x-5}{x} \times \dfrac{x^2}{x+1} =$

(A) $\dfrac{x^2-5x}{x+1}$ (B) $x-4$ (C) $\dfrac{x^3-5x^2}{3x}$

62. $\dfrac{(n+2n)}{n^4} \times \dfrac{(2n)^2}{(15n-5n)} =$

(A) $\dfrac{2n^2+4n^3}{15n^4-5n^5}$ (B) $\dfrac{6}{5n^2}$ (C) $\dfrac{n^7}{n^{16}}$

Drill 10

Simplify the following complex fractions.

63. $\dfrac{3}{3+\frac{3}{4}}$

64. $\dfrac{8}{2-\frac{2}{3}}$

65. $\dfrac{\frac{1}{2}+\frac{1}{3}}{\frac{7}{6}-\frac{3}{4}}$

66. $\dfrac{1}{1-\frac{1}{1-y}}$

A) $\dfrac{1}{1-y}$ B) $\dfrac{1-y}{y}$ C) $\dfrac{y-1}{y}$

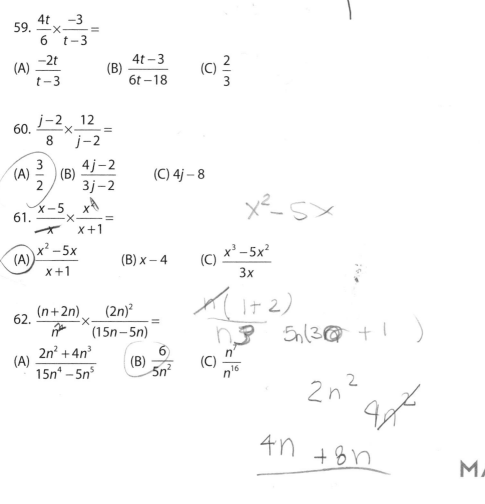

Drill Sets Solutions

Drill 1

1. The denominators are the same, but the numerator of $\frac{3}{4}$ is larger, so $\frac{3}{4} > \frac{1}{4}$.

2. The numerators are the same, but the denominator of $\frac{1}{5}$ is smaller, so $\frac{1}{5} > \frac{1}{6}$.

3. In the first fraction, $\frac{53}{52}$, the numerator is bigger than the denominator, so the fraction is greater than 1. In the second fraction, $\frac{85}{86}$, the denominator is bigger than the numerator, so the fraction is less than 1. $\frac{53}{52} > \frac{85}{86}$.

4. The second fraction, $\frac{6}{10}$, has both a smaller numerator and a larger denominator than the first fraction. Therefore, $\frac{6}{10} < \frac{7}{9}$. Or, cross-multiply.

5. The first fraction is greater than 1 but less than 2, because 700 is less than twice 360 ($2 \times 360 = 720$). The second fraction is greater than 2, because 590 is more than twice 290 ($2 \times 290 = 580$).

$$\frac{590}{290} > \frac{700}{360}$$

Drill 2

6. $\dfrac{7}{9} - \dfrac{2}{9} = \dfrac{7-2}{9} = \dfrac{5}{9}$

7. $\dfrac{2}{3} + \dfrac{5}{9} = \dfrac{2}{3} \times \dfrac{3}{3} + \dfrac{5}{9} = \dfrac{6}{9} + \dfrac{5}{9} = \dfrac{6+5}{9} = \dfrac{11}{9}$

8. $\dfrac{4}{9} + \dfrac{8}{11} = \dfrac{4}{9} \times \dfrac{11}{11} + \dfrac{8}{11} \times \dfrac{9}{9} = \dfrac{44}{99} + \dfrac{72}{99} = \dfrac{116}{99}$

9. $\dfrac{20}{12} - \dfrac{5}{3} = \dfrac{20}{12} - \dfrac{5}{3} \times \dfrac{4}{4} = \dfrac{20}{12} - \dfrac{20}{12} = 0$

10. Because the denominators are the same, add the numerators and reduce.

$$\frac{52}{11x} + \frac{25}{11x} = \frac{77}{11x} = \frac{7}{x}$$

11. Find a common denominator and subtract. Because both 6 and 4 are factors of 12, 12 is the lowest common denominator.

$$\frac{a}{12} - \frac{b}{6} - \frac{b}{4} = \frac{a}{12} - \frac{2b}{12} - \frac{3b}{12} = \frac{a-2b-3b}{12} = \frac{a-5b}{12}$$

12. The common denominator of $\dfrac{u}{v}$ and 1 is v.

$$\frac{u}{v}+1=\frac{u}{v}+\frac{v}{v}=\frac{u+v}{v}$$

13. $\sqrt{\dfrac{3}{2}}-\sqrt{\dfrac{2}{3}}=\dfrac{\sqrt{3}}{\sqrt{2}}-\dfrac{\sqrt{2}}{\sqrt{3}}=\dfrac{\sqrt{3}\sqrt{3}}{\sqrt{2}\sqrt{3}}-\dfrac{\sqrt{2}\sqrt{2}}{\sqrt{3}\sqrt{2}}=\dfrac{3}{\sqrt{6}}-\dfrac{2}{\sqrt{6}}=\dfrac{1}{\sqrt{6}}$

The answer is (B).

14. Start by simplifying the individual fractions. Dividing the common terms results in common denominators here and, in the case of the third fraction, dividing top and bottom by a and b also reduces both exponents by 1.

$$\frac{a\cancel{b}}{c\cancel{b}}+\frac{a}{c}-\frac{a^{\cancel{2}}b^{\cancel{3}2}}{\cancel{a}\,\cancel{b}c}=\frac{a}{c}+\frac{a}{c}-\frac{ab^2}{c}=\frac{2a-ab^2}{c}=\frac{a(2-b^2)}{c}$$

We can solve by using a common denominator of abc, but it will take a little more work. Look for opportunities to simplify up-front to save yourself time and effort!

$$\frac{ab}{cb}+\frac{a}{c}-\frac{a^2b^3}{abc}=\frac{a^2b}{abc}+\frac{a^2b}{abc}-\frac{a^2b^3}{abc}=\frac{2a^2b-a^2b^3}{abc}$$

Every term in the fraction has ab as a factor. Pull out ab from the numerator and simplify.

$$\frac{2a^2b-a^2b^3}{abc}=\frac{\cancel{ab}(2a-ab^2)}{\cancel{ab}c}=\frac{2a-ab^2}{c}=\frac{a(2-b^2)}{c}$$

No matter how you perform the addition, the answer is (B).

15. One way to approach this is to multiply the second term by 3/3 to get a common denominator:

$$\frac{24}{3\sqrt{2}}-\frac{4}{\sqrt{2}}=\frac{24}{3\sqrt{2}}-\frac{12}{3\sqrt{2}}=\frac{12}{3\sqrt{2}}=\frac{4}{\sqrt{2}}$$

But this fraction doesn't match our answer choices. In fact, none of the answer choices are even fractions! That means we need to find a way to get rid of the denominator. Normally, we could divide the numerator by the denominator, but we can't divide by a root. We can, however, get rid of the root on the bottom if we multiply the fraction by $\dfrac{\sqrt{2}}{\sqrt{2}}$.

$$\frac{4}{\sqrt{2}}\times\frac{\sqrt{2}}{\sqrt{2}}=\frac{4\sqrt{2}}{2}=2\sqrt{2}$$

The answer is (A).

Drill 3

16. $\dfrac{9}{4} = \dfrac{8+1}{4} = \dfrac{8}{4} + \dfrac{1}{4} = 2 + \dfrac{1}{4} = 2\frac{1}{4}$

17. $\dfrac{31}{7} = \dfrac{28+3}{7} = \dfrac{28}{7} + \dfrac{3}{7} = 4 + \dfrac{3}{7} = 4\frac{3}{7}$

18. $\dfrac{47}{15} = \dfrac{45+2}{15} = \dfrac{45}{15} + \dfrac{2}{15} = 3 + \dfrac{2}{15} = 3\frac{2}{15}$

19. $\dfrac{70}{20} = \dfrac{60+10}{20} = \dfrac{60}{20} + \dfrac{10}{20} = 3 + \dfrac{10}{20} = 3 + \dfrac{1}{2} = 3\frac{1}{2}$

20. $\dfrac{91}{13} = 7$

Drill 4

21. $3\frac{2}{3} = 3 + \dfrac{2}{3} = \dfrac{3\times3}{1\times3} + \dfrac{2}{3} = \dfrac{9}{3} + \dfrac{2}{3} = \dfrac{11}{3}$

22. $2\frac{1}{6} = 2 + \dfrac{1}{6} = \dfrac{2\times6}{1\times6} + \dfrac{1}{6} = \dfrac{12}{6} + \dfrac{1}{6} = \dfrac{13}{6}$

23. $6\frac{3}{7} = 6 + \dfrac{3}{7} = \dfrac{6\times7}{1\times7} + \dfrac{3}{7} = \dfrac{42}{7} + \dfrac{3}{7} = \dfrac{45}{7}$

24. $4\frac{5}{9} = 4 + \dfrac{5}{9} = \dfrac{4\times9}{1\times9} + \dfrac{5}{9} = \dfrac{36}{9} + \dfrac{5}{9} = \dfrac{41}{9}$

25. $12\frac{5}{12} = 12 + \dfrac{5}{12} = \dfrac{12\times12}{1\times12} + \dfrac{5}{12} = \dfrac{144}{12} + \dfrac{5}{12} = \dfrac{149}{12}$

Drill 5

26. $\dfrac{5}{8} - \dfrac{4}{8} = \dfrac{5-4}{8} = \dfrac{1}{8}$

27. $\dfrac{7}{9} - \dfrac{2}{9} = \dfrac{7-2}{9} = \dfrac{5}{9}$

28. $\dfrac{9}{11} + \dfrac{20}{11} = \dfrac{9+20}{11} = \dfrac{29}{11}$ OR $2\frac{7}{11}$

29. $\dfrac{3}{4} - \dfrac{10}{4} = \dfrac{3-10}{4} = \dfrac{-7}{4}$ OR $-1\frac{3}{4}$

30. We begin by simplifying the square root in the numerator. When simplifying a square root, always look for factors that are perfect squares; in this example, we have $18 = 2 \times 9 = 2 \times 3^2$. Therefore:

$$\frac{2\sqrt{18}}{15} = \frac{2\sqrt{2 \times 3 \times 3}}{15} = \frac{2 \times \cancel{3} \times \sqrt{2}}{\cancel{3} \times 5} = \frac{2\sqrt{2}}{5}$$

31. $\dfrac{17^2 \times 22}{11 \times 34} = \dfrac{17 \times \cancel{17} \times \cancel{2} \times \cancel{11}}{\cancel{11} \times \cancel{2} \times \cancel{17}} = 17$

32. $\dfrac{14x^2 y}{42x} = \dfrac{\cancel{2} \times \cancel{7} \times \cancel{x} \times x \times y}{\cancel{2} \times 3 \times \cancel{7} \times \cancel{x}} = \dfrac{xy}{3}$

33. To begin, we simplify the square roots in the numerator and denominator by looking for factors that have pairs:

$$\sqrt{54} = \sqrt{2 \times 3 \times 3 \times 3} = 3\sqrt{2 \times 3} = 3\sqrt{6}$$
$$\sqrt{12} = \sqrt{2 \times 2 \times 3} = 2\sqrt{3}$$

Because the numbers remaining inside the square roots have a factor of 3 in common, we can simplify even further:

$$3\sqrt{6} = 3\sqrt{2 \times 3} = 3\sqrt{2}\sqrt{3}$$

Therefore:

$$\frac{2r\sqrt{54}}{r^2 s\sqrt{12}} = \frac{\cancel{2} \times \cancel{r} \times 3 \times \sqrt{2} \times \cancel{\sqrt{3}}}{\cancel{2} \times r \times s \times \cancel{2} \times \cancel{\sqrt{3}}} = \frac{3\sqrt{2}}{rs}$$

34. There are several good ways to simplify a fraction with variables raised to powers. One approach is to use exponent rules to rewrite the expression so that the cancelations are more clear:

$$\frac{6x^8 yz^5}{46x^6 y^2 z^3} = \frac{\cancel{2} \times 3 \times \cancel{x^6} \times x^2 \times \cancel{y} \times \cancel{z^3} \times z^2}{\cancel{2} \times 23 \times \cancel{x^6} \times \cancel{y} \times y \times \cancel{z^3}} = \frac{3x^2 z^2}{23y}$$

Alternatively, we can consider only one variable at a time and use other exponent rules to simplify:

$$\frac{6}{46} \times \frac{x^8}{x^6} \times \frac{y}{y^2} \times \frac{z^5}{z^3} = \frac{3}{23} x^2 y^{-1} z^2$$

To combine these into one fraction, we can put x^2 and z^2 in the numerator. $y^{-1} = \dfrac{1}{y}$. Place y in the denominator.

$$\frac{3}{23} x^2 y^{-1} z^2 = \frac{3x^2 z^2}{23y}$$

35. We begin by simplifying the square roots by searching for factors that have pairs:

$$\sqrt{50} = \sqrt{2 \times 5 \times 5} = 5\sqrt{2}$$
$$\sqrt{18a^2} = \sqrt{2 \times 3 \times 3 \times a \times a} = 3a\sqrt{2}$$

Notice that the a^2 inside the second square root became an a outside the square root. We then have:

$$\frac{3ab^2\sqrt{50}}{\sqrt{18a^2}} = \frac{\cancel{3}\,\cancel{a}b^2 \times 5\cancel{\sqrt{2}}}{\cancel{3}\,\cancel{a}\,\cancel{\sqrt{2}}} = 5b^2$$

Drill 6

36. $\dfrac{14}{20} \times \dfrac{15}{21} = \dfrac{2\times7\times3\times5}{2\times2\times5\times7\times3} = \dfrac{\cancel{2}\times\cancel{7}\times\cancel{3}\times\cancel{5}}{2\times\cancel{2}\times\cancel{5}\times\cancel{7}\times\cancel{3}} = \dfrac{1}{2}$

37. $\dfrac{6}{25} \div \dfrac{9}{10} = \dfrac{6}{25} \times \dfrac{10}{9} = \dfrac{2\times3\times2\times5}{5\times5\times3\times3} = \dfrac{2\times\cancel{3}\times2\times\cancel{5}}{5\times\cancel{5}\times\cancel{3}\times3} = \dfrac{4}{15}$

38. $\dfrac{3}{11} \div \dfrac{3}{11} = \dfrac{3}{11} \times \dfrac{11}{3} = \dfrac{\cancel{3}\times\cancel{11}}{\cancel{11}\times\cancel{3}} = 1$

39. Before multiplying the fractions, look to cancel common factors.

$$\frac{a^2b}{cd^2} \times \frac{d^3}{abc} = \frac{\cancel{a}\times a\times\cancel{b}}{c\times\cancel{d}\times\cancel{d}} \times \frac{d\times\cancel{d}\times\cancel{d}}{\cancel{a}\times\cancel{b}\times c} = \frac{ad}{c^2}$$

40. Before multiplying the fractions, look to cancel common factors.

$$\frac{3^2}{4^2} \times \frac{2^2}{5^2} \times \frac{10}{3} = \frac{\cancel{3}\times3}{\cancel{2}\times\cancel{2}\times\cancel{2}\times2} \times \frac{\cancel{2}\times\cancel{2}}{\cancel{5}\times5} \times \frac{\cancel{2}\times\cancel{5}}{\cancel{3}} = \frac{3}{10}$$

41. Begin by simplifying the roots.

$$\frac{\sqrt{25}}{\sqrt{10}} \times \frac{\sqrt{8}}{\sqrt{15}} = \frac{5}{\sqrt{2}\times\sqrt{5}} \times \frac{2\sqrt{2}}{\sqrt{3}\times\sqrt{5}}$$

$\sqrt{2}$ can be canceled from the numerator and denominator. Also note that $\sqrt{5}$ appears twice in the denominator, and $\sqrt{5}\times\sqrt{5} = 5$.

$$\frac{5}{\cancel{\sqrt{2}}\times\sqrt{5}} \times \frac{2\cancel{\sqrt{2}}}{\sqrt{3}\times\sqrt{5}} = \frac{2\times5}{\sqrt{3}\times\sqrt{5}\times\sqrt{5}} = \frac{2\times\cancel{5}}{\cancel{5}\sqrt{3}} = \frac{2}{\sqrt{3}}$$

42. Begin by simplifying the roots.

$$\frac{\sqrt{12}}{5} \times \frac{\sqrt{60}}{2^4} \times \frac{\sqrt{45}}{3^2} = \frac{2\sqrt{3}}{5} \times \frac{2\sqrt{3}\times\sqrt{5}}{2\times2\times2\times2} \times \frac{3\sqrt{5}}{3\times3}$$

Look to cancel common factors before multiplying. Remember you can cancel across fractions because they are being multiplied.

$$\frac{\cancel{2}\sqrt{3}}{5} \times \frac{\cancel{2}\sqrt{3} \times \sqrt{5}}{\cancel{2} \times \cancel{2} \times 2 \times 2} \times \frac{\cancel{3}\sqrt{5}}{\cancel{3} \times 3} = \frac{\sqrt{3} \times \sqrt{3} \times \sqrt{5} \times \sqrt{5}}{2 \times 2 \times 3 \times 5}$$

Now we can combine the roots in the numerator.

$$\frac{\sqrt{3} \times \sqrt{3} \times \sqrt{5} \times \sqrt{5}}{2 \times 2 \times 3 \times 5} = \frac{\cancel{3} \times \cancel{5}}{2 \times 2 \times \cancel{3} \times \cancel{5}} = \frac{1}{4}$$

43. To divide by a fraction, multiply by its reciprocal.

$$\frac{\sqrt{10}}{\sqrt{8}} \div \frac{\sqrt{9}}{\sqrt{10}} = \frac{\sqrt{10}}{\sqrt{8}} \times \frac{\sqrt{10}}{\sqrt{9}}$$

The numerator simplifies to 10. Simplify the roots on the bottom and combine the fractions.

$$\frac{\sqrt{10}}{\sqrt{8}} \times \frac{\sqrt{10}}{\sqrt{9}} = \frac{10}{2\sqrt{2} \times 3}$$

Now cancel common factors.

$$\frac{10}{2\sqrt{2} \times 3} = \frac{\cancel{2} \times 5}{\cancel{2}\sqrt{2} \times 3} = \frac{5}{3\sqrt{2}}$$

44. To divide, multiply by the reciprocal.

$$\frac{xy^3z^4}{x^3y^4z^2} \div \frac{x^6y^2z}{x^3y^5z^2} = \frac{xy^3z^4}{x^3y^4z^2} \times \frac{x^3y^5z^2}{x^6y^2z}$$

We can deal with each variable separately. Combine like variables and use exponent rules to simplify.

$$\frac{xy^3z^4}{x^3y^4z^2} \times \frac{x^3y^5z^2}{x^6y^2z} = \frac{x \times x^3}{x^3 \times x^6} \times \frac{y^3 \times y^5}{y^4 \times y^2} \times \frac{z^4 \times z^2}{z^2 \times z} =$$

$$x^{1+3-3-6}y^{3+5-4-2}z^{4+2-2-1} = x^{-5}y^2z^3 = \frac{y^2z^3}{x^5}$$

45. Begin by multiplying by the reciprocal.

$$\frac{39^2}{2^4} \div \frac{13^3}{4^2} = \frac{39^2}{2^4} \times \frac{4^2}{13^3}$$

To do fewer messy calculations, break the numbers into their prime factors and cancel common factors.

$$\frac{39^2}{2^4} \times \frac{4^2}{13^3} = \frac{(3 \times 13)^2}{2^4} \times \frac{(2^2)^2}{13^3} = \frac{3 \times 3 \times \cancel{13} \times \cancel{13}}{\cancel{2 \times 2 \times 2 \times 2}} \times \frac{\cancel{2 \times 2 \times 2 \times 2}}{\cancel{13} \times \cancel{13} \times 13} = \frac{9}{13}$$

Drill 7

46. When the numerator of a fraction consists of two or more terms added together, but the denominator is a single term, we can split the fraction into two fractions with a common denominator and then simplify further:

$$\frac{6x+8}{2x} = \frac{6x}{2x} + \frac{8}{2x}$$

Now we need to simplify both fractions.

$$\frac{6x}{2x} + \frac{8}{2x} = \frac{\cancel{2} \times 3 \times \cancel{x}}{\cancel{2} \times \cancel{x}} + \frac{\cancel{2} \times 2 \times 2}{\cancel{2} \times x} = 3 + \frac{4}{x}$$

If you left the expressions as one fraction, then you could have factored a 2 out of each term in the expression:

$$\frac{6x+8}{2x} = \frac{\cancel{2}(3x+4)}{\cancel{2} \times x} = \frac{3x+4}{x}$$

Either version is correct.

47. We can split this fraction into two fractions with a common denominator of $5xy$ and then simplify further:

$$\frac{10x+3y}{5xy} = \frac{10x}{5xy} + \frac{3y}{5xy} = \frac{5\cancel{x} \times 2}{5\cancel{x} \times y} + \frac{\cancel{y} \times 3}{\cancel{y} \times 5x} = \frac{2}{y} + \frac{3}{5x}$$

Now we have a match. The correct answer is (C).

48. We must be careful when dealing with addition or subtraction in the denominator; the best we can do is identify factors common to all terms and cancel these. Every term within the fraction contains $3a$ as a factor:

$$\frac{6a}{33a+21ab} = \frac{3a \times 2}{(3a \times 11)+(3a \times 7b)} = \frac{\cancel{3a} \times 2}{\cancel{3a}(11+7b)} = \frac{2}{11+7b}$$

49. We begin by simplifying the square roots in the denominator:

$$\frac{3x\sqrt{3}}{6x\sqrt{12}-x\sqrt{27}} = \frac{3x\sqrt{3}}{6x(2\sqrt{3})-x(3\sqrt{3})} = \frac{3x\sqrt{3}}{12x\sqrt{3}-3x\sqrt{3}}$$

Because the subtraction is taking place in the denominator, we must identify common factors and cancel. These terms have a common factor of $3x\sqrt{3}$. Factor $3x\sqrt{3}$ out of the denominator.

$$\frac{3x\sqrt{3}}{12x\sqrt{3} - 3x\sqrt{3}} = \frac{3x\sqrt{3}}{3x\sqrt{3}(4-1)}$$

Now we can cancel $3x\sqrt{3}$ from the numerator and denominator.

$$\frac{\cancel{3x\sqrt{3}}}{\cancel{3x\sqrt{3}}(4-1)} = \frac{1}{3}$$

50. When dealing with addition or subtraction in the denominator, the best we can do is look for common factors among all of the terms. In this case, every coefficient present is a multiple of 8 and every term has at least one factor of x. Factor $8x$ out of the numerator and denominator.

$$\frac{8x^2 + 40x}{32x - 24x^2} = \frac{8x(x+5)}{8x(4-3x)}$$

Now we can cancel $8x$ from the numerator and denominator.

$$\frac{\cancel{8x}(x+5)}{\cancel{8x}(4-3x)} = \frac{x+5}{4-3x}$$

Drill 8

Simplify the following expressions. Final answers should be in their most simplified forms.

51. Begin by simplifying each fraction.

$$\frac{3+4}{1+2} - \frac{1+2}{3+4} = \frac{7}{3} - \frac{3}{7}$$

Because 3 and 7 share no common factors, the least common denominator is $3 \times 7 = 21$.

$$\frac{49}{21} - \frac{9}{21} = \frac{40}{21}$$

52. $\dfrac{3}{x+2} \times \dfrac{1}{5} = \dfrac{3 \times 1}{(x+2) \times 5} = \dfrac{3}{5x+10}$

53. $\dfrac{7}{n+3} \times \dfrac{n+1}{2} = \dfrac{7 \times (n+1)}{(n+3) \times 2} = \dfrac{7n+7}{2n+6}$

54. $\dfrac{x+2}{4} + \dfrac{x+3}{4} = \dfrac{(x+2)+(x+3)}{4} = \dfrac{2x+5}{4}$

55. $\dfrac{-t+1}{t-2} \times \dfrac{-t}{2} = \dfrac{(-t+1) \times (-t)}{(t-2) \times 2} = \dfrac{t^2 - t}{2t-4}$

MANHATTAN
GMAT

56. When subtracting fractions with more than one term in the numerator, put the subtracted term in parentheses to remind yourself to distribute the negative:

$$\frac{b+6}{6} - \frac{3+b}{6} = \frac{b+6-(3+b)}{6} = \frac{b+6-3-b}{6} = \frac{3}{6} = \frac{1}{2}$$

57. $$\frac{x(3+\sqrt{3})}{9} - \frac{x}{3} = \frac{3x + x\sqrt{3}}{9} - \frac{3x}{9} = \frac{(3x + x\sqrt{3}) - (3x)}{9} = \frac{x\sqrt{3}}{9}$$

58. Because the first fraction doesn't reduce, we need to multiply to find a common denominator:

$$\frac{3x^2 + 3y}{40} + \frac{x^2 + y}{8} = \frac{3x^2 + 3y}{40} + \frac{5x^2 + 5y}{40} = \frac{(3x^2 + 3y) + (5x^2 + 5y)}{40} = \frac{8x^2 + 8y}{40}$$

We're not done, because all the terms in the fraction are divisible by 8. We can still reduce this fraction further.

$$\frac{8x^2 + 8y}{40} = \frac{\cancel{8}(x^2 + y)}{\cancel{8} \times 5} = \frac{x^2 + y}{5}$$

Drill 9

59. Begin by breaking down the fractions so that we can reduce common factors before we multiply. Remember that you can cancel across fractions because they're multiplied.

$$\frac{4t}{6} \times \frac{-3}{t-3} = \frac{\cancel{2} \times 2 \times t}{\cancel{2} \times \cancel{3}} \times \frac{(-1) \times \cancel{3}}{(t-3)} = \frac{2 \times t \times -1}{t-3} = \frac{-2t}{t-3}$$

The answer is (A).

60. Begin by looking for common factors to cancel before we multiply.

$$\frac{j-2}{8} \times \frac{12}{j-2} = \frac{(j-2)}{2 \times 2 \times 2} \times \frac{2 \times 2 \times 3}{(j-2)}$$

Because $(j-2)$ is a factor of both the numerator and denominator, we can cancel it along with other common factors.

$$\frac{\cancel{(j-2)}}{\cancel{2} \times \cancel{2} \times 2} \times \frac{\cancel{2} \times \cancel{2} \times 3}{\cancel{(j-2)}} = \frac{3}{2}$$

The answer is (A).

61. Break down each fraction and look for common denominators.

$$\frac{x-5}{x} \times \frac{x^2}{x+1} = \frac{(x-5)}{\cancel{x}} \times \frac{\cancel{x} \times x}{(x+1)} = \frac{(x-5) \times x}{(x+1)} = \frac{x^2-5x}{x+1}$$

The answer is A.

62. Be careful—we can simplify the numerator of the first fraction and the denominator of the second fraction.

$$\frac{(n+2n)}{n^4} \times \frac{(2n)^2}{(15n-5n)} = \frac{3n}{n^4} \times \frac{4n^2}{10n}$$

Don't forget to simplify before you multiply:

$$\frac{3n}{n^4} \times \frac{4n^2}{10n} = \frac{3 \times \cancel{n} \times \cancel{2} \times 2 \times \cancel{n} \times \cancel{n}}{\cancel{n} \times \cancel{n} \times \cancel{n} \times n \times \cancel{2} \times 5 \times n} = \frac{3 \times 2}{n \times 5 \times n} = \frac{6}{5n^2}$$

The answer is B.

Drill 10

63. Begin by simplifying the denominator.

$$\frac{3}{3 + \frac{3}{4}} = \frac{3}{\frac{12}{4} + \frac{3}{4}} = \frac{3}{\frac{15}{4}}$$

Dividing by (15/4) is the same as multiplying by (4/15).

$$\frac{3}{\frac{15}{4}} = 3 \times \frac{4}{15} = \cancel{3} \times \frac{4}{\cancel{3} \times 5} = \frac{4}{5}$$

64. Begin by simplifying the denominator.

$$\frac{8}{2 - \frac{2}{3}} = \frac{8}{\frac{6}{3} - \frac{2}{3}} = \frac{8}{\frac{4}{3}}$$

Now we can divide 8 by the fraction (4/3), which is the same as multiplying by (3/4).

$$\frac{8}{\frac{4}{3}} = 8 \times \frac{3}{4} = (2 \times \cancel{4}) \times \frac{3}{\cancel{4}} = 6$$

65. To begin, simplify the numerator and the denominator.

$$\frac{\frac{1}{2} + \frac{1}{3}}{\frac{7}{6} - \frac{3}{4}} = \frac{\frac{3}{6} + \frac{2}{6}}{\frac{14}{12} - \frac{9}{12}} = \frac{\frac{5}{6}}{\frac{5}{12}}$$

Now we can divide.

$$\frac{\frac{5}{6}}{\frac{5}{12}} = \frac{5}{6} \times \frac{12}{5}$$

Simplify before you multiply.

$$\frac{5}{6} \times \frac{12}{5} = \frac{\cancel{5}}{\cancel{6}} \times \frac{\cancel{6} \times 2}{\cancel{5}} = 2$$

66. First we have to combine the terms in the denominator.

$$\frac{1}{1 - \dfrac{1}{1-y}} = \frac{1}{\dfrac{1-y}{1-y} - \dfrac{1}{1-y}} = \frac{1}{\dfrac{(1-y) - (1)}{1-y}} = \frac{1}{\dfrac{-y}{1-y}}$$

Now we can divide.

$$\frac{1}{\dfrac{-y}{1-y}} = 1 \times \frac{1-y}{-y} = \frac{1-y}{-y}$$

Be careful. The fraction we have doesn't match any of the answer choices. Notice that the denominator we have is $-y$, while two of the answer choices have a denominator of y. Let's factor (-1) out of the fraction.

$$\frac{1-y}{-y} = \frac{-1(y-1)}{-1(y)} = \frac{y-1}{y}$$

Now we have a match. The answer is C.

Chapter 5
of Foundations of GMAT Math

Fractions, Decimals, Percents, & Ratios

In This Chapter...

Chapter 5:
Fractions, Decimals, Percents, & Ratios

In This Chapter:

• Relationships among fractions, decimals, percents, & ratios

Four Ways to Express Parts of a Whole

Say you have the shaded part of this orange. You can express how much you have in four ways.

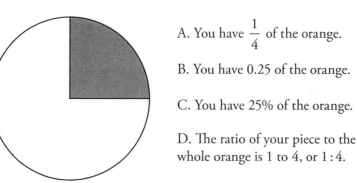

A. You have $\frac{1}{4}$ of the orange. **Fraction**

B. You have 0.25 of the orange. **Decimal**

C. You have 25% of the orange. **Percent**

D. The ratio of your piece to the whole orange is 1 to 4, or 1 : 4. **Ratio**

Any of these four forms can express a **part-to-whole relationship**. The main difference between the forms is how you think about the whole.

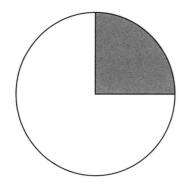

$\frac{1}{4}$ = 1 out of 4 pieces of the whole.

0.25 = 0.25 of the whole itself.

25% = 25 out of 100 pieces of the whole.

"1 to 4" = 1 out of 4 pieces of the whole.

In other words, what is each form "out of"? What is the whole that you are dividing by?

Fractions are *out of* the denominator (4 in this case).

Decimals are *out of* 1 (the whole). You've already done the division.

Percents are *out of* 100. *Percent* literally means "per hundred," or divided by 100.

Ratios are *out of* the second term in the ratio (4 in this case). So ratios are very similar to fractions, and you can quickly rewrite any ratio as a fraction. For instance, a ratio of 3 to 7 is $\frac{3}{7}$.
Another word for ratio is **proportion**.

Which form is most useful depends on the problem at hand. You might say any of the following:

The container is $\frac{1}{2}$ full.
The container is filled to 0.5 of its capacity.
The container is 50% full.
The ratio of the contents of the container to its capacity is 1 to 2.

By the way, the "part" can be greater than the whole.

I ate $\frac{5}{4}$ of a box of cereal. (I ate more than one box.)
I ate 1.25 boxes of cereal.
I ate 125% of a box of cereal.
The ratio of what I ate to a whole box of cereal was 5 to 4.

Convert 0.25 to 25%: Move The Decimal Point Two Places Right

Decimals are out of 1. Percents are out of 100. So, **to convert a decimal to a percent, move the decimal point two places to the right.** Add zeroes if necessary.

$$0.53 = 53\% \qquad 0.4 = 40\% \qquad 0.03 = 3\% \qquad 1.7 = 170\%$$

A percent might still contain a visible decimal point when you're done.

$$0.4057 = 40.57\% \qquad 0.002 = 0.2\% \qquad 0.0005 = 0.05\%$$

Just keep track of which decimal is part of the percent and which one is the "pure" decimal.

To convert a percent to a decimal, go in reverse. That is, move the decimal point two places to the *left*. If the decimal point isn't visible, it's actually just before the % sign. Add zeroes if necessary as you move left.

$$39\% = 39.\% = 0.39 \qquad 60\% = 0.60 = 0.6 \qquad 8\% = 0.08 \qquad 225\% = 2.25$$

13.4% = 0.134   0.7% = 0.007   0.001% = 0.00001

If you...	Then you...	Like this:
Want to convert a decimal to a percent	Move the decimal point two places to the right	$0.036 = 3.6\%$
Want to convert a percent to a decimal	Move the decimal point two places to the left	$41.2\% = 0.412$

Check Your Skills

1. Convert 0.035 to a percent.

Answer can be found on page 225.

Convert 0.25 or 25% to 1/4: Put 25 over 100 and Simplify

The decimal 0.25 is twenty-five one-hundredths. So rewrite that as 25 over 100:

$$0.25 = \frac{25}{100}$$

Now simplify by cancelling common factors from top and bottom.

$$0.25 = \frac{25}{100} = \frac{\overset{1}{\cancel{25}}}{\underset{4}{\cancel{100}}} = \frac{1}{4}$$

When you convert a decimal to a fraction, put a power of 10 (10, 100, 1,000, etc.) **in the denominator of the fraction.** Which power of 10? It depends on how far the decimal goes to the right.

Put as many zeroes in your power of 10 as you have digits to the right of the decimal point.

$0.3 = \dfrac{3}{10}$	$0.23 = \dfrac{23}{100}$	$0.007 = \dfrac{7}{1,000}$
Zero point three	is	three tenths, or three over ten

Zero point three | is | three tenths, or three over ten

Zero point two three | is | twenty-three one-hundredths

Zero point zero zero seven | is | seven one-thousandths.

Don't forget to cancel.

$$0.4 = \frac{4}{10} = \frac{\overset{2}{\cancel{4}}}{\underset{5}{\cancel{10}}} = \frac{2}{5} \qquad 0.375 = \frac{375}{1,000} = \frac{\overset{3}{\cancel{375}}}{\underset{8}{\cancel{1,000}}} = \frac{3}{8}$$

In the second case, you cancel 125 from top and bottom, leaving 3 and 8.

When you put the digits on top, keep any zeroes in the middle, such as the 0 between the 1 and the 2 in 0.0102. Otherwise, drop any zeroes (such as the 0's to the left of the 1).

$$0.0102 = \frac{102}{10,000} = \frac{\overset{51}{\cancel{102}}}{\underset{5,000}{\cancel{10,000}}} = \frac{51}{5,000}$$

To convert a percent to a fraction, write the percent "over one hundred." Remember that *percent* literally means "per hundred."

$$45\% = \frac{45}{100} = \frac{\overset{9}{\cancel{45}}}{\underset{20}{\cancel{100}}} = \frac{9}{20} \qquad 8\% = \frac{8}{100} = \frac{\overset{2}{\cancel{8}}}{\underset{25}{\cancel{100}}} = \frac{2}{25}$$

Alternatively, you can first convert the percent to a decimal by moving the decimal place. Then follow the process given earlier.

$$2.5\% = 0.025 = \frac{25}{1,000} = \frac{\overset{1}{\cancel{25}}}{\underset{40}{\cancel{1,000}}} = \frac{1}{40}$$

If you don't convert to a decimal first, be sure to write the fraction over 100.

$$2.5\% = \frac{2.5}{100}$$

That fraction ultimately reduces to $\frac{1}{40}$, but we'll look at the process of dividing decimals a little further on.

If you...	Then you...	Like this:
Want to convert a decimal to a fraction	Put the digits to the right of the decimal point over the appropriate power of 10, then simplify	$0.036 = \dfrac{36}{1,000}$ $= \dfrac{9}{250}$
Want to convert a percent to a fraction	Write the percent "over 100," then simplify	$4\% = \dfrac{4}{100}$ $= \dfrac{1}{25}$
	OR Convert first to a decimal, then follow the process for converting decimals to fractions	$3.6\% = 0.036$ $0.036 = \dfrac{9}{250}$

Check Your Skills

2. Convert 0.375 to a fraction.
3. Convert 24% to a fraction.

Answers can be found on page 225.

Convert 1/4 to 0.25 or 25%: Long-Divide 1 by 4

A fraction represents division. The decimal equivalent is the result of that division.

To convert a fraction to a decimal, long-divide the numerator by the denominator.

$$\frac{1}{4} = ?$$ Divide 1 by 4.

$$
\begin{array}{r}
0.25 \\
4\overline{)\,1.00} \\
-0.80 \\
\hline
0.20 \\
-0.20 \\
\hline
0
\end{array}
$$

$$\frac{1}{4} = 0.25$$

$$\frac{5}{8} = ?$$ Divide 5 by 8.

$$
\begin{array}{r}
0.625 \\
8\overline{)\,5.000} \\
-4.800 \\
\hline
0.200 \\
-0.160 \\
\hline
0.040 \\
-0.040 \\
\hline
0
\end{array}
$$

$$\frac{5}{8} = 0.625$$

In some cases, the decimal never ends because the long division never ends. You get a repeating decimal.

$$\frac{1}{3} = 0.333... = 0.\overline{3}$$

$$
\begin{array}{r}
0.33.. \\
3\overline{)\,1.000} \\
-0.900 \\
\hline
0.100 \\
-0.090 \\
\hline
0.010 \\
...
\end{array}
$$

If the denominator contains only 2's and/or 5's as factors, the decimal will end. In that case, you can take a shortcut to find the decimal equivalent: **make the denominator a power of 10 by multiplication.**

$$\frac{1}{4} = \frac{1 \times 25}{4 \times 25} = \frac{25}{100} = 0.25 \qquad \frac{5}{8} = \frac{5 \times 125}{8 \times 125} = \frac{625}{1,000} = 0.625$$

Since $4 = 2^2$, you multiply by 25 ($= 5^2$) to get 100 ($= 10^2$). Likewise, you multiply 8 ($= 2^3$) by 125 ($= 5^3$) to get 1,000 ($= 10^3$).

5

To convert a fraction to a percent, first c~~...~~ **to a per-cent.**

$$\frac{1}{2} = \frac{1 \times 5}{2 \times 5} = \frac{5}{10} = 0.5 = 50\%$$

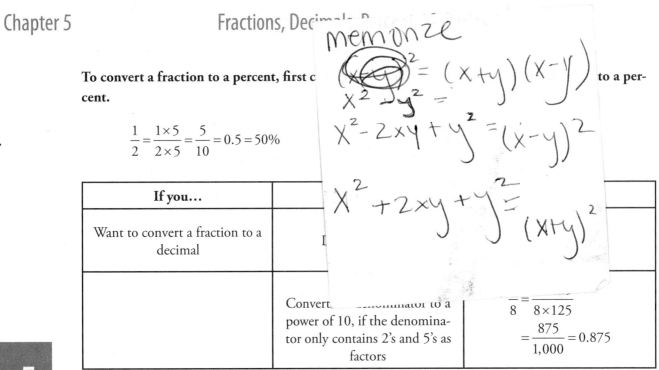

If you...		
Want to convert a fraction to a decimal		
	Convert ~~the denomi~~nator to a power of 10, if the denominator only contains 2's and 5's as factors	$\frac{}{8} = \frac{}{8 \times 125}$ $= \frac{875}{1,000} = 0.875$

Know the following conversions.

Fraction	Decimal	Percent
1/100	0.01	1%
1/20	0.05	5%
1/10	0.1	10%
1/8	0.125	12.5%
1/5	0.2	20%
1/4	0.25	25%
3/10	0.3	30%
1/3	0.3333…	33.33…%
3/8	0.375	37.5%
2/5	0.4	40%
1/2	0.5	50%
3/5	0.6	60%
5/8	0.625	62.5%
2/3	0.6666…	66.66…%
7/10	0.7	70%
3/4	0.75	75%
4/5	0.8	80%
7/8	0.875	87.5%
9/10	0.9	90%
1	1	100%
6/5	1.2	120%
5/4	1.25	125%
3/2	1.5	150%

Check Your Skills

4. Change 3/5 to a decimal.
5. Convert 3/8 to a percent.

Answers can be found on page 225.

Multiply a Decimal by a Power of Ten: Shift the Decimal Point

Decimals are tenths, hundredths, thousandths, and so on. One tenth is a power of 10—namely, 10^{-1}. One hundredth is also a power of 10—namely, 10^{-2}.

You can write any decimal as a fraction with a power of 10 in the denominator, or as a product involving a power of 10. **The power of 10 determines where the decimal point is.**

So **if you multiply or divide a decimal by a power of 10, you move the decimal point.**

If you multiply by 10 itself, you shift the decimal point one place to the right.

$$0.004 \times 10 = 0.04$$

The 10 cancels with one power of 10 in the denominator.

$$\frac{4}{1,000} \times 10 = \frac{4}{1,00\cancel{0}} \times \cancel{10} = \frac{4}{100}$$

You can also see it in terms of exponents. The additional 10 increases the overall exponent from –3 to –2.

$$4 \times 10^{-3} \times 10 = 4 \times 10^{-2}$$

If you multiply by 100, or 10^2, you shift the decimal point two places to the right.

$$0.004 \times 100 = 0.4 \qquad \text{That is, } \frac{4}{1,000} \times 100 = \frac{4}{10} \qquad 4 \times 10^{-3} \times 10^2 = 4 \times 10^{-1}$$

When you multiply by a power of 10, the exponent of that power is the number of places you move the decimal.

$$43.8723 \times 10^3 = 43,872.3 \qquad \text{Move the decimal 3 places to the right.}$$

If you divide by a power of 10, you just move to the left instead.

$$782.95 \div 10 = 78.295 \qquad \text{Move the decimal 1 place to the left.}$$

$$57,234 \div 10^4 = 5.7234 \qquad \text{Move the decimal 4 places to the left.}$$

If you encounter negative powers of 10, flip them to positive powers of 10 and change from multiplication to division or vice versa.

Multiplying by a negative power of 10 is the same as dividing by a positive power.

$$0.004 \times 10^{-3} = 0.004 \div 10^3 = 0.000004 \quad \text{Move 3 places to the left.}$$

Likewise, dividing by a negative power of 10 is the same as multiplying by a positive power.

$$62 \div 10^{-2} = 62 \times 10^2 = 6{,}200 \qquad \text{Move 2 places to the right.}$$

All of these procedures work the same for repeating decimals.

$$\frac{1}{3} \times 10 = 0.333... \times 10 = 3.33... \qquad \text{Move 1 place to the right.}$$

If you…	Then you…	Like this:
Multiply a decimal by a power of 10	Move the decimal point right a number of places, corresponding to the exponent of 10	$0.007 \times 10^2 = 0.7$
Divide a decimal by a power of 10	Move the decimal point left a number of places, corresponding to the exponent of 10	$0.6 \div 10^3 = 0.0006$

Check Your Skills

6. $32.753 \times 10^2 =$

7. $43{,}681 \times 10^{-4} =$

Answers can be found on page 225.

Add or Subtract Decimals: Line Up the Decimal Points

When you add or subtract decimals, write the decimals vertically, with the decimal points lined up.

$0.3 + 0.65 = \qquad\qquad\qquad 0.65 - 0.5 =$

$$\begin{array}{r} 0.3 \\ + \ \ 0.65 \\ \hline 0.95 \end{array} \qquad\qquad \begin{array}{r} 0.65 \\ - \ \ 0.50 \\ \hline 0.15 \end{array}$$

You can add zeroes on the right to help you line up. For instance, turn 0.5 into 0.50 before you subtract it from 0.65.

If you...	Then you...	Like this:
Add or subtract decimals	Line up the decimal points vertically	4.035 +0.120 ——— 4.155

Check Your Skills

8. $3.128 + 0.045 =$

9. $1.8746 - 0.313 =$

Answers can be found on page 225.

Multiply Two Decimals: Ignore Decimal Points At First

Consider this example:

$0.25 \times 0.5 =$

First, multiply the numbers together as if they were integers. In other words, ignore the decimal points.

$25 \times 5 = 125$

Now count all the digits to the right of the original decimal points.

0.25 has 2 digits to the right.   0.5 has 1 digit to the right.

There were a total of 3 digits originally to the right. So we move the decimal point of our answer 3 places to the *left*, in order to compensate.

125 becomes 0.125   Therefore, $0.25 \times 0.5 = 0.125$

You can see why this process works using powers of 10.

$0.25 = 25 \times 10^{-2}$ $0.5 = 5 \times 10^{-1}$

$0.25 \times 0.5 = (25 \times 10^{-2}) \times (5 \times 10^{-1}) = 125 \times 10^{-3} = 0.125$

The powers of 10 just tell you where to put the decimal point. Here is another example:

$3.5 \times 20 =$

$35 \times 20 = 700$ We originally had one digit to the right of a decimal point.
                       Move the final decimal point one place to the left.

$3.5 \times 20 = 70.0 = 70$

Count the zeroes to the right of the decimal point as well.

$0.001 \times 0.005 =$

$1 \times 5 = 5$ We originally had six digits to the right, including zeroes.

Move the final decimal point six places to the left.

$0.001 \times 0.005 = 0.000005$

If you…	Then you…	Like this:
Multiply two decimals	Ignore the decimal points, multiply integers, then place the decimal point by counting the original digits on the right	$0.2 \times 0.5 = ?$ $2 \times 5 = 10$ $10 \rightarrow 0.10$ $0.2 \times 0.5 = 0.1$

Check Your Skills

10. $0.6 \times 1.4 =$

11. $0.0004 \times 0.032 =$

Answers can be found on pages 225–226.

Multiply a Decimal and a Big Number: Trade Decimal Places

Now consider this example:

$4,000,000 \times 0.0003 =$

When one number is very big and the other one is very small, you can trade powers of 10 from the big one (4,000,000) to the small one (0.0003). In other words, move one decimal point *left* and the other one *right*. Just make sure you move the same number of places.

This multiplication would be easier if we got rid of the decimal altogether. To do so, we need to move the decimal in 0.0003 to the right 4 places. So to compensate, we move the decimal in 4,000,000 to the left 4 places. That makes that number more manageable anyway.

$4,000,000 \times 0.0003 = 4,000,000 \times 0.0003 = 400 \times 3 = 1,200$

You can justify these maneuvers with powers of 10.

$4,000,000 \times 0.0003 = (4 \times 10^6) \times (3 \times 10^{-4}) = 12 \times 10^{6-4} = 12 \times 10^2 = 1,200$

If you...	Then you...	Like this:
Multiply a decimal and a big number	Trade decimal places from the big number to the decimal	$50,\underline{000} \times 0.0\underline{07} =$ $50 \times 7 = 350$

Check Your Skills

12. $520,000 \times 0.0004 =$

Answers can be found on page 226.

Divide Two Decimals: Move Points in the Same Direction To Kill Decimals

When you divide decimals, first write the division as a fraction if it isn't in that form already.

$$\frac{300}{0.05} =$$

Now move the decimals in the *same* direction on top and bottom. This is the same as multiplying top and bottom by the same power of 10. Do this to eliminate decimals.

In this case, you want to turn 0.05 into 5 by moving its decimal 2 places to the right. Just do the same thing on top. Add zeroes as necessary.

$$\frac{300}{0.05} = \frac{300}{0.05} = \frac{30,000}{5} = 6,000$$

This is equivalent to multiplying top and bottom by 100.

$$\frac{300}{0.05} = \frac{300 \times 100}{0.05 \times 100} = \frac{30,000}{5} = 6,000$$

One decimal may need more moves than the other. Try this example:

$$\frac{12.39}{0.003} =$$

The 12.39 only needs 2 moves to get rid of the decimal, while 0.003 needs 3 moves. Go with the larger number of moves. You can always add zeroes to the other number.

5

$$\frac{12.39}{0.003} = \frac{12.39}{0.003} = \frac{12,390}{3} = 4,130$$

If you...	Then you...	Like this:
Divide two decimals	Move the decimal points in the same direction to eliminate decimals as far as you can	$\frac{0.002}{0.0004} = \frac{20}{4} = 5$

Check Your Skills

13. $\dfrac{0.00084}{0.00007} =$

Answers can be found on page 226.

"20% Of $55" = 0.2 × $55

In everyday life, percents are the most common way of expressing part-to-whole relationships. You often see signs advertising "25% off," but you don't see as many signs advertising "$\frac{1}{4}$ off" or "0.75 of the original price." So your intuition about percents is probably good, and that's useful on the GMAT.

However, percents are the least useful form for actual *computation*. **If you need to crunch numbers, convert percents to decimals or fractions.**

Consider this problem:

30% of $60 =

"Of" means "times." In a percent problem, "of" indicates multiplication.

So convert 30% to a decimal, and then multiply.

30% of $60 = 0.30 × $60 = 3 × $6 = $18

Of course, you can use the fraction form of 30% instead.

$$30\% \text{ of } \$60 = \frac{30}{100} \times \$60 = \frac{3\cancel{0}}{10\cancel{0}} \times \$60 = \frac{3}{1\cancel{0}} \times \$6\cancel{0} = \$18$$

The problem could be worded as a question.

What is 20% of $55?

In the "Word Problems" chapter, we'll do more with translating words into math. For now, though, you should know these translations:

What   can be translated as   *x*   (some variable)

is   can be translated as   =   (the equals sign)

So you can translate the full question to math as follows:

$$\text{What} \quad \text{is} \quad 20\% \quad \text{of} \quad \$55?$$
$$x \quad = \quad 0.20 \quad \times \quad \$55$$

Now you can crunch the numbers on the right.

$0.20 \times \$55 =$ Compute $2 \times \$55 = \$110$, then move the decimal point.

$0.20 \times \$55 = \$11$

Of course, you could translate 20% to a fraction rather than to a decimal.

$$20\% = \frac{20}{100} = \frac{1}{5}$$

$$\frac{1}{5} \times \$55 = \frac{1}{\cancel{5}} \times {}^{11}\cancel{\$55} = \$11$$

The translation gets a little tougher when you encounter the phrase "what percent."

What percent of 125 is 25?

You should still use *x* to translate "what."

The word "percent" by itself means "divided by 100." You can show that as " /100" or "$\frac{}{100}$".

As a result, **"what percent" can be translated as *x*/100, or $\frac{x}{100}$.**

Translate the question now.

$$\text{What percent} \quad \text{of} \quad 125 \quad \text{is} \quad 25?$$
$$\frac{x}{100} \quad \times \quad 125 \quad = \quad 25$$

You can now find the answer by solving for *x*. Solving equations for *x* will be covered in depth in the "Equations" chapter on page 257.

$$\frac{x}{100} \times 125 = 25$$

$$\frac{x}{\cancel{100}_{4}} \times {}^{5}\cancel{125} = 25$$

$$\frac{x}{4} \times 5 = 25$$

$$\frac{x}{4} = 5$$

$$x = 20$$

In practice, you should use something other than × to indicate multiplication when you have an x around, so that you don't mix up × and x on your paper. You can use parentheses or a big dot.

$$\left(\frac{x}{100}\right)125 = 25 \qquad \frac{x}{100} \cdot 125 = 25$$

Here's a last example:

16 is 2% of what?

Translate word by word. Change 2% either to 0.02 or to $\frac{2}{100} = \frac{1}{50}$.

16	is	2%	of	what?
16	=	0.02	×	x

Now solve for x.

$$16 = (0.02)x$$

$$\frac{16}{0.02} = x$$

$$\frac{16}{0.0\overset{\rightarrow\rightarrow}{2}} = x$$

$$\frac{1,600}{2} = x$$

$$800 = x$$

If you...	Then you...	Like this:
See "30% of"	Convert 30% into a decimal or fraction, then multiply	30% of 200 = $0.30 \times 200 = 60$
See "what percent of"	Turn "what percent" into $\dfrac{x}{100}$, then multiply	What percent of 200 is 60? $\left(\dfrac{x}{100}\right)200 = 60$

Check Your Skills

Translate the following and solve.

14. 21 is 30% of what number?

Answers can be found on page 226.

Percent Change: Divide Change in Value by Original Value

Consider this example.

> You have $200 in a bank account. You deposit an additional $30 in that account. By what percent did the value of the bank account change?

Whenever some amount changes and you care about percents, set up this equation:

Original + Change = New

This equation holds true in two ways. First, it holds true for the actual amounts or values, which in this case are in dollars. This is unsurprising.

Original value	+	Change in value	=	New value
$200	+	$30	=	$230

This equation *also* holds true for percents, as long as you mean percents *of the original value.*

Original Percent (% of original)	+	Change Percent (% of original)	=	New Percent (% of original)
100%	+	?	=	?

The original percent is always 100%, since the original value is always 100% of itself.

The change percent is better known as the **percent change**. This equals **the change in value divided by the original value.**

$$\text{Percent Change (as \% of original)} = \frac{\text{Change in value}}{\text{Original value}}$$

The new percent is related to the new value by the same kind of formula.

$$\text{New Percent (as \% of original)} = \frac{\text{New value}}{\text{Original value}}$$

You can rewrite these equations by multiplying through by the original value.

$$\text{Percent Change (as \% of original)} \times \text{Original value} = \text{Change in value}$$

$$\text{New Percent (as \% of original)} \times \text{Original value} = \text{New value}$$

To solve this problem, you can find the percent change using either form of the equation.

$$\text{Percent Change (as \% of original)} = \frac{\text{Change in value}}{\text{Original value}}$$

$$\frac{\text{Change in value}}{\text{Original value}} = \frac{\$30}{\$200} = \frac{\overset{15}{\cancel{\$30}}}{\underset{100}{\cancel{\$200}}} = \frac{15}{100} = 15\%$$

The additional $30 corresponds to a 15% change in the value of the account.

You can also use "Percent Change × Original value = Change in value." That's equivalent to this question:

What percent of $200 is $30?

Turn "what percent" into $\dfrac{x}{100}$, translate the rest and solve for x.

$$\left(\frac{x}{100}\right)200 = 30$$

$$\left(\frac{x}{\cancel{100}}\right)2\cancel{00} = 30$$

$$2x = 30$$

$$x = 15$$

Again, the $30 increase represents a 15% increase in the account's value.

You can also find the new percent if you want:

Original Percent (% of original)	+	Change Percent (% of original)	=	New Percent (% of original)
100%	+	15%	=	115%

In other words, $230 is 115% of $200, the original value of the account.

If the value of the account decreases, the equations still hold true. You just have a negative change. In other words, you subtract the change.

> You again have $200 in a bank account. You make a withdrawal that reduces the value of the account by 40%. How much money remains in the account?

This time, solve for the new percent first. A 40% decrease is a −40% change.

Original Percent (% of original)	+	Change Percent (% of original)	=	New Percent (% of original)
100%	+	−40%	=	60%

If you take out 40%, what's left is 60% of the original. Now find the new value.

> New Percent (as % of original) × Original value = New value

$$60\% \times \$200 = \text{New value}$$

$$\left(\frac{60}{100}\right)200 = x$$

$$\left(\frac{60}{100}\right)2\cancel{00} = x$$

$$120 = x$$

$120 remains in the account.

Alternatively, you could figure out the change in value, then subtract that from the original value. However, it's often faster to turn the percent change into the new percent, then convert that into a convenient fraction or decimal and multiply by the original value.

Learn these shortcuts.

A percent INCREASE of...	... is the same as this NEW percent...	... which is the same as multiplying the ORIGINAL VALUE by...
10%	110%	1.1
20%	120%	1.2, or $\dfrac{6}{5}$
25%	125%	1.25, or $\dfrac{5}{4}$
50%	150%	1.5, or $\dfrac{3}{2}$
100%	200%	2

A percent DECREASE of...	... is the same as this NEW percent...	... which is the same as multiplying the ORIGINAL VALUE by...
10%	90%	0.9
20%	80%	0.8, or $\dfrac{4}{5}$
25%	75%	0.75, or $\dfrac{3}{4}$
50%	50%	0.5, or $\dfrac{1}{2}$
75%	25%	0.25, or $\dfrac{1}{4}$

"Percent more than" is just like "percent increase." You do exactly the same math.

$230 is what percent more than $200?

Think of $230 as the new value and $200 as the original value. Again, you'll get 15%. You just call it the **percent difference** rather than the percent change.

Likewise, **"percent less than" is just like "percent decrease."**

$120 is what percent less than $200?

Think of $120 as the new value and $200 as the original value. Again, you'll get a 40% "decrease" or difference.

Which number you call the original value matters. **The original value is always after the "than."** It's the value you're comparing the other value *to*.

> $230 is what percent more than $200?

$200 is the original value. You're comparing $230 to $200, not the other way around.

Finally, be sure not to misread a "percent OF" as a "percent MORE THAN" or vice versa.

> 35 is what percent of 20?
> 35 is what percent more than 20?

The answer to the first question is 175, since 35 is 175 percent *of* 20.

The answer to the second question is 75, since 35 is 75 percent *more than* 20.

Keep "percent of" and "percent more than/less than" distinct.

If you…	Then you…	Like this:
Need to find a percent change	Divide the change in value by the original value	Add $30 to $200 $$\frac{\$30}{\$200} = 15\%$$
Need to find a new value from the percent change and the original value	Find the new "percent of" using Original + Change = New, then multiply by the original value	$60 + 25% = ? New % = 125% $$= \frac{5}{4}$$ $$\left(\frac{5}{4}\right)\$60 = \$75$$
Need to find a "percent more than" or "percent less than"	Treat the problem like a percent increase or a percent decrease	$230 is what % more than $200? $$\frac{\$30}{\$200} = 15\%$$

Check Your Skills

15. What is the percent decrease from 90 to 72?

Answers can be found on page 226.

Percent Of a Percent Of: Multiply Twice

Consider this example.

What is 120% of 150% of 30?

These are "percents of," so you turn the percents into decimal or fractional equivalents and multiply 30 by *both* of those equivalents.

Fraction equivalents are particularly handy for successive percent changes, because frequently we can cancel.

$$120\% = \frac{6}{5} \qquad 150\% = \frac{3}{2}$$

$$120\% \text{ of } 150\% \text{ of } 30 = \frac{6}{5} \times \frac{3}{2} \times 30 = \frac{\cancel{6}^{3}}{5} \times \frac{3}{\cancel{2}} \times 30 = \frac{9}{\cancel{5}} \times \cancel{30}^{6} = 54$$

Percent changes often come one after the other. **When you have successive percent changes, multiply the original value by each "new percent"** (converted to a suitable fraction or decimal).

The price of a share, originally $50, goes up by 10% on Monday and then by 20% on Tuesday. What is the overall change in the price of a share, in dollars?

A percent increase of 10% is equivalent to a "new percent" of 110%, or multiplying the original value by 1.1 or $\frac{11}{10}$.

A percent increase of 20% is equivalent to a "new percent" of 120%, or multiplying the original value by 1.2 or $\frac{6}{5}$.

Compute the new value by multiplying the original value by both of these factors.

$$\$50 \times \frac{11}{10} \times \frac{6}{5} = \cancel{\$50} \times \frac{11}{\cancel{10}} \times \frac{6}{\cancel{5}} = 11 \times 6 = \$66$$

So the change in value is $66 − $50 = $16.

Notice that that change is *not* 30% of $50 = $15. **Never add successive percents** (e.g., 10% and 20%). The answer will be approximately right ($15 is *close* to $16) and precisely wrong.

If you...	Then you...	Like this:
Have successive percent changes	Multiply the original value by the "new percents" for *both* percent changes	$50 + 10\%$, then $+ 20\%$ $$\$50\left(\frac{11}{10}\right)\left(\frac{6}{5}\right) = \$66$$

Check Your Skills

16. What is 80% of 75% of 120?

Answers can be found on page 226.

Ratio: One Quantity Divided By Another

Ratios or proportions express a particular kind of relationship between two quantities. That relationship is division. Consider this example:

> For every 2 boys in a certain kindergarten class, there are 3 girls.

This relationship can be rewritten this way:

$$\frac{\text{Number of boys}}{\text{Number of girls}} = \frac{2}{3}$$

In words, the number of boys divided by the number of girls is $\frac{2}{3}$.

The language and symbols of ratios are peculiar. Note the following equivalent expressions:

> For every 2 boys, there are 3 girls.
> There are 2 boys for every 3 girls.
> The ratio of boys to girls is 2 to 3.
> The ratio of boys to girls is 2 : 3.
> The ratio of boys to girls is $\frac{2}{3}$.

None of this means that there are only 2 boys and 3 girls in the class.

There *could* be 2 boys and 3 girls in the class. But there could also be 4 boys and 6 girls, or 6 boys and 9 girls, or 20 boys and 30 girls, and so on. The only constraint is that the number of boys divided by the number of girls must equal $\frac{2}{3}$.

By the way, use full words for the units "boys" and "girls." *Never* write 2B to mean 2 boys or 3G to mean 3 girls. You will confuse yourself terribly. Single letters (such as B and G) should always be variables, not units. The expression 2B would mean "2 times the number of boys."

If you know that the ratio of boys to girls is 2 to 3 and you are told what one of the numbers is, then you can figure out the other one. For instance, if you are told that there are 15 girls, then you can figure out that there must be 10 boys, since $\frac{10 \text{ boys}}{15 \text{ girls}} = \frac{2}{3}$. Likewise, if you are told that there are 12 boys, then there must be 18 girls, to keep the ratio at 2:3.

Every possible set of numbers reduces to $\frac{2}{3}$, if you write the set as a fraction.

$$\frac{10 \text{ boys}}{15 \text{ girls}} = \frac{10}{15} = \frac{\overset{2}{\cancel{10}}}{\underset{3}{\cancel{15}}} = \frac{2}{3} \qquad\qquad \frac{12 \text{ boys}}{18 \text{ girls}} = \frac{12}{18} = \frac{\overset{2}{\cancel{12}}}{\underset{3}{\cancel{18}}} = \frac{2}{3}$$

Let's write the common factors explicitly before cancelling them out.

$$\frac{10 \text{ boys}}{15 \text{ girls}} = \frac{10}{15} = \frac{2 \times 5}{3 \times 5} = \frac{2 \times \cancel{5}}{3 \times \cancel{5}} = \frac{2}{3} \qquad\qquad \frac{12 \text{ boys}}{18 \text{ girls}} = \frac{12}{18} = \frac{2 \times 6}{3 \times 6} = \frac{2 \times \cancel{6}}{3 \times \cancel{6}} = \frac{2}{3}$$

The number of boys and the number of girls must have a common factor that cancels out to leave 2 and 3, respectively. We call that common factor the **unknown multiplier** and usually give it the letter x.

So the number of boys must be 2 times that common factor x.

> Number of boys = $2x$

Likewise, the number of girls must be 3 times that common factor x.

> Number of girls = $3x$

This formulation *guarantees* the ratio of 2 to 3.

$$\frac{\text{Number of boys}}{\text{Number of girls}} = \frac{2x}{3x} = \frac{2\cancel{x}}{3\cancel{x}} = \frac{2}{3}$$

The unknown multiplier x is the common factor that cancels out to leave $\frac{2}{3}$.

If you are given one quantity, you can always figure out the other quantity directly from the proportion. Or you can figure out the unknown multiplier first, then the other quantity. Although the second way might seem roundabout, it can save you computational effort.

> The ratio of apples to bananas in a certain display is 7 to 10. If there are 63 apples, how many bananas are there?

You can solve this problem in your head if you use the unknown multiplier.

Set the number of apples equal to 7x, and solve for x.

$7x = 63$ $x = 9$

You can think of 9 as the number of "basic sets" of apples and bananas. A basic set contains exactly the numbers in the ratio: 7 apples and 10 bananas. Any possible quantity of fruit in the display must contain some number of these basic sets.

You've now figured out that there are 9 basic sets of apples and bananas. The multiplier is no longer unknown. If each set has 10 bananas, how many total bananas are there?

Total number of bananas = $10x = 10(9) = 90$

There are 90 bananas in the display.

If you...	Then you...	Like this:
See that the ratio of sharks to dolphins is 3 to 13	Write the proportion of sharks to dolphins as a fraction	$\dfrac{\text{Sharks}}{\text{Dolphins}} = \dfrac{3}{13}$
	Write each quantity in terms of an unknown multiplier	Sharks = $3x$ Dolphins = $13x$

Check Your Skills

17. The ratio of blue marbles to white marbles in a bag is $3:5$. If there are 15 white marbles in the bag, how many blue marbles are there?

Answers can be found on page 227.

Part : Part : Whole Ratios—Write Part + Part: Whole and Use the Unknown Multiplier

If there are 2 boys for every 3 girls in the kindergarten class, then you can also say something about the total number of students in the class.

Write each quantity in terms of the unknown multiplier again.

Number of boys = $2x$
Number of girls = $3x$

You also know that Boys + Girls = Total Students.

Total number of students = $2x + 3x = 5x$

All three quantities (boys, girls, and students) have the same multiplier.

This means that you can write a **Part : Part : Whole ratio** relating boys, girls, and total students. The Whole number is just the sum of the two Parts.

Boys : Girls : Students   =   2 : 3 : 5

Here's another way to think about this concept. Each "basic set" of 2 boys and 3 girls has a total of 5 students. Once you know the number of basic sets (that is, the unknown multiplier), you know *three* things—the number of boys, the number of girls, *and* the total number of students.

For all this to work, you have to have just two distinct parts in the whole. This lets you sum to the whole from the Boys : Girls ratio.

You can now write two-way ratios between any two components.

Boys : Girls = 2 : 3
Boys : Students = 2 : 5
Girls : Students = 3 : 5

Furthermore, you can determine percents of the whole. The 2 : 3 ratio of boys to girls guarantees a 2 : 5 ratio of boys to students. Thus, $\frac{2}{5}$, or 40%, of the students are boys. Likewise, $\frac{3}{5}$, or 60%, of the students are girls.

Here are a few other common Part : Part ratios and the resulting percents of the whole.

Boys : Girls	Boys : Girls : Students	Boys : Students	Girls : Students
1 : 1	1 : 1 : 2	1 : 2 50%	1 : 2 50%
1 : 2	1 : 2 : 3	1 : 3 33.33...%	2 : 3 66.66...%
1 : 3	1 : 3 : 4	1 : 4 25%	3 : 4 75%

Consider this problem:

A bouquet contains white roses and red roses. If the ratio of white to red roses is 5 : 3, what percent of all the roses are red?

(A) 37.5%   (B) 40%   (C) 60%   (D) 62.5%   (E) 80%

Set up a Part : Part : Whole ratio. The Whole number is just $5 + 3 = 8$.

White : Red : Total Roses   = $5 : 3 : 8$

So the ratio of Red to Total is 3 to 8. The fraction you want is $\frac{3}{8}$. As a percent, $\frac{3}{8} = 37.5\%$. The correct answer is (A).

If you have the percents of the two parts of the whole, you can set up a Part : Part : Whole ratio with the percents. Use 100 for the Whole. Then reduce the ratio by removing common factors.

If 20% of the animals in a zoo are skunks, what is the ratio of non-skunk animals to skunks in the zoo?

Here, the "Part + Part = Whole" equation is Skunks + Non-skunks = Animals. If 20% of the animals are skunks, then 100% - 20% = 80% are non-skunks.

Skunks : Non-skunks : Animals   = $20 : 80 : 100$

Now reduce the ratio. You can take out a common factor of 20, leaving $1 : 4 : 5$.

Thus, the ratio of non-skunk animals to skunks is 4 to 1. Be careful of the order in any ratio, and answer the question as given.

You didn't need the unknown multiplier in these problems, but now try this one:

A car lot contains only sedans and trucks. There are 4 sedans for every 5 trucks on the lot. If there are 12 sedans on the lot, how many total vehicles are there?

Set up the Part : Part : Whole ratio.

Sedans : Trucks : Total vehicles   = $4 : 5 : 9$

You are told that there are actually 12 sedans on the lot. So now use the unknown multiplier x.

Number of sedans = $4x = 12$ sedans

$x = 3$

Now plug in this multiplier to find the total number of vehicles.

Total number of vehicles = $9x = 9(3) = 27$ vehicles.

Notice that when the quantities are counting real things, you have to stick to positive integers—the counting numbers 1, 2, 3, etc. In that case, the unknown multiplier itself is restricted to counting numbers as well. This means that the parts and the whole must be multiples of the numbers in the ratio.

Take the kindergarten class again.

Boys : Girls : Students =   2 : 3 : 5

The number of boys is $2x$, and x must be an integer, so the number of boys must be even (a multiple of 2).

Likewise, the number of girls must be a multiple of 3, and the total number of students must be a multiple of 5. If the GMAT asks you what *could* be the total number of students, then the right answer will be a multiple of 5, and the 4 wrong answers will not be.

In real life, you encounter ratios in recipes. You usually have more than two ingredients. But you can still use the unknown multiplier.

Take this recipe:

3 cups of olive oil
+ 1 cup of vinegar
+ ½ cup of lemon juice
+ ½ cup of mustard   = 5 cups of salad dressing

What if you need 10 cups of salad dressing for a big party? Set up the unknown multiplier.

Cups of salad dressing = $5x = 10$ so $x = 2$

The multiplier is 2. This means that you double the recipe, as you probably figured out immediately. Recognize that this is what the multiplier in a ratio does: it multiplies every ingredient by the same factor (2 in this case).

Cups of olive oil $= 3x$ $= 3(2)$ $= 6$ cups
Cups of vinegar $= 1x$ $= 1(2)$ $= 2$ cups
Cups of lemon juice $= ½x$ $= ½(2)$ $= 1$ cup
Cups of mustard $= ½x$ $= ½(2)$ $= 1$ cup

If you...	Then you...	Like this:
Have two parts that make a whole and that have a ratio of 3 to 4	Write the Part : Part : Whole ratio as 3 : 4 : 7 and use the unknown multiplier as needed	Lefties $= 3x$ Righties $= 4x$ so People $= 7x$

Check Your Skills

18. A flowerbed contains only roses and tulips. If the ratio of tulips to the total number of flowers in the bed is 5 : 11, and there are 121 flowers in the bed, how many roses are there?

Answers can be found on page 227.

Check Your Skills Answer Key

1. **3.5%:** Move the decimal to the right 2 places. $0.035 \rightarrow 3.5\%$

2. $\dfrac{3}{8}$: $0.375 = \dfrac{\overset{75}{\cancel{375}}}{\underset{200}{\cancel{1,000}}} = \dfrac{\overset{3}{\cancel{75}}}{\underset{8}{\cancel{200}}} = \dfrac{3}{8}$

3. $\dfrac{6}{25}$: $24\% = \dfrac{\overset{6}{\cancel{24}}}{\underset{25}{\cancel{100}}} = \dfrac{6}{25}$

4. **0.6:** Perform long division to convert a fraction to a decimal.

$$\begin{array}{r} 0.6 \\ 5\overline{)3.0} \\ -30 \\ \hline 0 \end{array}$$

5. **37.5%:** Begin by performing long division.

$$\begin{array}{r} 0.375 \\ 8\overline{)3.000} \\ 24 \\ \hline 60 \\ 56 \\ \hline 40 \\ 40 \\ \hline 0 \end{array}$$

6. **3,275.3:** $32.753 \times 10^2 = 3,275.3$

7. **4.3681:** $43,681 \times 10^{-4} = 4.3681$

8. **3.173:**

$$\begin{array}{r} 3.128 \\ +\ 0.045 \\ \hline 3.173 \end{array}$$

9. **1.5616:**

$$\begin{array}{r} 1.8746 \\ -\ 0.313 \\ \hline 1.5616 \end{array}$$

10. **0.84:** $0.6 \times 1.4 =$
$6 \times 14 = 84$
$0.6 \times 1.4 = 0.84$

11. **0.0000128:** 0.0004×0.032

$$4 \times 32 = 128$$

$$0.0004 \times 0.032 = 0.0000128$$

12. **208:** Move the decimal in 520,000 to the left four places and move the decimal in 0.0004 to the right four places. $520{,}000 \times 0.0004 = 52 \times 4 = 208$.

13. **12:** Move each decimal to the right 5 places. $\dfrac{0.00084}{0.00007} = \dfrac{84}{7} = 12$.

14. **70:**

21	=	$\dfrac{30}{100}$	×	x
21	is	30 percent	of	what number?

$$21 = \frac{30}{100}x$$

$$\frac{10\cancel{0}}{3\cancel{0}} \times 21 = x$$

$$\frac{10 \times \overset{7}{\cancel{21}}}{\underset{1}{\cancel{3}}} = x$$

$$70 = x$$

15. **20%:** If we want to find the percent decrease, then we should focus on the amount by which 90 was reduced. $90 - 72 = 18$, so:

$$\frac{\overset{2}{\cancel{18}}}{\underset{10}{\cancel{90}}} = \frac{2}{10} = 20\%$$

16. **72:** Convert 80% and 75% to fractions. $80\% = \dfrac{4}{5}$ and $75\% = \dfrac{3}{4}$.

$$x = \frac{\cancel{4}}{5} \times \frac{3}{\cancel{4}} \times 120$$

$$x = \frac{3}{\underset{1}{\cancel{5}}} \times \cancel{120}^{24}$$

$$x = 3 \times 24 = 72$$

17. **9:** If there are 15 white marbles, then we can set the 15 equal to $5x$, to solve for the unknown multiplier.

$$5x = 15$$
$$x = 3$$

So the number of blue marbles is $3x$, which is $3(3) = 9$.

18. **66:** If the ratio of tulips to all flowers is $5:11$, then the ratio of roses to tulips to all flowers must be $6:5:11$.

We can use the total number of flowers to find the unknown multiplier.

$$11x = 121$$
$$x = 11$$

That means that the total number of roses is $6x$, which is $6(11) = 66$.

5

Chapter Review: Drill Sets

Drill 1

1. Fill in the missing information in the chart below:

Fraction	Decimal	Percent
1/100	0.01	1%
1/20	0.05	5%
1/10	0.1	10%
1/8	0.125	12.5%
2/10 = 1/5	0.2	20%
1/4	.25	25%
3/10	0.3	30%
1/3	0.333	33.33…%
3/8	.375	37.5%
4/10 = 2/5	.40	40%
1/2	.50	50%
6/10 3/5	0.6	60%
2/3	.666	66.66…%
7/10	.70	70%
3/4	0.75	75%
4/5	0.8	80%
7/8	0.875	
9/10	.90	90%
10/10	1	100%

$6/5 = 120\%$
$5/4 = 125\%$
$3/2 = 150\%$

Drill 2

2. Convert 45% to a decimal.   .45
3. Convert 0.20 to a percent.   20%
4. Convert 4/5 to a percent.   80%
5. Convert 13.25% to a decimal.   .1325
6. Convert 6/20 to a percent.   3/10 = 30%
7. Convert 0.304 to a percent.   30.4%
8. Convert 0.02% to a decimal.   .0002
9. Convert 0.375 to a fraction.   3/8
10. Convert 3/2 to a percent.   150%

229

Drill 3

Simplify the following expressions. Answers in the explanation may appear in more than one form (e.g., fraction and decimal).

11. $\frac{1}{2} \times 50\%$

12. $25\% - 0.1$

13. $\frac{2}{3} + 0.3$

14. $1.2 \div \frac{2}{5}$

15. $\frac{3}{8} \div 10\%$

16. What is twenty percent of $7.50?

17. What is 0.3 times 110%?

18. $\frac{2}{5} + 20\% + 0.7$

19. $1.5 \div \left(\frac{5}{8} - 50\%\right)$

20. $190\% - \left(1.2 \div \frac{4}{5}\right)$

Drill 4

Simplify the following expressions.

21. $6.75 \times 10^3 =$

22. $1 + 0.2 + 0.03 + 0.004 =$

23. $0.27 \times 2 =$

24. $72.12 \times 10^{-4} =$

25. $0.2 \times 0.2 =$

26. $0.48 + 0.02 =$

27. $4 / 0.2 =$

28. $20 \times 0.85 =$

29. $54.197 / 10^2 =$

30. $12.6 / 0.3 =$

MANHATTAN
GMAT

Drill 5

Simplify the following expressions.

31. $2,346 \times 10^{-3} =$ 2.346
32. $1.21 + 0.38 =$ 1.59
33. $6 / 0.5 =$
34. $2.1 \times 0.08 =$ .168
35. $0.03 \times 0.005 =$ 0.0015
36. $0.370 + 0.042 =$
37. $3.20 / 0.04 =$ 80
38. $0.75 (80) + 0.50 (20) =$ 70
39. $0.49 / 0.07 =$ 7
40. $100 \times 0.01 \times 0.01 =$ 10^{-2}

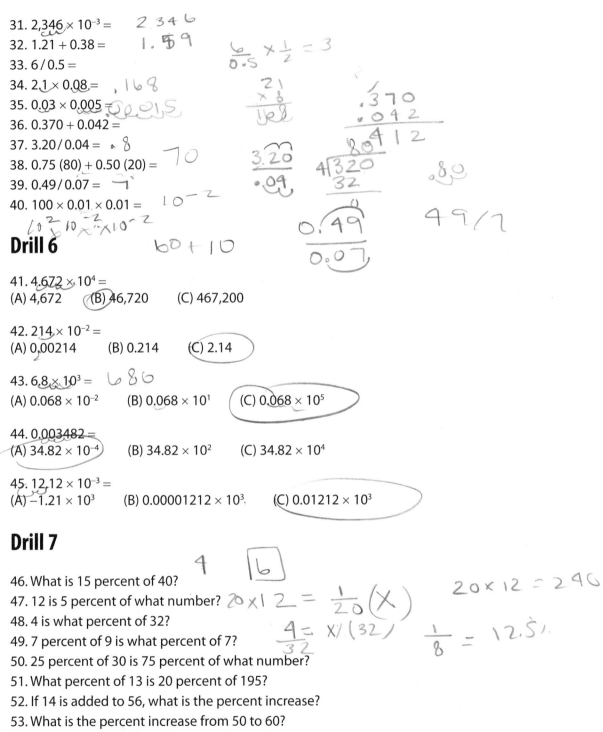

Drill 6

41. $4.672 \times 10^4 =$
(A) 4,672   (B) 46,720   (C) 467,200

42. $214 \times 10^{-2} =$
(A) 0.00214   (B) 0.214   (C) 2.14

43. $6.8 \times 10^3 =$ 686
(A) 0.068×10^{-2} (B) 0.068×10^1 (C) 0.068×10^5

44. $0.003482 =$
(A) 34.82×10^{-4} (B) 34.82×10^2 (C) 34.82×10^4

45. $12.12 \times 10^{-3} =$
(A) -1.21×10^3 (B) 0.00001212×10^3 (C) 0.01212×10^3

Drill 7

46. What is 15 percent of 40?
47. 12 is 5 percent of what number?
48. 4 is what percent of 32?
49. 7 percent of 9 is what percent of 7?
50. 25 percent of 30 is 75 percent of what number?
51. What percent of 13 is 20 percent of 195?
52. If 14 is added to 56, what is the percent increase?
53. What is the percent increase from 50 to 60?
54. What number is 40% more than 30?
55. What is 60% less than 60?

Drill 8

56. If *x* is reduced by 30%, the resulting number is 63. *x* =
57. 75 reduced by *x*% is 54. *x* =
58. If *x* is 15% more than 20, what is 30% of *x*?
59. What is 50% of 12% of 50?
60. What is 230% of 15% of 400?
61. 45% of 80 is *x*% more than 24. *x* =
62. 10 percent of 30 percent of what number is 200 percent of 6?
63. If *y* ≠ 0, what percent of *y* percent of 50 is 40 percent of *y*?
64. If *a* ≠ 0, 200 percent of 4 percent of *a* is what percent of $\frac{a}{2}$?
65. If positive integer *m* is increased by 20%, decreased by 25%, and then increased by 60%, the resulting number is what percent of *m*?

Drill 9

66. If there are 20 birds and 6 dogs in a park, which of the following represents the ratio of dogs to birds?
(A) 3 : 13   (B) 3 : 10   (C) 10 : 3

67. In a class of 24 students, 12 are boys. Which of the following is the ratio of boys to girls in the class?
(A) 1 : 1   (B) 1 : 2   (C) 2 : 1

68. If there are 24 white marbles and 36 blue marbles in a bag, which of the following is the ratio of blue to white marbles?
(A) 3 : 5   (B) 2 : 3   (C) 3 : 2

69. If there are 7 bananas and 14 strawberries in a basket, then which of the following is the ratio of strawberries to the total pieces of fruit in the basket.
(A) 1 : 2   (B) 1 : 3   (C) 2 : 3

Drill 10

70. Fill in the missing information in the table below.

1 : 2	=	3 : 6	=	7 : 14	=	11 : 22
1 : 5	=	4 : 20	=	5 : 25	=	15 : 75
3 : 4	=	6 : 8	=	27 : 36	=	33 : 44
5 : 7	=	20 : 28	=	40 : 56	=	60 : 84
4 : 11	=	8 : 22	=	36 : 99	=	48 : 132

Drill 11

71. The ratio of cheese to sauce for a single pizza is 1 cup to ½ cups. If Bob used 15 cups of sauce to make pizzas, how much cheese did he use?

30

72. Laura plans a rose and tulip garden by planting 4 tulips to every 1 rose. If there are 50 total flowers in the garden, how many of the flowers are tulips?

40 tulips

73. The ratio of oranges to peaches to strawberries in a fruit basket is 2 : 3 : 4. If there are 8 oranges, how many pieces of fruit are in the basket?

36

74. A certain automotive dealer sells only cars and trucks and currently has 51 trucks for sale. If the ratio of cars for sale to trucks for sale is 1 to 3, how many cars are for sale?

17

75. Arjun has a record of winning 3 tennis matches for every 2 he loses. If he played 30 matches, how many did he win?

18

76. A steel manufacturer combines 98 ounces of iron with 2 ounces of carbon to make one sheet of steel. How much iron is used in ½ of a sheet of steel?

49?

77. To bake 36 cupcakes, Maria uses a recipe of 8 cups of flour, 12 cups of milk, and 4 cups of sugar. How much of each ingredient, in cups, must Maria use if she only wants to make 9 cupcakes?

(handwritten work)

$$\frac{40}{56} = \frac{20}{28} = \frac{10}{14} \quad \frac{5}{7}$$

5

Drill Sets Solutions

Drill 1

1.

Fraction	Decimal	Percent
1/100	0.01	1%
1/20	0.05	5%
1/10	0.1	10%
1/8	0.125	12.5%
1/5	0.2	20%
1/4	0.25	25%
3/10	0.3	30%
1/3	0.3333…	33.33…%
3/8	0.375	37.5%
2/5	0.40	40%
1/2	0.50	50%
3/5	0.6	60%
2/3	0.6666…	66.66…%
7/10	0.7	70%
3/4	0.75	75%
4/5	0.8	80%
7/8	0.875	87.5%
9/10	0.9	90%
1	1.0	100%

Drill 2

2. **0.45:** 45% becomes 0.45

3. **20%:** 0.20 becomes 20%

4. **80%:**

Step 1: $4 \div 5 = 0.8$

$$5\overline{)4.0}\quad \frac{0.8}{}$$

Step 2: 0.8 becomes 80%

5. **0.1325:** 13.25% becomes 0.1325

6. **30%:** Step 1: $6 \div 20 = 0.30$

$$20\overline{)6.0}\quad \frac{0.3}{}$$

Step 2: 0.30 becomes 30%

7. **30.4%:** 0.304 becomes 30.4%

8. **0.0002:** 0.02% becomes 0.0002

9. $\frac{3}{8}$: 0.375 becomes $\frac{375}{1,000}$, which reduces to 3/8

10. **150%:**

Step 1: $3 \div 2 = 1.5$

$$2\overline{)3.0}^{1.5}$$

Step 2: 1.5 becomes 150%

Drill 3

11. **1/4 or 25%**:

$\dfrac{1}{2} \times 50\%$ Convert percent to fraction because fractions are

$\dfrac{1}{2} \times \dfrac{50}{100}$ easier to multiply than percents.

$\dfrac{1}{2} \times \dfrac{1}{2}$ Simplify before you multiply.

$\dfrac{1}{4}$

12. **15% or 0.15**:

$25\% - 0.1$ Convert decimal to percent because decimals that end in

$25\% - 10\%$ the tenths or hundredths digit are easy to convert to percents.

15%

13. $\dfrac{\mathbf{29}}{\mathbf{30}}$:

$\dfrac{2}{3} + 0.3$ Convert decimal to fraction because fractions that have a

$\dfrac{2}{3} + \dfrac{3}{10}$ denominator that is a multiple of 3 cannot be converted into an easy decimal.

$\dfrac{20}{30} + \dfrac{9}{30}$ Get common denominators.

$\dfrac{29}{30}$

14. **3**:

$1.2 \div \dfrac{2}{5}$ Convert fraction to decimal because 1.2 is a simple multiple of 0.4.

$1.2 \div 0.4$

$\dfrac{1.2}{0.4}$

$\dfrac{12}{4}$ Multiply by $\dfrac{10}{10}$ to convert decimals to integers.

3

15. **3.75 or $\frac{15}{4}$ or $3\frac{3}{4}$:**

$\frac{3}{8} \div 10\%$ Convert percent to fraction because (1) three−eighths is a difficult

$\frac{3}{8} \div \frac{1}{10}$ fraction to convert and (2) fractions are easier to divide than percents.

$\frac{3}{8} \times \frac{10}{1}$

$\frac{3}{4} \times \frac{5}{1}$

$\frac{15}{4}$

16. **$1.50:**

20% of $7.50   Convert percent to fraction because 1) 20% is a simple fraction

$\frac{1}{5} \times \$7.50$ to convert and 2) fractions are easier to multiply than decimals.

$1.50

17. **0.33 or 33/100 or 33%:**

0.3 × 110%   Convert percent to decimal because percents are difficult to multiply.
0.3 × 1.1
0.33

18. **13/10 or 1.3 or 130%**

$\frac{2}{5} + 20\% + 0.7$ Convert all terms to fractions because all terms can be easily

$\frac{2}{5} + \frac{20}{100} + \frac{7}{10}$ converted to a common denominator.

$\frac{4}{10} + \frac{2}{10} + \frac{7}{10}$

$\frac{13}{10}$

19. **12 or 1,200%**

$1.5 \div \left(\frac{5}{8} - 50\% \right)$ Convert percent to fraction because 50% is easier to convert than 5/8.

$1.5 \div \left(\frac{5}{8} - \frac{1}{2} \right)$

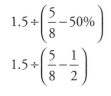

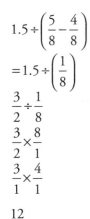

$$1.5 \div \left(\frac{5}{8} - \frac{4}{8} \right)$$

$$= 1.5 \div \left(\frac{1}{8} \right)$$

$$\frac{3}{2} \div \frac{1}{8}$$

Convert decimal to fraction because (1) 1.5 is easier to convert than

$$\frac{3}{2} \times \frac{8}{1}$$

1/8 and (2) it's easier to divide fractions.

$$\frac{3}{1} \times \frac{4}{1}$$

12

20. **40% or 0.4 or $\frac{2}{5}$** :

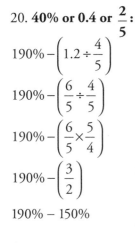

$$190\% - \left(1.2 \div \frac{4}{5} \right)$$

Convert decimal to fraction because (1) fractions are easier

$$190\% - \left(\frac{6}{5} \div \frac{4}{5} \right)$$

to divide than decimals and (2) 4/5 is not a simple multiple of 1.2.

$$190\% - \left(\frac{6}{5} \times \frac{5}{4} \right)$$

$$190\% - \left(\frac{3}{2} \right)$$

$$190\% - 150\%$$

Convert fraction to percent because 3/2 is easier to convert than 190%.

40%

Drill 4

21. $6.75 \times 10^3 =$ **6,750**   Move the decimal to the right 3 places.

22. **1.234:**
       1.000
    + 0.200
    + 0.030
    + 0.004
    ───────
       1.234

23. **0.54:**
    $0.27 \times 2 =$
    $27 \times 2 = 54$ Move the decimal to the left 2 places.
    $0.27 \times 2 = 0.54$

24. $72.12 \times 10^{-4} =$ **0.007212**   Move the decimal to the left 4 places

25. **0.04:**

   $0.2 \times 0.2 =$

   $2 \times 2 = 4$ Move the decimal to the left 2 places.

   $0.2 \times 0.2 = 0.04$

26. **0.50:**

   $0.\overset{1}{4}8$
   $+\,0.02$
   _____
   0.50

27. **20:**

   $$\frac{4}{0.2} \times \frac{10}{10} = \frac{40}{2} = 20$$

28. **17:**

   $20 \times 0.85 =$

   $20 \times 85 = 1{,}700$ Move the decimal to the left 2 places.

   $20 \times 0.85 = 17$

29. $54.197 \,/\, 10^2 = $ **0.54197**   Because we are dividing by 10^2, we move the decimal to the **left** 2 places.

30. **42:**

   $$\frac{12.6}{0.3} \times \frac{10}{10} = \frac{126}{3} = 42$$

Drill 5

31. $2{,}346 \times 10^{-3} = $ **2.346**   Move the decimal to the left 3 places.

32. **1.59:**

   1.21
   $+\,0.38$
   _____
   1.59

33. **12:**

   $$\frac{6}{0.5} \times \frac{10}{10} = \frac{60}{5} = 12$$

34. **0.168:**

   $2.1 \times 0.08 =$

   $21 \times 8 = 168$ Move the decimal to the left 3 places.

   $2.1 \times 0.08 = 0.168$

35. **0.00015:**

$0.03 \times 0.005 =$

$3 \times 5 = 15$ Move the decimal to the left 5 places.

$0.03 \times 0.005 = 0.00015$

36. **0.412:**

$$
\begin{array}{r}
0.\overset{1}{3}70 \\
+\ 0.042 \\
\hline
0.412
\end{array}
$$

37. **80:**

$$\frac{3.20}{0.04} \times \frac{100}{100} = \frac{320}{4} = 80$$

38. **70:**

$0.75(80) + 0.50(20) =$

$0.75 \times 80 = 60$

$0.50 \times 20 = 10$

$60 + 10 = 70$

39. **7:**

$$\frac{0.49}{0.07} \times \frac{100}{100} = \frac{49}{7} = 7$$

40. **0.01:**

$100 \times 0.01 \times 0.01 =$

$10^2 \times 10^{-2} \times 10^{-2} =$

$10^{2 + (-2) + (-2)} = 10^{-2} = 0.01$

Drill 6

41. **(B) 46,720:** The answer choices indicate that we need to rewrite the value 4.672×10^4 without using a power of 10. When we multiply by 10^4, we are making the number larger by 4 decimal places; in other words, moving the decimal 4 spaces to the right.

$$4.6720\underset{\curvearrowright\curvearrowright\curvearrowright\curvearrowright}{}$$

Therefore, we can rewrite 4.672×10^4 as 46,720.

42. **(C) 2.14:** The answer choices indicate that we need to rewrite the value 214×10^{-2} without using a power of 10. When we multiply by 10^{-2}, we are making the number smaller by 2 decimal places; in other words, moving the decimal 2 spaces to the left.

$$214.\underset{\curvearrowleft\curvearrowleft}{}$$

Therefore, we can rewrite 214×10^{-2} as 2.14.

43. **(C) 0.068×10^5:** The answer choices indicate that we need to rewrite the value 6.8×10^3 as 0.068 times 10 to some power. Therefore, we must compare the relative sizes of 6.8 and 0.068. To move from 6.8 to 0.068, we must move the decimal to the left 2 spaces to make our number smaller.

06.8

In order to balance the decrease in 6.8 of 2 decimal places, we must increase the power of ten by 2: $10^{3+2} = 10^5$. Therefore, we can rewrite 6.8×10^3 as 0.068×10^5.

Alternatively, we could convert the original and all answer choices to numbers without a power of 10 and look for a match (though this will take much longer).

For 6.8×10^3 we multiply through with the 10^3, moving the decimal to the right 3 spaces (making it larger):

6.800

The result is 6,800. Now we must compare this number to the answer choices.

For choice A, 0.068×10^{-2}, we multiply through with the 10^{-2}, moving the decimal to the left 2 spaces (making it smaller):

00.068

The result is 0.00068, NOT the same as our desired answer.

For choice B, 0.068×10^1, we multiply through with the 10^1, moving the decimal to the right 1 space (making it larger):

0.068

The result is 0.68, NOT the same as our desired answer.

For choice C, 0.068×10^5, we multiply through with the 10^5, moving the decimal to the right 5 spaces, (making it larger):

0.06800

The result is 6,800; this is same as our desired answer.

44. **(A) 34.82×10^{-4}:** The answer choices indicate that we need to rewrite the value 0.003482 as 34.82 times 10 to some power. Therefore, we must compare the relative sizes of 0.003482 and 34.82. To move from 0.003482 to 34.82, we must move the decimal to the right 4 spaces to make our number larger.

0.003482

In order to balance the increase in 0.003482 of 4 decimal places, we must reduce the power of 10 by 4. We can write the original number this way: 0.003482×10^0 (note that $10^0 = 1$). Therefore, we want to reduce the starting power of 0 by 4: $0.003482 \times 10^0 = 34.82 \times 10^{-4}$.

45. **(B) 0.00001212×10^3:** The answer choices indicate that we need to rewrite the value 12.12×10^{-3} as some number times 10^3. Therefore, we must compare the relative sizes of our powers of 10; what must be done to 10^{-3} to make it 10^3? We can ask the question: what plus -3 equals 3? Because $6 + -3 = 3$, our exponent on the power of 10 increased by 6. To counter this increase, the number 12.12 must decrease by 6 decimal spaces; we move the decimal 6 spaces to the left.

000012.12

Therefore, we can rewrite 12.12×10^{-3} as 0.00001212×10^3.

Drill 7

46. **6:**

What	is	15 percent	of	40?
x	$=$	15/100	$\times$	40

$$x = \frac{15}{100} \times 40$$

$$x = \frac{3}{20} \times 40$$

$$x = \frac{3}{\cancel{20}} \times (\cancel{20} \times 2) = 6$$

47. **240:**

12	is	5 percent	of	what number?
12	$=$	5/100	$\times$	x

$$12 = \frac{5}{100} \times x$$

$$12 = \frac{1}{20} \times x$$

$$20(12) = x$$

$$x = 240$$

48. **12.5:**

4	is	what percent	of	32?		
4	=	$x/100$	×	32		

$$4 = \frac{x}{100} \times 32$$

$$400 = x \times 32$$

$$\frac{400}{32} = x$$

$$\frac{100}{8} = x$$

$$12.5 = x$$

49. **9:**

7 percent	of	9	is	what percent	of	7
7/100	×	9	=	$x/100$	×	7

$$\frac{7}{100} \times 9 = \frac{x}{100} \times 7 \qquad \text{Multiply both sides by 100.}$$

$$7 \times 9 = x \times 7$$

$$9 = x$$

50. **10:**

25 percent	of	30	is	75 percent	of	what?
25/100	×	30	=	75/100	×	x

$$\frac{25}{100} \times 30 = \frac{75}{100} \times x \qquad \text{Multiply both sides by 100.}$$

$$25 \times 30 = 75 \times x$$

$$25 \times 3 \times 10 = 75 \times x$$

$$75 \times 10 = 75 \times x$$

$$10 = x$$

Alternatively, at step 2, divide both sides by 75 and cancel terms.

$$25 \times 30 = 75 \times x$$

$$\frac{25\times30}{75}=x$$

$$\frac{\cancel{25}\times30}{\cancel{25}\times3}=x$$

$$10=x$$

51. 300:

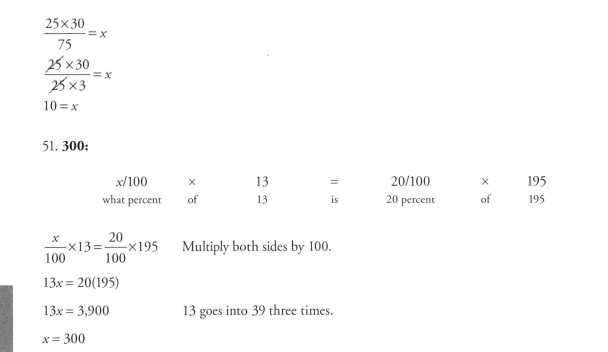

$x/100$	$\times$	13	$=$	$20/100$	$\times$	195
what percent	of	13	is	20 percent	of	195

$$\frac{x}{100}\times13=\frac{20}{100}\times195 \qquad \text{Multiply both sides by 100.}$$

$$13x=20(195)$$

$$13x=3{,}900 \qquad \text{13 goes into 39 three times.}$$

$$x=300$$

52. 25% increase: In this problem, the change is 14 and the original number is 56. Therefore, we can translate the question to the following: "14 is what percent of 56?"

$$14=\frac{x}{100}\times56$$

$$1=\frac{x}{100}\times4$$

$$\frac{100}{4}=x$$

$$25=x$$

Notice that we never need to find the new number (14 + 56 = 70), as we have only been asked about the percent increase, not the new value.

53. 20% increase: We have been asked about the increase from 50 to 60, which is 60 − 50 = 10. So now we need to answer the question "What percent of 50 is 10?"

$$\frac{x}{100}\times50=10$$

$$\frac{x}{2}=10$$

$$x=20$$

54. 42: We have two ways to represent "40% more than 30." The first is a literal translation—30 plus an additional 40% of 30:

$$x=30+\frac{40}{100}\times30$$

However, we can also work with the idea that 40% more than a number is the same as 100% of that number plus an additional 40%, or 140%. With that in mind, we can represent "40% more than 30" this way:

$$x = \frac{140}{100} \times 30$$

This method often lends itself to a decimal approach, so we can avoid working with multiples of 100. This leads us to a final, simpler translation of the problem:

$x = 1.4(30)$
$x = 42$

Note that we can translate $(1.4)(30)$ to $(14)(3)$ to make the multiplication easier. You can "swap" decimals between two multiplied numbers—take away a decimal place from one number (30) and give it to the other (1.4).

55. **24:** We can use fractions to set this up:

$$x = 60 - \frac{60}{100} \times 60$$

However, decimals allow us to simplify the problem more quickly:

$x = 1(60) - (0.6)60 = 0.4(60)$

This is a good skill to practice until it becomes automatic. To tackle complex GMAT problems, it helps to be able to translate directly to this last step. We see "60% less than 60" and instantly express this as the remaining 40% of 60, or 0.4(60).

$x = 0.4(60) = 24$

Note that we can translate $(0.4)(60)$ to $(4)(6)$ to make the multiplication easier. You can "swap" decimals between two multiplied or divided numbers—take away a decimal place from one number (60) and give it to the other (0.4).

Drill 8

56. **90:** Because 30% less than x is the same as 70% of x, we can translate as follows:

$0.7x = 63$
$7x = 630$
$x = 90$

When shifting decimal places, it is a good idea to check the final answer for reasonableness. If 90 is reduced by 30%, does it make sense for the result to be 63? That seems fairly reasonable. If we had gotten an answer of 9 or 900, we would want to check our work.

57. **28:** Because we don't know the value of x, we can't go straight to a decimal translation. Here, a fraction translation of the problem works best. "75 minus x percent of 75 is 54."

$$75 - \frac{x}{100} \times 75 = 54$$
$$75 - 54 = \frac{75x}{100}$$
$$21 = \frac{3x}{4}$$
$$7 = \frac{x}{4}$$
$$28 = x$$

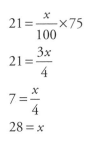

We might also start by looking at the change from 75 to 54. 75 has been reduced by 21, so we can translate the problem as "21 is x% of 75."

$$21 = \frac{x}{100} \times 75$$
$$21 = \frac{3x}{4}$$
$$7 = \frac{x}{4}$$
$$28 = x$$

58. **6.9 or 69/10:** Notice that we have two equations—" x is 15% more than 20" and "what is 30% of x?" Also, we have been given a variable named x, so we need to translate the word "what" as a different variable. Let's use y.

$$x = \frac{115}{100} \times 20$$
$$y = \frac{30}{100} \times x$$

A fractional representation works well here, because both 20 and 30 cancel well with 100. Use the first equation to solve for x, then plug into the second equation to find y.

$$x = \frac{115}{5}$$

$$x = 23$$

$$y = \frac{3}{10} \times (23)$$

$$y = \frac{69}{10}$$

$$y = 6.9$$

59. **3:** Because multiplying decimals together can be rather labor–intensive, let's use a fractional representation here:

$$x = \frac{50}{100} \times \frac{12}{100} \times 50$$

$$x = \frac{1}{2} \times \frac{6}{\cancel{50}} \times \cancel{50}$$

$$x = \frac{1}{2} \times 6$$

$$x = 3$$

60. **138:**

$$x = \frac{23\cancel{0}}{10\cancel{0}} \times \frac{15}{1\cancel{00}} \times 4\cancel{00}$$

$$x = \frac{23}{10} \times 15 \times 4$$

$$x = \frac{23}{1\cancel{0}} \times 6\cancel{0}$$

$$x = 23 \times 6$$

$$x = 138$$

61. **50:** We can solve this through direct translation:

$$\frac{45}{10\cancel{0}}\times8\cancel{0}=24+\frac{x}{100}\times24$$

$$\frac{45}{10}\times8=24+\frac{24x}{100}$$

$$\frac{9}{2}\times8=24+\frac{24x}{100}$$

$$36=24+\frac{24x}{100}$$

$$12=\frac{24x}{100}$$

$$1=\frac{2x}{100}$$

$$\frac{100}{2}=x$$

$$50=x$$

5

However, it might be helpful to start by simplifying things in smaller pieces. If we figure out what 45% of 80 is (36), then we can come up with a simpler problem: "36 is x% more than 24." Our increase (36 − 24) is 12, so we can rephrase once more as "12 is x% of 24." If we recognize that 12 is half of 24, we can solve for x right away. 12 is 50% of 24, so $x = 50$.

62. **400:** Again, multiplying percents is usually easiest in fraction form. If we are comfortable with percent equivalents, however, we might skip the first step below and start by writing the second equation, in which 200% is just 2.

$$\frac{10}{100}\times\frac{30}{100}\times x=\frac{200}{100}\times6$$

$$\frac{1}{10}\times\frac{3}{10}\times x=2\times6$$

$$\frac{3}{100}\times x=12$$

$$x=12\times\frac{100}{3}$$

$$x=4\times100$$

$$x=400$$

63. **80:** The question already contains a variable (y). We'll need to use another variable to represent the value we want. We'll represent "what" with the variable x, so we need to isolate x to solve. Notice that by the end, our y variables cancel out.

$$\frac{x}{100} \times \frac{y}{2\,\cancel{100}} \times \cancel{50} = \frac{\cancel{4}\cancel{0}}{10\cancel{0}} \times y$$

$$\frac{x}{100} \times \frac{y}{2} = \frac{4y}{10}$$

$$\frac{xy}{200} = \frac{4y}{10}$$

$$x = \frac{4\cancel{0}}{1\cancel{0}} \times \frac{20\cancel{0}}{\cancel{0}}$$

$$x = 4 \times 20$$

$$x = 80$$

64. **16:**

$$\frac{2\cancel{00}}{1\cancel{00}} \times \frac{4}{100} \times a = \frac{x}{100} \times \frac{a}{2}$$

$$2 \times \frac{4}{100} \times a = \frac{x}{100} \times \frac{a}{2} \qquad \text{Divide both sides by 100}$$

$$8a = \frac{xa}{2} \qquad \text{Divide both sides by } a$$

$$8 = \frac{x}{2}$$

$$16 = x$$

This is another case where we might benefit by solving the problem in smaller pieces. 200% of 4% is the same as 2 × 4% (note that 200% equals the plain number 2), or 8%. So we can rephrase as "8% of a is what percent of $\frac{a}{2}$?" Without even translating to an equation, we can simplify by multiplying both sides of our "equation" by 2 (remember that "is" means "equals"):

8% of a is what percent of $\frac{a}{2}$?

16% of a is what percent of a?

The answer is 16.

65. **144:** Notice that both sides of our equation below are multiplied by the variable m. We can cancel it immediately (since it is not zero) and solve for x.

$$m \times \frac{120}{100} \times \frac{75}{100} \times \frac{160}{100} = \frac{x}{100} \times m \qquad \text{Divide both sides by } m$$

$$\frac{6}{5} \times \frac{3}{4} \times \frac{8}{5} = \frac{x}{100}$$

$$\frac{144}{100} = \frac{x}{100}$$

$$144 = x$$

Drill 9

66. **(B) 3 : 10.** If there are 6 dogs and 20 birds in the park, the ratio of dogs to birds is 6 : 20. Because 6 and 20 have common factors, we can divide through by their Greatest Common Factor (GCF) to simplify. The GCF of 6 and 20 is 2; the reduced ratio is 6 ÷ 2 : 20 ÷ 2 or 3 : 10.

67. **(A) 1 : 1.** If 12 of 24 students in the class are boys, then the remainder, 24 − 12 = 12, are girls. Therefore the ratio of boys to girls in the class is 12 : 12. Because 12 and 12 have common factors, we can divide by their GCF (12) to find the reduced ratio. 12 ÷ 12 : 12 ÷ 12 or 1 : 1.

68. **(C) 3:2.** If there are 36 blue marbles and 24 white marbles, the ratio of blue to white is 36 : 24. Because 36 and 24 have common factors, we can divide through by their GCF to simplify. The GCF of 36 and 24 is 12; the reduced ratio is 36 ÷ 12 : 24 ÷ 12 or 3 : 2.

69. **(C) 2:3.** If there are 7 bananas and 14 strawberries, then there are 7 + 14 = 21 total pieces of fruit. The ratio of strawberries to the total would therefore be 14 : 21. Because 14 and 21 have common factors, we can divide through by their Greatest Common Factor (GCF) to simplify. The GCF of 14 and 21 is 7; the reduced ratio is 14 ÷ 7 : 21 ÷ 7 or 2 : 3.

Drill 10

70.

1 : 2	=	3 : **6**	=	**7** : 14	=	**11** : 22
1 : **5**	=	4 : 20	=	**5** : 25	=	15 : **75**
3 : **4**	=	**6** : 8	=	**27** : 36	=	33 : 44
5 : 7	=	20 : **28**	=	40 : 56	=	60 : **84**
4 : 11	=	**8** : 22	=	36 : **99**	=	**48** : 132

Drill 11

71. 30 cups: We're given information about the two parts of a recipe (cheese and sauce) and asked to solve for a specific amount (cheese). We can manipulate the Part : Part ratio to solve. If the ratio of cheese to sauce is 1: ½, and Bob uses 15 cups of sauce, then we find our unknown multiplier by asking the question, "what times ½ equals 15?"

$½x = 15$
$x = 15(2)$
$x = 30$

Therefore, our uknown multiplier is 30. The actual amounts are $30 \times 1 : 30 \times ½$ or 30 : 15. Bob used 30 cups of cheese and 15 cups of sauce to make the pizzas.

72. 40 tulips: We're given information about the two parts of the garden (tulips and roses) as well as the total number of flowers. We can manipulate the Part : Part : Whole ratio to solve. If the ratio of tulips to roses is 4 : 1, then the Part : Part : Whole relationship would be 4 tulips to 1 rose to $4 + 1 = 5$ total flowers or 4 : 1 : 5.

If there are 50 total flowers in the garden, then we find our uknown multiplier by using the ratio entry for total flowers (5) and asking the question, "what times 5 equals 50?"

$5x = 50$

$$x = \frac{50}{5} = 10$$

Therefore, our uknown multiplier is 10. The actual amounts are $10 \times 4 : 10 \times 1 : 10 \times 5$ or 40 : 10 : 50. Laura has 40 tulips, 10 roses and 50 total flowers in her garden.

73. 36 pieces of fruit: We're given information about the three parts of the fruit basket (oranges, peaches and strawberries) and asked to solve for the total number of pieces of fruit. We can manipulate a Part : Part : Whole ratio to solve. If the ratio of oranges to peaches to strawberries is 2 : 3 : 4, then the Part : Part : Whole relationship would include the total of $2 + 3 + 4 = 9$, or 2 : 3 : 4 : 9.

If there are 8 oranges in the basket, then we find our uknown multiplier by using the ratio entry for oranges (2) and asking the question, "what times 2 equals 8?"

$2x = 8$

$$x = \frac{8}{2} = 4$$

Therefore, our uknown multiplier is 4. The actual amounts are $4 \times 2 : 4 \times 3 : 4 \times 4 : 4 \times 9$ or 8 : 12 : 16 : 36. The fruit basket contains 8 oranges, 12 peaches, 16 strawberries and 36 total pieces of fruit.

74. **17 cars:** This problem only discusses the individual parts on sale (cars and trucks) so a good way to handle this would be to manipulate a Part : Part ratio. The ratio of cars to trucks is 1 : 3. If there are 51 trucks for sale, then we find our uknown multiplier by asking the question, "what times 3 equals 51?"

$$3x = 51$$

$$x = \frac{51}{3} = 17$$

Therefore, our uknown multiplier is 17. The actual amounts are $17 \times 1 : 17 \times 3$ or 17 : 51. The automotive dealer has 17 cars and 51 trucks for sale.

75. **18 games:** We're given information about both parts (wins and losses) as well as a whole (total number of matches, or wins and losses combined). We can manipulate a Part : Part : Whole ratio to solve. If the ratio of wins to losses is 3 to 2, then the Part : Part : Whole relationship of wins to losses to all games would include the total of 3 + 2 = 5 games or 3 : 2 : 5.

If Arjun played 30 matches, then we find our uknown multiplier by using the ratio entry for total matches (5) and asking the question, "what times 5 equals 30?"

$$5x = 30$$

$$x = \frac{30}{5} = 6$$

Therefore, our uknown multiplier is 6. The actual amounts are $6 \times 3 : 6 \times 2 : 6 \times 5$ or 18 : 12 : 30. Arjun wins 18 matches and loses 12 for a total of 30 matches.

76. **49 ounces:** We're given information about the two parts of production (iron and carbon) as well as the total output (1 sheet of steel). We can manipulate a Part : Part : Whole ratio to solve. The ratio of iron to carbon to sheets of steel is 98 : 2 : 1. If we want the ratio for ½ sheet of steel, then we find our uknown multiplier by asking the question, "what times 1 equals ½?"

$$1x = ½$$
$$x = ½$$

Therefore, our uknown multiplier is ½. The actual amounts are $½ \times 98 : ½ \times 2 : ½ \times 1$ or 49 : 1: ½. The manufacturer would combine 49 ounces of iron with 1 ounce of carbon to produce ½ sheet of steel.

77. **2 cups of flour, 3 cups of milk, and 1 cup sugar:** We're given information about the three parts of a recipe (flour, milk and sugar) as well as the total number of cupcakes. We can manipulate a Part : Part : Whole ratio to solve. We can write the ratio of flour to milk to sugar to cupcakes as 8 : 12 : 4 : 36. If Maria wants to make only 9 cupcakes, we find our uknown multiplier by asking the question, "what times 36 equals 9?"

$$36x = 9$$

$$x = \frac{9}{36} = \frac{1}{4}$$

Therefore, our unknown multiplier is $\frac{1}{4}$. The actual amounts are $\frac{1}{4} \times 8 : \frac{1}{4} \times 12 : \frac{1}{4} \times 4 : \frac{1}{4} \times 36$ or 2 : 3 : 1 : 9. The amounts of flour, milk, and sugar are 2 cups, 3 cups, and 1 cup, respectively.

5

Chapter 6
Foundations of GMAT Math

Equations

In This Chapter...

Chapter 6:

Equations

In This Chapter:

- Manipulate expressions and equations to solve for variables

Manipulating expressions and equations is at the core of algebra. First, you need to make sure that you understand the distinction between expressions and equations.

Expressions Don't Have Equals Signs

An **expression** such as $3y + 8z$ ultimately represents a number. It has a value, although you may not know that value. The expression $3y + 8z$ contains numbers that are known (3, 8) and unknown (y, z) and that are linked by arithmetic operations (+ and ×).

Here are more expressions.

$$12 \qquad x - y \qquad 2w^3 \qquad 4(n + 3)(n + 2) \qquad \frac{\sqrt{x}}{3b - 2}$$

Don't mix up expressions and equations. An expression never contains an equals sign.

When you **simplify** an expression, you reduce the number of separate terms, or you pull out and maybe cancel common factors. In other words, you make the expression simpler. However, **you never change the expression's value as you simplify**.

Unsimplified		Simplified	How
$3x + 4x$	$\rightarrow$	$7x$	Combine like terms
$\dfrac{2y^2}{3} + \dfrac{3y^2}{5}$	$\rightarrow$	$\dfrac{19y^2}{15}$	Find a common denominator and then combine
$x + xy$	$\rightarrow$	$x(1 + y)$	Pull out a common factor

$\dfrac{3x^2}{6x}$	$\longrightarrow$	$\dfrac{x}{2}$	Cancel common factors

At times you might go in reverse. For instance you might **distribute** a common factor.

$$x(1+y) \qquad \longrightarrow \qquad x+xy$$

Or you might multiply the top and bottom of a fraction by the same number to change its look. The result may seem even *less* simplified, temporarily. But by finding a common denominator, you can add fractions and get a simpler final result.

Unsimplified		**Even Less Simple**		**Simplified**
$\dfrac{w}{2}+\dfrac{w}{3}$	$\longrightarrow$	$\dfrac{w\times3}{2\times3}+\dfrac{w\times2}{3\times2}$	$\longrightarrow$	$\dfrac{5w}{6}$

The point is that as you simplify an expression (or even complicate one), the value of the expression must never change.

When you **evaluate** an expression, you figure out its value—the actual number represented by that expression.

To evaluate an expression, **substitute numbers in for any variables, then simplify**. In other words, **swap out the variables**, replacing them with numbers. Then do the arithmetic.

Some people say "**plug and chug**." You *plug* in the values of the variables, then you *chug* through the simplification. Some people also call this "**subbing in**."

Whatever you call this process, you have to know the values of the variables to evaluate the expression. Otherwise you're stuck.

And of course, never inadvertently change the value of the expression by doing the arithmetic wrong. Always apply PEMDAS.

Evaluate the expression $3\sqrt{2x}$ given that x has the value of 8.

First, substitute in 8 for x.

$3\sqrt{2x}$ becomes $3\sqrt{2(8)}$

Now simplify the expression.

$$3\sqrt{2(8)}=3\sqrt{16}=3\times4=12$$

You have now evaluated the expression $3\sqrt{2x}$ when $x = 8$. For that particular value of x, the value of the expression is 12.

Pay attention to negative signs, especially if the value you're subbing in is negative. Put in parentheses to obey PEMDAS.

If $y = -2$, what is the value of $3y^2 - 7y + 4$?

Substitute -2 for y. Put parentheses around the -2 to clarify that you're subbing in negative 2, not subtracting 2 somehow.

$3y^2 - 7y + 4$ becomes $3(-2)^2 - 7(-2) + 4$

Now simplify.

$3(-2)^2 - 7(-2) + 4 = 3(4) - (-14) + 4 = 12 + 14 + 4 = 30$

Be sure to square the negative sign and to subtract -14 (in other words, add 14). The value of the expression is 30.

You might have to plug into expressions in answer choices.

If $y = 6$, then which of the following expressions has the value of 20?

    (A) $y + 14$ (B) $y - 14$ (C) $20y$

When you substitute 6 in for y in the answer choices, only $y + 14$ gives you 20. The answer is (A).

Other expressions involving y could also equal 20, such as $2y + 8$ or $y^2 - 16$. You would not be forced to pick between these expressions, because they'd all be correct answers to this question.

If you...	Then you...	Like this:
Simplify an expression	Never do anything to change its value	$3x + 4x$ becomes $7x$
Evaluate an expression	Substitute numbers in for unknowns, then simplify	$7x$ becomes $7(2)$ or 14 when $x = 2$

An Equation Says "Expression A = Expression B"

An equation is a complete sentence that has a subject, a verb, and an object. The sentence always takes this form:

Subject *equals* object.

One expression equals another expression.

$$2x \quad - \quad z \quad = \quad y \quad + \quad 4$$

Two x   minus   z   equals   y   plus   four.

An equation always sets one expression ($2x - z$) equal to another expression ($y + 4$).

Everything you know about simplifying or evaluating expressions applies in the world of equations, because equations contain expressions.

You can *simplify* an expression on just one side of an equation, because you are not changing the value of that expression. So the equation still holds true, even though you're ignoring the other side.

For instance, simplify the left side but leave the right side alone.

$$\frac{x}{3} + \frac{x}{5} = y \qquad \text{becomes} \qquad \frac{5x}{15} + \frac{3x}{15} = y \qquad \text{and finally} \qquad \frac{8x}{15} = y$$

You can also *evaluate* an expression on just one side. For instance, say you have $\dfrac{8x}{15} = y$ and you know that $x = 5$. Then you can plug and chug just on the left side:

$$\frac{8x}{15} = y \qquad \text{becomes} \qquad \frac{8(5)}{15} = y \qquad \text{and finally} \qquad \frac{8}{3} = y$$

Throughout all these changes on the left side, the right side has remained y.

If all you could do to equations was simplify or evaluate expressions, then your toolset would be limited. However, you can do much more.

You can truly *change* both sides. You can actually alter the values of the two expressions on either side of an equation.

You just have to follow the Golden Rule.

Golden Rule of Equations: Do Unto One Side As You Do Unto The Other

You can change the value of the *left* side any way you want…

… as long as you change the *right* side in **exactly the same way**.

Take this simple example.

$$x + 5 = 8$$

If you subtract 5 from the left side, you must subtract 5 from the right side. You get a new equation with new expressions. If the first equation isn't lying, then the second equation is true, too.

$$
\begin{array}{rcl}
x + 5 &=& 8 \\
-\,5 && -\,5 \\
\hline
x &=& 3
\end{array}
$$

Here is a table of the major Golden Rule moves you can do to both sides of an equation.

1) **Add the same thing** to both sides. • That "thing" can be a number or a variable expression. • You should actually show the addition underneath to be safe.	$$\begin{array}{rcl} y - 6 &=& 15 \\ +\,6 && +\,6 \\ \hline y &=& 21 \end{array}$$
2) **Subtract the same thing** from both sides.	$$\begin{array}{rcl} z + 4 &=& k \\ -\,4 && -\,4 \\ \hline z &=& k - 4 \end{array}$$
3) **Multiply both sides by the same thing** (except 0, of course). • Put parentheses in so that you multiply *entire* sides.	$$n + m = \frac{3w}{4}$$ $$4 \times (n + m) = \left(\frac{3w}{4}\right) \times 4$$ $$4n + 4m = 3w$$
4) **Divide both sides by the same thing** (except 0, of course). • Extend the fraction bar all the way so that you divide *entire* sides.	$$a + b = 5d$$ $$\frac{a + b}{5} = \frac{5d}{5}$$ $$\frac{a + b}{5} = d$$
5) **Square both sides**, cube both sides, etc. • Put parentheses in so you square or cube *entire* sides.	$$x + \sqrt{2} = \sqrt{7w}$$ $$\left(x + \sqrt{2}\right)^2 = \left(\sqrt{7w}\right)^2$$ $$\left(x + \sqrt{2}\right)^2 = 7w$$

6) **Take the square root of both sides**, the cube root of both sides, etc. • Extend the radical so you square-root or cube-root *entire* sides.	$z^3 = 64$ $\sqrt[3]{z^3} = \sqrt[3]{64}$ $z = 4$

One warning about square-rooting both sides of an equation: **the equation usually splits into *two* separate equations**.

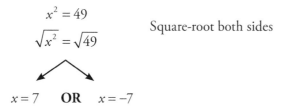

$$x^2 = 49$$
$$\sqrt{x^2} = \sqrt{49}$$

Square-root both sides

$$x = 7 \quad \textbf{OR} \quad x = -7$$

The reason is that there are two numbers that, when squared, equal 49. When negative numbers are squared, they become positive. When you take a square root of a squared number, always remember to find the negative solution as well.

When you square $y = 6$ you always get $y^2 = 36$

But if you square-root $y^2 = 36$ you get $y = 6$ **OR** $y = -6$

Perform the same action to an *entire* side of an equation. Pretend that the expression on each side of the equation is surrounded by parentheses—and actually write those parentheses in as necessary. Consider this equation:

$$x + 4 = \frac{x}{2}$$

To multiply both sides by 2, add in parentheses:

$$2(x + 4) = \left(\frac{x}{2}\right)2$$

Now simplify. Distribute the 2 to both the *x* and the 4. Cancel the 2's on the right:

$$2x + 8 = x$$

This is why multiplying to get rid of a denominator is sometimes called **cross-multiplication**. You can imagine that the 2 that *was* in the denominator on the right side moves to the left side, where it is multiplied by the *x* + 4. Cross-multiplication is even more useful when both sides have denominators to begin with.

Let's go back to the equation at hand. You can do more Golden Rule moves further by subtracting x from both sides, and then subtracting 8.

$$
\begin{array}{rcl}
2x + 8 & = & x \\
-x & & -x \\
\hline
x + 8 & = & 0 \\
-8 & & -8 \\
\hline
x & & = -8
\end{array}
$$

You now have x by itself on one side, so the equation tells you the value of x—namely, negative 8. What you did here was **isolate the variable** or **solve for the variable**.

To isolate x, **get x by itself on one side of the equation**. The equation should wind up reading "$x = \ldots$"

The thing on the right side is often a number, as in the case above ($x = -8$).

In a more complicated equation, the right side could be a variable expression. Either way, the important thing when you isolate x on the left is that **the right side can't contain any terms containing x**. Otherwise, you haven't truly *isolated* the x on the left side.

You can isolate the x on the *right* side if you want, of course. Just make sure that the *left* side contains no terms containing x.

When you get "x = a number" or "a number = x," then you have **solved the equation**. The number you get is a **solution** to the equation.

When you plug a solution into an equation (that is, into the *variable* in an equation), you make the equation true.

> "4 is a solution to the equation $2x + 7 = 15$."

> This sentence means that if $x = 4$, that equation is true.

To find the solution to the equation, **don't guess and check**. Instead, isolate the variable.

If you have more than one variable in an equation, you may still want to isolate one variable for some reason.

> If $3x + 5y = 12$, what is x in terms of y?

"x in terms of y" is an expression that equals x and only contains y (and known numbers).

In other words, "x in terms of y" is the right side of this equation:

> x = blah blah y blah blah y^2 blah blah…

There cannot be any x's on the right side.

To get x in terms of y, isolate x on one side by applying Golden Rule moves to the given equation.

$$\begin{array}{rl} 3x + 5y &= 12 \\ -5y & -5y \\ \hline 3x & = 12 - 5y \end{array}$$

So x in terms of y is this expression: $\dfrac{12-5y}{3}$. This contains no x's. If you're looking for "x in terms of y," the answer will contain y's, not x's.

If you want y in terms of x instead, then isolate y on one side. You'll get this expression on the other side: $\dfrac{12-3x}{5}$.

If you...	Then you...	Like this:
Want to change an expression on one side of an equation	Apply the Golden Rule: change both sides in exactly the same way.	$$\begin{array}{rl} y - 3 &= 9 \\ +3 & +3 \\ \hline y & = 12 \end{array}$$
Want to isolate the variable x in an equation	Do Golden Rule moves and simplify until the equation reads "$x =$ something else."	$$\begin{array}{rl} 7x + 4 &= 18 \\ -4 & -4 \\ \hline \dfrac{7x}{7} & = \dfrac{14}{7} \\ x &= 2 \end{array}$$
Need x in terms of y	Isolate x. Do Golden Rule moves and simplify until the equation reads "$x =$ something containing only y's."	$$\begin{array}{rl} 7x + 4 &= y \\ -4 & -4 \\ \hline \dfrac{7x}{7} & = \dfrac{y-4}{7} \\ x &= \dfrac{y-4}{7} \end{array}$$

MANHATTAN
GMAT

Check Your Skills

1. If $\sqrt{x+2}=4$, what is x?

2. If $\dfrac{y-3}{x}=2$, what is y in terms of x?

Answers can be found on page 283.

Isolate a Variable: Work Your Way In by Doing PEMDAS in Reverse

If an expression is complicated, you might get confused about how to isolate the variable inside.

Consider the following equation:

$$5(x-1)^3 - 30 = 10$$

The expression on the left side is a complicated recipe that builds from the inside out.

1)	Start with x.	x
2)	Subtract 1.	$x-1$
3)	Cube the result.	$(x-1)^3$
4)	Multiply by 5.	$5(x-1)^3$
5)	Subtract 30.	$5(x-1)^3 - 30$

The recipe follows PEMDAS, as you'd expect. The result of this recipe equals 10, because that's what the equation says:

$$5(x-1)^3 - 30 = 10$$

To isolate x on the left, you need to work your way through from the outside in. So you need to **undo the PEMDAS steps *in reverse order*.**

The last step of the recipe was to subtract 30. To undo that step first, you add 30 to both sides.

$$
\begin{array}{r}
5(x-1)^3 - 30 = 10 \\
+30 \quad +30 \\
\hline
5(x-1)^3 \quad\;\; = 40
\end{array}
$$

You have now gotten rid of 30 on the left side. You've "moved" it to the other side.

Now undo the previous step of the original recipe, which was to multiply by 5. So you divide both sides by 5.

$$\frac{\cancel{5}(x-1)^3}{\cancel{5}} = \frac{40}{5}$$

$$(x-1)^3 = 8$$

Next, undo the cubing. The opposite of exponents is roots. So take the cube root of both sides.

$$\sqrt[3]{(x-1)^3} = \sqrt[3]{8}$$
$$(x-1) = 2$$

You don't need the parentheses anymore, so drop them.

$$x - 1 = 2$$

Finally, undo the subtraction by adding 1 to both sides, and you get $x = 3$.

In summary, you **added** 30, then **divided** by 5, then got rid of the **exponent**, then simplified what was inside **parentheses**. You did PEMDAS backwards, from the outside in.

If you want to isolate a variable deep inside an expression, but you are unsure about the order of steps to perform, do PEMDAS in reverse. Try another example.

If $4\sqrt{x-6} + 7 = 19$, then $x = ?$

A/S

M/D

E

P

Here's the solution path. First, **subtract** 7 from both sides.

$$4\sqrt{x-6} + 7 = 19$$
$$\underline{-7 \quad -7}$$
$$= 12$$

Next, **divide** both sides by 4.

$$\frac{\cancel{4}\sqrt{x-6}}{\cancel{4}} = \frac{12}{4}$$
$$\sqrt{x-6} = 3$$

Now undo the square root by **squaring** both sides.

$$\sqrt{x-6} = 3$$
$$\left(\sqrt{x-6}\right)^2 = (3)^2$$
$$x-6 = 9$$

Finally, **add** 6 to both sides, and you end up with $x = 15$.

The original equation did not contain explicit parentheses, but the square root symbol extended over two terms: $\sqrt{x-6}$. That's just like putting parentheses around $x - 6$ and raising that whole quantity to the 1/2 power: $(x - 6)^{\frac{1}{2}}$.

A square root sign acts like parentheses when it extends over more than one term. Likewise, a fraction bar acts like parentheses when it's stretched.

If you…	Then you…	Like this:
Want to isolate a variable inside an expression	Follow PEMDAS in reverse as you undo the operations in the expression—in other words, work your way in from the outside	$2y^3 - 3 = 51$ $\underline{+3\ \ +3}$ $\dfrac{2y^3}{2} \quad = \dfrac{54}{2}$ $y^3 \quad = 27$ $\sqrt[3]{y^3} = \sqrt[3]{27}$ $y = 3$

Check Your Skills

Solve for x.

3. $3(x + 4)^3 - 5 = 19$
4. $\sqrt[3]{(x + 5)} - 7 = -8$

Answers can be found on page 283.

Clean Up an Equation: Combine Like Terms and Eliminate Denominators

What happens when x shows up in multiple places in an equation?

$$\text{If } \frac{5x-3(4-x)}{2x}=10, \text{ what is } x?$$

To isolate x, you have to get all the x's together, or as many of them as you can. How? **Combine like terms.**

You should also **get rid of the denominator** right away, especially if the denominator contains x. **Always get variables out of denominators.**

This should be the first move in the case above. Undo the division by multiplying both sides by the entire denominator, which is $2x$:

$$2x\left(\frac{5x-3(4-x)}{2x}\right)=(10)2x$$
$$5x-3(4-x)=20x$$

At this point, to combine like terms, you need to get x out of the parentheses. Distribute the 3 on the left side:

$$5x-3(4-x)=20x$$
$$5x-12+3x=20x$$

(Remember to distribute the negative sign!) Now combine like terms. First add $5x$ and $3x$ on the left side.

$$5x-12+3x=20x$$
$$8x-12=20x$$

Next, subtract $8x$ from both sides and immediately combine like terms on the right.

$$
\begin{array}{r}
8x-12=20x \\
-8x \qquad -8x \\
\hline
-12=12x
\end{array}
$$

The right side could be written as $20x - 8x$, but you should combine into $12x$ as you perform the subtraction.

Why subtract $8x$ rather than $20x$? If you subtract $8x$, you get all the x terms on one side and numbers on the other side. You also get a positive coefficient on the x (12). These results are both nice to have.

Finally, divide by 12 to isolate x on the right.

$$\frac{-12}{12} = \frac{12x}{12}$$
$$-1 = x$$

You now have the answer to the question. $x = -1$.

If you…	Then you…	Like this:
Have a variable in multiple places in an equation	Combine like terms, which might be on different sides of the equation.	$9y + 30 = 12y$ $\underline{-9y \qquad\quad -9y}$ $30 = 3y$
Have a variable in a denominator	Multiply to eliminate the denominator right away.	$\dfrac{2z-3}{z} = 4$ $(z)\left(\dfrac{2z-3}{z}\right) = 4(z)$ $2z - 3 = 4z$

Check Your Skills

Solve for x.

5. $\dfrac{2x + 6(9 - 2x)}{x - 4} = -3$

Answers can be found on page 283.

Variables in the Exponent: Make the Bases Equal

If a variable is in the exponent, none of the typical PEMDAS moves are going to help much.

> If $3^x = 27^4$, what is x?

The key is to **rewrite the terms so they have the same base**. Usually, the best way to do this is to **factor bases into primes**.

On the left side, 3 is already a prime, so leave it alone. On the right side, 27 is not prime. Since $27 = 3^3$, replace 27 with 3^3. Put in parentheses to keep the exponents straight.

> $3^x = (3^3)^4$

Simplify the right side by applying the "two-exponent" rule: $(3^3)^4 = 3^{3\times4} = 3^{12}$.

$$3^x = 3^{12}$$

In words, this equation says, "Three raised to the power of x is equal to three raised to the power of 12."

This is only true if x itself is equal to 12.

$$3^x = 3^{12} \quad \longrightarrow \quad x = 12$$

Once the bases are the same, the exponents must be the same.

This rule has exactly three exceptions: a base of 1, a base of 0, and a base of –1. The reason is that more than one exponent of these particular bases results in the same number.

$$1^2 = 1^3 = \ldots = 1 \qquad 0^2 = 0^3 = \ldots = 0 \qquad (-1)^2 = (-1)^4 = 1, \text{ while } (-1)^1 = (-1)^3 = -1$$

However, for every other base, the rule works. Try this example:

If $4^y = 8^{y+1}$, then $2^y =$

(A) –8   (B) $\dfrac{1}{8}$ (C) $\dfrac{1}{4}$ (D) 1   (E) 8

Look at the answer choices. Since none of them contain a y, we will have to find the value of y.

Now look at the given equation. The variable y is in two exponents.

$$4^y = 8^{y+1}$$

To figure out what this tells you about y, make the bases the same. Rewrite both 4 and 8 as powers of 2.

$$4 = 2^2 \qquad\qquad 8 = 2^3$$

$$4^y = 8^{y+1} \quad \longrightarrow \quad (2^2)^y = (2^3)^{y+1}$$

Next, apply the "two exponent" rule on both sides.

$$(2^2)^y = (2^3)^{y+1}$$

$$2^{2y} = 2^{3(y+1)}$$

Now that the bases are the same (and the common base is not 1, 0, or –1), you can set the exponents equal to each other. Write a brand-new equation that expresses this fact.

$$2y = 3(y + 1)$$

At this point, solve for y. Distribute the 3 on the right:

$2y = 3y + 3$

Subtract $2y$ from both sides to combine like terms:

$0 = y + 3$

Finally, subtract 3 from both sides:

$-3 = y$

Now that you've solved for y, find the value of 2^y, which is what the question asks for. Replace y with -3.

$2^y = 2^{(-3)} = \dfrac{1}{8}$ The correct answer is (B).

If you…	Then you…	Like this:
Have a variable in an exponent or exponents	Make the bases equal, usually by breaking the given bases down to primes	$3^x = 27^4$ $3^x = (3^3)^4$ $3^x = 3^{12}$ $x = 12$

Check Your Skills

6. If $4^6 = 64^{2x}$, then $16^x = ?$

Answers can be found on page 282.

Systems of Equations

Many GMAT problems will force you to deal with two variables. In most of those cases, you'll also have two equations. For example:

(a) $2x - 3y = 16$ (b) $y - x = -7$

A group of more than one equation is often called a **system of equations**. Solving a system of two equations with two variables x and y means finding values for x and y that make both equations true *at the same time.*

The systems of equations discussed in this section only have 1 solution. That is, only one set of values of x and y makes the system work.

To solve a system of two equations and two unknowns, you can use either of two good strategies:

(A) **Isolate, then Substitute**   (B) **Combine Equations**

These strategies are similar at a high level. In both, here's what you do:

1) Kill off one equation and one unknown.
2) Solve the remaining equation for the remaining unknown.
3) Plug back into one of the original equations to solve for the other variable.

However, the two strategies take very different approaches to step #1: how to kill off one equation and one unknown. Let's examine these approaches in turn.

Kill an Equation and an Unknown: (A) Isolate, then Substitute

This strategy is also known as **substitution**. Consider this system again:

$$(a) \qquad 2x - 3y = 16 \qquad\qquad (b) \qquad y - x = -7$$

To follow the substitution strategy, first isolate one variable in one of the equations. Then substitute into the other equation.

Which variable should you isolate? The one you *don't* ultimately want. **If the problem asks for x, first isolate y.**

Why *y*? Because the variable you first isolate is the one you will then kill off. You're left with one equation in *x*—the variable you want. This way, you save work.

Conversely, if the problem asks for *y*, first isolate *x* so you can kill it off early.

Let's say that the question asks for the value of *x*. Then you want to isolate *y* in one of the given equations.

Which equation should you isolate your variable in? The one that's easier to deal with.

It looks easier to isolate *y* in equation (b). All you have to do is add *x* to both sides. So go ahead and do that.

$$
\begin{array}{lll}
(a) \quad 2x - 3y = 16 \qquad & (b) \quad & y - x = -7 \\
& & \underline{+x \qquad +x} \\
& & y \quad = -7 + x \\
& & y \quad = x - 7
\end{array}
$$

By the way, when you use this method, it's good practice to write the two equations in the system side by side. That way, you can do algebra down your page to isolate one variable without running into the other equation.

Now you have expressed *y* in terms of *x*. Since $y = x - 7$, you can replace *y* with $(x - 7)$ anywhere you see *y*. So you can remove any references to *y* in the first equation. In essence, you are killing off *y*.

(a) $2x - 3y = 16$ (b) $y - x = -7$

$$\frac{+x \qquad\quad +x}{}$$

$$y \quad\; = -7 + x$$

$$y \quad\; = x - 7$$

$2x - 3(x - 7) = 16$

When you sub in an expression such as $x - 7$, place parentheses around the expression. This way, you avoid PEMDAS errors.

Now that you have killed off one variable (y) and one equation (the second one), you have just one variable left (x) in one equation. Solve for that variable:

$$
\begin{aligned}
2x - 3(x - 7) &= 16 \\
2x - 3x + 21 &= 16 \qquad &&\text{Distribute the 3} \\
-x + 21 &= 16 \qquad &&\text{Combine } 2x \text{ and } -3x \text{ (like terms)} \\
-x &= -5 \qquad &&\text{Subtract 21 from both sides} \\
x &= 5 \qquad &&\text{Multiply both sides by } -1
\end{aligned}
$$

At this point, you're done if the question only asks for x. If the question asks for $x + y$ or some other expression involving both x and y, then you need to solve for y. Do so by plugging your value of x into either of the original equations.

Which equation should you plug back into? The one in which you isolated y. In fact, you should plug into the revised form of that equation—the one that looks like "$y =$ something." This is the easiest way to solve for y.

$y = x - 7$

Swap out x and replace it with 5, since you found that $x = 5$.

$y = (5) - 7$
$y = -2$

Now you have the complete solution: $x = 5$ and $y = -2$. These are the values that make **both** of the original equations true at the same time:

(a) $2x - 3y = 16$ (b) $y - x = -7$

$2(5) - 3(-2) = 16$ $(-2) - (5) = -7$

True   True

If you...	Then you...	Like this:
Have two equations and two unknowns	Isolate one unknown, then substitute into the other equation	$2x - 3y = 16$ and $y - x = -7$ $y = -7 + x = x - 7$ $2x - 3(x - 7) = 16$ ... $x = 5$ $y = -2$

Check Your Skills

Solve for x and y.

7. $6y + 15 = 3x$
$\ x + y = 14$

Answers can be found on page 284.

Kill an Equation and an Unknown: (B) Combine Equations

Substitution will always work. But some GMAT problems can be solved more easily with another method, known as **combination**.

Here's how combination works. You can always **add two equations together**. Just add the left sides up and put the result on the left. Then add the right sides up and put that result on the right.

$$
\begin{aligned}
x &= 4 \\
+ \quad y &= 7 \\
\hline
x + y &= 4 + 7
\end{aligned}
$$

Why is this allowed? You are actually adding the same thing to both sides of an equation. Since y equals 7, you can legally add y on the left side of $x = 4$ and add 7 on the right side. You are making the same change on each side of the first equation.

In this example, the resulting equation ($x + y = 11$) is more complicated than the starting equations. However, adding equations can sometimes actually kill off a variable—**and that's why you do it**.

Consider this system of equations:

$a + b = 11$ $a - b = 5$

What happens when you add these equations together?

$$a + b = 11$$
$$+ \quad \underline{a - b = 5}$$
$$2a = 16$$

The b's cancel out of the resulting equation completely. It's now easy to solve for a.

$$2a = 16 \quad \longrightarrow \quad a = 8$$

Finally, solve for b by plugging back into one of the original equations.

$$a + b = 11 \quad \longrightarrow \quad (8) + b = 11 \quad \longrightarrow \quad b = 3$$

So the complete solution to the original system of equations is $a = 8$ and $b = 3$.

If you solve that system by substitution, you will need to take a few more steps. Every extra step takes time and presents an additional opportunity for error. If you learn to combine equations, you can often kill off a variable easily and safely.

Combination isn't restricted to adding equations. You can also subtract equations. Say you are given these two equations:

$$5n + m = 17 \qquad 2n + m = 11$$

Since "$+ m$" shows up in both equations, we can kill m by subtracting the second equation from the first.

$$5n + m = 17$$
$$- \quad \underline{2n + m = 11}$$
$$3n = 6$$

Realize that you are subtracting the whole left side, as well as the right side. If you are concerned that you might not follow PEMDAS, put in parentheses around the whole equation.

$$5n + m = 17$$
$$- \quad \underline{(2n + m = 11)}$$
$$3n = 6$$

Now you can solve for n, then plug back in to get m.

$$3n = 6 \quad \longrightarrow \quad n = 2$$
$$2n + m = 11 \quad \longrightarrow \quad 2(2) + m = 11 \quad \longrightarrow \quad m = 7$$

To set up a good elimination, you can even multiply a whole equation by a number. That's the same thing as multiplying the left side and the right side by the same number. This is a Golden Rule move.

Consider this system of equations from earlier:

(a) $2x - 3y = 16$ (b) $y - x = -7$

To take the combination approach, first rewrite the equations vertically and line up the variables. Here, you *want* to write one equation below the other (not *next to* each other as you do with substitution). Space the terms to line up x with x and y with y.

$$2x - 3y = 16$$
$$-x\ +y = -7$$

If you add the equations now, neither variable will die. So that's not helpful.

However, if you multiply the second equation by 2 on both sides, you'll be able to cancel when you add.

$$2x - 3y = 16 \qquad \longrightarrow \qquad 2x - 3y = 16$$
$$2(-x\ +y) = (-7)2 \qquad \longrightarrow \qquad -2x + 2y = -14$$

Now add. The $2x$ term will cancel with the $-2x$ term.

$$2x - 3y = 16$$
$$+ \quad -2x + 2y = -14$$
$$-y = 2$$
$$y = -2$$

Finally, use this value of y in one of the original equations to solve for x.

$$y - x = -7 \quad \longrightarrow \quad (-2) - x = -7 \quad \longrightarrow \quad -x = -5 \quad \longrightarrow \quad x = 5$$

This is the same solution as before. In this case, you only saved a little work by combining equations rather than isolating and substituting. However, some problems are *much* easier to solve by combining equations. Take a look at this last example:

$$\frac{1}{2}x + \frac{1}{3}y = 3$$
$$2x + y = 11$$

For this system of equations, what is the value of $x + y$?

If you try direct substitution, you will need to make a lot of messy calculations involving fractions.

Instead, try combination. First, multiply the top equation through by 6 to eliminate all fractions.

$$6\left(\frac{1}{2}x + \frac{1}{3}y\right) = (3)6$$
$$3x + 2y = 18$$

Now line up the two given equations, which now look much better.

$$3x + 2y = 18$$
$$2x + y = 11$$

Before going further, consider: what does the question specifically ask for? It does not ask for x or y separately. Rather, it asks for $x + y$.

You can certainly solve for one of the variables, then find the other. But there's a shortcut.

You can solve for $x + y$ directly, simply by subtracting the equations:

$$3x + 2y = 18$$
$$-\ (2x + y = 11)$$
$$\overline{x + y = 7}$$

Ta-da! The answer to the question is 7.

Combination isn't always appropriate. Become very comfortable with substitution as a default method. But as you spot opportunities to kill off a variable by adding or subtracting equations, seize those opportunities.

6

If you...	Then you...	Like this:
Have two equations and two unknowns	Add or subtract equations to kill a variable	$2x - 3y = 16$ and $y - x = -7$ Multiply 2nd equation by 2: $2(y - x) = (-7)2$ Add equations: $-2x + 2y = -14$ $\underline{+2x - 3y = 16}$ $-y = 2$ $y = -2$

Check Your Skills

Solve for x and y.

8. $x + 4y = 10$
$y - x = -5$

Answers can be found on page 284.

Three or More Variables: Isolate the Expression You Want

A few problems involve even more than two variables. Fortunately, all the procedures you've learned so far still work.

Focus on exactly what the question asks for and isolate that on one side of the equation. Try this example:

If $\sqrt{\dfrac{a}{b}} = c$ and $bc \neq 0$, what is the value of b in terms of a and c?

Since the question asks for b, you should isolate b. The answer will contain a and c, because the question asks for an expression "in terms of" a and c.

Take the given equation and do Golden Rule moves to isolate b.

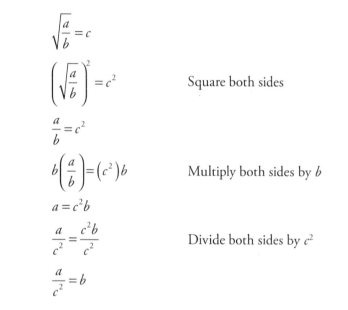

$$\sqrt{\dfrac{a}{b}} = c$$

$$\left(\sqrt{\dfrac{a}{b}}\right)^2 = c^2 \qquad \text{Square both sides}$$

$$\dfrac{a}{b} = c^2$$

$$b\left(\dfrac{a}{b}\right) = \left(c^2\right)b \qquad \text{Multiply both sides by } b$$

$$a = c^2 b$$

$$\dfrac{a}{c^2} = \dfrac{c^2 b}{c^2} \qquad \text{Divide both sides by } c^2$$

$$\dfrac{a}{c^2} = b$$

The answer to the question is $\dfrac{a}{c^2}$.

By the way, the "non-equation" $bc \neq 0$ was only there to prevent division by zero. You rarely wind up using this sort of information in any other way.

Here is another tough question:

$$\dfrac{w}{x-y} = 3 \qquad -y + x = 4$$

In the system of equations above, what is the value of w?

(A) -12　　　(B) $\dfrac{-3}{4}$　　　(C) $\dfrac{3}{4}$　　　(D) $\dfrac{4}{3}$　　　(E) 12

You are asked for the value of w, so you want to manipulate the equations to get "$w = \ldots$"

Notice that the answer choices are all numbers. This means that the other variables x and y must disappear along the way.

One approach is to isolate x or y in the second equation, then substitute into the first equation. This way, you at least get rid of one variable. It's a start—let's see where it goes.

Isolate y by adding x to both sides of the second equation.

$$
\begin{array}{r}
y - x = 4 \\
\underline{+\ x\ \ +x} \\
y\ \ \ = x + 4
\end{array}
$$

Now substitute $x + 4$ into the first equation in place of y. Be sure to put parentheses around $x + 4$.

$$\frac{w}{x-y} = 3 \quad\longrightarrow\quad \frac{w}{x-(x+4)} = 3 \quad\longrightarrow\quad \frac{w}{x-x-4} = 3 \quad\longrightarrow\quad \frac{w}{-4} = 3$$

Look what happened—the variable x disappeared as well. This is a good sign. If x didn't cancel out, then you'd be in trouble. You can solve for w now:

$$\frac{w}{-4} = 3 \quad\longrightarrow\quad w = -12 \qquad \text{The answer is (A).}$$

Another approach to the problem is to recognize that $x - y$ is very similar to $y - x$. In fact, they are opposites of each other:

$$x - y = -(y - x)$$

If you recognize this, then multiply the second equation by -1 so that it has $x - y$ on one side:

$$
\begin{array}{c}
y - x = 4 \\
(-1)\,(y - x) = (4)(-1) \\
x - y = -4
\end{array}
$$

Now you can **substitute for a whole expression**. That is, you can swap out $x - y$ in the first equation and replace that entire thing with -4.

$$\frac{w}{x-y} = 3 \qquad \boxed{x - y = -4}$$

$$\frac{w}{(-4)} = 3$$

This gets you to the same point as the first method, and you end up with $w = -12$.

6

However many variables and equations you have, pay close attention to what the question is asking for.

- If the question asks for the variable *x*, isolate *x*, so you have "*x* = …"
- If the question asks for *x* in terms of *y*, the other side should contain *y*.
- If the question asks for *x* + *y*, isolate that expression, so you have "*x* + *y* = …"
- If a variable does not appear in the answer choices, help it vanish. Isolate it and substitute for it in another equation.
- If an expression such as *x* − *y* shows up in two different equations, feel free to substitute for it, so that the whole thing disappears.

If you…	Then you…	Like this:
Have three or more unknowns	Isolate whatever the question asks for, and use substitution to eliminate unwanted variables	If $a + b - c = 12$ and $c - b = 8$, what is the value of *a*? Isolate *a*: $a = 12 + c - b$ Substitute for $c - b$: $a = 12 + (8)$ $a = 20$

Check Your Skills

9. If $\dfrac{a}{c} + \dfrac{b}{3c} = 1$, what is *c* in terms of *a* and *b*?

Answers can be found on page 285.

Check Your Skills Answer Key:

1. **14:** In order to find the value of x, we need to isolate x on one side of the equation.

$$\sqrt{x+2} = 4$$
$$(\sqrt{x+2})^2 = (4)^2$$
$$x + 2 = 16$$
$$x = 14$$

2. **$2x + 3$:** In order to find y in terms of x, we need to isolate y on one side of the equation.

$$\frac{y-3}{x} = 2$$
$$\cancel{x} \times \left(\frac{y-3}{\cancel{x}}\right) = (2) \times x$$
$$y - 3 = 2x$$
$$y = 2x + 3$$

3. **$x = -2$:**

$$3(x+4)^3 - 5 = 19$$
$$3(x+4)^3 = 24 \qquad \text{Add 5 to both sides}$$
$$(x+4)^3 = 8 \qquad \text{Divide both sides by 3}$$
$$(x+4) = 2 \qquad \text{Take the cube root of both sides}$$
$$x = -2 \qquad \text{Remove the parentheses, subtract 4 from both sides}$$

4. **$x = -6$:**

$$\sqrt[3]{(x+5)} - 7 = -8$$
$$\sqrt[3]{(x+5)} = -1 \qquad \text{Add 7 to both sides}$$
$$x + 5 = -1 \qquad \text{Cube both sides, remove parentheses}$$
$$x = -6 \qquad \text{Subtract 5 from both sides}$$

5. **$x = 6$:**

$$\frac{2x + 6(9 - 2x)}{x - 4} = -3$$
$$2x + 6(9 - 2x) = -3(x - 4) \qquad \text{Multiply by the denominator } (x - 4)$$
$$2x + 54 - 12x = -3x + 12 \qquad \text{Simplify grouped terms by distributing}$$
$$-10x + 54 = -3x + 12 \qquad \text{Combine like terms } (2x \text{ and } -12x)$$
$$54 = 7x + 12 \qquad \text{Add } 10x \text{ to both sides}$$
$$42 = 7x \qquad \text{Subtract 12 from both sides}$$
$$6 = x \qquad \text{Divide both sides by 7}$$

6. **16:** We could answer this question by breaking each base down to a power of 2, but notice that all three bases in the question (4, 64, and 16) are powers of 4. Solve for x by rewriting 64 as 4^3.

$$4^6 = 64^{2x}$$
$$4^6 = (4^3)^{2x}$$
$$4^6 = 4^{6x}$$
$$6 = 6x$$
$$1 = x$$

If $x = 1$, then $16^x = 16^1 = 16$.

7. **$x = 11, y = 3$:**

$6y + 15 = 3x$	
$x + y = 14$	
$2y + 5 = x$	Divide the first equation by 3
$(2y + 5) + y = 14$	Substitute $(2y + 5)$ for x in the second equation
$3y + 5 = 14$	Combine like terms ($2y$ and y)
$3y = 9$	Subtract 5 from both sides
$y = 3$	Divide both sides by 3
$x + (3) = 14$	Substitute (3) for y in the second equation to solve for x
$x = 11$	

8. **$x = 6, y = 1$:** Notice we have positive x in the first equation and negative x in the second equation. Rearrange the second equation and line it up under the first equation.

$$\begin{aligned} x + 4y &= 10 \\ \underline{-x + y} &= \underline{-5} \\ 5y &= 5 \\ y &= 1 \end{aligned}$$

Now that we know $y = 1$, we can plug it back into either equation to solve for x.

$$x + 4y = 10$$
$$x + 4(1) = 10$$
$$x = 6$$

9. $\dfrac{3a+b}{3}$ **OR** $a+\dfrac{b}{3}$: We have to isolate c on one side of the equation. First combine the fractions on

the left side of the equation.

$$\frac{a}{c}+\frac{b}{3c}=1$$

$$\frac{3a}{3c}+\frac{b}{3c}=1$$

$$\frac{3a+b}{3c}=1$$

$$3a+b=3c$$

$$\frac{3a+b}{3}=c$$

If you split the numerator, then you would get:

$$\frac{3a+b}{3}=c$$

$$\frac{\not3a}{\not3}+\frac{b}{3}=c$$

$$a+\frac{b}{3}=c$$

6

Chapter Review: Drill Sets

Drill 1

1. If $x = 2$, then $x^2 - 4x + 3 =$

2. If $x = 3$, what is the value of $x + \sqrt{48x}$?

3. What is the value of $-y^3 - \dfrac{3y-2}{4}$ when $y = -2$?

4. If $p = 300c^2 - c$, what is the value of p when $c = 100$?

5. What is the value of y if $y - 3 = \dfrac{xy}{2}$ and $x = 3$?

Drill 2

Solve for the variable in the following equations.

6. $14 - 3x = 2$

7. $3(7 - x) = 4(1.5)$

8. $7x + 13 = 2x - 7$

9. $3t^3 - 7 = 74$

10. $\dfrac{z-4}{3} = -12$

11. $1{,}200x + 6{,}000 = 13{,}200$

12. $\sqrt{x} = 3 \times 5 - 20 \div 4$

13. $+(x)^3 = 64$

14. $\dfrac{\sqrt{3x+1}}{2} - 1 = 3$

15. $5\sqrt[3]{x} + 6 = 51$

Drill 3

Isolate x in the following equations.

16. $3x + 2(x + 2) = 2x + 16$

17. $\dfrac{3x+7}{x} = 10$

18. $4(-3x - 8) = 8(-x + 9)$

19. $3x + 7 - 4x + 8 = 2(-2x - 6)$

20. $2x(4 - 6) = -2x + 12$

21. $\dfrac{3(6-x)}{2x} = -6$

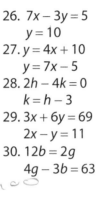

22. $\dfrac{13}{x+13} = 1$

23. $\dfrac{10(-3x+4)}{10-5x} = 2$

24. $\dfrac{8-2(-4+10x)}{2-x} = 17$

25. $\dfrac{50(10+3x)}{50+7x} = 50$

Drill 4

Solve for the values of both variables in each system of equations using substitution. The explanations will use substitution to solve.

26. $7x - 3y = 5$
    $y = 10$

27. $y = 4x + 10$
    $y = 7x - 5$

28. $2h - 4k = 0$
    $k = h - 3$

29. $3x + 6y = 69$
    $2x - y = 11$

30. $12b = 2g$
    $4g - 3b = 63$

Drill 5

Solve for the values of both variables in each system of equations using elimination. The explanations will use elimination to solve.

31. $x - y = 4$
    $2x + y = 5$

32. $x + 2y = 5$
    $x - 4y = -7$

33. $a + b = 8$
    $2a + b = 13$

34. $r - 2s = 1$
    $5r + s = 5$

35. $y - 2x - 1 = 0$
    $x - 3y - 1 = 0$

36. $\dfrac{1}{3}r - \dfrac{1}{6}s = 0$
    $2r + \dfrac{1}{2}s - 3 = 0$

Drill 6

Solve for the values of both variables in each system of equations. Decide whether to use substitution or elimination. Explanation will use one of the two methods and explain why that is the better solution method.

37. $5x + 2y = 12$

    $y = \dfrac{1}{2}x + 3$

    (handwritten) $5x + 2\left(\frac{1}{2}x + 3\right) = 12$

    $5x + 1 + 6 = 12$

    $x = 1 \dfrac{-7}{\frac{5}{5}}$

38. $y - 1 = x + 2$

    $2y = x + 1$

39. $r + 2s - 1 = 0$

    $s - r + 2 = 0$

40. $3x = 6 - y$

    $6x - y = 3$

    (handwritten) $3x + y = 6$

    $6x - y = 3$

    $9x = 9 \qquad x = 1$

41. $x = 2y - \dfrac{1}{2}$

    $y - x = -\dfrac{3}{2}$

    (handwritten) $-2y + x = -\frac{1}{2}$

    $y - x = -\frac{3}{2}$

    $-1y = +\frac{4}{2}$

    $-y = -2$

Drill 7

Solve for the desired value in each system of equations.

42. $4x + y + 3z = 34$

    $x - 1 \left(4x + 3z = 21 \right)$

    What is y?

43. $2p = \dfrac{m-5}{n+2}$

    (handwritten) $2p(n+2) + 5 = m$

    What is m in terms of n and p?

44. $3x + 5y + 2z = 20$

    $x - 1 \mid 6x + 4z = 10$

    (handwritten) $3x + 5y + 2z = 20$

    $-3x \qquad -2z = 5$

    $5y = 15 \qquad y = 3$

    What is y?

45. $\dfrac{a-b}{4} = c + 1$

    $c = b + 2$

    (handwritten) $\dfrac{a-b}{4} = (b+2)4$

    $4b + 2 = a - b$

    $5b + 2 = a$

    What is b in terms of a?

Drill 8

Solve for the desired value in each system of equations.

46. $\dfrac{(a+b)}{(c+d)} = 10$

    $3d = \dfrac{15 - 3c}{3}$

    (handwritten) $a + b = 10c + 10d$

    $10c + 50 - 5c$

    $d = 5 - c$

    What is $a + b$?

47. $x = \dfrac{y}{5}$

    $2z - 1 = \dfrac{x+y}{2}$

    (handwritten) $z = \qquad y = 5x$

    $2z - 1 = \dfrac{x + 5x}{2}$

    $2z - 1 = \dfrac{6x}{2} + 1$

    What is z in terms of x?

48. $2^{x+y} = \sqrt{z-2}$

    $x = 2 - y$

    What is z?

49. (1) $\dfrac{2j}{3k+1} = 3$

    (2) $\dfrac{k}{2} = \dfrac{h}{3}$

    What is $j - 3h$?

Drill Sets Solutions

Drill 1

1. To evaluate the expression, we need to replace x with (2).

$x^2 - 4x + 3 =$
$(2)^2 - 4(2) + 3 =$
$4 - 8 + 3 = -1$

2. To evaluate the expression, replace x with (3).

$x + \sqrt{48x} =$
$3 + \sqrt{48(3)} =$
$3 + \sqrt{144} =$
$3 + 12 = 15$

3. To evaluate the expression, replace y with (-2) everywhere in the equation. Be extra careful with the negative signs.

$-y^3 - \dfrac{3y - 2}{4} =$
$-(-2)^3 - \dfrac{3(-2) - 2}{4} =$
$-(-8) - \dfrac{-6 - 2}{4} =$
$8 - \dfrac{-8}{4} =$
$8 - (-2) = 10$

4. To find the value of p, we first need to replace c with 100.

$p = 300c^2 - c$
$p = 300(100)^2 - 100$
$p = 300(10,000) - 100$
$p = 3,000,000 - 100 = 2,999,900$

5. First we need to replace x with (3) in the equation.

$y - 3 = \dfrac{xy}{2}$
$y - 3 = \dfrac{(3)y}{2}$
$y - 3 = \dfrac{3y}{2}$

Now, to find the value of y, we need to isolate y on one side of the equation.

$$y - 3 = \frac{3y}{2}$$
$$2(y - 3) = 3y$$
$$2y - 6 = 3y$$
$$-6 = y$$

Drill 2

6. $14 - 3x = 2$

       $-3x = -12$ Subtract 14

       $x = 4$ Divide by -3

7. $3(7 - x) = 4(1.5)$

       $21 - 3x = 6$ Simplify

       $-3x = -15$ Subtract 21

       $x = 5$ Divide by -3

8. $7x + 13 = 2x - 7$

       $5x + 13 = -7$ Subtract $2x$

       $5x = -20$ Subtract 13

       $x = -4$ Divide by 5

9. $3t^3 - 7 = 74$

       $3t^3 = 81$

       $t^3 = 27$

       $t = 3$

10. $\dfrac{(z - 4)}{3} = -12$

       $z - 4 = -36$ Multiply by 3

       $z = -32$ Add 4

11. $1,200x + 6,000 = 13,200$

       $1,200x = 7,200$

       $x = 6$

12. $\sqrt{x} = 3 \times 5 - 20 \div 4$

       $\sqrt{x} = 15 - 5$

       $\sqrt{x} = 10$

       $x = 100$

13. $-(x)^3 = 64$

      $(x)^3 = -64$

      $x = -4$

14. $\dfrac{\sqrt{3x+1}}{2} - 1 = 3$

    $\dfrac{\sqrt{3x+1}}{2} = 4$

    $\sqrt{3x+1} = 8$

    $3x + 1 = 64$

    $3x = 63$

    $x = 21$

15. $5\sqrt[3]{x} + 6 = 51$

    $5\sqrt[3]{x} = 45$

    $\left(\sqrt[3]{x} = 9\right)^3$

    $x = 9^3 = 729$

Drill 3

16. $3x + 2(x + 2) = 2x + 16$

    $3x + 2x + 4 = 2x + 16$

    $5x + 4 = 2x + 16$

    $3x + 4 = 16$

    $3x = 12$

    $x = 4$

17. $\dfrac{3x + 7}{x} = 10$

    $3x + 7 = 10x$

    $7 = 7x$

    $1 = x$

18. $4(-3x - 8) = 8(-x + 9)$

    $-12x - 32 = -8x + 72$

    $-32 = 4x + 72$

    $-104 = 4x$

    $-26 = x$

19. $3x + 7 - 4x + 8 = 2(-2x - 6)$

    $-x + 15 = -4x - 12$

    $3x + 15 = -12$

    $3x = -27$

    $x = -9$

20. $2x(4-6) = -2x + 12$

$$2x(-2) = -2x + 12$$
$$-4x = -2x + 12$$
$$-2x = 12$$
$$x = -6$$

21. $$\dfrac{3(6-x)}{2x} = -6$$

$$3(6-x) = -6(2x)$$
$$18 - 3x = -12x$$
$$18 = -9x$$
$$-2 = x$$

22. $$\dfrac{13}{x+13} = 1$$

$$13 = 1(x+13)$$
$$13 = x + 13$$
$$0 = x$$

23. $$\dfrac{10(-3x+4)}{10-5x} = 2$$

$$10(-3x+4) = 2(10-5x)$$
$$-30x + 40 = 20 - 10x$$
$$40 = 20 + 20x$$
$$20 = 20x$$
$$1 = x$$

24. $$\dfrac{8 - 2(-4+10x)}{2-x} = 17$$

$$8 - 2(-4+10x) = 17(2-x)$$
$$8 + 8 - 20x = 34 - 17x$$
$$16 - 20x = 34 - 17x$$
$$16 = 34 + 3x$$
$$-18 = 3x$$
$$-6 = x$$

25. $$\dfrac{50(10+3x)}{50+7x} = 50$$

$$50(10+3x) = 50(50+7x)$$
$$500 + 150x = 2{,}500 + 350x$$
$$500 = 2{,}500 + 200x$$
$$-2{,}000 = 200x$$
$$-10 = x$$

MANHATTAN
GMAT

Drill 4

26. Eq. (1): $7x - 3y = 5$ Eq. (2): $y = 10$

$7x - 3(10) = 5$	Substitute (10) for y in Eq. (1).
$7x - 30 = 5$	Solve for x. Simplify grouped terms.
$7x = 35$	Add 30.
$x = 5$	Divide by 7.

Answer: $x = 5$, $y = 10$

27. Eq. (1): $y = 4x + 10$ Eq. (2): $y = 7x - 5$

$(4x + 10) = 7x - 5$	Substitute $(4x + 10)$ for y in Eq. (2).
$10 = 3x - 5$	Solve for x. Subtract $4x$.
$15 = 3x$	Add 5.
$5 = x$	Divide by 3.
$y = 4(5) + 10$	Substitute (5) for x in Eq. (1). Solve for y.
$y = 30$	Simplify.

Answer: $x = 5$, $y = 30$

28. Eq. (1): $2h - 4k = 0$ Eq. (2): $k = h - 3$

$2h - 4(h - 3) = 0$	Substitute $(h - 3)$ for k in Eq. (1).
$2h - 4h + 12 = 0$	Solve for h.
$-2h = -12$	Combine like terms.
$h = 6$	Divide by -2.
$k = (6) - 3$	Substitute (6) for h in Eq. 2 and solve for k.
$k = 3$	Simplify.

Answer: $h = 6$, $k = 3$

29. Eq. (1): $3x + 6y = 69$ Eq. (2): $2x - y = 11$

$2x - y = 11$	Isolate y in Eq. (2). Subtract $2x$.
$-y = -2x + 11$	
$y = 2x - 11$	Divide by -1.
$3x + 6(2x - 11) = 69$	Substitute $(2x - 11)$ for y in Eq. (1).
$3x + 12x - 66 = 69$	Solve for x.
$15x - 66 = 69$	Combine like terms.
$15x = 135$	Add 66.
$x = 9$	Divide by 15.
$2(9) - y = 11$	Substitute (9) for x in Eq. (2). Solve for y.
$18 - y = 11$	Simplify.

6

$18 = 11 + y$ Add y.
$7 = y$ Subtract 11.

Answer: $x = 9$, $y = 7$

30. Eq. (1): $12b = 2g$ Eq. (2): $4g - 3b = 63$

$12b = 2g$
$6b = g$ Isolate g in Eq. (1). Divide by 2.

$4(6b) - 3b = 63$ Substitute $(6b)$ for g in Eq. (2).
$24b - 3b = 63$ Solve for b. Simplify.
$21b = 63$ Combine like terms.
$b = 3$ Divide by 21.
$12(3) = 2g$ Substitute (3) for b in Eq. (1). Solve for g.
$36 = 2g$ Simplify.
$g = 18$ Divide by 2.

Answer: $b = 3$, $g = 18$

Drill 5

31. Notice that the first equation has the term $-y$ while the second equation has the term $+y$. Because these terms will cancel, we do not need to do any manipulations before adding the equations together:

$$\begin{array}{r} x - y = 4 \\ +(2x + y = 5) \\ \hline 3x = 9 \end{array}$$

Therefore $x = 3$ and plugging this back in to the first equation yields:

$x - y = 4$
$(3) - y = 4$
$-1 = y$

Answer: $x = 3$ and $y = -1$

32. Both equations have the term $+x$, so we can eliminate the variable x by subtracting the second equation from the first:

$$\begin{array}{r} x + 2y = 5 \\ -(x - 4y = -7) \\ \hline 2y + 4y = 5 + 7 \end{array}$$

The new equation simplifies to $6y = 12$, or $y = 2$. Then, we plug this value for y into the first equation to get $x + 2(2) = 5$, or $x = 1$.

Notice that we must be very careful to change the sign of each term in the second equation when subtracting (for example, $-4y$ becomes $-(-4y) = +4y$ and -7 becomes $-(-7) = +7$). Alternatively, we could have multiplied the entire second equation by -1 to get $-x + 4y = 7$ and then added this equation to the first:

$$\begin{array}{r} x + 2y = 5 \\ + (-x + 4y = 7) \\ \hline 6y = 12 \end{array}$$

This yields the same solution: $y = 2$ and $x = 1$.

33. Both equations have the term $+b$, so we can eliminate the variable b by subtracting the second equation from the first:

$$\begin{array}{r} a + b = 8 \\ - (2a + b = 13) \\ \hline -a = -5 \end{array}$$

Hence $a = 5$. Then, we plug this value for a into the first equation to get $(5) + b = 8$, or $b = 3$.

Answer: $a = 5$, $b = 3$

34. Neither of the variables will be eliminated if we add or subtract the equations as they are currently written, so we need to multiply one of the equations by an appropriately chosen constant. Notice that the s in the first equation has coefficient -2 and the s in the second equation has coefficient $+1$, so the easiest way to match up coefficients is to multiply the second equation by 2. After making this adjustment, the second equation is $10r + 2s = 10$ and we have:

$$\begin{array}{r} r - 2s = 1 \\ + (10r + 2s = 10) \\ \hline 11r = 11 \end{array}$$

Therefore $r = 1$ and after plugging this value into the first equation we have $1 - 2s = 1$, or $s = 0$.

Answer: $r = 1$, $s = 0$

35. We first manipulate the two equations so that the variables are nicely aligned on the left hand side and the constant terms are all on the right:

$$\begin{array}{r} -2x + y = 1 \\ x - 3y = 1 \end{array}$$

At this point, neither of the variables will be eliminated if we simply add or subtract the equations, so we must multiply one of the equations by an appropriately chosen constant. While there are many cor-

rect ways to do this, the simplest is to multiply the second equation by 2, thereby replacing it with the equation $2x - 6y = 2$. Then add the original first equation to the new second equation:

$$-2x + y = 1$$
$$\underline{+(2x - 6y = 2)}$$
$$-5y = 3$$

Therefore $y = -\dfrac{3}{5}$. After solving for one of the variables in a system of equations, we can actually plug this value into *any* of the equations we have used so far. For this problem, the simplest option is the original second equation because the x in that equation has coefficient 1, which means we won't have to divide in order to isolate the x:

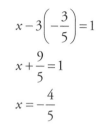

This yields the solution $x = -\dfrac{4}{5}$ and $y = -\dfrac{3}{5}$.

36. When faced with a system of equations in which none of the coefficients match up nicely, we must multiply one of the equations by an appropriately chosen constant before adding or subtracting. Since there are many correct ways to do this, it is worth taking a few seconds to determine which option will result in the easiest numbers.

For the problem at hand, multiplying the first equation by 3 will both cancel out the fractional coefficient of r and (more importantly) change the coefficient of s to $(-1/2)$, which will cancel with the $+(1/2)$ s in the second equation:

$$r - \dfrac{1}{2}s = 0$$
$$\underline{+(2r + \dfrac{1}{2}s = 3)}$$
$$3r = 3$$

We then plug $r = 1$ into the second equation to get:

$$2(1) + \dfrac{1}{2}s - 3 = 0$$
$$\dfrac{1}{2}s = 1$$
$$s = 2$$

Therefore $r = 1$ and $s = 2$.

Drill 6

37. When one of the two equations is already solved for one of the variables, substitution is almost always the better method. In this particular problem, the second equation is solved for y, so we take the right-hand side of this equation and substitute it for y in the first equation:

$$5x + 2\left(\frac{1}{2}x + 3\right) = 12$$
$$5x + x + 6 = 12$$
$$6x = 6$$

Therefore $x = 1$. We can now plug this value for x in to either of the original equations to solve for y, but it will be easiest to plug in to the equation that was used for the substitution (after all, it is already solved for y). Hence $y = (1/2) \times (1) + 3 = 3.5$.

Answer: $x = 1$, $y = 3.5$

38. For this system of equations, either method would be appropriate. Both equations would require some manipulation before we could simply stack-and-add and neither equation is already solved for one of its variables. When neither method seems to have an advantage, pick whichever you like best.

If we use substitution, it is best to solve the first equation for y, giving us $y = x + 3$, and then substitute this into the second equation:

$$2(x + 3) = x + 1$$
$$2x + 6 = x + 1$$
$$x = -5$$

We then plug this into the equation used for the substitution step to get $y = (-5) + 3 = -2$.

Answer: $x = -5$, $y = -2$

39. Even though some manipulations will be required to line up the variables nicely in this system, stack-and-add is the optimal method because the $+r$ in the first equation will cancel the $-r$ in the second. Rearranging the two equations yields:

$$r + 2s = 1$$
$$-r + s = -2$$

We then add them together:

$$
\begin{array}{r}
r + 2s = 1 \\
+(-r + s = -2) \\
\hline
3s = -1
\end{array}
$$

Therefore $s = -1/3$ and $r + 2(-1/3) = 1$, so $r = 1 + \dfrac{2}{3} = \dfrac{5}{3}$.

Answer: $s = -1/3$, $r = 5/3$

40. For this system of equations, either method would be appropriate. Both equations would require some manipulation before we could simply stack-and-add and neither equation is already solved for one of its variables. When neither method seems to have an advantage, pick whichever you like best.

To solve this system of equations by substitution, we isolate y in the first equation, which gives us $y = 6 - 3x$, and then substitute this for y in the second equation:

$$6x - (6 - 3x) = 3$$
$$6x - 6 + 3x = 3$$
$$9x = 9$$

We then plug $x = 1$ into the equation used for the substitution step, so $y = 6 - 3(1) = 3$.

To solve using the stack-and-add method, we rearrange the first equation to get $3x + y = 6$ and then add the equations together to eliminate y:

$$3x + y = 6$$
$$\underline{+(6x - y = 3)}$$
$$9x = 9$$

This time, we can plug $x = 1$ into the first equation to get $3(1) + y = 6$, which simplifies to $y = 3$.

Answer: $x = 1$, $y = 3$

41. Even though the first equation is solved for x, we should always look for terms that might cancel out easily when we stack-and-add. Notice that the first equation has $+x$ on the left side while the second equation has $-x$. Therefore, with a few quick manipulations we could eliminate the x by adding the two equations together. (Note: either method would work here, though).

To solve using the stack-and-add method, we rearrange the first equation to get $x - 2y = -1/2$ and then add the equations together to eliminate the x:

$$x - 2y = -\frac{1}{2}$$
$$\underline{+(-x + y = -\frac{3}{2})}$$
$$-y = -2$$

Therefore $y = 2$ and we plug this into the second equation to get $-x + (2) = -3/2$, which simplifies to $-x = -1.5 - 2$. That means $-x = -3.5$, so $x = 3.5$.

Answer: $x = 3.5$, $y = 2$

MANHATTAN
GMAT

To solve by substitution, we take the first equation, which is already solved for *x*, and substitute into the second equation:

$$y - \left(2y - \frac{1}{2}\right) = -\frac{3}{2}$$

$$y - 2y + \frac{1}{2} = -\frac{3}{2}$$

$$-y = -\frac{3}{2} + \frac{1}{2}$$

This simplifies to $-y = -2$, or $y = 2$, which we then plug into the first equation to get $x = 2(2) - 1/2 = 3.5$.

Answer: $x = 3.5$, $y = 2$

Drill 7

42. This question contains only two equations, but three variables. To isolate *y*, we need to get rid of both *x* and *z*. The only way to eliminate two variables at the same time is with elimination. Notice that the coefficients of *x* and *z* are the same in both equations. We can subtract the second equation from the first to eliminate *x* and *z*.

$$\begin{array}{r} 4x + y + 3z = 34 \\ -(4x + 3z = 21) \\ \hline y = 13 \end{array}$$

43. In order to find the value of *m* in terms of *n* and *p*, we need to isolate *m* on one side of the equation. Begin by getting rid of the fraction on the right side of the equation.

$$2p = \frac{m-5}{n+2}$$

$$2p(n+2) = m-5$$

$$2np + 4p = m-5$$

$$2np + 4p + 5 = m$$

We have isolated *m* on one side of the equation.
$m = 2np + 4p + 5$

44. In order to isolate *y*, we need to eliminate both *x* and *z*. Because we only have two equations, we have to find a way to eliminate both *x* and *z* at the same time. Elimination is our only option.

Notice that the coefficients for *x* and *z* in the second equation (6 and 4, respectively) are exactly double their coefficients in equation 1 (3 and 2, respectively). If we divide the second equation by 2, the coefficients will be the same.

$3x + 5y + 2z = 20$ → $3x + 5y + 2z = 20$

$6x + 4z = 10$ → $3x + 2z = 5$

Now we can subtract the second equation from the first.

$$3x + 5y + 2z = 20$$
$$\underline{-(3x + 2z = 5)}$$
$$5y = 15$$
$$y = 3$$

45. To solve for b in terms of a, we need to isolate b on one side of an equation. Furthermore, we need to eliminate the variable c, because the question does not mention c. The second equation is already solved for c. If we replace (c) in the first equation with ($b + 2$), then the first equation will only contain a and b.

$$\frac{a - b}{4} = c + 1$$

$$\frac{a - b}{4} = (b + 2) + 1$$

Now isolate b on one side of the equation.

$$\frac{a - b}{4} = b + 3$$
$$a - b = 4(b + 3)$$
$$a - b = 4b + 12$$
$$a - 12 = 5b$$
$$\frac{a - 12}{5} = b$$

Drill 8

46. In order to find the value of $a + b$, we need to eliminate c and d from the first equation. More specifically, we need to find a way to eliminate ($c + d$). That means that we need to find a way to manipulate the second equation so that it gives us a value for ($c + d$). Start by isolating c and d on the same side of the equation.

$3d = 15 - 3c$

$3c + 3d = 15$

If we divide by 3, then we will have $c + d$ on the left side of the equation.

$3c + 3d = 15$

$c + d = 5$

Now we can replace $(c + d)$ with (5) in the first equation, and isolate $a + b$.

$$\frac{(a+b)}{(c+d)} = 10$$
$$\frac{(a+b)}{(5)} = 10$$
$$a + b = 50$$

The sum $a + b = 50$.

47. In order to solve for z in terms of x, we need to isolate z on one side of an equation that contains only the variable x on the other side of the equals sign. The second equation contains both z and x, but also contains y. We need to eliminate y from the second equation. Isolate y in the first equation.

$$x = \frac{y}{5}$$
$$5x = y$$

Now we can replace (y) in the second equation with $(5x)$.

$$2z - 1 = \frac{x + y}{2}$$
$$2z - 1 = \frac{x + (5x)}{2}$$

Now isolate z.

$$2z - 1 = \frac{x + (5x)}{2}$$
$$2z - 1 = \frac{6x}{2}$$
$$2z - 1 = 3x$$
$$2z = 3x + 1$$
$$z = \frac{3x + 1}{2}$$

48. In order to isolate z, we have to eliminate x and y from the first equation. In this case, we have to eliminate $(x + y)$ from the first equation. That means we have to isolate $(x + y)$ in the second equation.

$$x = 2 - y$$
$$x + y = 2$$

Now we can replace $(x + y)$ with (2) in the first equation and solve for z.

$$2^{x+y} = \sqrt{z-2}$$
$$2^{(2)} = \sqrt{z-2}$$
$$4 = \sqrt{z-2}$$
$$(4)^2 = (\sqrt{z-2})^2$$
$$16 = z-2$$
$$18 = z$$

49. To find the value of $j - 3h$, we need j and h in the same equation. Notice that the first equation contains j but not h, the second equation contains h but not j, and both equations contain k. If we can get j or h in terms of k, then we can replace k in one of the equations.

We can begin simplifying both equations by getting rid of fractions.

$$\frac{2j}{3k+1} = 3 \qquad\qquad \frac{k}{2} = \frac{h}{3}$$
$$2j = 3(3k+1) \qquad\qquad 3k = 2h$$

Notice that we have $3k$ in both equations. Replace $(3k)$ in the first equation with $(2h)$.

$$2j = 3(3k + 1)$$
$$2j = 3((2h) + 1)$$

$$2j = 6h + 3$$

We're looking for the value of $j - 3h$, so isolate j and h on one side of the equation.

$$2j = 6h + 3$$
$$2j - 6h = 3$$

Notice that $(2j - 6h)$ is exactly twice $(j - 3h)$. Divide the equation by 2.

$$2j - 6h = 3$$
$$j - 3h = 3/2$$

Chapter 7
of
Foundations of GMAT Math

Quadratic Equations

In This Chapter...

Mechanics of Quadratic Equations

Distribute $(a + b)(x + y)$ ➤ Use FOIL

Factor $x^2 + 5x + 6$ ➤ Guess the Original Numbers in $(x + ...)(x + ...)$

Solve a Quadratic Equation: Set Quadratic Expression Equal to 0, Factor, Then Set Factors to 0

Solve a Quadratic Equation with No x Term: Take Positive and Negative Square Roots

Solve a Quadratic Equation with Squared Parentheses: Take Positive and Negative Square Roots

Higher Powers: Solve Like A Normal Quadratic

See a Special Product: Convert to the Other Form

Chapter 7:
Quadratic Equations

In This Chapter:

• Manipulating quadratic expressions and solving quadratic equations

Mechanics of Quadratic Equations

In high school algebra, you learned a number of skills for dealing with quadratic equations. For the GMAT, you need to relearn those skills.

Let's define terms first. A **quadratic expression** contains a squared variable, such as x^2, and no higher power. The word "quadratic" comes from the Latin word for "square." Here are a few quadratic expressions:

$$z^2 \qquad\qquad y^2 + y - 6 \qquad\qquad x^2 + 8x + 16 \qquad\qquad w^2 - 9$$

A quadratic expression can also be disguised. You might not see the squared exponent on the variable explicitly. Here are some disguised quadratic expressions.

$$z \times z \qquad\qquad (y+3)(y-2) \qquad\qquad (x+4)^2 \qquad\qquad (w-3)(w+3)$$

If you multiply these expressions out—that is, if you **distribute** them—then you see the exponents on the variables. Note that the second list corresponds to the first list exactly.

A **quadratic equation** contains a quadratic expression and an equals sign.

Quadratic expression = something else

A quadratic equation usually has two solutions. That is, in most cases, *two* different values of the variable each make the equation true. Solving a quadratic equation means finding those values.

Before you can solve quadratic equations, you have to be able to distribute and factor quadratic expressions.

Distribute $(a + b)(x + y)$ ➤ Use FOIL

Recall that distributing means applying multiplication across a sum.

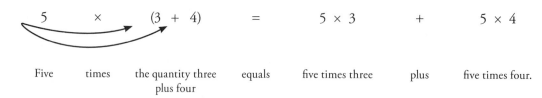

Five	times	the quantity three plus four	equals	five times three	plus	five times four.

You can omit the multiplication sign next to parentheses. Also, the order of the product doesn't matter, and subtraction works the same way as addition. Here are more examples:

$$3(x + 2) = 3x + 6 \qquad (z - 12)y = zy - 12y \qquad w(a + b) = wa + wb$$

What if you have to distribute the product of two sums?

$$(a + b)(x + y) =$$

The process is straightforward. **Multiply every term in the first sum by every term in the second sum, then add all the products up.** This is just distribution on steroids.

To make the products, use the acronym **FOIL**: **F**irst, **O**uter, **I**nner, **L**ast (or **F**irst, **O**utside, **I**nside, **L**ast).

$(\boldsymbol{a} + b)(\boldsymbol{x} + y)$ F – multiply the First term in each of the parentheses: $a \times x = ax$
$(\boldsymbol{a} + b)(x + \boldsymbol{y})$ O – multiply the Outer term in each: $a \times y = ay$
$(a + \boldsymbol{b})(\boldsymbol{x} + y)$ I – multiply the Inner term in each: $b \times x = bx$
$(a + \boldsymbol{b})(x + \boldsymbol{y})$ L – multiply the Last terms in each: $b \times y = by$

Now add up the products:

$$(a + b)(x + y) = ax + ay + bx + by$$

By the way, you can even FOIL numbers.

What is 102×301?

If you express 102 as $100 + 2$ and 301 as $300 + 1$, you can rewrite the question as a product of two sums:

What is $(100 + 2)(300 + 1)$?

Now FOIL it out.

$$(100 + 2)(300 + 1) \qquad = 100 \times 300 + 100 \times 1 + 2 \times 300 + 2 \times 1$$
$$= 30{,}000 + 100 + 600 + 2$$
$$= 30{,}702$$

You get the same answer if you multiply these numbers in longhand. In fact, longhand multiplication is just distribution. You're essentially FOILing as you multiply the digits and adding up the results.

$$\begin{array}{r} 102 \\ \times\, 301 \\ \hline 102 \\ 30{,}600 \\ \hline 30{,}702 \end{array}$$

Now try to FOIL this disguised quadratic expression: $(x + 2)(x + 3)$.

$(\boldsymbol{x} + 2)(\boldsymbol{x} + 3)$ F – multiply the First term in each of the parentheses: $x \times x = x^2$
$(\boldsymbol{x} + 2)(x + \boldsymbol{3})$ O – multiply the Outer term in each: $x \times 3 = 3x$
$(x + \boldsymbol{2})(\boldsymbol{x} + 3)$ I – multiply the Inner term in each: $2 \times x = 2x$
$(x + \boldsymbol{2})(x + \boldsymbol{3})$ L – multiply the Last terms in each: $2 \times 3 = 6$

Add up the products.

$$(x + 2)(x + 3) = x^2 + 3x + 2x + 6$$

Notice that you can combine the like terms in the middle ($3x$ and $2x$).

$$(x + 2)(x + 3) = x^2 + 3x + 2x + 6 = x^2 + 5x + 6$$

Now compare the expression you started with and the expression you ended up with.

$$(x + 2)(x + 3) \qquad\qquad x^2 + 5x + 6$$

Study how the numbers on the left relate to the numbers on the right.

> The 2 and the 3 *multiply* to give you the 6.
> The 2 and the 3 *add* to give you the 5 in $5x$.

What if you have subtraction? Just attach the minus signs to the numbers themselves. Then multiply according to the rules of arithmetic and add the products. Try this example:

$$(y - 5)(y - 2) =$$

First, FOIL. Keep track of minus signs. Put them in the products.

$(y - 5)(y - 2):$ F – multiply First terms $(y)(y) = y^2$

$(y-5)(y-2)$:	O – multiply Outer terms	$(y)(-2) = -2y$
$(y-5)(y-2)$:	I – multiply Inner terms	$(-5)(y) = -5y$
$(y-5)(y-2)$:	L – multiply Last terms	$(-5)(-2) = 10$

Finally, add the products and combine like terms.

$$(y-5)(y-2) = y^2 - 2y - 5y + 10 = y^2 - 7y + 10$$

Again, study how the numbers on the left relate to the numbers on the right.

The -5 and the -2 *multiply* to give you the positive 10.
The -5 and the -2 *add* to give you the -7 in $-7y$.

Here's one last wrinkle. In the course of doing these problems, you might encounter a sum written as $4 + z$ rather than as $z + 4$. You can FOIL it as is, or you can flip the sum around so that the variable is first. Either way works fine.

If you...	Then you...	Like this:
Want to distribute $(x+5)(x-4)$	FOIL it out and combine like terms (which will be the x terms)	$(x+5)(x-4)$ $= x^2 - 4x + 5x - 20$ $= x^2 + x - 20$

Check Your Skills

FOIL the following expressions:

1. $(x+4)(x+9)$
2. $(y+3)(y-6)$

Answers can be found on page 327.

Factor $x^2 + 5x + 6$ ➤ Guess the Original Numbers in $(x + ...)(x + ...)$

FOILing is a form of distribution. So going in reverse is a form of **factoring**. To factor a quadratic expression such as $x^2 + 5x + 6$ means to **rewrite the expression as a product of two sums**:

$$x^2 + 5x + 6 = (x + ...)(x + ...)$$

The form on the right is called the **factored** form. (You can call $x^2 + 5x + 6$ the distributed form.)

You already know the answer, because earlier you turned $(x + 2)(x + 3)$ into $x^2 + 5x + 6$.

$$(x + \mathbf{2})(x + \mathbf{3}) = x^2 + 3x + 2x + 6 = x^2 + \mathbf{5}x + \mathbf{6}$$

Consider the relationship between the numbers one more time.

$2 + 3 = 5$, the coefficient of the x term $2 \times 3 = 6$, the "constant" term on the end

This is true in general. The two numbers in the factored form **add to the x coefficient**, and they **multiply to the constant**.

Now think about how to work *backwards*:

$x^2 + \mathbf{5}x + \mathbf{6} = (x + \ldots)(x + \ldots)$

You need two numbers that multiply together to 6 and add to 5.

Look first for factor pairs of the constant—in this case, two numbers that multiply to 6. Then check the sum.

2 and 3 are a factor pair of 6, because $2 \times 3 = 6$.

2 and 3 also add to 5, so you're done.

$x^2 + \mathbf{5}x + \mathbf{6} = (x + \mathbf{2})(x + \mathbf{3})$

Try this slightly different example:

$y^2 + \mathbf{7}y + \mathbf{6} = (y + \ldots)(y + \ldots)$

The constant is the same: 6. So you need a factor pair of 6. But now the pair has to add up to 7.

2 and 3 no longer work. But 1 and 6 are also a factor pair of 6. So you factor $y^2 + 7y + 6$ like this:

$y^2 + \mathbf{7}y + 6 = (y + 1)(y + 6)$

Now try to factor this quadratic:

$z^2 + 7z + 12 = (z + \ldots)(z + \ldots)$

Again, start with the constant. Look for a factor pair of 12 that adds up to 7.

The only factor pair of 12 that adds up to 7 is 3 and 4.

$3 \times 4 = 12$ $3 + 4 = 7$

$z^2 + 7z + \mathbf{12} = (z + \mathbf{3})(z + \mathbf{4})$

What if you have subtraction? The same principles hold. Just think of the minus signs as part of the numbers themselves.

$x^2 - \mathbf{9}x + \mathbf{18} = (x + \ldots)(x + \ldots)$

You still need two numbers that multiply to 18, but now they have to add up to –9.

This means that both numbers must be negative.   Neg × Neg = Pos   Neg + Neg = Neg

To find these numbers, ignore the negative signs for a moment. Consider the normal, positive factor pairs of 18. Which pair adds up to 9?

The answer is 3 and 6. $3 \times 6 = 18$ $3 + 6 = 9$

So this same pair, **made negative**, fits the bill. $(-3) \times (-6) = 18$ $(-3) + (-6) = -9$

Now write the factored form of the quadratic expression:

$$x^2 - 9x + 18 = (x - 3)(x - 6)$$

If the constant is positive, then the two numbers in the factored form must both be positive or both be negative, depending on the sign of the x term.

$$z^2 + 7z + 12 = (z + 3)(z + 4) \qquad\qquad x^2 - 9x + 18 = (x - 3)(x - 6)$$
pos   pos   both positive   neg   pos   both negative

What if the constant is being subtracted? Again, **think of the minus sign as part of the number**. Try this example:

$$w^2 + 3w - 10 = (w + \ldots)(w + \ldots)$$

You need two numbers that multiply to negative 10 and that add up to 3.

For the product to be –10, one number must be positive and the other one must be negative. That's the only way to get a negative product of two numbers.

Pos × Neg = Neg

If the constant is negative, then one number in the factored form is positive, and the other one is negative.

This means that you are adding a positive and a negative to get 3.

Pos + Neg = 3

Here's a straightforward way to find the two numbers you want. First, pretend that the constant is positive. Think of the normal, positive factor pairs of 10. Which pair *differs* by 3?

The answer is 5 and 2. $5 \times 2 = 10$ $5 - 2 = 3$

Now make *one* of those numbers negative, so that the product is now –10 and the sum is now 3.

The answer is 5 and –2. $5 \times (-2) = -10$ $5 + (-2) = 3$

Notice that –5 and 2 would give you the correct product (–10) but the incorrect sum (–5 + 2 = –3).

Now you know where to place the signs in the factored form. Place the minus sign with the 2.

$$w^2 + 3w - 10 = (w + 5)(w - 2)$$

When the constant is negative, test factor pairs by pretending the constant is positive and asking which pair *differs* by the right amount.

Once you find a good factor pair for the constant (say 5 and 2), then make one number negative so that the product is correctly negative and the sum comes out right.

Consider this example:

$$y^2 - 4y - 21 = (y + \dots)(y + \dots)$$

You need two numbers that multiply to *negative* 21 and that add up to *negative* 4.

Again, one number must be positive, while the other is negative.

Temporarily pretend that the constant is positive 21. What factor pair of 21 differs by 4? You can ignore the sign on the –4 for a moment here as well.

Testing factor pairs, you quickly find that only 7 and 3 work. $7 \times 3 = 21$ $7 - 3 = 4$

Now you need to make one number negative, so that the product is now –21 and the *sum* is now –4.

Since the sum is negative, you need to make the 7 negative, since 7 is larger than 3.

$$(-7) \times 3 = -21 \quad (-7) + 3 = -4$$

Write the factored form:

$$y^2 - 4y - 21 = (y - 7)(y + 3)$$

Finally, the GMAT can make factoring a quadratic expression harder in a couple of ways.

(1) Every term in the expression is multiplied through by a common numerical factor, including the x^2 term.

$$3x^2 + 21x + 36 = \dots$$

In this case, **pull out the common factor first**. Put parentheses around what's left. Then factor the quadratic expression as usual.

$$3x^2 + 21x + 36 = \qquad 3(x^2 + 7x + 12) = 3(x + 3)(x + 4)$$

If the x^2 term is negative, factor out a common factor of –1 first. That will flip the sign on every term.

$$-x^2 + 9x - 18 = \dots$$

Pull out the –1, which just becomes a minus sign outside a set of parentheses. Then factor the quadratic expression as usual.

$$-x^2 + 9x - 18 = -(x^2 - 9x + 18) = -(x - 3)(x - 6)$$

Avoid fractional coefficients at all costs. If you cannot pull out a common factor from the x^2 term without turning coefficients into fractions, then you will need to keep a coefficient on one or even both x's in your factored form. At this point, **experiment with factor pairs of the constant** until you get a match.

$$2z^2 - z - 15 = \dots$$

Don't factor a 2 out of all the terms. Rather, set up the parentheses on the right. Put a $2z$ in one set.

$$2z^2 - z - 15 = (2z + \dots)(z + \dots)$$

At least you've got the F of FOIL covered.

What you already know how to do is still useful. Since the constant is negative (–15), one of the numbers must be negative, while the other must be positive.

Pretend for a minute that the constant is positive 15. You still need a factor pair of 15. There are only 2 factor pairs of 15:

$$1 \times 15 = 15 \qquad 3 \times 5 = 15$$

But which pair do you want? Which number becomes negative? And where does that one go—with the $2z$ or the z?

The middle term is your guide. The coefficient on the z term is only –1, so it's very unlikely that the "1 and 15" factor pair will work. The numbers must be 3 and 5, with a minus sign on exactly one of them. This covers the L of FOIL.

Finally, experiment. Try the numbers in different configurations. Examine only the OI of FOIL (Outer and Inner) to see whether you get the right middle term.

$$2z^2 - z - 15 = (2z + \dots)(z + \dots) = (2z + 3)(z - 5)? \quad \textit{FOIL} \longrightarrow (2z)(-5) + 3z \text{ does not equal } -z$$

Learn after each attempt. You probably want the 5 to multiply the z and the 3 to multiply the $2z$.

$2z^2 - z - 15 = (2z + \dots)(z + \dots) = (2z - 5)(z + 3)?$ $FOIL \longrightarrow (2z)(3) - 5z$ equals z, not $-z$

Switch the signs.

$2z^2 - z - 15 = (2z + \dots)(z + \dots) = (2z + 5)(z - 3)?$ $FOIL \longrightarrow (2z)(-3) + 5z$ equals $-z$ YES

So $2z^2 - z - 15$ factors into $(2z + 5)(z - 3)$. You can always check your work by FOILing the result:

$(2z + 5)(z - 3) = 2z^2 - 6z + 5z - 15 = 2z^2 - z - 15$

This example reinforces our last word of advice: **if you're ever in doubt, just FOIL it back out!**

If you…	Then you…	Like this:
Want to factor $x^2 + 11x + 18$	Find a factor pair of 18 that sums to 11	$x^2 + 11x + 18$ $= (x + 9)(x + 2)$ $9 + 2 = 11$ $9 \times 2 = 18$
Want to factor $x^2 - 8x + 12$	Find a factor pair of 12 that sums to 8, then make both numbers negative	$x^2 - 8x + 12$ $= (x - 6)(x - 2)$ $(-6) + (-2) = -8$ $(-6) \times (-2) = 12$
Want to factor $x^2 + 6x - 16$	Find a factor pair of 16 that *differs* by 6, then make the smaller number negative so that the sum is 6 and the product is -16	$x^2 + 6x - 16$ $= (x + 8)(x - 2)$ $8 + (-2) = 6$ $8 \times (-2) = -16$
Want to factor $x^2 - 5x - 14$	Find a factor pair of 14 that *differs* by 5, then make the bigger number negative so that the sum is -5 and the product is -14	$x^2 - 5x - 14$ $= (x - 7)(x + 2)$ $(-7) + 2 = -5$ $(-7) \times 2 = -14$
Want to factor $-2x^2 + 16x - 24$	Factor out -2 from all terms first, then factor the quadratic expression normally	$-2x^2 + 16x - 24$ $= -2(x^2 - 8x + 12)$ $= -2(x - 6)(x - 2)$

Check Your Skills

Factor the following expressions:

3. $x^2 + 14x + 33$
4. $x^2 - 14x + 45$
5. $x^2 + 3x - 18$
6. $x^2 - 5x - 66$

Answers can be found on page 327.

Solve a Quadratic Equation: Set Quadratic Expression Equal to 0, Factor, Then Set Factors to 0

So far, you've dealt with quadratic expressions—distributing them and factoring them.

Now, how do you solve quadratic *equations*?

If $x^2 + x = 6$, what are the possible values of x?

Notice that you are asked for *possible* values of x. Usually, two different values of x will make a quadratic equation true. In other words, you should expect the equation to have two solutions.

The best way to solve most quadratic equations involves a particular property of the number 0.

If $ab = 0$, then either $a = 0$ or $b = 0$ (or both, potentially).

In words, if the product of two numbers is zero, then you know that at least one of the numbers is zero.

This is true no matter how complicated the factors.

If $(a + 27)(b - 12) = 0$, then either $a + 27 = 0$ or $b - 12 = 0$ (or both).

If the quantity $a + 27$ times the quantity $b - 12$ equals 0, then at least one of those quantities must be zero.

This gives you a pathway to solve quadratic equations.

1) Rearrange the equation to make one side equal 0. The other side will contain a quadratic expression.
2) Factor the quadratic expression. The equation will look like this: (Something)(Something else) = 0.
3) Set each factor equal to 0.
   Something = 0   or   Something else = 0

These two equations will be much easier to solve. Each one will give you a possible solution for the original equation.

Try this with the problem above. First, rearrange the equation to make one side equal 0.

$$
\begin{aligned}
x^2 + x &= 6 \\
-6 &\ -6 \\
\hline
x^2 + x - 6 &= 0
\end{aligned}
$$

Next, factor the quadratic expression on the left side.

$$x^2 + x - 6 = 0$$
$$(x+3)(x-2) = 0$$

Finally, set each factor (the quantities in parentheses) equal to 0, and solve for x in each case.

$$x + 3 = 0 \qquad\qquad x - 2 = 0$$
$$\text{or}$$
$$x = -3 \qquad\qquad x = 2$$

Now you have the two possible values of x, which are the two solutions to the original equation:

$$x^2 + x = 6 \qquad x \text{ could be } -3 \qquad (-3)^2 + (-3) = 6$$
$$\text{or } x \text{ could be } 2 \qquad 2^2 + 2 = 6$$

By the way, the two equations you get at the end can't both be true at the same time. What $x^2 + x = 6$ tells you is that x must equal either –3 or 2. The value of x is one or the other; it's not both simultaneously. The variable has multiple *possible* values.

The solutions of a quadratic equation are also called its **roots**.

If an additional condition is placed on the variable, you can often narrow down to one solution. Try this example:

If $y < 0$ and $y^2 = y + 30$, what is the value of y?

First, solve the quadratic equation. Rearrange it so that one side equals 0.

$$y^2 \qquad\quad = \quad y + 30$$
$$\underline{-y - 30 \quad -y - 30}$$
$$y^2 - y - 30 = \ 0$$

Next, factor the quadratic expression.

$$y^2 - y - 30 = 0$$
$$(y-6)(y+5) = 0$$

Set each factor equal to zero.

$$y - 6 = 0 \qquad\qquad y + 5 = 0$$
$$\text{or}$$
$$y = 6 \qquad\qquad y = -5$$

At this point, you can definitively say that y is either 6 or –5. Go back to the question, which gives the additional condition that $y < 0$. Since y is negative, y cannot be 6. Thus, the answer to the question is –5. The quadratic equation gave you two possibilities, but only one of them fit the other constraint.

Occasionally, a quadratic equation has only one solution on its own.

If $w^2 - 8w + 16 = 0$, what is the value of w?

The quadratic equation already has one side equal to 0, so go ahead and factor the quadratic expression:

$$w^2 - 8w + 16 = 0$$
$$(w-4)(w-4) = 0$$

The two factors in parentheses happen to be identical. So you don't get two separate equations and two separate roots.

$$w - 4 = 0 \qquad \text{so} \qquad w = 4 \qquad \text{The only solution is 4.}$$

Lastly, **never factor before you set one side equal to 0**.

If z is positive and $z^2 + z - 6 = 6$, what is the value of z?

You might be tempted to factor the left side right away. Avoid that temptation. Instead, rearrange to make the right side zero first.

$$\begin{aligned} z^2 + z - 6 &= 6 \\ -6 \quad &-6 \\ \hline z^2 + z - 12 &= 0 \end{aligned}$$

Now you should factor the left side.

$$z^2 + z - 12 = 0$$
$$(z+4)(z-3) = 0$$

Finally, set each factor equal to 0 and solve for z.

$$z + 4 = 0 \qquad \text{or} \qquad z - 3 = 0$$

Thus, z equals either -4 or 3. Since you are told that z is positive, z must be 3.

It's legal to factor a quadratic expression whenever you want to. But if you factor the expression *before* setting one side equal to zero, your factors don't tell you anything useful. You can't set them individually to zero.

When you solve a quadratic equation, always set one side equal to zero before you factor.

If you...	Then you...	Like this:
Want to solve $x^2 + 11x = -18$	Rearrange to make one side 0, factor the quadratic side, then set the factors equal to 0	$x^2 + 11x = -18$ $x^2 + 11x + 18 = 0$ $(x + 9)(x + 2) = 0$ $x + 9 = 0$ or $x + 2 = 0$ $x = -9$ or $x = -2$

Check Your Skills

Solve the following quadratic equations.

7. $x^2 + 2x - 35 = 0$
8. $x^2 - 15x = -26$

Answers can be found on pages 327–328.

Solve a Quadratic Equation with No *x* Term: Take Positive and Negative Square Roots

Occasionally you encounter a quadratic equation with no *x* term.

> If *x* is negative and $x^2 = 9$, what is *x*?

Here's the fast way to solve. **Take positive and negative square roots**.

$$x^2 = 9 \quad \longrightarrow \quad \sqrt{x^2} = \sqrt{9} \quad \longrightarrow \quad x = 3 \text{ OR } -3$$

Since you are told that *x* is negative, the answer to the question is –3.

You can also solve this problem using the method of the previous section. Although the method is longer in this case, it's worth seeing how it works.

1) Rearrange the equation to make one side zero.

$$x^2 = 9 \quad \longrightarrow \quad x^2 - 9 = 0$$

2) Factor the quadratic expression. The strange thing is that there is no *x* term, but you can imagine that it has a coefficient of 0:

$$x^2 - 9 = 0 \quad \longrightarrow \quad x^2 + 0x - 9 = 0$$

Because the constant (–9) is negative, you look for a factor pair of 9 that *differs* by 0. In other words, you need 3 and 3. Make one of these numbers negative to fit the equation as given:

$$x^2 + 0x - 9 = 0$$
$$(x + 3)(x - 3) = 0$$

You can FOIL the result back out to see how the x terms cancel in the middle:

$$(x + 3)(x - 3) = x^2 - 3x + 3x - 9 = x^2 - 9$$

3) Finally, set each of the factors in parentheses equal to zero, and solve for x.

$$x + 3 = 0 \quad \text{or} \quad x - 3 = 0$$

Thus, x equals either -3 or 3. Again, the question tells you that x is negative, so you choose the negative root.

Obviously, the second method is overkill in this case. However, you should be able to carry out the steps in a pinch. More importantly, you should be able to factor $x^2 - 9$ into $(x + 3)(x - 3)$. We'll come back to that point later in this chapter.

If you...	Then you...	Like this:
Want to solve $x^2 = 25$	Take the positive and negative square roots of both sides	$x^2 = 25$ $\sqrt{x^2} = \sqrt{25}$ $x = 5$ or $x = -5$

Check Your Skills

9. If $x^2 - 3 = 1$, what are all the possible values of x?

Answers can be found on page 328.

Solve a Quadratic Equation with Squared Parentheses: Take Positive and Negative Square Roots

Try this example:

If $(y + 1)^2 = 16$, what are the possible values of y?

You can do this problem in either of two ways.

One way is to treat $y + 1$ as if it were a new variable z. In other words, $z = y + 1$.

Solve $z^2 = 16$ by taking positive and negative square roots.

$$(y + 1)^2 = 16 \quad \longrightarrow \quad z^2 = 16 \quad \longrightarrow \quad z = 4 \text{ or } z = -4$$

Go back to y.

$$(y + 1)^2 = 16 \quad\rightarrow\quad z^2 = 16 \quad\rightarrow\quad z = 4 \text{ or } z = -4 \quad\rightarrow\quad y + 1 = 4 \text{ or } y + 1 = -4$$

In fact, you didn't need z. You could have just taken the positive and negative square roots right away.

$$(y + 1)^2 = 16 \quad\rightarrow\quad y + 1 = 4 \text{ or } y + 1 = -4$$

Finally, solve the simpler equations for y. You get $y = 3$ or $y = -5$.

The alternative approach to this problem is to expand $(y + 1)^2$ into $(y + 1)(y + 1)$. FOIL this product out.

$$(y + 1)(y + 1) = y^2 + y + y + 1 = y^2 + 2y + 1$$

Now solve the quadratic equation normally: set one side equal to zero and factor.

$$y^2 + 2y + 1 = 16 \quad\rightarrow\quad y^2 + 2y - 15 = 0 \quad\rightarrow\quad (y + 5)(y - 3) = 0 \quad\rightarrow\quad y = -5 \text{ or } 3$$

Which way is faster depends on the numbers involved. With big numbers, the first way is easier.

If you…	Then you…	Like this:
Want to solve $(z - 7)^2 = 625$	Take the positive and negative square roots of both sides	$(z - 7)^2 = 625$ $\sqrt{(z - 7)^2} = \sqrt{625}$ $z - 7 = 25 \text{ or } z - 7 = -25$ $z = 32 \text{ or } z = -18$

Check Your Skills

10. If $(z + 2)^2 = 225$, what are the possible values of z?

Answers can be found on page 328.

Higher Powers: Solve Like A Normal Quadratic

If you have a higher power of x in the equation, look for solutions as if the equation were a typical quadratic: set one side equal to zero, factor as much as you can, then set factors equal to zero.

$$x^3 = 3x^2 - 2x$$

What is the product of all the roots of the equation above?

(A) −2   (B) −1   (C) 0   (D) 1   (E) 2

Recall that a "root" of an equation is a solution—a value for the variable that makes the equation true.

First, set one side of the equation equal to zero.

$$x^3 = 3x^2 - 2x$$
$$\underline{-3x^2 + 2x \qquad -3x^2 + 2x}$$
$$x^3 - 3x^2 + 2x = 0$$

You may notice that every term on the left contains an x. That means that x is a common factor. You might be tempted to divide both sides by x to eliminate that factor.

Resist that temptation. **Never divide an equation by x unless you know for sure that x is not zero ($x \neq 0$).** You could be dividing by 0 without realizing it.

The problem doesn't tell you that $x \neq 0$. So, rather than divide away the x, simply pull it out to the left and keep it around.

$$x^3 - 3x^2 + 2x = 0$$
$$x\left(x^2 - 3x + 2\right) = 0$$

Now factor the quadratic expression in the parentheses normally and rewrite the equation.

$$x\left(x^2 - 3x + 2\right) = 0$$
$$x\left(x - 2\right)\left(x - 1\right) = 0$$

You have *three* factors on the left side: x, $(x - 2)$, and $(x - 1)$. So you can set each one of them to 0, and you get *three* solutions to the original equation.

$$x = 0 \qquad\qquad x - 2 = 0 \qquad\qquad x - 1 = 0$$
$$x = 2 \qquad\qquad\qquad x = 1$$

By the way, the presence of the x^3 term should alert you that there could be three solutions.

If you had divided away the x earlier, you would have missed the $x = 0$ solution. The question asks for the product of the roots, so the answer is $0 \times 2 \times 1 = 0$, or (C).

If you...	Then you...	Like this:
Want to solve $x^3 = x$	Solve like a normal quadratic: set the equation equal to zero, factor, and set factors equal to zero	$x^3 = x$ $x^3 - x = 0$ $x(x^2 - 1) = 0$ $x(x + 1)(x - 1) = 0$ $x = 0$ or $x + 1 = 0$ or $x - 1 = 0$ $x = 0$ or -1 or 1

Check Your Skills

11. What are all the possible solutions to the equation $x^3 - 2x^2 = 3x$?

Answers can be found on page 328.

Other Instances of Quadratics

You will come across quadratic expressions in various circumstances other than the ones already given. Fortunately, the skills of FOILing and factoring are still relevant as you try to simplify the problem.

See a Quadratic Expression in a Fraction: Factor and Cancel

Take a look at this problem:

If $x \neq -1$, then $\dfrac{x^2 - 2x - 3}{x + 1} =$

(A) $x + 1$ (B) $x + 3$ (C) $x - 3$

This question doesn't involve a typical quadratic equation. However, the numerator of the fraction is a quadratic. To simplify the fraction, **factor the quadratic expression**.

$x^2 - 2x - 3 = (x - 3)(x + 1)$

Now substitute the factored form back into the fraction.

$$\frac{x^2 - 2x - 3}{x + 1} = \frac{(x - 3)(x + 1)}{x + 1}$$

Finally, you can cancel a common factor from top and bottom of the fraction. The common factor is the entire quantity $x + 1$. Since that is the denominator, you cancel the whole thing out, and the fraction is gone.

$$\frac{x^2 - 2x - 3}{x + 1} = \frac{(x - 3)(x + 1)}{(x + 1)} = \frac{(x - 3)\,\cancel{(x + 1)}}{\cancel{(x + 1)}} = x - 3$$

The correct answer is (C).

As before, the constraint that $x \neq -1$ is mentioned only to prevent division by 0 in the fraction. You don't have to use this fact directly.

If you see a quadratic expression in a numerator or denominator, try factoring the expression. Then cancel common factors.

Common factors can be disguised, of course, even when you don't have quadratics.

$$\text{If } x \neq y, \text{ then } \frac{y-x}{x-y} =$$

(A) -1 (B) $x^2 - y^2$ (C) $y^2 - x^2$

The numerator $y - x$ may look different from the denominator $x - y$. However, these two expressions are actually identical except for a sign change throughout.

$$y - x = -(x - y) \qquad \text{because} \qquad -(x - y) = -x + y = y - x$$

In other words, these expressions only differ by a factor of -1. The GMAT loves this little disguise. **Expressions that only differ by a sign change are only different by a factor of -1.**

Rewrite the numerator:

$$\frac{y-x}{x-y} = \frac{-(x-y)}{x-y}$$

Now you can cancel $x - y$ from both top and bottom. You are left with -1 on top. So the whole fraction is equal to -1.

$$\frac{y-x}{x-y} = \frac{-(x-y)}{(x-y)} = \frac{-\cancel{(x-y)}}{\cancel{(x-y)}} = -1$$

The correct answer is (A).

Try this last example:

$$\text{If } y \neq -8, \text{ then } \frac{(y+7)^2 + y + 7}{y+8} =$$

(A) $y + 7$ (B) $y + 8$ (C) $2y + 14$

The long way to solve this is to expand $(y + 7)^2$, then add $y + 7$, then factor and cancel. This approach will work. Fortunately, there's a faster way.

Put parentheses around the last $y + 7$ on top of the fraction:

$$\frac{(y+7)^2 + y + 7}{y+8} = \frac{(y+7)^2 + (y+7)}{y+8}$$

This subtle change can help you see that you can factor the numerator. You can **pull out a common factor**—namely, $y + 7$—from both the $(y + 7)^2$ and from the $(y + 7)$.

When you pull out $(y + 7)$ from $(y + 7)^2$, you are left with $(y + 7)$.

When you pull out $(y + 7)$ from $(y + 7)$, you are left with 1.

$$\frac{(y+7)^2+(y+7)}{y+8}=\frac{(y+7)\big[(y+7)+1\big]}{y+8}$$

Since $y + 7 + 1 = y + 8$, you can simplify the second factor on top.

$$\frac{(y+7)^2+(y+7)}{y+8}=\frac{(y+7)\big[(y+7)+1\big]}{y+8}=\frac{(y+7)(y+8)}{y+8}$$

Finally, cancel the $y + 8$ quantity from top and bottom as a common factor of both.

$$\frac{(y+7)^2+(y+7)}{y+8}=\frac{(y+7)\big[(y+7)+1\big]}{y+8}=\frac{(y+7)(y+8)}{(y+8)}=\frac{(y+7)\,\cancel{(y+8)}}{\cancel{(y+8)}}=y+7$$

The correct answer is (A).

The recurring principle is this: look for ways to pull out common factors from complicated fractions and cancel them.

If you...	Then you...	Like this:
See a quadratic expression in a fraction	Factor the quadratic and cancel common factors	$\dfrac{z^2+5z+6}{z+3}=\dfrac{(z+2)(z+3)}{z+3}$ $=z+2$ (as long as $z \neq -3$)

Check Your Skills

Simplify the following fraction by factoring the quadratic expression.

12. If $x \neq -3$, $\dfrac{x^2+7x+12}{x+3}=$

Answers can be found on page 329.

See a Special Product: Convert to the Other Form

Three quadratic expressions are so important on the GMAT that we call them **special products**. Here they are:

$$(x + y)^2 = x^2 + 2xy + y^2 \qquad (x - y)^2 = x^2 - 2xy + y^2 \qquad (x + y)(x - y) = x^2 - y^2$$

Square of a sum   **Square of a difference**   **Difference of squares**

You should memorize these forms and learn to go both ways quickly: factoring or distributing. If you learn to recognize these templates, you'll save time.

The GMAT often disguises these forms using different variables, numbers, roots, and so on.

$$x^2 + 8x + 16 \qquad\qquad a^2 - 4ab + 4b^2 \qquad\qquad \left(1 + \sqrt{2}\right)\left(1 - \sqrt{2}\right)$$

Square of a sum   Square of a difference   Difference of squares

The first example can be factored normally.

$$x^2 + 8x + 16 = (x + 4)(x + 4) = (x + 4)^2$$

The test likes "square of a sum" (as well as "square of a difference") because they can create quadratic equations that have only one solution. For instance:

$$x^2 + 8x + 16 = 0$$
$$(x + 4)^2 = 0$$

This means that $x + 4 = 0$, or $x = -4$. The only number that makes $x^2 + 8x + 16 = 0$ true is -4.

The second example above, $a^2 - 4ab + 4b^2$, is tougher to factor. First, recognize that the first and last term are both perfect squares:

$$a^2 = \text{the square of } a \qquad\qquad 4b^2 = \text{the square of } 2b$$

This should give us a hint as to how to factor. Set up $(a - 2b)^2$, and FOIL it to check that it matches.

$$(a - 2b)^2 = (a - 2b)(a - 2b) = a^2 - 2ba - 2ba + 4b^2 = a^2 - 4ab + 4b^2$$

The third example above, $\left(1 + \sqrt{2}\right)\left(1 - \sqrt{2}\right)$, matches the factored form of the **difference of squares**, the most important of the three special products.

In distributed or expanded form, the difference of squares has no middle term. In the process of FOIL-ing, the Outer and the Inner terms cancel.

$$\left(1+\sqrt{2}\right)\left(1-\sqrt{2}\right)=1^2+\left(-\sqrt{2}\right)+\sqrt{2}+\sqrt{2}\left(-\sqrt{2}\right)$$
$$=1^2-\left(\sqrt{2}\right)^2$$
$$=1-2$$
$$=-1$$

It's not a coincidence that the middle terms cancel. If you multiply $x + y$ by $x - y$, the middle terms or **cross-terms** will be $-xy$ and $+xy$, which add up to 0 and drop out every time.

As a result, you shouldn't FOIL every time you multiply a sum of two things by the difference of those same two things. You'll waste time.

Rather, match up to the "difference of squares" template. Square the first thing, and subtract the square of the second thing. Try this problem:

$$\left(3+2\sqrt{3}\right)\left(3-2\sqrt{3}\right)=$$

The two things being added are 3 and $2\sqrt{3}$. Always make sure that the other expression in parentheses is the *difference* of the same exact terms. Since that's true, you can just square the 3, square the $2\sqrt{3}$ and subtract the second from the first.

$$\left(3+2\sqrt{3}\right)\left(3-2\sqrt{3}\right)=3^2-\left(2\sqrt{3}\right)^2$$
$$=9-(4)(3)$$
$$=9-12$$
$$=-3$$

Try this example going the other direction:

$16x^4 - 9y^2 =$

To treat this as a difference of squares, figure out what each term is the square of.

$16x^4 = (4x^2)^2 \qquad\qquad 9y^2 = (3y)^2$

So the first term of the difference ($16x^4$) is the square of $4x^2$, and the second term ($9y^2$) is the square of $3y$.

Take those square roots ($4x^2$ and $3y$) and place them in two sets of parentheses.

$16x^4 - 9y^2 = (4x^2 \quad 3y) (4x^2 \quad 3y)$

Put a + sign in one place and a − sign in the other.

$16x^4 - 9y^2 = (4x^2 + 3y) (4x^2 - 3y)$

Now you have factored a difference of squares.

A couple of sections ago, you saw $x^2 - 9 = 0$. You should now recognize the left side as the difference of squares and be able to factor it:

$$x^2 - 9 = (x + 3)(x - 3)$$

To match a special products template, you might have to rearrange an equation.

If $x^2 + y^2 = -2xy$, what is the sum of x and y?

You need to find $x + y$. Look at the equation. It doesn't match a special product, but it's close. Rearrange the equation:

$$\begin{array}{r} x^2 + y^2 = -2xy \\ + 2xy + 2xy \\ \hline x^2 + 2xy + y^2 = 0 \end{array}$$

The left side now matches the square of a sum.

$$x^2 + 2xy + y^2 = 0$$
$$\left(x + y\right)^2 = 0$$

The right side is also now equal to 0—a double benefit of the first move you made.

Since the square of $x + y$ equals 0, you know that $x + y$ itself must equal 0. That is the answer to the question.

If you...	Then you...	Like this:
See a special product	Consider converting it to its other form, especially when you see the difference of squares	$4w^2 - 25z^4$ $= (2w)^2 - (5z^2)^2$ $= (2w + 5z^2)(2w - 5z^2)$
See something close to a special product	Rearrange the equation to try to fit the special product template	$n^2 + m^2 = 2nm$ $n^2 - 2nm + m^2 = 0$ $(n - m)^2 = 0$ $n - m = 0$ $n = m$

Check Your Skills

Factor the following quadratic expressions.

13. $25a^4b^6 - 4c^2d^2$

14. $4x^2 + 8xy + 4y^2$

Answers can be found on page 329.

7

Check Your Skills Answer Key

1. $(x + 4)(x + 9)$

$(\boldsymbol{x} + 4)(\boldsymbol{x} + 9)$ F – multiply the First term in each parentheses: $x \times x = x^2$

$(\boldsymbol{x} + 4)(x + \boldsymbol{9})$ O – multiply the Outer term in each: $x \times 9 = 9x$

$(x + \boldsymbol{4})(\boldsymbol{x} + 9)$ I – multiply the Inner term in each: $4 \times x = 4x$

$(x + \boldsymbol{4})(x + \boldsymbol{9})$ L – multiply the Last term in each: $4 \times 9 = 36$

$x^2 + 9x + 4x + 36 \longrightarrow \boldsymbol{x^2 + 13x + 36}$

2. $(y + 3)(y - 6)$

$(\boldsymbol{y} + 3)(\boldsymbol{y} - 6)$ F – multiply the First term in each parentheses: $y \times y = y^2$

$(\boldsymbol{y} + 3)(y - \boldsymbol{6})$ O – multiply the Outer term in each: $y \times -6 = -6y$

$(y + \boldsymbol{3})(\boldsymbol{y} - 6)$ I – multiply the Inner term in each: $3 \times y = 3y$

$(y + \boldsymbol{3})(y - \boldsymbol{6})$ L – multiply the Last term in each: $3 \times -6 = -18$

$y^2 - 6x + 3y - 18 \longrightarrow \boldsymbol{y^2 - 3y - 18}$

3. 1 & 33 and 3 & 11 multiply to 33. 3 & 11 sum to 14.

$\boldsymbol{(x + 3)(x + 11)}$

4. 1 & 45, 3 & 15, and 5 & 9 multiply to 45. 5 & 9 sum to 14.

$\boldsymbol{(x - 5)(x - 9)}$

5. Middle term is positive, so the larger of the two numbers (6) is positive.
1 & 18, 2 & 9, and 3 & 6 multiply to 18. The difference of 3 & 6 is 3.

$\boldsymbol{(x + 6)(x - 3)}$

6. 1 & 66, 2 & 33, 3 & 22, and 6 & 11 multiply to 66. The difference of 6 and 11 is 5.

$\boldsymbol{(x + 6)(x - 11)}$

7. 5 & 7 multiply to 35 and their difference is 2. Middle term is positive, so the larger of the two numbers (7) is positive.

$(x - 5)(x + 7) = 0$

$\boldsymbol{x = 5 \text{ OR } -7}$

8. $x^2 - 15x = -26$
        $x^2 - 15x + 26 = 0$ Add 26 to both sides so that the expression equals 0

        2 & 13 multiply to 26 and sum to 15
        $(x - 2)(x - 13) = 0$

        $x = 2$ OR 13

9. The easiest way to solve this equation for x is to isolate x^2 on one side of the equation then take the square root of both sides.

        $x^2 - 3 = 1$
        $x^2 = 4$
        $\sqrt{x^2} = \sqrt{4}$

        $x = 2$ OR -2

10. We can begin by taking the square root of both sides. Remember to include the negative solution as well.

        $(z + 2)^2 = 225$
        $\sqrt{(z + 2)^2} = \sqrt{225}$

        $z + 2 = 15$ OR $z + 2 = -15$
        $z = 13$ **$z = -17$**

11. To find all the solutions, we need to treat this equation like a quadratic. Begin by isolating x on one side of the equation.

        $x^3 - 2x^2 = 3x$
        $x^3 - 2x^2 - 3x = 0$

Notice that all the terms contain x. Factor x out of the left side of the equation then factor the quadratic.

        $x^3 - 2x^2 - 3x = 0$
        $x(x^2 - 2x - 3) = 0$
        $x(x - 3)(x + 1) = 0$

The three values of x that will make the equation true are **0, 3, and -1**.

12. To begin, factor the numerator.

$$\frac{x^2 + 7x + 12}{x+3} = \frac{(\cancel{x+3})(x+4)}{(\cancel{x+3})} = x+4$$

13. $(5a^2b^3 + 2cd)$ $(5a^2b^3 - 2cd)$: Any expression that contains one term subtracted from another can be expressed as a difference of squares. Take the square root of each term. The square root of $25a^4b^6$ is $5a^2b^3$, and the square root of $4c^2d^2$ is $2cd$. In one set of parentheses, add the square roots; in the other, subtract: $(5a^2b^3 + 2cd)$ $(5a^2b^3 - 2cd)$.

14. $(2x + 2y)^2$: This is a more complicated version of the form $(x + y)^2 = x^2 + 2xy + y^2$. Take the square root of the first term to get $(2x)$ and the square root of the last term to get $(2y)$. $4x^2 + 8xy + 4y^2 = (2x + 2y)(2x + 2y)$.

Chapter Review: Drill Sets

Drill 1

Distribute the following expressions.

1. $(x + 2)(x - 3) =$
2. $(2s + 1)(s + 5) =$
3. $(5 + a)(3 + a) =$
4. $(3 - z)(z + 4) =$
5. $(2x - y)(x + 4y) =$

Drill 2

Solve the following equations. List all possible solutions.

6. $x^2 - 2x = 0$
7. $z^2 = -5z$
8. $y^2 + 4y + 3 = 0$
9. $y^2 - 11y + 30 = 0$
10. $y^2 + 3y = 0$
11. $y^2 + 12y + 36 = 0$
12. $a^2 - a - 12 = 0$
13. $x^2 + 9x - 90 = 0$
14. $2a^2 + 6a + 4 = 0$
15. $x^3 - 5x^2 + 4x = 0$

Drill 3

Simplify the following expressions.

16. If $a \neq b$, $\dfrac{a^2 - b^2}{a - b} =$

(A) $a - b$ (B) $a + b$ (C) $a^2 + b^2$

17. If $|r| \neq |s|$, $\dfrac{r^2 + 2rs + s^2}{r^2 - s^2} =$

(A) $\dfrac{r + s}{r - s}$ (B) $\dfrac{r - s}{r + s}$ (C) $2rs$

18. If $x \neq 1$, $\dfrac{5x^3}{x - 1} - \dfrac{5x^2}{x - 1} =$

(A) $\dfrac{x}{x - 1}$ (B) $5x^2$ (C) 0

19. If $t \neq 1/2$, $\dfrac{2t - 1 + (2t - 1)^2}{2t - 1} =$

(A) $2t$ (B) $2t - 1$ (C) $2t - 2$

20. If $m \neq -7$, $\dfrac{m^2 + 2m}{m + 7} + \dfrac{49 + 12m}{m + 7} =$

(A) 1 (B) $(m + 7)^2$ (C) $m + 7$

Drill 4

Simplify the following expressions.

21. If $x \neq -3$, $\dfrac{3x^2 - 6x - 45}{3x + 9} =$

(A) $5 - x$ (B) $x - 5$ (C) $x + 5$

22. $\dfrac{5ab + abc}{abc^2 + 10abc + 25ab} =$

(A) $\dfrac{1}{(c + 5)^2}$ (B) $c + 5$ (C) $\dfrac{1}{c + 5}$

23. $\dfrac{\left(x^5 - x^3\right)}{\left(x^3 - x^2\right)} \times \dfrac{x}{5} =$

(A) $\dfrac{x^2}{5}$ (B) $\dfrac{x^3 - x^2}{5}$ (C) $\dfrac{x^3 + x^2}{5}$

24. $(a^2 + 2ab + b^2) \times \dfrac{a - b}{a + b} =$

(A) $a^2 - 2ab + b^2$ (B) $a^2 - b^2$ (C) $a - b$

25. $\dfrac{x^2 - 6x + 9}{3 - x} =$

(A) $x - 3$ (B) $3 - x$ (C) $(x - 3)^2$

Drill Set Answers:

Drill 1

1. $(x + 2)(x - 3) = x^2 - 3x + 2x - 6 = \mathbf{x^2 - x - 6}$

2. $(2s + 1)(s + 5) = 2s^2 + 10s + s + 5 = \mathbf{2s^2 + 11s + 5}$

3. $(5 + a)(3 + a) = 15 + 5a + 3a + a^2 = \mathbf{a^2 + 8a + 15}$

4. $(3 - z)(z + 4) = 3z + 12 - z^2 - 4z = \mathbf{-z^2 - z + 12}$

5. $(2x - y)(x + 4y) = 2x^2 + 8xy - xy - 4y^2 = \mathbf{2x^2 + 7xy - 4y^2}$

Drill 2

6. $\mathbf{x = 0}$ **OR 2:**
$x^2 - 2x = 0$
$x(x - 2) = 0$
$x = 0$
OR $(x - 2) = 0 \rightarrow x = 2$

7. $\mathbf{z = 0}$ **OR −5:**
$z^2 = -5z$
$z^2 + 5z = 0 \rightarrow z(z + 5) = 0$
$z = 0$
OR $(z + 5) = 0 \rightarrow z = -5$

8. $y = \mathbf{-1}$ **OR −3:**
$y^2 + 4y + 3 = 0$
$(y + 1)(y + 3) = 0$
$(y + 1) = 0 \rightarrow y = -1$
$(y + 3) = 0 \rightarrow y = -3$

9. $\mathbf{y = 5}$ **OR 6:**
$y^2 - 11y + 30 = 0$
$(y - 5)(y - 6) = 0$
$(y - 5) = 0 \rightarrow y = 5$
OR $(y - 6) = 0 \rightarrow y = 6$

10. **$y = 0$ OR -3:**

$y^2 + 3y = 0$

$y(y + 3) = 0$

$y = 0$

OR $(y + 3) = 0 \rightarrow y = -3$

11. **$y = -6$:**

$y^2 + 12y + 36 = 0$

$(y + 6)(y + 6) = 0$

$(y + 6) = 0 \rightarrow y = -6$

OR $(y + 6) = 0 \rightarrow y = -6$

12. **$a = 4$ OR -3:**

$a^2 - a - 12 = 0$

$(a - 4)(a + 3) = 0$

$(a - 4) = 0 \rightarrow a = 4$

OR $(a + 3) = 0 \rightarrow a = -3$

13. **$x = -15$ OR 6:**

$x^2 + 9x - 90 = 0$

$(x + 15)(x - 6) = 0$

$(x + 15) = 0 \rightarrow x = -15$

OR $(x - 6) = 0 \rightarrow x = 6$

14. **$a = -2$ OR -1:**

$2a^2 + 6a + 4 = 0$

$2(a^2 + 3a + 2) = 0 \rightarrow 2(a + 2)(a + 1) = 0$

$(a + 2) = 0 \rightarrow a = -2$

OR $(a + 1) = 0 \rightarrow a = -1$

15. **$x = 0$ OR 1 OR 4:**

$x^3 - 5x^2 + 4x = 0$

$x(x^2 - 5x + 4) = 0 \rightarrow x(x - 1)(x - 4) = 0$

$x = 0$

OR $(x - 1) = 0 \rightarrow x = 1$

OR $(x - 4) = 0 \rightarrow x = 4$

Drill 3

16. **(B)** $a + b$: The key to simplifying this expression is to recognize the special product:

$$a^2 - b^2 = (a + b)(a - b)$$

After replacing the original numerator with $(a + b)(a - b)$, we can cancel the $(a - b)$ in the numerator with the $(a - b)$ in the denominator:

$$\frac{a^2 - b^2}{a - b} = \frac{(a + b)\,\cancel{(a - b)}}{\cancel{(a - b)}} = a + b$$

17. **(A)** $\dfrac{r + s}{r - s}$: We have one special product in the numerator and another in the denominator. After factoring each of these, we find a common term that cancels:

$$\frac{r^2 + 2rs + s^2}{r^2 - s^2} = \frac{\cancel{(r + s)}(r + s)}{\cancel{(r + s)}(r - s)} = \frac{r + s}{r - s}$$

18. **(B)** $5x^2$: First perform the subtraction to combine the two terms:

$$\frac{5x^3}{x - 1} - \frac{5x^2}{x - 1} = \frac{5x^3 - 5x^2}{x - 1}$$

Because we have a common factor in both terms of the numerator, we can divide that factor out in order to simplify further. This is often a useful move when we are asked to add or subtract exponents with the same base:

$$\frac{5x^3 - 5x^2}{x - 1} = \frac{5x^2\,\cancel{(x - 1)}}{\cancel{(x - 1)}} = 5x^2$$

19. **(A)** $2t$: It is tempting to expand the quadratic term in the numerator, but we should try to simplify first. Notice that none of the answer choices are fractions. Therefore, we need to look for a way to cancel $(2t - 1)$ from the denominator. To make this task easier, enclose every $(2t - 1)$ term in parentheses and then simplify. We can factor $(2t - 1)$ out of the numerator:

$$\frac{(2t - 1) + (2t - 1)^2}{(2t - 1)} =$$
$$\frac{\cancel{(2t - 1)}[(1) + (2t - 1)]}{\cancel{(2t - 1)}} =$$
$$1 + (2t - 1) = 2t$$

Alternatively, we can introduce a new variable x defined as $x = 2t - 1$. In general, it is not a good idea to introduce more variables than strictly necessary, but in this case the new variable can make it easier to see how the math works:

$$\frac{(2t-1)+(2t-1)^2}{(2t-1)} = \frac{x+x^2}{x}$$

We can then simplify the expression in terms of x:

$$\frac{x+x^2}{x} = \frac{\cancel{x}(1+x)}{\cancel{x}} = x+1$$

And we then finish by replacing x with $2t - 1$:

$$x + 1 = (2t - 1) + 1 = 2t$$

20. **(C)** $m + 7$: The denominators are the same, so add the fractions:

$$\frac{m^2+2m}{m+7} + \frac{49+12m}{m+7} = \frac{m^2+14m+49}{m+7}$$

None of the answer choices are fractions, so we need to find a way to eliminate the denominator. Factor the numerator:

$$\frac{m^2+14m+49}{m+7} = \frac{\cancel{(m+7)}(m+7)}{\cancel{(m+7)}} = m+7$$

Drill 4

21. **(B)** $x - 5$: We can make this problem a lot simpler if we begin by factoring 3 out of both the numerator and the denominator:

$$\frac{3x^2-6x-45}{3x+9} = \frac{\cancel{3}(x^2-2x-15)}{\cancel{3}(x+3)} = \frac{x^2-2x-15}{x+3}$$

The answers are not fractions, so we'll have to get rid of the denominator. Factor the numerator:

$$\frac{x^2-2x-15}{x+3} = \frac{(x-5)\cancel{(x+3)}}{\cancel{(x+3)}} = x-5$$

22. **(C)** $\dfrac{1}{c+5}$: This might seem nearly impossible to factor down until we take out the common term:

ab. Then, we are left with one of our familiar special products in the denominator:

$$\frac{5ab+abc}{abc^2+10abc+25ab}=$$

$$\frac{\cancel{ab}(5+c)}{\cancel{ab}(c^2+10c+25)}=$$

$$\frac{(5+c)}{(c+5)(c+5)}=$$

$$\frac{\cancel{(c+5)}}{\cancel{(c+5)}(c+5)}=\frac{1}{c+5}$$

23. **(C)** $\dfrac{x^3+x^2}{5}$: There's no obvious way to proceed through this question. The best bet is to try to

simplify before multiplying. Notice that x^3 can be factored out of the numerator and x^2 can be factored out of the denominator:

$$\frac{(x^5-x^3)}{(x^3-x^2)}\times\frac{x}{5}=\frac{x^3(x^2-1)}{x^2(x-1)}\times\frac{x}{5}$$

Notice now that we can cancel x^2 from the fraction. Also, we have (x^2-1) in the numerator, which we can factor:

$$\frac{x^3(x^2-1)}{x^2(x-1)}\times\frac{x}{5}=$$

$$\frac{\cancel{x^2}\times x(x+1)\cancel{(x-1)}}{\cancel{x^2}\cancel{(x-1)}}\times\frac{x}{5}=$$

$$\frac{x(x+1)\times x}{5}$$

We don't have a match with any of the answer choices yet. None of the numerators in the answer choices have parenthetical expressions. We should multiply the numerator:

$$\frac{x(x+1)\times x}{5}=\frac{x^2(x+1)}{5}=\frac{x^3+x^2}{5}$$

24. **(B) $a^2 - b^2$:** Save yourself time and look to cancel common factors before multiplying. ($a^2 + 2ab + b^2$) factors to $(a + b)^2$:

$$(a^2 + 2ab + b^2) \times \frac{a-b}{a+b} =$$

$$\cancel{(a+b)}(a+b) \times \frac{(a-b)}{\cancel{(a+b)}} =$$

$$(a+b)(a-b) = a^2 - b^2$$

25. **(B) $3 - x$:** None of the answer choices are fractions, so we need to cancel the denominator. Factor the numerator:

$$\frac{x^2 - 6x + 9}{3 - x} = \frac{(x-3)(x-3)}{3-x}$$

Neither of the expressions in the numerator matches the denominator. However, $(x - 3) = -(3 - x)$. We can factor out a (-1) from the denominator, then cancel:

$$\frac{(x-3)(x-3)}{3-x} = \frac{\cancel{(x-3)}(x-3)}{-\cancel{(x-3)}} = \frac{x-3}{-1} = 3 - x$$

Chapter 8
Foundations of GMAT Math

Beyond Equations:
Inequalities & Absolute Value

In This Chapter...

Chapter 8:
Beyond Equations:
Inequalities & Absolute Value

In This Chapter:

- Introduction to inequalities
- Solving inequalities
- Working with absolute value

An Inequality With a Variable: A Range on the Number Line

Inequalities use $<$, $>$, $\leq$ or $\geq$ to describe the relationship between two expressions.

$$5 > 4 \qquad y \leq 7 \qquad x < 5 \qquad 2x + 3 \geq 0$$

Like equations, **inequalities are full sentences.** Always read from left to right.

$x < y$	x is less than y	
$x > y$	x is greater than y	
$x \leq y$	x is less than or equal to y	x is at most y
$x \geq y$	x is greater than or equal to y	x is at least y

We can also have two inequalities in one statement. Just make a compound sentence.

$9 < g < 200$	9 is less than g, and g is less than 200
$-3 < y \leq 5$	-3 is less than y, and y is less than or equal to 5
$7 \geq x > 2$	7 is greater than or equal to x, and x is greater than 2

To visualize an inequality that involves a variable, **represent the inequality on a number line.** Recall that "greater than" means "to the right of" on a number line. Likewise, "less than" means "to the left of."

y is to the right of 5. 5 is *not* included in the line (as shown by the empty circle around 5), because 5 is not a part of the solution—*y* is greater than 5, but not equal to 5.

b is to the left of 2 (or on top of 2). Here, 2 is included in the solution, because *b* can equal 2. A solid black circle indicates that you include the point itself.

Any number covered by the black arrow will make the inequality true and so is a possible solution to the inequality. Any number not covered by the black arrow is not a solution.

If you...	Then you...	Like this:
Want to visualize an inequality	Put it all on a number line, where < means "to the left of" and > means "to the right of"	$y > 5$ 5

Check Your Skills

Represent the following equations on the number line provided:

1. $x > 3$

2. $b \geq -2$

3. $y = 4$

Translate the following into inequality statements:

4. *z* is greater than *v*.
5. The total amount is greater than $2,000.

Answers can be found on page 351.

Many Values "Solve" an Inequality

What does it mean to "solve an inequality"?

The same thing as it means for an equation: find the value or values of *x* that make the inequality true. When you plug a solution back into the original equation or inequality, you get a *true statement*.

Here's what's different. Equations have only one (or just a few) values as solutions. In contrast, **inequalities give a whole range of values as solutions**—way too many to list individually.

Equation: $x + 3 = 8$

The solution to $x + 3 = 8$ is $x = 5$. 5 is the **only** number that will make the equation true.

Plug back in to check:
$5 + 3 = 8$. True.

Inequality: $x + 3 < 8$

The solution to $x + 3 < 8$ is $x < 5$. Now, 5 itself is not a solution because $5 + 3 < 8$ is not a true statement. But 4 is a solution because $4 + 3 < 8$ is true. For that matter, 4.99, 3, 2, 2.87, −5, and −100 are also solutions. The list goes on. Whichever of the correct answers you plug in, you arrive at something that looks like this:

(Any number less than 5) $+ 3 < 8$. True.

Check Your Skills

6. Which of the following numbers are solutions to the inequality $x < 10$?

    (A) −3
    (B) 2.5
    (C) −3/2
    (D) 9.999
    (E) All of the above

The answer can be found on page 351.

Solve Inequalities: Isolate Variable by Transforming Each Side

As with equations, your objective is to isolate our variable on one side of the inequality. When the variable is by itself, you can see what the solution (or range of solutions) really is.

$2x + 6 < 12$ and $x < 3$ provide the same information. But you understand the full range of solutions more easily when you see the second inequality, which literally says that "x is less than 3."

Many manipulations are the same for inequalities as for equations. First of all, you are *always* allowed to simplify an expression on just one side of an inequality. Just don't change the expression's value.

    $2x + 3x < 45$ is the same as $5x < 45$

The inequality sign isn't involved in this simplification.

Next, some "Golden Rule" moves work the same way for inequalities as for equations. For instance, you can **add anything you want to both sides of an inequality**. Just do it to both sides. You can also **subtract anything you want from both sides of an inequality.**

$$\begin{array}{r} a - 4 > 6 \\ +4 \quad +4 \\ \hline a \quad\quad > 10 \end{array} \qquad\qquad \begin{array}{r} y + 7 < 3 \\ -7 \quad -7 \\ \hline y \quad\quad < -4 \end{array}$$

We can also add or subtract variables from both sides of an inequality. It doesn't matter what the sign of the variables is.

If you...	Then you...	Like this:
Want to add or subtract something on both sides of an inequality	Go ahead and do it	$x + y > -4$ $\underline{-y \quad -y}$ $x > -4 - y$

Check Your Skills

Isolate the variable in the following inequalities.

7. $x - 6 < 13$
8. $y + 11 \geq -13$
9. $x + 7 > 7$

Answers can be found on page 351.

Multiply an Inequality by a Negative: Flip > to < or Vice Versa

If you multiply both sides of an inequality by a positive number, leave the inequality sign alone. The same is true for division.

$$\frac{x}{3} < 7$$
$$3\left(\frac{x}{3}\right) < (7)3$$
$$x < 21$$

$$4y > 12$$
$$\frac{4y}{4} > \frac{12}{4}$$
$$y > 3$$

However, **if you multiply both sides of an inequality by a negative number, flip the inequality sign.** "Greater than" becomes "less than" and vice versa.

$$-2x > 10$$
$$\frac{-2x}{-2} < \frac{10}{-2}$$
$$x < -5$$

$$-b \geq 10$$
$$-1 \times (-b) \leq (10) \times (-1)$$
$$b \leq -10$$

If you didn't switch the sign, then true inequalities such as 5 < 7 would become false when you multiplied them by, say, −1. You must flip the sign.

$5 < 7$ but $-5 > -7$
5 is less than 7   −5 is greater than −7

What about multiplying or dividing an inequality by a variable? The short answer is... try not to do it! The issue is that you don't know the sign of the "hidden number" that the variable represents. If the variable has to be positive (e.g., it counts people or measures a length), then you can go ahead and multiply or divide. But still keep your eyes peeled for danger.

If you...	Then you...	Like this:
Multiply or divide both sides of an inequality by a number	Flip the inequality sign if the number is negative	$45 < -5w$ $$\frac{45}{-5} > \frac{-5w}{-5}$$ $-9 > w$

Check Your Skills

Isolate the variable in each equation.

10. $x + 3 \geq -2$
11. $-2y < -8$
12. $a + 4 \geq 2a$

Answers can be found on page 351.

Absolute Value: The Distance from Zero

The **absolute value** of a number describes how far that number is away from 0. It is the distance between that number and 0 on a number line.

The symbol for absolute value is |number|. For instance, write the absolute value of −5 as |−5|.

The absolute value of 5 is 5. $|5| = 5$

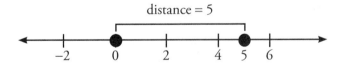

The absolute value of −5 is also 5. $|-5| = 5$

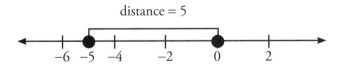

When you face an expression like |4 − 7|, treat the absolute value symbol like parentheses. Solve the arithmetic problem *inside* first, and then find the absolute value of the answer.

$|4 - 7| = ?$ $4 - 7 = -3$

$|-3| = 3$

8

Check Your Skills

Mark the following expressions as TRUE or FALSE.

13. $|3| = 3$
14. $|-3| = -3$
15. $|3| = -3$
16. $|-3| = 3$
17. $|3 - 6| = 3$
18. $|6 - 3| = -3$

Answers can be found on pages 351–352.

Replace |x| with x in One Equation and with −x in Another

You often see a variable inside the absolute value signs.

> Example: $|y| = 3$

This equation has **two solutions.** There are *two* numbers that are 3 units away from 0: namely, 3 and −3. So both of these numbers could be possible values for *y*. *y* is *either 3 or −3.*

When you see a variable inside an absolute value, look for the variable to have two possible values. Here is a step-by-step process for finding both solutions.

$\|y\| = 3$	Step 1: Isolate the absolute value expression on one side of the equation. Here, the expression is already isolated.
$+(y) = 3$ or $-(y) = 3$	Step 2: Drop the absolute value signs and **set up two equations.** The first equation has the positive value of what's inside the absolute value. The second equation puts in a negative sign.
$y = 3$ or $-y = 3$	Step 3: Solve both equations.
$y = 3$ or $y = -3$	
$y = 3$ or $y = -3$	You have two possible values.

You can take a shortcut and go right to "*y* equals plus or minus 3." This shortcut works as long as the absolute value expression is by itself on one side of the equation.

Here's a slightly more difficult problem:

> Example: $6 \times |2x + 4| = 30$

To solve this problem, you can use the same approach.

$6 \times |2x + 4| = 30$

$|2x + 4| = 5$ Step 1: Isolate the absolute value expression on one side of the equation or inequality.

$2x + 4 = 5$ or $-(2x + 4) = 5$ Step 2: Set up two equations—the positive and the negative values are
$ -2x - 4 = 5$ set equal to the other side.

$2x = 1$ or $-2x = 9$ Step 3: Solve both equations/inequalities.

$x = \dfrac{1}{2}$ or $x = \dfrac{-9}{2}$ Note: We have two possible values.

If you…	Then you…	Like this:
Have a variable inside absolute value signs	Drop the absolute value and set up two equations, one positive and one negative	$\|z\| = 4$ $+(z) = 4$ or $-(z) = 4$ $z = 4$ or $z = -4$

Check Your Skills

Solve the following equations with absolute values in them:

19. $|a| = 6$
20. $|x + 2| = 5$
21. $|3y - 4| = 17$
22. $4|x + 1/2| = 18$

Answers can be found on page 352.

Inequalities + Absolute Values: Set Up Two Inequalities

Some tough problems include both inequalities and absolute values. To solve these problems, combine what you have learned about inequalities with what you have learned about absolute values.

$|x| \geq 4$

The basic process for dealing with absolute values is the same for inequalities as it is for equations. The absolute value is already isolated on one side, so now drop the absolute value signs and **set up two inequalities**. The first inequality has the positive value of what was inside the absolute value signs, while the second inequality has the negative value.

$+(x) \geq 4$ or $-(x) \geq 4$

Now isolate the variable in each inequality, as necessary.

$+ (x) \geq 4$ $- (x) \geq 4$

$x \geq 4$ $-x \geq 4$ Divide by -1

          $x \leq -4$ Remember to flip the sign when dividing by a negative

So the two solutions to the original equation are $x \geq 4$ and $x \leq -4$. Represent that on a number line.

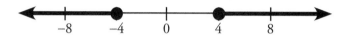

As before, any number that is covered by the black arrow will make the inequality true. Because of the absolute value, there are now two arrows instead of one, but nothing else has changed. Any number to the left of -4 will make the inequality true, as will any number to the right of 4.

Looking back at the inequality $|x| \geq 4$, you can also interpret it in terms of distance. $|x| \geq 4$ means "x is at least 4 units away from zero, in either direction." The black arrows indicate all numbers for which that statement is true.

Here is a harder example:

$|y + 3| < 5$

Once again, the absolute value is already isolated on one side, so set up the two inequalities.

$+ (y + 3) < 5$ and $- (y + 3) < 5$

Next, isolate the variable.

$y + 3 < 5$ $-y - 3 < 5$

$y < 2$ $-y < 8$

          $y > -8$

The two inequalities are $y < 2$ and $y > -8$. If you plot those results, something curious happens.

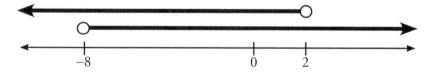

It seems as if every number should be a solution to the equation. But if you start testing numbers, you see that 5 doesn't work, because $|5 + 3|$ is not less than 5. In fact, the only numbers that make the inequality true are those that are true for *both* inequalities. The number line should look like this:

In the first example, x could be greater than or equal to 4 OR less than or equal to −4. For this example, however, it makes more sense to say that y is greater than −8 AND less than 2. If your two arrows do not overlap, as in the first example, any number that falls in the range of *either* arrow will be a solution to the inequality. If your two arrows overlap, as in the second example, only the numbers that fall in the range of *both* arrows will be solutions to the inequality.

You *can* interpret $|y + 3| < 5$ in terms of distance: "$(y + 3)$ is less than 5 units away from from zero, in either direction." The shaded segment indicates all numbers y for which this is true. As inequalities get more complicated, don't worry about interpreting their meaning—just solve them algebraically!

If you...	Then you...	Like this:
Have an inequality with variable inside absolute value signs	Drop the absolute value and set up two inequalities, one positive and one negative	$|z| > 4$ $+(z) > 4 \quad \text{or} \quad -(z) > 4$ $z > 4 \quad \text{or} \quad z < -4$

Check Your Skills

23. $|x + 1| > 2$
24. $|-x - 4| \geq 8$
25. $|x - 7| < 9$

Answers can be found on pages 352–353.

8

Check Your Skills Answer Key:

1.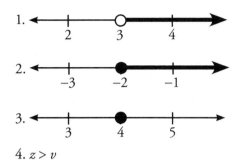

2.

3.

4. $z > v$

5. Let a = amount.

$a > \$2,000$

6. The answer is (E) All of the above! All of these numbers are to the left of 10 on the number line.

7. $x - 6 < 13$

$x < 19$

8. $y + 11 \geq -13$

$y \geq -24$

9. $x + 7 > 7$

$x > 0$

10. $x + 3 \geq -2$

$x \geq -5$

11. $-2y < -8$

$y > 4$

12. $a + 4 \geq 2a$

$4 \geq a$

13. True

14. False—(Note that absolute value is always positive!)

15. False

16. True

17. True ($|3 - 6| = |-3| = 3$)

18. False

19. $|a| = 6$

   $a = 6$ or $a = -6$

20. $|x + 2| = 5$

  $+$ $(x + 2) = 5$ or $-(x + 2) = 5$

    $x + 2 = 5$ or $-x - 2 = 5$

    $x = 3$ or $-x = 7$

            $x = -7$

21. $|3y - 4| = 17$

  $+$ $(3y - 4) = 17$ or $-(3y - 4) = 17$

    $3y - 4 = 17$ or $-3y + 4 = 17$

    $3y = 21$ or $-3y = 13$

    $y = 7$ or $y = -13/3$

22. $4|x + 1/2| = 18$

  $+$ $(x + 1/2) = 4.5$ or $-(x + 1/2) = 4.5$

    $x + 1/2 = 4.5$ or $-x - 1/2 = 4.5$

    $x = 4$ or $-x = 5$

            $x = -5$

23. $|x + 1| > 2$

  $+$ $(x + 1) > 2$ or $-(x + 1) > 2$

    $x + 1 > 2$ or $-x - 1 > 2$

    $x > 1$ or $-x > 3$

            $x < -3$

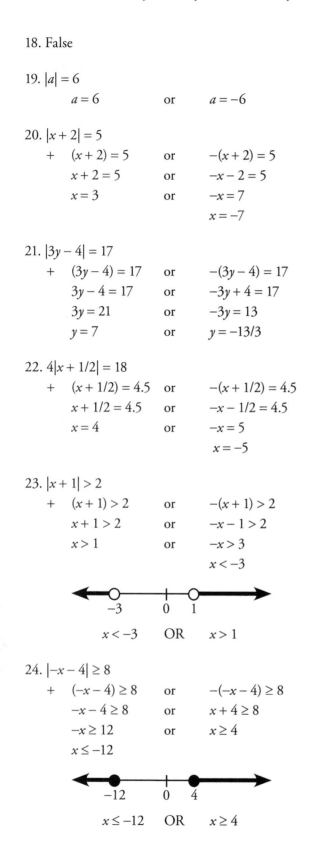

   $x < -3$ OR $x > 1$

24. $|-x - 4| \geq 8$

  $+$ $(-x - 4) \geq 8$ or $-(-x - 4) \geq 8$

    $-x - 4 \geq 8$ or $x + 4 \geq 8$

    $-x \geq 12$ or $x \geq 4$

    $x \leq -12$

   $x \leq -12$ OR $x \geq 4$

8

MANHATTAN
GMAT

25. $|x - 7| < 9$

     + $(x - 7) < 9$ or $-(x - 7) < 9$

         $x - 7 < 9$ or $-x + 7 < 9$

         $x < 16$ or $-x < 2$

                                     $x > -2$

$$\underset{-2\ \ 0 \hspace{2.5em} 16}{\circ\!\!\rule[0.5ex]{6em}{1pt}\!\!\circ\!\!\longrightarrow}$$

$x > -2$ AND $x < 16$, $-2 < x < 16$

Chapter Review: Drill Sets

Drill 1

Draw the following inequalities on the number line provided:

1. $x > 4$

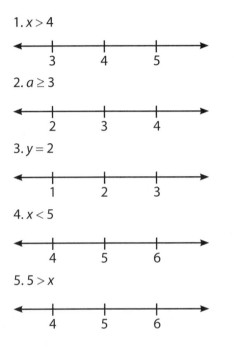

2. $a \geq 3$

3. $y = 2$

4. $x < 5$

5. $5 > x$

Drill 2

Translate the following into inequality statements:

6. a is less than b.

7. Five times x is greater than 10.

8. Six is less than or equal to $4x$.

9. The price of an apple is greater than the price of an orange.

10. The total number of members is at least 19.

Drill 3

Solve the following inequalities.

11. $x + 3 \leq -2$

12. $t - 4 \leq 13$

13. $3b \geq 12$

14. $-5x > 25$

15. $-8 < -4y$

Drill 4

Solve the following equations.

16. $2z + 4 \geq -18$

17. $7y - 3 \leq 4y + 9$

18. $b/5 \leq 4$

19. $d + 3/2 < 8$

20. $4x/7 \leq 15 + x$

Drill 5

Solve the following inequalities.

21. $3(x - 7) \geq 9$

22. $\dfrac{x}{3} + 8 < \dfrac{x}{2}$

23. $2x - 1.5 > 7$

24. $\dfrac{8(x + 6)}{9} \geq 0$

25. $\dfrac{2(3 - x)}{5x} \leq 4$, if $x > 0$

Drill 6

Solve the following inequalities.

26. $3\sqrt{2x + 3} > 12$

27. $\dfrac{2(8 - 3x)}{7} > 4$

28. $0.25x - 3 \leq 1$

29. $2(x - 1)^3 + 3 \leq 19$

30. $\dfrac{4\sqrt[3]{5x - 8}}{3} \geq 4$

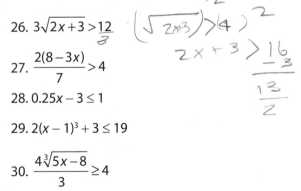

8

Drill 7

Solve the following absolute value equations.

31. $|x| = 5$
32. $|2y| = 6$
33. $|x + 6| = 3$
34. $|4y + 2| = 18$
35. $|1 - x| = 6$

Drill 8

Solve the following absolute value equations.

36. $3|x - 4| = 16$
37. $2|x + 0.32| = 7$
38. $|3x - 4| = 2x + 6$
39. $|5x - 17| = 3x + 7$
40. $\left|\dfrac{x}{4} + 3\right| = 0.5$

Drill 9

Solve each of the following inequalities, and then mark the solution on a number line.

41. $|x + 3| < 1$
42. $|3x| \geq 6$
43. $5 \geq |2y + 3|$
44. $7 \geq |-3a + 5|$
45. $|-12a| < 15$

Drill 10

Solve each of the following inequalities, and then mark the solution on a number line.

46. $|-x| \geq 6$
47. $|x + 4|/2 > 5$
48. $|x^3| < 64$
49. $|0.1x - 3| \geq 1$

50. $\left|\dfrac{3x}{2} + 7\right| \leq 11$

Drill 11

Solve each of the following inequalities, and then mark the solution on a number line.

51. $\left|-\dfrac{4x}{5} + \dfrac{2}{3}\right| \leq \dfrac{7}{15}$
52. $|3x + 7| \geq 2x + 12$
53. $|3 + 3x| < -2x$
54. $|-3 - 5x| \leq -4x$
55. $3\left|\dfrac{5x}{3} - 7\right| < \dfrac{2x}{3} + 18$

Drill Set Answers

Drill 1

Draw the following inequalities on the number line provided:

1. $x > 4$
2. $a \geq 3$
3. $y = 2$
4. $x < 5$
5. $5 > x$

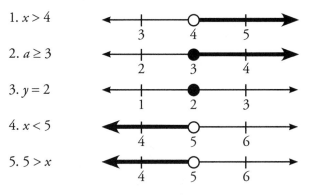

Note: We can flip inequalities around… $x < 5$ means the same thing as $5 > x$.
"x is less than 5" means the same thing as "5 is greater than x."

Drill 2

Translate the following into inequality statements:

6. a is less than b.

$a < b$

7. Five times x is greater than 10.

$5x > 10$

8. Six is less than or equal to $4x$.

$6 \leq 4x$

9. The price of an apple is greater than the price of an orange.

Let a = the price of an apple
Let o = the price of an orange

$a > o$

Note: In this problem, we set up our variables to refer to prices—not the number of apples and oranges.

10. The total number of members is at least 19.

Let m = the number of members
$m \geq 19$

Drill 3

11. $x + 3 \leq -2$
$x \leq -5$

12. $t - 4 \leq 13$
$t \leq 17$

13. $3b \geq 12$
$b \geq 4$

14. $-5x > 25$
$x < -5$

15. $-8 < -4y$
$2 > y$

Drill 4

16. $2z + 4 \geq -18$
$2z \geq -22$
$z \geq -11$

17. $7y - 3 \leq 4y + 9$
$3y - 3 \leq 9$
$3y \leq 12$
$y \leq 4$

18. $b/5 \leq 4$
$b \leq 20$

19. $d + 3/2 < 8$
$d < 8 - 3/2$
$d < 16/2 - 3/2$
$d < 13/2$

20. $4x/7 \leq 15 + x$
$4x \leq 105 + 7x$
$-3x \leq 105$
$x \geq -35$

Drill 5

21. $3(x - 7) \geq 9$
$x - 7 \geq 3$
$x \geq 10$

22. $\dfrac{x}{3} + 8 < \dfrac{x}{2}$ Multiply by 6 to get rid of fractions

$6\left(\dfrac{x}{3} + 8\right) < 6\left(\dfrac{x}{2}\right)$

$2x + 48 < 3x$

$48 < x$

23. $2x - 1.5 > 7$

$2x > 8.5$

$x > 4.25$

24. $\dfrac{8(x + 6)}{9} \geq 0$

$8(x + 6) \geq 0$

$x + 6 \geq 0$

$x \geq -6$

25. $\dfrac{2(3 - x)}{5x} \leq 4$

$2(3 - x) \leq 20x$ Since $x > 0$, you can multiply both sides by $5x$ and keep the inequality sign as

$3 - x \leq 10x$ is.

$3 \leq 11x$

$\dfrac{3}{11} \leq x$

Drill 6

8

26. $3\sqrt{2x + 3} > 12$

$\sqrt{2x + 3} > 4$

$2x + 3 > 16$ We can square both sides of an inequality as long as both sides are positive.

$2x > 13$

$x > \dfrac{13}{2}$

27. $\dfrac{2(8 - 3x)}{7} > 4$

$2(8 - 3x) > 28$

$8 - 3x > 14$

$-3x > 6$

$x < -2$

28. $0.25x - 3 \leq 1$

$\qquad 0.25x \leq 4$

$\qquad x \leq 16$

29. $2(x - 1)^3 + 3 \leq 19$

$\qquad 2(x - 1)^3 \leq 16$

$\qquad (x - 1)^3 \leq 8$

$\qquad x - 1 \leq 2$ We can take the cube root of both sides of an inequality.

$\qquad x \leq 3$

30. $\dfrac{4\sqrt[3]{5x - 8}}{3} \geq 4$

$\qquad 4\sqrt[3]{5x - 8} \geq 12$

$\qquad \sqrt[3]{5x - 8} \geq 3$ We can cube both sides of an inequality.

$\qquad 5x - 8 \geq 27$

$\qquad 5x \geq 35$

$\qquad x \geq 7$

Drill 7

31. $|x| = 5$

$\qquad + \quad (x) = 5$ or $-x = 5$

$\qquad\quad x = 5$ $x = -5$

$\qquad\quad x = 5$ or -5

32. $|2y| = 6$

$\qquad + \quad (2y) = 6$ or $-(2y) = 6$

$\qquad\quad 2y = 6$ $-2y = 6$

$\qquad\quad y = 3$ $y = -3$

$\qquad\quad y = 3$ or -3

33. $|x + 6| = 3$

$\qquad + \quad (x + 6) = 3$ or $-(x + 6) = 3$

$\qquad\quad x + 6$ $-x - 6 = 3$

$\qquad\quad x = -3$ $-x = 9$

$\qquad\qquad\qquad\qquad\qquad\qquad\quad x = -9$

$\qquad\quad x = -3$ or -9

8

34. $|4y + 2| = 18$

+ $(4y + 2) = 18$ or $-(4y + 2) = 18$

$4y + 2 = 18$ $-4y - 2 = 18$

$4y = 16$ $-4y = 20$

$y = 4$ $y = -5$

$y = 4$ or -5

35. $|1 - x| = 6$

+ $(1 - x) = 6$ or $-(1 - x) = 6$

$-x = 5$ $-1 + x = 6$

$x = -5$ $x = 7$

$x = -5$ or 7

Drill 8

36. $3|x - 4| = 16$

$$|x - 4| = \frac{16}{3}$$

+ $(x - 4) = 16/3$ or $-(x - 4) = 16/3$

$x - 4 = 16/3$ $-x + 4 = 16/3$

$x = 16/3 + 4$ $-x = 16/3 - 4$

$x = 16/3 + 12/3$ $-x = 16/3 - 12/3$

$x = 28/3$ $-x = 4/3$

          $x = -4/3$

$x = 28/3$ or $-4/3$

37. $2|x + 0.32| = 7$

$|x + 0.32| = 3.5$

+ $(x + 0.32) = 3.5$ or $-(x + 0.32) = 3.5$

$x + 0.32 = 3.5$ $-x - 0.32 = 3.5$

$x = 3.18$ $-x = 3.82$

          $x = -3.82$

$x = 3.18$ or -3.82

38. $|3x - 4| = 2x + 6$

+ $(3x - 4) = 2x + 6$ or $-(3x - 4) = 2x + 6$

$3x - 4 = 2x + 6$ $-3x + 4 = 2x + 6$

$x - 4 = 6$ $4 = 5x + 6$

$x = 10$ $-2 = 5x$

          $$-\frac{2}{5} = x$$

$x = 10$ or $-2/5$

39. $|5x - 17| = 3x + 7$

$+$ $(5x - 17) = 3x + 7$ or $-(5x - 17) = 3x + 7$

     $5x - 17 = 3x + 7$ $-5x + 17 = 3x + 7$

     $2x - 17 = 7$ $17 = 8x + 7$

     $2x = 24$ $10 = 8x$

     $x = 12$ $\dfrac{10}{8} = x$

                                       $\dfrac{5}{4} = x$

     $x = 12$ or $5/4$

40. $\left|\dfrac{x}{4} + 3\right| = 0.5$

$+$ $\left(\dfrac{x}{4} + 3\right) = 0.5$ or $-\left(\dfrac{x}{4} + 3\right) = 0.5$

     $\dfrac{x}{4} + 3 = 0.5$ $-\dfrac{x}{4} - 3 = 0.5$

     $\dfrac{x}{4} = -2.5$ $-\dfrac{x}{4} = -3.5$

     $x = -10$ $x = -14$

     $x = -10$ or -14

Drill 9

41. $|x + 3| < 1$

$+$ $(x + 3) < 1$ $-(x + 3) < 1$

    $x + 3 < 1$ $-x - 3 < 1$

    $x < -2$ $-x < 4$

    $x + 3 < 1$ $x > -4$

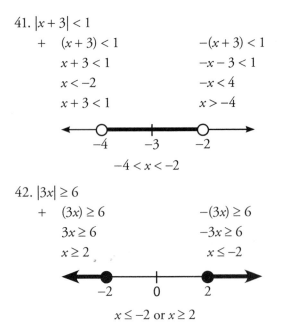

$-4 < x < -2$

42. $|3x| \geq 6$

$+$ $(3x) \geq 6$ $-(3x) \geq 6$

    $3x \geq 6$ $-3x \geq 6$

    $x \geq 2$ $x \leq -2$

$x \leq -2$ or $x \geq 2$

43. $5 \geq |2y + 3|$

$5 \geq (2y + 3)$	$5 \geq -(2y + 3)$
$5 \geq 2y + 3$	$5 \geq -2y - 3$
$2 \geq 2y$	$8 \geq -2y$
$1 \geq y$	$-4 \leq y$

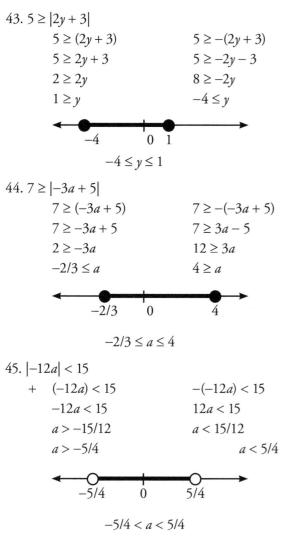

$-4 \leq y \leq 1$

44. $7 \geq |-3a + 5|$

$7 \geq (-3a + 5)$	$7 \geq -(-3a + 5)$
$7 \geq -3a + 5$	$7 \geq 3a - 5$
$2 \geq -3a$	$12 \geq 3a$
$-2/3 \leq a$	$4 \geq a$

$-2/3 \leq a \leq 4$

45. $|-12a| < 15$

+	$(-12a) < 15$	$-(-12a) < 15$
	$-12a < 15$	$12a < 15$
	$a > -15/12$	$a < 15/12$
	$a > -5/4$	$a < 5/4$

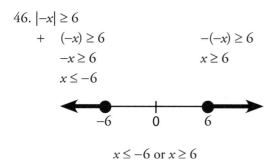

$-5/4 < a < 5/4$

Drill 10

46. $|-x| \geq 6$

+	$(-x) \geq 6$	$-(-x) \geq 6$
	$-x \geq 6$	$x \geq 6$
	$x \leq -6$	

$x \leq -6$ or $x \geq 6$

47. $|x + 4|/2 > 5$
   $|x + 4| > 10$
   + $(x + 4) > 10$ $-(x + 4) > 10$
       $x + 4 > 10$ $-x - 4 > 10$
       $x > 6$ $-x > 14$
                                $x < -14$

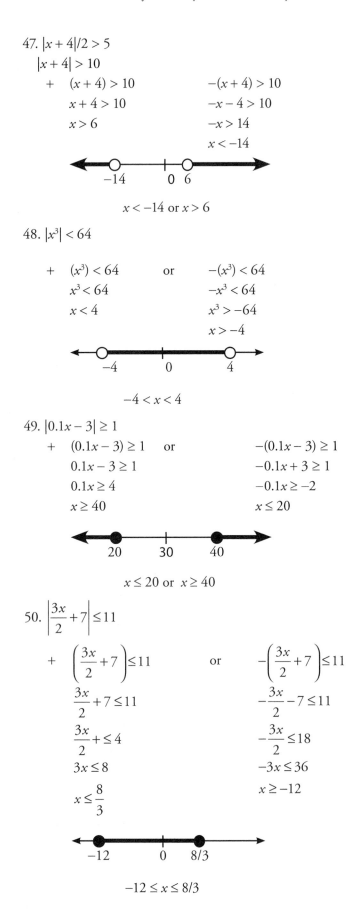

   $x < -14$ or $x > 6$

48. $|x^3| < 64$

   + $(x^3) < 64$ or $-(x^3) < 64$
       $x^3 < 64$ $-x^3 < 64$
       $x < 4$ $x^3 > -64$
                                 $x > -4$

   $-4 < x < 4$

49. $|0.1x - 3| \geq 1$
   + $(0.1x - 3) \geq 1$ or $-(0.1x - 3) \geq 1$
       $0.1x - 3 \geq 1$ $-0.1x + 3 \geq 1$
       $0.1x \geq 4$ $-0.1x \geq -2$
       $x \geq 40$ $x \leq 20$

   $x \leq 20$ or $x \geq 40$

50. $\left|\dfrac{3x}{2} + 7\right| \leq 11$

   + $\left(\dfrac{3x}{2} + 7\right) \leq 11$ or $-\left(\dfrac{3x}{2} + 7\right) \leq 11$

       $\dfrac{3x}{2} + 7 \leq 11$ $-\dfrac{3x}{2} - 7 \leq 11$

       $\dfrac{3x}{2} + \leq 4$ $-\dfrac{3x}{2} \leq 18$

       $3x \leq 8$ $-3x \leq 36$

       $x \leq \dfrac{8}{3}$ $x \geq -12$

   $-12 \leq x \leq 8/3$

Drill 11

51. $\left|\dfrac{-4x}{5}+\dfrac{2}{3}\right| \le \dfrac{7}{15}$

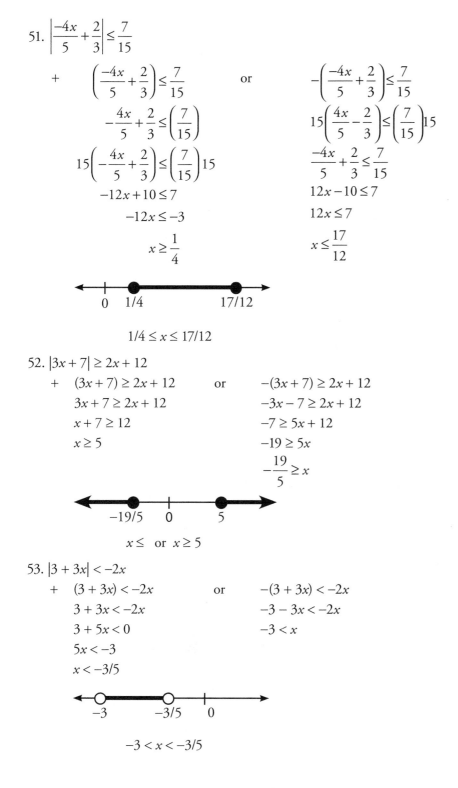

+ $\left(\dfrac{-4x}{5}+\dfrac{2}{3}\right) \le \dfrac{7}{15}$ or $-\left(\dfrac{-4x}{5}+\dfrac{2}{3}\right) \le \dfrac{7}{15}$

$\qquad\qquad -\dfrac{4x}{5}+\dfrac{2}{3} \le \left(\dfrac{7}{15}\right) \qquad\qquad 15\left(\dfrac{4x}{5}-\dfrac{2}{3}\right) \le \left(\dfrac{7}{15}\right)15$

$\qquad 15\left(-\dfrac{4x}{5}+\dfrac{2}{3}\right) \le \left(\dfrac{7}{15}\right)15 \qquad \dfrac{-4x}{5}+\dfrac{2}{3} \le \dfrac{7}{15}$

$\qquad\qquad -12x+10 \le 7 \qquad\qquad 12x-10 \le 7$

$\qquad\qquad\qquad -12x \le -3 \qquad\qquad\quad 12x \le 7$

$\qquad\qquad\qquad\qquad x \ge \dfrac{1}{4} \qquad\qquad\qquad x \le \dfrac{17}{12}$

$1/4 \le x \le 17/12$

52. $|3x + 7| \ge 2x + 12$

+ $(3x + 7) \ge 2x + 12$ or $-(3x + 7) \ge 2x + 12$

$\qquad 3x + 7 \ge 2x + 12 \qquad\qquad -3x - 7 \ge 2x + 12$

$\qquad x + 7 \ge 12 \qquad\qquad\qquad -7 \ge 5x + 12$

$\qquad x \ge 5 \qquad\qquad\qquad\qquad -19 \ge 5x$

$\qquad\qquad\qquad\qquad\qquad\qquad -\dfrac{19}{5} \ge x$

$x \le \quad$ or $\ x \ge 5$

53. $|3 + 3x| < -2x$

+ $(3 + 3x) < -2x$ or $-(3 + 3x) < -2x$

$\qquad 3 + 3x < -2x \qquad\qquad\quad -3 - 3x < -2x$

$\qquad 3 + 5x < 0 \qquad\qquad\qquad -3 < x$

$\qquad 5x < -3$

$\qquad x < -3/5$

$-3 < x < -3/5$

54. $|-3 - 5x| \leq -4x$

$$+ \quad (-3 - 5x) \leq -4x \qquad \text{or} \qquad -(-3 - 5x) \leq -4x$$

$$-3 - 5x \leq -4x \qquad\qquad\qquad 3 + 5x \leq -4x$$

$$-3 \leq x \qquad\qquad\qquad\qquad\quad 3 \leq -9x$$

$$\qquad\qquad\qquad\qquad\qquad\qquad -1/3 \geq x$$

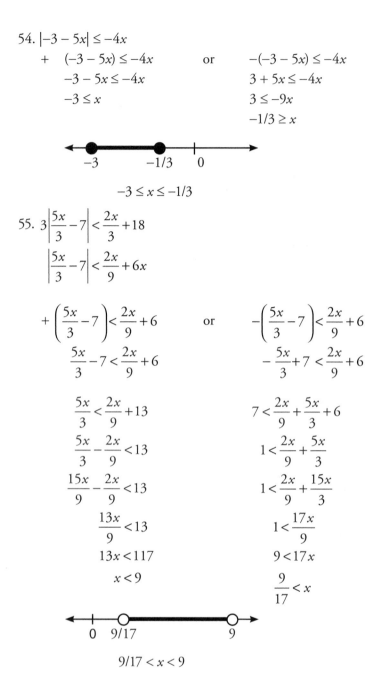

$$-3 \leq x \leq -1/3$$

55. $3\left|\dfrac{5x}{3} - 7\right| < \dfrac{2x}{3} + 18$

$$\left|\dfrac{5x}{3} - 7\right| < \dfrac{2x}{9} + 6x$$

$$+ \left(\dfrac{5x}{3} - 7\right) < \dfrac{2x}{9} + 6 \qquad \text{or} \qquad -\left(\dfrac{5x}{3} - 7\right) < \dfrac{2x}{9} + 6$$

$$\dfrac{5x}{3} - 7 < \dfrac{2x}{9} + 6 \qquad\qquad\qquad -\dfrac{5x}{3} + 7 < \dfrac{2x}{9} + 6$$

$$\dfrac{5x}{3} < \dfrac{2x}{9} + 13 \qquad\qquad\qquad\quad 7 < \dfrac{2x}{9} + \dfrac{5x}{3} + 6$$

$$\dfrac{5x}{3} - \dfrac{2x}{9} < 13 \qquad\qquad\qquad\quad 1 < \dfrac{2x}{9} + \dfrac{5x}{3}$$

$$\dfrac{15x}{9} - \dfrac{2x}{9} < 13 \qquad\qquad\qquad\quad 1 < \dfrac{2x}{9} + \dfrac{15x}{3}$$

$$\dfrac{13x}{9} < 13 \qquad\qquad\qquad\qquad\quad 1 < \dfrac{17x}{9}$$

$$13x < 117 \qquad\qquad\qquad\qquad\quad 9 < 17x$$

$$x < 9 \qquad\qquad\qquad\qquad\qquad \dfrac{9}{17} < x$$

$$9/17 < x < 9$$

Chapter 9 of

Foundations of GMAT Math

Word Problems

In This Chapter...

Chapter 9:

Word Problems

In This Chapter:

- How to solve word problems

Solve Word Problems: Follow Four Steps To Turn Words Into Math

Word problems are everywhere on the GMAT. They come in all sorts of shapes and sizes. The descriptions are confusing and unfamiliar.

Fortunately, the process for tackling almost all word problems is fundamentally the same. You can solve word problems by asking yourself the following four questions.

(1) What do they want?

> Identify what the problem is specifically asking for. Name that thing. This is the unknown that you care about the most.

(2) What do they give me?

> The problem typically gives you some numbers. It also gives you relationships between things. Clearly identify all this given information. You may have to name additional unknowns.

(3) How do I turn this information into equations?

> An equation is a sentence: *The left side equals the right side.* You can express most relationships using the equals sign (=). A few common relationships show up over and over again; you can learn to recognize them.

(4) How do I solve those equations for the desired value?

At this point, you do algebra, using methods from the Equations chapter, the Quadratic Equations chapter, and so on. Manipulate the equations you've created, eliminating secondary unknowns until you find the value you want.

Along the way, you will have to **write things down**. Do not wait for lightning to strike. Often, the entire process will not be completely clear from the beginning. That's fine—just be methodical and patient.

The four questions above correspond to the four steps of a general process of solving word problems.

Consider this example:

The annual profit for a mattress company is defined by the equation $p = 200m - 3,000$, where p is the profit (in dollars) and m is the number of mattresses sold. How much profit does the company make, in dollars, from the sale of 40 mattresses in a particular year?

Start with step #1: **What do they want?**

The question is asking for the *profit* in a particular year. This unknown has already been named for you. Profit is represented by p.

If you were not given a letter for the variable, you would make up your own.

Write "p = profit = ?" on your paper. By writing an actual question mark, you flag the most important unknown. Later you'll stay focused on the ultimate goal.

Next is step #2: **What do they give me?**

What specific information is given? You are given two things:

- The relationship between number of mattresses and profit.
- A specific number of mattresses.

Step #3: **How do I turn this information into equations?**

The first bit of information is already in equation form. Write "$p = 200m - 3,000$."

The same relationship could have been given in words: "The profit, in dollars, is $200 times the number of mattresses, less a $3,000 fixed cost." You would translate those words to the same equation.

The second bit of given information is straightforward: there are 40 mattresses. Write "$m = 40$." This is actually a second equation.

Don't just write "40." Put information down in the form of equations.

Finally, step #4: **How do I solve the equations for the desired value?**

$$p = 200m - 3,000 \qquad m = 40 \qquad p = \text{profit} = ?$$

To get p, you want to eliminate the variable m. Plug 40 in for m in the first equation and simplify.

$$p = 200(40) - 3,000 = 8,000 - 3,000$$
$$p = 5,000$$

The answer to the problem is $5,000.

Even as the problems become more complicated, follow these same 4 steps.

> A steel rod 50 meters long is cut into two pieces. If one piece is 14 meters longer than the other, what is the length, in meters, of the shorter piece?

Again, start with step #1: **What do they want?**

The question asks specifically for the "length… of the shorter piece." This length is the number you want.

Since the problem did not give you a letter to represent this length, you should pick one. Choose a letter that will easily remind you of what quantity it stands for. For instance, you might choose S for "shorter." Write this down:

$$S = \text{length of shorter piece} = ?$$

Step #2: **What do they give me?**

Reread the first sentence. "A steel rod 50 meters long is cut into two pieces."

It might not be obvious at first, but this sentence provides a relationship between a few lengths:

- The length of the whole rod, which is 50 meters.
- The length of the shorter piece, which you've already called S.
- The length of the longer piece (which must be longer, because the other piece is shorter).

Before trying to represent the relationship, you should name the length of the longer piece. Write this down:

$$L = \text{length of longer piece}$$

Now you can express the relationship between all the lengths. This relationship is very common:

Part + Part = Whole

If you break something into two parts, you can add the parts back up to get the original thing. That's true of lengths, weights, and so on.

Go ahead and do step #3 right now: **How do I turn this information into an equation?** Write this relationship down using the numbers and letters for each quantity.

$$S + L = 50$$

As you identify each relationship, you will often want to go ahead and express it on paper in the form of an equation right away. You can go back and forth between steps #2 and 3 easily.

$S + L = 50$ is a good start, but it's not enough on its own to solve for S. Go back to step #2 and ask: **What ELSE do they give me?**

Keep reading. "If one piece is 14 meters longer than the other…" Stop there. In a math problem, anything after an "if" is true. You are told that one piece is 14 meters longer than the other.

This relationship is also very common: **Different Values are Made Equal**. You have two different values that are definitely not equal. But you are told exactly how the values differ, so you can set up an equivalence.

If the shorter piece were 14 meters longer, it would have the *same* length as the longer piece. "Same" always means "equal":

Shorter piece, if made 14 meters longer = Longer piece

Now do step #3 again: **How do I turn THIS information into an equation?**

To make something 14 meters longer, add 14 meters to its length. Write the equation using letters and numbers:

$$S + 14 = L$$

Be careful not to write this equation down backward. If you need to check, mentally test a number for S and verify that the longer piece comes out longer.

At last you have two equations and two variables (S and L), and you have no more information to process from the problem. Move on to step #4: **How do I solve the equations for the desired value?**

$$S + L = 50 \qquad\qquad S + 14 = L \qquad\qquad S = ?$$

Since you ultimately want S, eliminate L by replacing it in the first equation with $S + 14$.

$$S + L = 50$$
$$S + (S + 14) = 50$$
$$2S + 14 = 50$$
$$2S = 36$$
$$S = 18$$

The answer to the question is 18.

Let's try a harder problem. Despite new challenges, the process remains the same. In practice, you will move fluidly between the first three steps: identify what the question asks for, identify given quantities and relationships, and represent those quantities as variables and those relationships as equations.

> Bob's Donuts sold an average of 80 donuts a day for the last 5 days. If Bob's Donuts sold an additional 500 donuts in total over the next 4 days, what was the average (arithmetic mean) number of donuts sold per day over the entire 9-day period?

Start by identifying what they want: the average number of donuts sold per day over 9 days. Use the letter a to represent this value.

a = average # of donuts sold a day = ?

Before going on, you should make note of the average formula. Every problem that mentions averages will make you use this formula in some way. The average of a group of numbers is the sum divided by the "count," which is the number of numbers you're averaging:

$$\text{Average} = \frac{\text{Sum}}{\text{Count}}$$

Write in units as well. The average is in "donuts a day," or donuts *per* day. "Per" means "divided by," so this unit is "donuts/day" or $\frac{\text{donuts}}{\text{day}}$. The sum is the total number of donuts, and you divide by the number of days. So write down the average formula customized for this problem:

$$\text{Average donuts per day} = \frac{\text{Total donuts}}{\text{Total days}}$$

This means that to find the average, you need both the total number of donuts and the total number of days.

Do you know either of these values? Yes. You are asked for the average "over the entire 9-day period." So the total number of days is 9.

However, the total number of donuts is unknown. Make up a variable—say, d for donuts.

Now rewrite the average formula:

$$a = \frac{d}{9}$$

You may not think that you've accomplished much yet, but now you know that to get a, you need d.

That's important. Now you should focus on d. What else can you find out about the total number of donuts sold over the 9 days?

Re-read the problem. The first sentence tells you something about the donuts sold during the first 5 days. The next sentence tells you that a total of 500 donuts were sold in the last 4 days. And you are looking for d, the total donuts sold over all 9 days.

What is the relationship between the donuts sold during these periods?

- Donuts sold over the first 5 days
- Donuts sold over the last 4 days
- Donuts sold over all 9 days

This is **Part + Part = Whole** again.

Donuts sold in the first 5 days	+	Donuts sold in the last 4 days	=	Total donuts sold over all 9 days

As word problems get harder, they make relationships harder to see. You also have to perform more steps.

Now you have two more unknowns to worry about on the left side of the equation above. Do you know either unknown?

Yes. You do know how many donuts were sold in the last 4 days: 500 donuts. However, the number of donuts sold in the first 5 days is still unknown. Use an n to represent that quantity, and rewrite the Part + Part = Whole equation:

$$n + 500 = d$$

You're almost there. If you can find n, you can find d. Then you can find a, and that's the answer.

What do you know about n, the number of donuts sold over the first 5 days? You know something about that period from the first sentence: on average, 80 donuts per day were sold. Once again, you can use the average formula to create an equation. Notice that you're focusing on a different period now—just the first 5 days.

9

$$\text{Average donuts per day} = \frac{\text{Total donuts}}{\text{Total days}} \qquad 80 = \frac{n}{5}$$

At last you can solve the problem. First, solve for n.

$$80 = \frac{n}{5} \qquad \longrightarrow \qquad 400 = n$$

Now find d.

$$n + 500 = d \quad \longrightarrow \quad 400 + 500 = d \quad \longrightarrow \quad 900 = d$$

Finally, solve for a.

$$a = \frac{d}{9} \qquad \longrightarrow \qquad a = \frac{900}{9} \qquad \longrightarrow \qquad a = 100$$

The average number of donuts sold per day over the entire 9-day period is 100. That is, on average, 100 donuts were sold each day for 9 days.

As you solve word problems, sometimes you'll notice relationships first. At other times, you'll notice unknowns first. The order is not important. Just keep extracting information from the problem and representing that information on paper.

Turn unknowns into letters, and turn relationships into equations. Observe how the equations hook together. In the previous problem, you ultimately wanted a, but you needed d first, and before that n.

The last value you solve for is the one you really want (a). When you identify other unknowns, realize that you will need to solve for them first.

If you...	Then you...	Like this:
Want to solve a word problem: Kelly is three times as old as Bill. In 5 years, Kelly will be twice as old as Bill will be. How old is Bill?	Follow the four steps: (1) Identify what they want (2) Identify what they give you (3) Represent relationships as equations (4) Solve the algebra	$B = ?$ $K = 3B$ $K + 5 = 2(B + 5)$ $(3B) + 5 = 2(B + 5)$ $3B + 5 = 2B + 10$ $B = 5$ Bill is 5 years old.

To help you translate, here are several phrases commonly found in word problems to describe mathematical relationships. Study this list.

Common Word Problem Phrases

Addition

Add, Sum, Total (of parts), More Than: +

The sum of x and y: $x + y$

The sum of the three funds combined: $a + b + c$

When fifty is added to his age: $a + 50$

Six pounds heavier than Dave: $d + 6$

A group of men and women: $m + w$

The cost is marked up: $c + m$

Subtraction

Minus, Difference, Less Than: −

x minus five: $x - 5$

The difference between Quentin's and Rachel's heights (if Quentin is taller): $q - r$

Four pounds less than expected: $e - 4$

The profit is the revenue minus the cost: $P = R - C$

Multiplication

The product of h and k: $h \times k$

The number of reds times the number of blues: $r \times b$

One fifth of y: $(1/5) \times y$

n persons have x beads each: total number of beads $= nx$

Go z miles per hour for t hours: distance $= zt$ miles

Ratios and Division

Quotient, Per, Ratio, Proportion: ÷ or /

Five dollars every two weeks: (5 dollars/2 weeks) ⟶ 2.5 dollars a week

The ratio of x to y: x/y

The proportion of girls to boys: g/b

Average or Mean (sum of terms divided by the total number of terms)

The average of a and b: $\dfrac{a+b}{2}$

The average salary of the three doctors: $\dfrac{x+y+z}{3}$

A student's average score on 5 tests was 87: $\dfrac{\text{sum}}{5} = 87$ or $\dfrac{a+b+c+d+e}{5} = 87$

Check Your Skills

1. The total weight of two jugs of milk is 2.2 kilograms. The lighter jug weighs 0.4 kilogram less than the heavier jug. What is the weight of the lighter jug?

2. Jan makes a salary of $10,000 per month for 3 months. Then her salary drops to $6,000 per month. After 9 months at $6,000 per month, what will Jan's average (arithmetic mean) monthly pay be for the whole period?

Answers can be found on page 391.

Express Total Cost as Price × Quantity

The GMAT expects you to know certain basic money relationships.

> At a certain store, 7 T-shirts cost $65.10. If every T-shirt has the same price, how much do 3 T-shirts cost, in dollars?

Solve the problem methodically. First, what is the question specifically asking for? It's asking for the total cost of 3 T-shirts, in dollars (represented by $).

What are you given? You are given the cost of 7 T-shirts ($65.10). You are also told that every T-shirt has the same price. And you are given another quantity of T-shirts to care about (3).

When every unit of something has the same price, you can use this equation:

Total Cost = Price × Quantity

Name the variables C, P, and Q.

$$C = P \times Q$$

What is the question asking for again? It asks for the total cost of 3 T-shirts. In other words, the question asks for the value of C when $Q = 3$.

$$C = P \times 3 = ?$$

To find C, then, you need P—the price of each shirt. Price is always in dollars *per unit*. It is the cost of one unit of whatever is being sold or bought—in this case, T-shirts.

How can you find the price of each shirt? You know something else related to the price: "… 7 T-shirts costs $65.10."

This is another instance of Total Cost = Price × Quantity. You have a different quantity (7) and a different total cost ($65.10), but the price is the same—because you are told it is. So P is the same in both equations.

Set up a second equation:

$$\$65.10 = P \times 7$$

9

Finally, you can solve for P and plug back into the prior equation to get C when the quantity is 3 shirts. Temporarily drop the $ sign as you calculate.

$$65.10 = P \times 7$$
$$\frac{65.10}{7} = \frac{7P}{7} = P$$

$$\begin{array}{r} 9.30 \\ 7\overline{)65.10} \\ \underline{63} \\ 2.1 \\ \underline{2.1} \\ 0 \end{array}$$

So $P = 9.30$. Each T-shirt costs $9.30.

Finally, solve the other equation for the total cost of 3 T-shirts by substituting 9.30 for P.

$$C = P \times 3$$
$$C = 9.30 \times 3$$
$$C = 27.90$$

The total cost of 3 T-shirts is $27.90.

Notice that you could express the problem from the store's point of view.

> A certain store sold 7 T-shirts for $65.10. If every T-shirt has the same price, how much revenue, in dollars, would the store receive from selling 3 T-shirts?

The answer is the same: $27.90. Instead of Total Cost, you can write Total Revenue:

> Total Revenue = Price × Quantity

Or you can simply focus on the units. The total on the left is in dollars, while the price is in dollars per shirt.

$$\text{Total Money (\$)} = \text{Price} \left(\frac{\$}{\text{shirt}} \right) \times \text{Quantity (shirts)}$$

Sometimes the word "cost" is even used for price, as in "Each shirt costs $9.30." Just be sure to distinguish between total dollar amounts and "per shirt" dollar amounts.

This Total Cost equation can be combined with Part + Part = Whole in the following way.

> Five apples and four bananas cost $2.10, while three apples and two bananas cost $1.20. If the cost of every apple is the same, and if the cost of every banana is the same, what is the cost of two apples and a banana?

Take this a step at a time.

9

You are told that the cost of 5 apples and 4 bananas is $2.10. This $2.10 is a whole made up of two parts: the cost of 5 apples and the cost of 4 bananas. Each of *those* costs is a price times a quantity.

Total Cost	=	**Price** × **Quantity**	+	**Price** × **Quantity**
		for apples		for bananas

What are you given? You are given the cost of 5 apples and 4 bananas ($2.10). You are also given the cost of 3 apples and 2 bananas ($1.20).

Furthermore, you are told that the cost (or price) of every apple is the same, and likewise for bananas. These last facts allow you to use the Total Cost = Price × Quantity relationship.

What are you asked for? The total cost of 2 apples and a banana.

The simplest unknowns to name are the price (or cost) of one apple and the price of one banana. Call these A and B. You can write everything in terms of these unknowns.

Express each given total cost as a separate equation.

Total Cost		**Price** × **Quantity**		**Price** × **Quantity**		
$2.10	=	$A \times 5$	+	$B \times 4$	=	$5A + 4B$
$1.20	=	$A \times 3$	+	$B \times 2$	=	$3A + 2B$

And you are looking for the cost of 2 apples and a banana: $A \times 2 + B \times 1 = 2A + B = ?$

Solve for A and B. Try combining the equations. First multiply the second equation by 2.

$$2.10 = 5A + 4B \qquad\qquad 1.20 = 3A + 2B$$
$$2.40 = 6A + 4B$$

Now subtract the first equation from the second.

$$2.40 = 6A + 4B$$
$$\underline{- (2.10 = 5A + 4B)}$$
$$0.30 = A$$

Plug back into one of the original equations to solve for B.

$$1.20 = 3A + 2B \quad \longrightarrow \quad 1.20 = 3(0.30) + 2B$$
$$1.20 = 0.90 + 2B$$
$$0.30 = 2B$$
$$0.15 = B$$

Finally, answer the question.

$$2A + B = 2(0.30) + (0.15) = 0.60 + 0.15 = 0.75$$

The cost of two apples and a banana is $0.75.

Sometimes the price is known and the quantity is not. The cost in dollars of x books priced at $12 each is $12x$. Notice that $12x$ is also the cost of 12 pens, if each pen costs $$x$. When you write a total cost as a product of price and quantity, keep track of which is which.

Occasionally, you encounter an upfront **fixed cost**. Cell phone minutes used to be priced this way: you have a fixed cost per call (including the first 2 or 3 minutes), and then you paid for additional minutes at a certain price per minute.

The equation looks like this:

> **Total Cost**   =   **Fixed Cost**   +   **Price** × *Additional* **Quantity**

Consider this example:

> The charge per seat to watch home games this season at Colossus Stadium is $1,000, which includes passes to 2 home games, plus $300 per additional home game. If Sam wants to spend no more than $4,000 to watch home games at Colossus Stadium, what is the maximum number of home games he can attend?

What is the question looking for? The maximum number of home games that Sam can attend. Call that n.

What information are you given? You are told that the total cost for someone to watch home games is $1,000 (which includes 2 home games), plus $300 per additional game. You are also told that Sam wants to spend only $4,000 on games.

Sam attends n games in all, but he had passes for 2 of them (included in the $1,000 up front).

So he attends $n - 2$ games at the $300 ticket price.

Write the equation.

Total Cost	=	Fixed Cost	+	Price × *Additional* Quantity
$4,000	=	$1,000	+	$300 × $(n - 2)$

Now solve for n.

$$4,000 = 1,000 + 300(n - 2)$$
$$3,000 = 300(n - 2)$$
$$10 = n - 2$$
$$12 = n$$

Sam can attend 12 home games.

Last but not least, don't forget this classic relationship:

Profit = Revenues − Costs

This one shows up in business school quite a bit, of course! You also need it on the GMAT, sometimes in combination with the other relationships above.

If you...	Then you...	Like this:
Encounter a money relationship: "The cost of 8 watches is $1,200..."	Write the equation: Total Cost = Price × Quantity, including more items or a fixed cost as necessary	P = Price of 1 watch $$\$1,200 = P \times 8$$ $$1,200 = 8P$$ $$150 = P$$ One watch costs $150

Check Your Skills

3. A candy shop sells 50 candy bars in January for $3 each. In February, the shop increases the price by $1, but its revenue from candy bar sales only increases by $10. By how many units did the number of candy bars sold decrease from January to February?

4. At the Initech Company store, seven staplers and five coffee mugs cost $36, while two staplers and a coffee mug cost $10. If every stapler costs the same, and if every coffee mug costs the same, how much more does a stapler cost than a coffee mug?

Answers can be found on pages 391–392.

Add Units: Add Apples to Apples

When you solve pure algebra problems, the numbers don't represent anything in particular. In contrast, word problems have a context. Every number has a meaning. That is, every number has a natural **unit** attached.

Up to this point, the units have worked out naturally. For instance, in the steel rod question (on page 371), all the lengths were already in meters. So you could ignore them.

S	+	L	=	50		S	+	14	=	L
meters		meters		meters		meters		meters		meters

If some units were meters and others were feet, you couldn't add or subtract them. **When you add or subtract quantities, they must have exactly the same units.**

What is $2 plus 45 cents, if $1 = 100 cents? Choose a common unit. It doesn't matter which one you pick, but you must express both quantities in that unit before you add.

$$2 + 0.45 = 2.45 \qquad 200 + 45 = 245$$
$$\text{dollars} \quad \text{dollars} \quad \text{dollars} \qquad \text{cents} \quad \text{cents} \quad \text{cents}$$

The result has the same unit as the original quantities. When you add or subtract units, the units do not change.

$$\text{meters} + \text{meters} = \text{meters} \qquad \text{dollars} - \text{dollars} = \text{dollars} \qquad \text{puppies} + \text{puppies} = \text{puppies}$$

Multiply and Divide Units: Treat Them Just Like Numbers or Variables

In contrast, when you multiply units, the result has a different unit. A good example is area.

If a room is 6 feet long and 9 feet wide, what is the area of the room?

You know that area is length times width, so multiply:

Area = 6 feet × 9 feet = 54...

What happens to the feet? Feet times feet equals feet squared.

Area = 6 feet × 9 feet = 54 feet squared = 54 feet^2 = 54 square feet

If you multiply two quantities that each have units, multiply the units too.

Not every multiplication in a word problem changes the units. If Alex is twice as old as Brenda, in years, then you can represent that relationship like so:

$$A = 2 \times B$$
$$\text{years} \qquad\qquad \text{years}$$

The word "twice" has no units (it just means "two times," or "2 ×").

Some units are naturally ratios of other units. Look for the words "per," "a," "for every," and so on.

$$3 \text{ books a week} = 3\,\frac{\text{books}}{\text{week}} \qquad\qquad 17 \text{ miles per gallon} = 17\,\frac{\text{miles}}{\text{gallon}}$$

Prices and averages often have units that are ratios of other units.

$$9 \text{ dollars a shirt} = 9\,\frac{\text{dollars}}{\text{shirt}} \qquad\qquad 100 \text{ donuts per day} = 100\,\frac{\text{donuts}}{\text{day}}$$

The average formula actually shows the division of units.

$$\text{Average donuts per day} = \frac{\text{Total donuts}}{\text{Total days}}$$

Likewise, the Total Cost relationship demonstrates how **units cancel in the same way as numbers and variables do**.

$$\text{Total Cost} = \quad \text{Price} \quad \times \text{Quantity}$$
$$\text{dollars} \quad = \frac{\text{dollars}}{\text{shirt}} \quad \times \quad \text{shirts}$$

The units match on both sides of the equation, because you can cancel the "shirt" unit just as you would with anything else in its place.

$$\text{dollars} \quad = \frac{\text{dollars}}{\cancel{\text{shirt}}} \quad \times \quad \cancel{\text{shirts}}$$

This cancellation property allows you to convert from a larger to a smaller unit, or vice versa.

How many minutes are in two days?

First, convert 2 days into hours. You know that 1 day = 24 hours. In your head, you can quickly convert 2 days to 48 hours, but do it on paper with unit cancellation:

$$2 \text{ days} \times \frac{24 \text{ hours}}{1 \text{ day}} = 48 \text{ hours} \qquad \cancel{\text{days}} \times \frac{\text{hours}}{\cancel{\text{day}}} = \text{hours}$$

Notice that the "day" unit cancels, leaving you with "hours" on top. The fraction you use to multiply is called a **conversion factor**. It's a fancy form of the number 1, because the top (24 hours) equals the bottom (1 day). When you write conversion factors, put the units in place first so that they cancel correctly. Then place the corresponding numbers so that the top equals the bottom.

Keep going to minutes. Set up the conversion factor using 60 minutes = 1 hour.

$$48 \text{ hours} \times \frac{60 \text{ minutes}}{1 \text{ hour}} = 2{,}880 \text{ minutes} \qquad \cancel{\text{hrs}} \times \frac{\text{min}}{\cancel{\text{hr}}} = \text{min}$$

By the way, always write out at least a few letters for every unit. "Hours" can be "hr," and "minutes" can be "min," but never write "h" or "m." You might confuse a single letter for a variable.

You can do two or more conversions in one fell swoop:

$$2 \text{ days} \times \frac{24 \text{ hours}}{1 \text{ day}} \times \frac{60 \text{ minutes}}{1 \text{ hour}} = 2{,}880 \text{ minutes} \qquad \cancel{\text{days}} \times \frac{\cancel{\text{hrs}}}{\cancel{\text{day}}} \times \frac{\text{min}}{\cancel{\text{hr}}} = \text{min}$$

9

A common conversion is between miles and kilometers. You don't have to know that 1 mile is approximately 1.6 kilometers; they will give you this information. However, you will have to be able to use this information to convert between these units.

A distance is 30 miles. What is the approximate distance in kilometers? (1 mile = 1.6 kilometers)

Multiply the given distance by the conversion factor, which you should set up to cancel units.

$$30 \text{ miles} \times \frac{1.6 \text{ kilometers}}{1 \text{ mile}} = 48 \text{ kilometers} \qquad \cancel{\text{miles}} \times \frac{\text{km}}{\cancel{\text{miles}}} = \text{km}$$

If you…	Then you…	Like this:
Add or subtract quantities with units	Ensure that the units are the same, converting first if necessary	30 minutes + 2 hours = 30 min + 120 min = 150 min *or* = ½ hr + 2 hrs = 2½ hr
Multiply quantities with units	Multiply the units, cancelling as appropriate	$10 \dfrac{\text{bagels}}{\text{hr}} \times 3 \text{ hrs} = 30 \text{ bagels}$
Want to convert from one unit to another	Multiply by a conversion factor and cancel	$20 \text{ min} \times \dfrac{60 \text{ sec}}{1 \text{ min}} = 1{,}200 \text{ sec}$

Check Your Skills

5. How many hours are there in two weeks? Do this problem with conversion factors.
6. How long after midnight is 3:04 am, in seconds?

Answers can be found on page 392.

In Rate × Time: Distance, Follow the Units

A **rate** or **speed** is expressed in "miles per hour" $\left(\dfrac{\text{miles}}{\text{hour}}\right)$ or in "feet per second" $\left(\dfrac{\text{feet}}{\text{sec}}\right)$.

The unit of this kind of rate is a *distance* unit (*miles, feet*) divided by a *time* unit (*hour, second*).

$$\text{Rate} = \frac{\text{Distance}}{\text{Time}} \qquad 60 \text{ miles per hour} = \frac{60 \text{ miles}}{1 \text{ hour}}$$

You can rearrange this relationship to isolate Distance on one side.

Rate × Time = Distance $60 \frac{\text{miles}}{\text{hour}} \times 1 \text{ hour} = 60 \text{ miles}$

This version is very similar to the Total Cost equation:

Price × Quantity = Total Cost $9 \frac{\text{dollars}}{\text{shirt}} \times 4 \text{ shirts} = 36 \text{ dollars}$

A price is kind of a rate, too, because it's "per" something. In distance problems, most rates are "per" time, but occasionally you see a rate "per" something else, such as miles per gallon.

Rate × Denominator = Numerator $11 \frac{\text{miles}}{\text{gallon}} \times 7 \text{ gallons} = 77 \text{ miles}$

Multiply a rate by the denominator's unit, and you'll get the numerator's unit.

Avoid expressing rates as time divided by distance. Instead, **always put time in the denominator**. It doesn't matter how the words are expressed. "It took Joe 4 hours to go 60 miles" means that Joe's rate was 60 miles ÷ 4 hours = 15 miles per hour.

You can combine the Rate × Time = Distance relationship with other relationships already covered. For instance, you have worked with the average formula, as in the "donuts per day" problem:

$$\text{Average donuts per day} = \frac{\text{Total donuts}}{\text{Total days}}$$

The same formula works for rates as well.

$$\text{Average miles per hour} = \frac{\text{Total miles}}{\text{Total hours}}$$

To get the totals on top and bottom, you often need another relationship you're familiar with:

Part + Part = Whole

Miles for first part of a trip + Miles for second part = Total Miles

Hours for first part of a trip + Hours for second part = Total Hours

Try this problem:

Nancy takes 2 hours to bike 12 kilometers from home to school. If she bikes back home by the same route at a rate of 4 kilometers per hour, what is her average rate, in kilometers per hour, for the entire trip?

9

Be careful. The average rate for a journey is the *total* distance divided by the *total* time. Do not simply take an average of the rates given.

You are asked for the average rate for the whole trip. Call this *a* and write an equation.

$$\text{Average kilometers per hour} = a \qquad a = \frac{\text{Total kilometers}}{\text{Total hours}}$$

Do you know either of the missing numbers on the right? Yes. You can quickly figure out the total kilometers. The route from home to school is 12 kilometers, and Nancy comes home by the *same* route, so the total kilometers = 12 + 12 = 24. This is Part + Part = Whole.

$$a = \frac{24}{\text{Total hours}}$$

Now, to find the total time in hours, use Part + Part = Whole again.

Total hours = Hours spent on the first part of the trip + Hours spent on the second part

Do you know either of *these* numbers? Yes—you have the first number directly from the problem.

Total hours = 2 hours + Hours spent on the second part

What do you know about the second part of the trip? You know that Nancy's rate was 4 kilometers per hour. You also know that this route was the *same* as for the first leg—so the distances are equal. It's easy to miss this information. Whenever the GMAT says "the same," pay attention! It always represents an equation.

Write Rate × Time = Distance again, this time just for the second leg of the journey.

$$\text{Rate} \times \text{Time} = \text{Distance} \qquad 4\,\frac{\text{kilometers}}{\text{hour}} \times \text{Time (hours)} = 12 \text{ kilometers}$$

You now have enough to solve. Call this time *t*.

$$4t = 12 \quad \longrightarrow \quad t = 3$$

Plug into the previous equation to find the total time spent on the trip.

Total hours = 2 hours + Hours spent on the second part

Total hours = 2 hours + 3 hours

Total hours = 5 hours

Finally, plug into the first equation you wrote.

$$a = \frac{24}{\text{Total hours}} = \frac{24}{5} = 4.8$$

Nancy's average rate for the whole trip is 4.8 kilometers per hour.

Rate problems can become tricky when you have to use the same relationship repeatedly (Rate × Time = Distance). To keep the various rates, times, and distances straight, you might use subscripts or even whole words.

$$t_1 = 2 \text{ hours} \qquad t_2 = 3 \text{ hours} \qquad \text{Time \#1} = 2 \text{ hrs} \qquad \text{Time \#2} = 3 \text{ hrs}$$

If you have more than one time in the problem, then using t everywhere for every time will only confuse you. Tables or grids can help keep quantities straight.

If you...	Then you...	Like this:
See a rate problem	Use Rate × Time = Distance, putting in units to keep the math correct	$7\,\dfrac{\text{miles}}{\text{hr}} \times 3 \text{ hrs} = 21 \text{ miles}$

Check Your Skills

7. Amanda ran 24 miles at a rate of 3 miles per hour, then took 4 hours to run an additional 6 miles. What was her average speed for the entire run?

The answer can be found on page 392.

In Rate × Time: Work, Define the Work Unit and Add Rates

Work problems are very similar to Rate-Time-Distance problems. The main difference is that work takes the place of distance.

$$\text{Rate} \times \text{Time} = \text{Distance} \qquad\qquad \text{Rate} \times \text{Time} = \text{Work}$$

$$20\,\frac{\text{miles}}{\text{hour}} \times 3 \text{ hours} = 60 \text{ miles} \qquad\qquad 20\,\frac{\text{chairs}}{\text{hour}} \times 3 \text{ hours} = 60 \text{ chairs}$$

Define work by the task done. It could be building chairs, painting houses, manufacturing soda cans, etc. One unit of output (chairs, houses, cans) is one unit of work.

Occasionally, it can be helpful to invent small units of work ("widgets") so that you avoid dealing with fractions. Instead of "half a warehouse per day," say that a warehouse contains 100 boxes. The rate becomes 50 boxes per day.

Again, always put time in the denominator. "It takes Sally 3 minutes to build a chair" should be translated this way, with an optional unit conversion.

$$\text{Rate} = 1 \text{ chair per 3 minutes} \qquad \text{Rate} = \frac{1 \text{ chair}}{3 \text{ minutes}} \times \frac{60 \text{ minutes}}{1 \text{ hour}} = 20 \frac{\text{chairs}}{\text{hour}}$$

If two people or machines work at the same time side by side, you can add their rates.

> Jay can build a chair in 3 hours. Kay can build a chair in 5 hours. How long will it take both of them, working together, to build 8 chairs?

First, focus on Jay. What is his rate of work? Put time in the denominator.

$$\text{Jay's rate} = 1 \text{ chair per 3 hours} = \frac{1}{3} \text{ chair per hour} \qquad \text{In 1 hour, Jay can build } \frac{1}{3} \text{ of a chair.}$$

Likewise, figure out Kay's rate of work.

$$\text{Kay's rate} = 1 \text{ chair per 5 hours} = \frac{1}{5} \text{ chair per hour} \qquad \text{In 1 hour, Kay can build } \frac{1}{5} \text{ of a chair.}$$

Together, then, Jay and Kay can build $\frac{1}{3} + \frac{1}{5}$ of a chair in an hour. This is the "adding rates" principle in action.

Simplify the sum of fractions.

$$\frac{1}{3} + \frac{1}{5} = \frac{5}{15} + \frac{3}{15} = \frac{8}{15} \qquad \text{They build } \frac{8}{15} \text{ of a chair in an hour.}$$

Now use the full Rate × Time = Work equation. The Work is 8 chairs. The Time is unknown.

$$\text{Rate} \times \text{Time} = \text{Work}$$

$$\frac{8}{15} \times T = 8 \text{ chairs}$$

$$\frac{8T}{15} = 8$$

$$8T = 8(15)$$

$$T = 15$$

It takes Jay and Kay 15 hours to build 8 chairs.

As with Rate-Time-Distance problems, keep the various quantities separate. If you decide to write the same equation more than once, distinguish the cases clearly. For instance, Jay working alone is different from Kay working alone, and the third case is them both working together.

If you...	Then you...	Like this:
See a work problem	Use Rate × Time = Work, choosing work units and often adding rates	$7\,\dfrac{\text{goblets}}{\text{hr}} \times 3\ \text{hrs} = 21\ \text{goblets}$

Check Your Skills

8. It takes Albert 6 hours to build a shelf. Betty can do the same work twice as fast. How many shelves can Albert and Betty, working together, build in a 24 hour period?

The answer can be found on page 393.

Fractions and Percents in Word Problems: "Of" Means "Times"

Many word problems involve fractional amounts or percents. Remember that word problems always have a real context. This means that fractional amounts are fractional amounts **of** something. Percents are percents **of** something. Neither fractions nor percents live in a vacuum.

As you already know, "of" means "times" in the context of fractions and percents.

> At a birthday party, kids can choose one of the following 3 flavors of ice cream: chocolate, vanilla, and strawberry. If 1/2 of the kids choose chocolate, 20% of the kids choose vanilla, and the remaining 15 kids choose strawberry, how many kids are at the party?

First, identify what the question asks for. It asks for the total number of kids at the party. Label that number *n*.

The problem contains a Part + Part = Whole relationship—or rather, Part + Part + Part = Whole.

> Kids who choose chocolate + Kids who choose vanilla + Kids who choose strawberry = Total kids

Replace all of these with variables for the moment.

> $c + v + s = n$

The question gives you *s* directly. 15 kids choose strawberry.

> $c + v + 15 = n$

How many kids choose chocolate? You don't have an absolute number, but you know that 1/2 of the kids choose this flavor. To emphasize the point, you can say that 1/2 of *all* kids choose chocolate. Express this as an equation:

$\dfrac{1}{2}$ of all kids = choose chocolate $\dfrac{1}{2}n = c$

Likewise, 20% of the kids (all kids) choose vanilla.

20% of all kids = choose vanilla $0.2n = v$

Rewrite $\dfrac{1}{2}n$ as $0.5n$. Replace c and v in the main Part + Part + Part equation.

$c + v + 15 = n$

$0.5n + 0.2n + 15 = n$

Now solve for n.

$$0.7n + 15 = n$$
$$15 = 0.3n$$
$$150 = 3n$$
$$50 = n$$

There are 50 kids at the party.

If you...	Then you...	Like this:
See a fraction or a percent in a word problem	Figure out what the fraction or percent is of, and write of as "times."	$\dfrac{1}{2}$ of kids choose chocolate $\dfrac{1}{2}n = c$ 20% of kids choose vanilla $0.2n = v$

Check Your Skills

9. Every junior at Central High School has to study exactly one language. 75% of the juniors study Gaelic, one sixth of the juniors study Spanish, and the other 7 juniors study Tagalog. How many juniors are in the junior class at Central High School?

The answer can be found on page 393.

Check Your Skills Answer Key:

1. H = weight of heavier jug

    L = weight of lighter jug = ?

    $H + L = 2.2$ Sum of weights

    $H - 0.4 = L$ Second relationship between weights

    $H = L + 0.4$ Rearrange

    $H + L = 2.2$ → $(L + 0.4) + L = 2.2$ Substitute

    $2L + 0.4 = 2.2$ Simplify

    $2L = 1.8$

    $L = 0.9$

    The lighter jug weighs 0.9 kilograms.

2. First 3 months: $\text{Average monthly pay} = \dfrac{\text{Total pay for 3 months}}{\text{Months}}$

    $\$10{,}000 = \dfrac{\text{Total pay for 3 mo's}}{3}$

    Total pay for first 3 months = $\$10{,}000 \times 3 = \$30{,}000$

    Last 9 months: $\text{Average monthly pay} = \dfrac{\text{Total pay for 9 months}}{\text{Months}}$

    $\$6{,}000 = \dfrac{\text{Total pay for 9 mo's}}{9 \text{ months}}$

    Total pay for last 9 months = $\$6{,}000 \times 9 = \$54{,}000$

    Total pay for all months = Pay for first 3 months + pay for last 9 months

    Total pay for all months = $\$30{,}000 + \$54{,}000 = \$84{,}000$

    Total months = $3 + 9 = 12$

    All months: $\text{Average monthly pay} = \dfrac{\text{Total pay for all months}}{\text{All months}}$ $a = \dfrac{84{,}000}{12}$

    $a = 84{,}000 \div 12 = 7{,}000$

    The average pay for the whole period is $7,000 per month.

3. January: Total revenue = Price × Quantity = 50 candy bars × $3 per bar = $150

    February: New price = Old price + $1 = $3 + $1 = $4 per bar

    New total revenue = Old revenue + $10 = $150 + $10 = $160

    February: Total revenue = Price × Quantity

    $\$160 = \$4$ per bar $\times Q$

    40 candy bars = Q

    The quantity decreased from 50 bars to 40 bars, for a decrease of 10 units.

391

4. S = price of 1 stapler
C = price of 1 coffee mug
$7S + 5C = \$36$ $2S + C = \$10$ $S - C = ?$
Combine equations to solve. Multiply the second equation by 4:
$2S + C = 10$ → $8S + 4C = 40$
Subtract the first equation

$$
\begin{array}{r}
8S + 4C = 40 \\
- (7S + 5C = 36) \\
\hline
S - C = 4
\end{array}
$$

A stapler costs \$4 more than a coffee mug.

5.   1 week = 7 days

$2 \text{ weeks} \times \dfrac{7 \text{ days}}{1 \text{ week}} = 14 \text{ days}$ $\cancel{\text{weeks}} \times \dfrac{\text{days}}{\cancel{\text{week}}} = \text{days}$

1 day = 24 hours

$14 \text{ days} \times \dfrac{24 \text{ hours}}{1 \text{ day}} = 336 \text{ hours}$ $\cancel{\text{days}} \times \dfrac{\text{hours}}{\cancel{\text{day}}} = \text{hours}$

Or, in one line:

$2 \text{ weeks} \times \dfrac{7 \text{ days}}{1 \text{ week}} \times \dfrac{24 \text{ hours}}{1 \text{ day}} = 336 \text{ hours}$

6.   Convert 3 hours and 4 minutes to seconds. Do in pieces.

$3 \text{ hours} \times \dfrac{60 \text{ minutes}}{1 \text{ hour}} \times \dfrac{60 \text{ seconds}}{1 \text{ minute}} = 10{,}800 \text{ seconds}$

$4 \text{ minutes} \times \dfrac{60 \text{ seconds}}{1 \text{ minute}} = 240 \text{ seconds}$

10,800 seconds + 240 seconds = 11,040 seconds

7.   First 24 miles: Rate × Time = Distance   3 miles per hour × t = 24 miles
t = 8 hours
Total time = 8 hours + 4 hours = 12 hours
Total distance = 24 miles + 6 miles = 30 miles
Entire run: Rate × Time = Distance r × 12 hours = 30 miles

$r = \dfrac{30 \text{ miles}}{12 \text{ hours}} = 2.5 \text{ miles per hour}$

8.   Albert: Rate × Time = Work $r \times 6$ hours = 1 shelf

Albert's rate is $\frac{1}{6}$ shelf per hour.

Betty can work twice as fast, so her rate is $2 \times \frac{1}{6} = \frac{1}{3}$ shelf per hour.

Together, their work rates add: $\frac{1}{6} + \frac{1}{3} = \frac{1}{6} + \frac{2}{6} = \frac{3}{6} = \frac{1}{2}$ shelf per hour

1 day = 24 hours

Together: Rate × Time = Work $\frac{1}{2}$ shelf per hour × 24 hours = 12 shelves

9. J = total number of juniors = ?

75% of juniors study Gaelic: $\frac{3}{4}J = G$

One sixth of juniors study Spanish: $\frac{1}{6}J = S$

The other 7 study Tagalog: $7 = T$

Part + Part + Part = Whole

$G + S + T = J$

Substitute: $\frac{3}{4}J + \frac{1}{6}J + 7 = J$ → $\frac{9}{12}J + \frac{2}{12}J + 7 = J$

$\frac{11}{12}J + 7 = J$ → $7 = \frac{1}{12}J$ → $7(12) = 84 = J$

There are 84 juniors in the class.

9

Chapter Review: Drill Sets

Drill 1

Translate and solve the following problems.

1. There are five more computers in the office than employees. If there are 10 employees in the office, how many computers are there?

2. If −5 is 7 more than *z*, what is *z*/4?

3. Two parking lots can hold a total of 115 cars. The Green lot can hold 35 fewer cars than the Red lot. How many cars can the Red lot hold?

4. Norman is 12 years older than Michael. In 6 years, he will be twice as old as Michael. How old is Norman now?

5. 3 lawyers earn an average of $300 per hour. How much money have they earned in total after each has worked 4 hours?

6. A clothing store bought a container of 100 shirts for $20. If the store sold all of the shirts at $0.50 per shirt, what is the store's gross profit on the box?

7. There are two trees in the front yard of a school. The trees have a combined height of 60 feet, and the taller tree is 3 times the height of the shorter tree. How high is the shorter tree?

8. Louise is three times as old as Mary. In 5 years, Louise will be twice as old as Mary. How old is Mary now?

9. The average of 2, 13 and *x* is 10. What is *x*?

10. Three friends sit down to eat 14 slices of pizza. If two of the friends eat the same number of slices, and the third eats two more slices than each of the other two, how many slices are eaten by the third friend?

Drill 2

Translate and solve the following problems.

11. Movie theater X charges $6 per ticket, and each movie showing costs the theatre $1,750. If 300 people bought tickets for a certain showing, and the theater averaged $2 in concessions (popcorn, etc.) per ticket-holder, what was the theater's profit for that showing?

12. Toshi is 7 years older than his brother Kosuke, who is twice as old as their younger sister Junko. If Junko is 8 years old, how old is Toshi?

13. A plane leaves Chicago in the morning and makes three flights before returning. The first flight traveled twice as far as the second flight, and the second flight traveled three times as far as the third flight. If the third flight was 45 miles, how many miles was the first flight?

14. It costs a certain bicycle factory $10,000 to operate for one month, plus $300 for each bicycle produced during the month. Each of the bicycles sells for a retail price of $700. The gross profit of the factory is measured by total income from sales minus the production costs of the bicycles. If 50 bicycles are produced and sold during the month, what is the factory's gross profit?

15. Arnaldo earns $11 for each ticket that he sells, and a bonus of $2 per ticket for each ticket he sells over 100. If Arnaldo was paid $2,400, how many tickets did he sell?

16. If the average of the five numbers $x - 3$, x, $x + 3$, $x + 4$, and $x + 11$ is 45, what is the value of x?

17. Amar is 30 years younger than Lauri. In 5 years, Lauri will be three times as old as Amar. How old will Lauri be in 10 years?

18. John buys 5 books with an average price of $12. If John then buys another book with a price of $18, what is the average price of the six books?

19. Alicia is producing a magazine that costs $3 per magazine to print. In addition, she has to pay $10,500 to her staff to design the issue. If Alicia sells each magazine for $10, how many magazines must she sell to break even?

20. Every week, Renee is paid 40 dollars per hour for the first 40 hours she works, and 80 dollars per hour for each hour she works after the first 40 hours. If she earned $2,000 last week, how many hours did she work?

9

Drill 3

Translate and solve the following unit conversion problems.

21. An American football field is 100 yards long. What is this length in feet? (1 yard = 3 feet)

22. How many gallons of water would it take to fill a tank with a capacity of 200 pints? (1 gallon = 8 pints)

23. A 44 kilogram suitcase weighs how much in terms of pounds? (1 kilogram = 2.2 pounds)

24. The weather man reported that Boston received 2.25 feet of snow yesterday. How many inches of snow did Boston receive? (1 foot = 12 inches)

25. What is the temperature in Fahrenheit when it is 30 degrees Celsius? $\left(C = \dfrac{5}{9}(F - 32) \right)$

26. How many minutes are in a week?

27. Joe's car can travel 36 miles per gallon of fuel. Approximately how many kilometers can the car travel on 10 liters of fuel? (5 miles = approximately 8 kilometers; 1 gallon = approximately 4 liters)

28. A recipe calls for 1.6 cups of sugar and 2 quarts of flour. How many gallons is the resulting mixture of sugar and flour? (1 gallon = 4 quarts; 1 quart = 4 cups) Leave your answer in decimal form. (For you chefs: ignore the difference between solid measures and liquid measures.)

29. How many 1-inch square tiles would it take to cover the floor of a closet that has dimensions 5 feet by 4 feet? (1 foot = 12 inches)

30. A pool has sprung a leak and is losing water at a rate of 5.5 milliliters per second. How many liters of water is this pool losing per hour? (1 liter = 1,000 milliliters)

Drill 4

Translate and solve the following rate problems.

31. Jiang begins driving away from Marksville at a constant speed of 64 miles per hour. How far will she be from Marksville after 2 hours and 15 minutes?

32. Tom begins the 180-mile drive from Smithton to Johnsonville at 1:00 pm. He drives at a speed of 60 miles per hour for 2 hours. He completes the rest of the drive at a speed of 45 miles per hour. At what time will he arrive in Johnsonville?

33. If Roger walks to a store that is 3 miles away in 2 hours, and then runs home along the same path in 1 hour, what is Roger's average rate, in miles per hour, for the round trip?

34. Sue and Rob are both running a 10-mile path around a lake. Sue runs at a constant rate of 8 miles per hour. Rob runs at a constant rate of 6 ⅔ miles per hour. If they began running at the same time at the beginning of the path, how long will Sue have to wait at the end of the path before Rob finishes?

35. Svetlana is running a 10-kilometer race. She runs the first 5 kilometers of the race at a speed of 12 kilometers per hour. At what speed will she have to run the last 5 kilometers of the race if she wants to complete the 10 kilometers in 55 minutes?

9

Drill 5

Translate and solve the following work problems.

36. A factory must complete production of 1,500 plastic bottles in 4 hours. How many bottles must be produced per hour (at a constant rate) to meet this deadline?

37. A standard machine can fill 15 gallons of paint per hour. A deluxe machine fills gallons of paint at twice the rate of a standard machine. How long will it take a deluxe machine to fill 130 gallons of paint?

38. Machine A produces 15 widgets per minute. Machine B produces 18 widgets per minute. How many widgets will the machines produce together in 20 minutes?

39. A hose is placed into an empty pool and turned on at 2:00 pm. The pool, which holds 680 gallons of water, reaches its capacity at 5:24 pm. How many gallons of water per hour did the hose add to the pool?

40. It takes Machine A, which produces 15 golf clubs per hour, 6 hours to fill a production lot. Machine B can fill the same production lot in 1.5 hours. How many golf clubs does Machine B produce per hour?

Drill 6

Translate and solve the following word problems.

41. If Ken's salary were 20% higher, it would be 20% less than Lorena's. If Lorena's salary is $60,000, what is Ken's salary?

42. A $10 shirt is marked up by 30%, then by an additional 50%. What is the new price of the shirt?

43. A share of Stock Q increases in value by 20%, then decreases in value by 10%. The new value of a share of Stock Q is what percent of its initial value?

44. 40 students in a class of 200 got A's on their test. 64 got B's, 18 got D's and 6 got F's. If students can only get A, B, C, D, or F as grades, what percent of the students got C's?

45. If Naiila has $10 and spends 70 cents, what percent of her money has she spent?

    (A) 0.7%   (B) 7%   (C) 70%

Drill 7

Translate and solve the following word problems.

46. Lily is staying up all night to watch meteors from her roof. 10% of the meteors visible from her roof tonight are exceptionally bright, and of these, 80% inspire Lily to write a haiku. If Lily is inspired to write haiku by 20 exceptionally bright meteors, how many meteors are visible from her roof tonight?

47. Bingwa the African elephant can lift 6% of his body weight using his trunk alone. If Bingwa weighs 1,000 times as much as a white handed gibbon, how many gibbons can Bingwa lift at once with his trunk?

48. The temperature in Limerick is 3/4 that in Cairo, where the temperature is 8/5 that in Halifax. If the temperature in Limerick is 66°, what is the temperature in Halifax?

49. In Farrah's workday playlist, 1/3 of the songs are jazz, 1/4 are R&B, 1/6 are rock, 1/12 are country, and the remainder are world music. What fraction of the songs in Farrah's playlist are world music?

50. At a convention of monsters, 2/5 have no horns, 1/7 have one horn, 1/3 have two horns, and the remaining 26 have three or more horns. How many monsters are attending the convention?

Drill 8

Translate and solve the following word problems.

51. Sal is looking for a clean, unwrinkled shirt to wear to work. 2/3 of his shirts are dirty, and of the remainder, 1/3 are wrinkled. If Sal has a total of 36 shirts, how many shirts does he have to choose from for work?

52. One dose of secret formula is made from 1/6 ounce of Substance X and 2/3 ounce of Substance Z. How many doses are in a 10-ounce vial of secret formula?

53. Of the movies in Santosh's collection, 1/3 are animated features, 1/4 are live-action features, and the remainder are documentaries. If 2/5 of the documentaries are depressing, what fraction of the films in Santosh's collection are depressing documentaries?

54. Of all the homes on Gotham Street, 1/3 are termite-ridden, and 3/5 of these are collapsing. What fraction of the homes are termite-ridden, but NOT collapsing?

55. 3/4 of supernatural creatures are invisible. Of the invisible supernatural creatures, 1/3 are ghosts. If there are 6,000,000 visible supernatural creatures, how many ghosts are there? (Note: assume that there are no visible ghosts.)

Drill Set Solutions:

Drill 1

1. **15:**
Let c = number of computers
Let e = number of employees

$c = e + 5$
If $e = 10$, then $c = (10) + 5$
$c = 15$

2. **–3:**
$-5 = z + 7$
$z = -12$
$z/4 = -3$

3. **75:**
Let g = the number of cars that the Green lot can hold
Let r = the number of cars that the Red lot can hold

$g + r = 115$
$g = r - 35$

$(r - 35) + r = 115$
$2r - 35 = 115$
$2r = 150$
$r = 75$

4. **18 years old:**

Let N = Norman's age now	$(N + 6)$ = Norman's age in 6 years.
Let M = Michael's age now	$(M + 6)$ = Michael's age in 6 years.

$N = M + 12$ Translate the first sentence into an equation.
$N + 6 = 2 (M + 6)$ Translate the second sentence into an equation.

$N - 12 = M$ Rewrite the first equation to put it in terms of M.

$N + 6 = 2(N - 12 + 6)$ Insert $N - 12$ for M in the second equation.
$N + 6 = 2(N - 6)$
$N + 6 = 2N - 12$

$18 = N$ Solve for N.

9

5. **$3,600:**

Each lawyer worked 4 hours, earning $300 per hour. $4 \times \$300 = \$1,200$
There are 3 lawyers. $\$1,200 \times 3 = \$3,600$

6. **$30 profit:**

Let p = profit
Let r = revenue
Let c = cost

Profit = Revenue − Cost
$p = r - c$
$r = 100 \times \$0.50$
$c = \$20$

$p = (100 \times \$0.50) - (\$20)$
$p = \$50 - \$20 = \$30$

7. **15 feet:**

Let s = the height of the shorter tree
Let t = the height of the taller tree

$s + t = 60$
$3s = t$

$s + (3s) = 60$
$4s = 60$

$s = 15$

8. **5 years old:**

Let L = Louise's age now ($L + 5$) = Louise's age 5 years from now
Let M = Mary's age now   ($M + 5$) = Mary's age 5 years from now

$L = 3M$ Translate the first sentence into an equation.
$(L + 5) = 2(M + 5)$ Translate the second sentence into an equation.

$(3M + 5) = 2(M + 5)$ Insert $3M$ for L in the second equation.
$3M + 5 = 2M + 10$ Make sure you distribute the 2.
$M = 5$ Solve for M.

9. **15:** Average $= \dfrac{\text{Sum}}{\text{Number}}$

Here, the average is 10, the sum of the 3 terms is $2 + 13 + x$, and 3 is the number of terms.

$$\frac{2+13+x}{3} = 10$$
$$2 + 13 + x = 30$$
$$15 + x = 30$$
$$x = 15$$

10. **6 slices of pizza:**

Let P = the number of slices of pizza eaten by each of the two friends who eat the same amount.

Let T = the number of slices of pizza eaten by the third friend.

$$T = P + 2$$
$$P + P + T = 14$$
$$P + P + (P + 2) = 14$$
$$3P + 2 = 14$$
$$3P = 12$$
$$P = 4$$

$$T = P + 2 = 4 + 2 = 6$$

Drill 2

11. **$650:**

Profit = Revenue − Cost

Revenue $= 300 \times 6 + 300 \times 2 = 1,800 + 600 = 2,400$

Cost $= 1,750$

Profit $= 2,400 - 1,750 = 650$

12. **23 years old:**

Let T = Toshi's age

Let K = Kosuke's age

Let J = Junko's age

$$J = 8$$
$$K = 2 \times J = 2 \times (8) = 16$$
$$T = K + 7 = (16) + 7 = 23$$

9

13. **270 miles:**

Let F = the distance of the first flight
Let S = the distance of the second flight
Let T = the distance of the third flight

$F = 2S$
$S = 3T$
$T = 45$

$S = 3 \times (45) = 135$
$F = 2 \times (135) = 270$

14. **$10,000:**

Profit = Revenue − Cost
Revenue = $50 \times 700 = 35{,}000$
Cost = $10{,}000 + (50 \times 300) = 10{,}000 + 15{,}000 = 25{,}000$
Profit = $35{,}000 − 25{,}000 = 10{,}000$

15. **200 tickets:**

Let x = the total number of tickets sold.

Therefore, $(x − 100)$ = the number of tickets Arnoldo sold beyond the first 100

$11x + 2(x − 100) = 2{,}400$
$11x + 2x − 200 = 2{,}400$
$13x = 2{,}600$
$x = 200$

16. **42:** $\dfrac{(x-3)+(x)+(x+3)+(x+4)+(x+11)}{5} = 45$

$\dfrac{5x+15}{5} = 45$

$x + 3 = 45$
$x = 42$

17. **50 years old:**

Let A = Amar's age now $(A + 5)$ = Amar's age 5 years from now
Let L = Lauri's age now $(L + 5)$ = Lauri's age 5 years from now

We're looking for Lauri's age in 10 years: $L + 10$

$A = L − 30$ Translate the first sentence into an equation.
$L + 5 = 3 (A + 5)$ Translate the second sentence into an equation.

$L + 5 = 3(L − 30 + 5)$ Insert $L − 30$ for A in the second equation.

9

$L + 5 = 3(L - 25)$
$L + 5 = 3L - 75$
$80 = 2L$
$40 = L$

Remember, we're looking for Lauri's age in 10 years:

$L + 10 = 40 + 10 = 50$

18. **$13:** $\dfrac{\text{Sum}}{\text{Number}} = \text{Average}$

First, we need to know the cost of the 5 books.

Sum = (Average)(Number) = ($12)(5) = $60

Sum of the cost of all 6 books = $60 + $18 = $78
Number of total books = 6

$\dfrac{\$78}{6} = \text{Average}$

19. **1,500 magazines:**
Let m = the number of magazines sold
Total cost = $3m + 10,500$
Total revenue = $10m$

Breaking even occurs when total revenue equals total cost, so:

$3m + 10,500 = 10m$
$10,500 = 7m$
$1,500 = m$

20. **45 hours:**
Let h = number of hours Renee worked

$40(40) + (h - 40)(80) = 2,000$
$1,600 + 80h - 3,200 = 2,000$
$80h - 1,600 = 2,000$
$80h = 3,600$
$h = 45$

9

Drill 3

21. **300 feet:** $100 \; \cancel{\text{yards}} \times \dfrac{3 \text{ feet}}{1 \; \cancel{\text{yard}}} = 300 \text{ feet}$

22. **25 gallons:** $200 \; \cancel{\text{pints}} \times \dfrac{1 \text{ gallon}}{8 \; \cancel{\text{pints}}} = \dfrac{200}{8} \text{ gallons} = 25 \text{ gallons}$

23. **96.8 pounds:** $44 \; \cancel{\text{kilograms}} \times \dfrac{2.2 \text{ pounds}}{1 \; \cancel{\text{kilogram}}} = 44 \times 2.2 \text{ pounds}$

Perform long multiplication to find the product.

$$
\begin{array}{r}
44 \\
\times 2.2 \\
\hline
88 \\
880 \\
\hline
96.8
\end{array}
$$

Because the two terms we're multiplying contain, collectively, one decimal place, include a decimal place in the product. That is, place the decimal not at the end (968.) but between the 6 and the 8 (96.8).

24. **27 inches:** $2.25 \; \cancel{\text{feet}} \times \dfrac{12 \text{ inches}}{1 \; \cancel{\text{foot}}} = 27 \text{ inches}$

25. **86° Fahrenheit:** Use the conversion formula, replacing the variable C with the temperature in Celsius:

$$C = \frac{5}{9}(F - 32)$$

$$30 = \frac{5}{9}(F - 32)$$

Solve for the temperature in Fahrenheit, F, by first multiplying both sides of the equation by 9/5 (the reciprocal of 5/9):

$$30 = \frac{5}{9}(F - 32)$$

$$30 \times \frac{9}{5} = F - 32$$

$$54 = F - 32$$

And then add 32 to both sides:

$54 + 32 = F$

$86 = F$

MANHATTAN
GMAT

26. **10,080 minutes:** One week contains 7 days and each of those days has 24 hours (7 × 24 = 168 total hours). Each of those hours has 60 minutes (168 × 60 = 10,080 total minutes). Using conversion ratios:

$$1 \text{ week} \times \frac{7 \text{ days}}{1 \text{ week}} \times \frac{24 \text{ hours}}{1 \text{ day}} \times \frac{60 \text{ minutes}}{1 \text{ hour}} =$$

10,080 minutes

27. **144 kilometers:** Convert miles per gallon to kilometers per liter by multiplying by the conversion ratios such that both the miles and gallons units are canceled out:

$$\frac{36 \text{ miles}}{\text{gallon}} \times \frac{8 \text{ kilometers}}{5 \text{ miles}} = \frac{288 \text{ kilometers}}{5 \text{ gallons}}$$

$$\frac{288 \text{ kilometers}}{5 \text{ gallons}} \times \frac{1 \text{ gallon}}{4 \text{ liters}} =$$

$$\frac{288 \text{ kilometers}}{20 \text{ liters}} = \frac{14.4 \text{ kilometers}}{\text{liter}}$$

The car has 10 liters of fuel in the tank.

$$10 \text{ liters} \times \frac{14.4 \text{ kilometers}}{\text{liter}} = 144 \text{ kilometers}$$

28. **0.6 gallons:** Convert both 1.6 cups and 2 quarts into gallons using conversion ratios:

$$1.6 \text{ cups} \times \frac{1 \text{ quart}}{4 \text{ cups}} \times \frac{1 \text{ gallon}}{4 \text{ quarts}} =$$

$$\frac{1.6}{16} \text{ gallons} = 0.1 \text{ gallons}$$

$$2 \text{ quarts} \times \frac{1 \text{ gallon}}{4 \text{ quarts}} = \frac{2}{4} \text{ gallons} = 0.5 \text{ gallons}$$

0.1 gallons + 0.5 gallons = 0.6 gallons.

29. **2,880 tiles:** There is a hidden trap in this question. Remember that the dimensions of this room are ft², not ft (because 5 feet × 4 feet = 20 square feet). To avoid this trap, we should convert the dimensions to inches first, then multiply.

$$5 \text{ feet} \times \frac{12 \text{ inches}}{1 \text{ foot}} = 60 \text{ inches}$$

$$4 \text{ feet} \times \frac{12 \text{ inches}}{1 \text{ foot}} = 48 \text{ inches}$$

The dimensions of the closet in inches are 60 inches by 48 inches, or 60 × 48 = 2,880 square inches. Each tile is 1 square inch, so it will take 2,880 tiles to cover the floor.

30. **19.8 liters/hour:** There is no mandatory order for processing the conversions. Start with 5.5 milliliters per second, and make the appropriate conversions:

$$\frac{5.5 \text{ milliliters}}{\text{second}} \times \frac{60 \text{ seconds}}{1 \text{ minute}} \times \frac{60 \text{ minutes}}{1 \text{ hour}} =$$

$$\frac{5.5 \times 60 \times 60 \text{ milliliters}}{\text{hour}}$$

$$\frac{5.5 \times 60 \times 60 \text{ milliliters}}{\text{hour}} \times \frac{1 \text{ liter}}{1{,}000 \text{ milliliters}} =$$

$$\frac{5.5 \times 3{,}600 \text{ liters}}{1{,}000 \text{ hours}}$$

To make the calculations as painless as possible, look to cancel before you multiply.

$$\frac{5.5 \times 3{,}600 \text{ liters}}{1{,}000 \text{ hours}} = \frac{5.5 \times 36 \text{ liters}}{10 \text{ hours}} =$$

$$\frac{198 \text{ liters}}{10 \text{ hours}} = \frac{19.8 \text{ liters}}{\text{hour}}$$

Drill 4

31. **144 miles:** The $D = RT$ formula allows us to solve for Jiang's distance. Note that the time must be converted so that it is expressed only in hours rather than hours and minutes.

$$15 \text{ min} \times \left(\frac{1 \text{ hr}}{60 \text{ min}} \right) = \frac{1}{4} \text{ hr} = 0.25 \text{ hr}$$

Therefore, 2 hours and 15 minutes is equivalent to 2.25 hours.

D (mi)	$=$	R (mi/hr)	$\times$	T (hr)
d	$=$	64	$\times$	2.25

$$\frac{64 \text{ miles}}{\text{hour}} \times 2.25 \text{ hours} = 144 \text{ miles} \qquad 64 \times 2.25 = 64 \times \frac{9}{4} = 16 \times 9 = 144$$

32. **4:20 pm:** To solve this problem, we can split Tom's journey into two portions: the first portion when he traveled 60 miles per hour and the second portion when he traveled 45 miles per hour.

For the first portion, we know that Tom traveled for 2 hours at 60 miles per hour. We can use these values in the $D = RT$ formula to figure out how far he went.

D (mi)	$=$	R (mi/hr)	$\times$	T (hr)
d	$=$	60	$\times$	2

$$\frac{60 \text{ miles}}{\text{hour}} \times 2 \text{ hours} = 120 \text{ miles}$$

Since Tom traveled 120 miles during the first portion of his journey he has $180 - 120 = 60$ miles to travel during the second part. We know that, during this portion, he traveled at 45 miles per hour, allowing us to use the $D = RT$ equation to calculate how long this portion of the journey took.

D (mi)	$=$	R (mi/hr)	$\times$	T (hr)
60	$=$	45	$\times$	t

$$60 = 45t$$

$$t = \frac{60}{45} \text{ hours} = \frac{4}{3} \text{ hours} = 1 \text{ hour } 20 \text{ minutes}$$

Tom's entire journey took 3 hours and 20 minutes: 2 hours for the first portion and 1 hour 20 minutes for the second portion. Finally, we must add 3 hours and 20 minutes to Tom's starting time of 1:00 pm to calculate when Tom completed his journey, 4:20 pm.

33. **2 miles per hour:** We can find the average rate by dividing the total distance traveled by the total time spent traveling. In this case, Roger travels 3 miles to and back from a store, covering a total of 6 miles in 3 hours. Thus, we can calculate his average rate using the relationship $R = \dfrac{D}{T}$:

$$R = \frac{6 \text{ miles}}{3 \text{ hours}} = 2\frac{\text{miles}}{\text{hour}}$$

34. **15 minutes:** The $D = RT$ equation allows us to calculate how long it will take each individual to run the path.

Sue runs the 10-mile path at a rate of 8 miles per hour.

D (mi)	$=$	R (mi/hr)	$\times$	T (hr)
10	$=$	8	$\times$	t

$$10 = 8t$$

$$\frac{5}{4} = t$$

Therefore, she completes the path in 1 hour 15 minutes.

Rob runs the 10-mile path at a rate of $6\frac{2}{3}$ mi/hr $=\frac{20}{3}$ mi/hr.

D (mi)	=	R (mi/hr)	×	T (hr)
10	=	20/3	×	t

$$10=\frac{20}{3}t$$

$$\frac{3}{2\cancel{0}}\times1\cancel{0}=t$$

$$\frac{3}{2}=t$$

Therefore, Rob runs the path in 1 hour 30 minutes.

Finally, we can subtract Sue's time from Rob's time to calculate how long she will have to wait.

1 hour 30 min − 1 hour 15 min = 15 min

35. **10 kilometers per hour:** In order to calculate Svetlana's speed during the second half of the race, we must first calculate how long it took her to run the first half of the race. We are told the first half of the race is 5 kilometers in length, and Svetlana ran at a speed of 12 kilometers per hour. These values can be used in the $D = RT$ formula.

D (km)	=	R (km/hr)	×	T (hr)
5	=	12	×	t

$$5=12t$$

$$t=\frac{5}{12}\text{ hr}$$

To calculate the time Svetlana has to run the second half of the race, we can subtract her time from the first half of the race from her goal time for the entire race. To do this calculation, first we must convert her goal time from minutes to hours.

$$55\text{ min }\times\frac{1\text{ hr}}{60\text{ min}}=\frac{55}{60}\text{ hr}=\frac{11}{12}\text{ hr}$$

Then we subtract Svetlana's time for the first half of the race from this value.

9

$$\frac{11}{12}\ \text{hr} - \frac{5}{12}\ \text{hr} = \frac{6}{12}\ \text{hr} = \frac{1}{2}\ \text{hr} = 0.5\ \text{hr}$$

We now know that Svetlana must complete the second 5 kilometers in 0.5 hours, allowing us to use this information in the $D = RT$ equation to solve for Svetlana's speed.

D (km)	=	R (km/hr)	×	T (hr)
5	=	r	×	0.5

$5 = 0.5r$
$10 = r$

Svetlana must run the second half of the race at a speed of 10 kilometers per hour to finish the entire race in 55 minutes.

Drill 5

Translate and solve the following work problems.

36. **375 bottles per hour:** We can use the $W = RT$ formula to solve for the number of bottles produced per hour.

W (bot)	=	R (bot/hr)	×	T (hr)
1,500	=	r	×	4

$1,500 = 4r$
$375 = r$

The rate is 375 bottles per hour.

37. **4 hours 20 minutes:**

First, we calculate the rate of the deluxe machine by multiplying the rate of the standard machine by 2.

15 gal/hr × 2 = 30 gal/hr

We can use this rate in the $W = RT$ formula to solve for the amount of time the machine takes to fill 130 gallons of paint.

W (gal)	=	R (gal/hr)	×	T (hr)
130	=	30	×	t

411

$$130 = 30t$$

$$t = \frac{13\cancel{0}}{3\cancel{0}} = \frac{13}{3} = 4\frac{1}{3} = 4 \text{ hr } 20 \text{ min}$$

38. 660 widgets: We can use two separate $W = RT$ charts, one for Machine A and one for Machine B, to calculate how many widgets each machine produces in 20 minutes.

	W (wid)	$=$	R (wid/min)	$\times$	T (min)
Machine A	a	$=$	15	$\times$	20
Machine A	b	$=$	18	$\times$	20

Machine A: $a = 15 \times 20 = 300$ widgets

Machine B: $b = 18 \times 20 = 360$ widgets

To calculate the total number of widgets produced, we add the values for the individual machines.

300 widgets + 360 widgets = 660 widgets

39. 200 gallons per hour: First, we must calculate the time it took to fill the pool.

5:24 pm – 2:00pm = 3 hours 24 minutes

Next, we need to convert the minutes portion of this time to hours.

$$24 \text{ min} \times \left(\frac{1 \text{ hr}}{60 \text{ min}} \right) = \frac{24}{60} \text{ hr} = \frac{2}{5} \text{ hr} = 0.4 \text{ hr}$$

Now we know that it takes 3.4 hours to fill the pool and the capacity of the pool is 680 gallons, allowing us to use the $W = RT$ equation to solve for the rate.

W (gal)	$=$	R (gal/hr)	$\times$	T (hr)
680	$=$	r	$\times$	3.4

$$680 = 3.4r$$

$$r = \frac{680}{3.4} = \frac{6800}{34} = 200 \frac{\text{gallons}}{\text{hour}}$$

40. 60 golf clubs per hour: First, we can calculate the size of a production lot using the information about Machine A. Machine A has a rate of 15 golf clubs per hour and completes a production lot in 6 hrs. We can use this information in the $W = RT$ formula.

W (clubs)	$=$	R (clubs/hr)	$\times$	T (hr)
w	$=$	15	$\times$	6

w = (15 clubs per hour)(6 hours) = 90 clubs

Therefore, a production lot consists of 90 golf clubs. We also know that Machine B can complete the lot in 1.5 hours. We can now use the $RT = W$ chart to calculate the rate for Machine B.

W (clubs)	$=$	R (clubs/hr)	$\times$	T (hr)
90	$=$	r	$\times$	1.5

We can make the calculation easier by converting 1.5 hours to $\dfrac{3}{2}$ hours.

$$90 = \frac{3}{2}r$$
$$\frac{2}{3} \times 90 = r$$
$$2 \times 30 = r$$
$$r = 60 \text{ clubs per hour}$$

Drill 6

Translate and solve the following word problems.

41. $40,000: We can use decimal equivalents here, using 1 (or 100%) as a starting point and adding to 1 for an increase or subtracting from 1 for a decrease. For example, "If Ken's salary were 20% higher" can be translated as 1 + (20%)(1) = 1 + 0.2 = 1.2. Similarly, "20% less than" can be translated as 1 − (20%)(1) = 1 − 0.2 = 0.8. Therefore 120% of Ken's salary is equal to 80% of Lorena's salary:

$1.2K = 0.8(60,000)$

$$K = \frac{0.8(60,000)}{1.2} \times \frac{10}{10}$$

$$K = \frac{\overset{2}{\cancel{8}}(60,000)}{\underset{3}{\cancel{12}}}$$

$$K = \frac{2(60,000)}{3}$$

$$K = 2(20,000)$$

$$K = 40,000$$

Ken's salary is $40,000.

42. **$19.50:** When we are asked to multiply percents, the most straightforward method is usually to use a fractional representation:

$$\$10 \times \frac{13\cancel{0}}{10\cancel{0}} \times \frac{15\cancel{0}}{10\cancel{0}}$$

$$= \$\cancel{10} \times \frac{13}{\cancel{10}} \times \frac{15}{10}$$

$$= \$13 \times \frac{3}{2}$$

$$= \$19.50$$

43. **108%:** If the stock increases 20%, then the new value is 120% of the original. If the stock then goes down 10%, the final value is 90% of the new value.

$\frac{120}{100}$	×	$\frac{90}{100}$	×	Q	=	$\frac{x}{100}$	×	Q
120 percent	of	90 percent	of	Q	is	what percent	of	Q ?

$$\frac{120}{100} \times \frac{90}{100} \times Q = \frac{x}{100} \times Q \qquad \text{Divide both sides by Q and reduce fractions}$$

$$\frac{6}{5} \times \frac{9}{10} = \frac{x}{100}$$

$$\frac{54}{50} = \frac{x}{100}$$

$$\overset{2}{\cancel{100}} \times \frac{54}{\cancel{50}_1} = x$$

$$108 = x$$

44. **36%:** We're given information about the parts of the class (the number of A's, B's, D's and F's) as well as the total number of students; we can handle this with a Parts Sum to a Total relationship. Because they all add to 200, we can write the following equation:

$A + B + C + D + E = \text{Total}$
$40 + 64 + C + 18 + 6 = 200$
$128 + C = 200$
$C = 200 - 128$
$C = 72$

$\frac{72}{200}$ of the grades are C's. Percents are defined in terms of 100. If we divide the top and bottom by 2, we can find the percent directly.

$$\frac{72}{200} \times \frac{\frac{1}{2}}{\frac{1}{2}} = \frac{36}{100}$$

Therefore 36% of the students got a C.

45. **(B) 7%:** The question is asking "70 cents is what percent of $10." We can translate this as follows. Don't forget to convert 70 cents to 0.7 dollars before performing the calculation.

0.7	=	$\frac{x}{100}$	×	10
0.7 dollars	is	what percent	of	10 dollars?

$$0.7 = \frac{x}{100} \times 10$$
$$0.7 = \frac{x}{10}$$
$$7 = x$$

Drill 7

Translate and solve the following word problems.

46. **250 meteors:** The 20 meteors that inspire Lily represent 80% of 10% of the visible meteors. Let's call the number we want m:

$$20 = (0.8)(0.1)m$$

We can simplify our equation by multiplying both sides by 10 to eliminate the 0.1, and then converting 0.8 to a fraction for ease of calculation:

$$200 = 0.8m$$

$$200 = \frac{4}{5}m$$
$$\frac{5}{\cancel{4}_1} \times \cancel{200}^{50} = m$$
$$5 \times 50 = m$$
$$250 = m$$

47. **60 gibbons:** We don't know how many pounds Bingwa weighs, but we know he weighs 1,000 gibbons. Therefore, he can lift 6% of this weight with his trunk.

$$\frac{6}{100} \times 1,000 \text{ gibbons} = 6 \times 10 \text{ gibbons} = 60 \text{ gibbons}$$

9

48. **55°:** When we are given two relationships in one sentence, we need to follow the grammar carefully to make sure we produce the right equations. The first sentence of the problem gives us two relationships:

The temperature in Limerick is 3/4 that in Cairo.
The temperature in Cairo is 8/5 that in Halifax.

$$L = \frac{3}{4}C$$

$$C = \frac{8}{5}H$$

We can now combine the two equations.

$$L = \frac{3}{4}\left(\frac{8}{5}H\right)$$

$$L = \frac{6}{5}H$$

And finally we can plug in the value we have been given for Limerick.

$$66 = \frac{6}{5}H$$

$$\frac{5}{6} \times 66 = H$$

$$5 \times 11 = H$$

$$55 = H$$

49. **1/6:** To determine the fraction of the songs that are world music, we need to figure out what fraction of the songs are not world music. We can do this by adding up the fractions we have been given for the other music types. We can use 12 as the common denominator because all of the denominators here are factors of 12.

$$\frac{1}{3} + \frac{1}{4} + \frac{1}{6} + \frac{1}{12} = \frac{4}{12} + \frac{3}{12} + \frac{2}{12} + \frac{1}{12} = \frac{10}{12} = \frac{5}{6}$$

5/6 of the songs in Farrah's playlist are not world music, so the remaining 1/6 of the songs are world music.

50. **210:** This is a common GMAT setup—we have been given several fractions and one actual number. Once we know what fraction of the whole that number represents, we can solve for the total (we'll call the total m). Notice that all of the denominators are primes, so they don't share any factors. Therefore we will have to multiply them all together to find a common denominator. $5 \times 7 \times 3 = 105$:

$$m = \frac{2}{5}m + \frac{1}{7}m + \frac{1}{3}m + 26$$

$$m = \frac{42}{105}m + \frac{15}{105}m + \frac{35}{105}m + 26$$

$$m = \frac{92}{105}m + 26$$

$$\frac{105}{105}m - \frac{92}{105}m = 26$$

$$\frac{13}{105}m = 26$$

$$m = 26\left(\frac{105}{13}\right)$$

$$m = 210$$

Drill 8

Translate and solve the following word problems.

51. **8:** We have to watch the grammar here. It would be easy to read the second sentence as "2/3 of his shirts are dirty, and 1/3 are wrinkled." However, what we have is slightly different—2/3 are dirty, and 1/3 of the remainder are wrinkled. This means that 1 − 2/3 = 1/3 of the shirts are clean, and of these clean shirts, 1/3 are wrinkled. So the fraction of wrinkled shirts is 1/3 × 1/3 = 1/9 of the total.

Now we know that 2/3 of the shirts are dirty, and 1/9 are wrinkled. Let's see what is left:

$\frac{2}{3}$ of 36 = 24 dirty shirts.

$\frac{1}{9}$ of 36 = 4 wrinkled shirts.

36 − 24 − 4 = 8 clean, unwrinkled shirts

52. **12 doses:** To find the number of doses in the vial, we need to divide the total volume of the formula in the vial by the volume of one dose.

One dose = $\frac{1}{6}$ oz. + $\frac{2}{3}$ oz. = $\frac{1}{6}$ oz. + $\frac{4}{6}$ oz. = $\frac{5}{6}$ oz. (Note that "oz." is the abbreviation for ounce.)

$$\frac{10}{\frac{5}{6}} = 10 \times \frac{6}{5} = 2 \times 6 = 12 \text{ doses}$$

9

53. **1/6:** Let's begin by finding what fraction of the movies are documentaries. We'll use M for the total number of movies, and d for the number of documentaries:

$$M = \frac{1}{3}M + \frac{1}{4}M + d$$

$$M = \frac{4}{12}M + \frac{3}{12}M + d$$

$$M = \frac{7}{12}M + d$$

$$\frac{12}{12}M - \frac{7}{12}M = d$$

$$\frac{5}{12}M = d$$

5/12 of the movies are documentaries. Of these, 2/5 are depressing.

$$\frac{\cancel{5}}{12}M \times \frac{2}{\cancel{5}} = \frac{2}{12}M = \frac{1}{6}M$$

1/6 of the movies in Santosh's collection are depressing documentaries.

54. $\dfrac{2}{15}$: If 3/5 of the termite-ridden homes are collapsing, then $1 - 3/5 = 2/5$ of the termite–ridden homes are NOT collapsing. We were asked to calculate something about all of the homes, not just the termite–ridden homes. We want to include the fraction of homes that ARE termite–ridden (1/3) but NOT collapsing (2/5). If h is the total number of houses, then:

$$h \times \frac{1}{3} \times \frac{2}{5} = \frac{2}{15}h$$

55. If 3/4 of supernatural creatures are invisible, then 1/4 are visible. Thus 6,000,000 is 1/4 of the total. There are 24,000,000 supernatural creatures in all. Now we can apply both of our fractions to this figure to find out the number of ghosts:

$$g = 24,000,000 \times \frac{3}{4} \times \frac{1}{3} = 24,000,000 \times \frac{1}{4} = 6,000,000$$

We ended up back at 6,000,000. This indicates that there might have been a quicker way to get to the answer. One way would be to start by calculating the fraction of all supernatural creatures that are ghosts:

3/4 × 1/3 = 1/4. That is, 1/4 of all supernatural creatures are ghosts. Because 6,000,000 already represents 1/4 of the total, we don't need to calculate anything else.

Chapter 10
of
Foundations of GMAT Math

Geometry

In This Chapter...

Chapter 10:

Geometry

In This Chapter:

- Basic shapes that the GMAT tests
- The key elements of each shape
- The equations that define the relationships between these elements
- How to apply these equations to solve GMAT geometry problems
- The coordinate plane

For many students, geometry brings to mind complicated shapes and the need to memorize lots of formulas. However, on the GMAT, geometry is fundamentally about the relationships between the various elements, or features, of a shape.

Each geometric shape has a set of basic elements. For instance, a circle has a radius, a diameter, a circumference, and an area. The key relationships among these elements are described by equations (usually not more than 4 or 5 per shape). For example, the relationship between a circle's radius and its area is described by the equation Area $= \pi r^2$ (where $r =$ radius).

In this chapter we'll go over the basic properties of the basic shapes most commonly tested on the GMAT. Then we'll discuss how the GMAT tests your knowledge of these shapes and how to work your way through Geometry questions.

Circles

A circle is a set of points that are all the same distance from a central point. By definition, every circle has a center, usually labeled O, which is not itself a point on the circle. The **radius** of a circle is the distance between the center of the circle and a point on the circle. *Any* line segment connecting the center and *any* point on the circle is a radius (usually labeled r). All radii in the same circle have the same length.

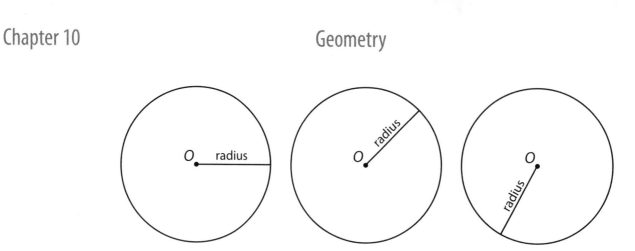

Know One Thing about a Circle: Know Everything Else

Now imagine a circle of radius 7. What else can you figure out about that circle?

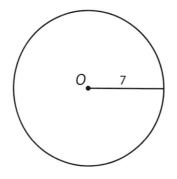

The next easiest thing to figure out is the **diameter** (usually labeled *d*), which passes through the center of a circle and connects 2 opposite points on the circle.

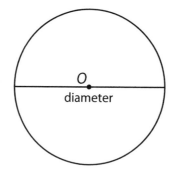

A diameter is 2 radii laid end to end, so it will always be exactly twice the length of the radius. This relationship can be expressed as $d = 2r$. A circle with radius 7 has a diameter of 14.

The **circumference** (usually referred to as *C*) is a measure of the distance around a circle. The circumference is essentially the perimeter of a circle.

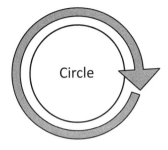

For any circle, the circumference and the diameter have a consistent relationship. If you divide the circumference by the diameter, you always get the same number—3.14… a number known by the Greek letter π (pi). To recap:

$$\frac{\text{circumference}}{\text{diameter}} = \pi. \text{ Or } \pi d = C.$$

In a circle with a diameter of 14, the circumference is $\pi(14) = 14\pi$. Most of the time you will not approximate this as 43.96 (which is 14 × 3.14). Instead, keep it as 14π.

You can relate the circumference directly to the radius, since the diameter is twice the radius. This relationship is commonly expressed as $C = 2\pi r$. Be comfortable with using either equation.

Finally, the **area** (usually labeled *A*) is the space inside the circle.

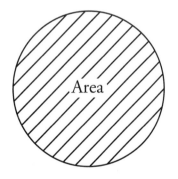

The area of a circle and its radius always have the same relationship. If you know the radius of the circle, then you can find the area using $A = \pi r^2$. For a circle of radius 7, the area is $\pi(7)^2 = 49\pi$. To recap, **once you know the radius, you can find the diameter, the circumference, and the area.**

10

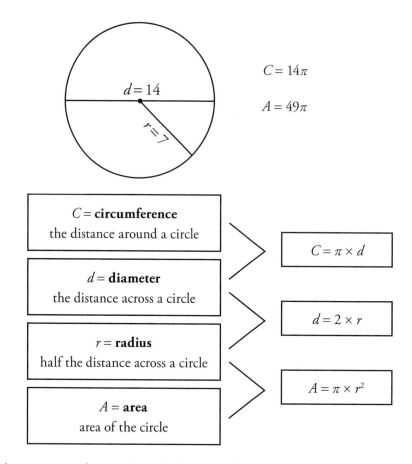

These relationships are true of any circle. What's more, **if you know *any* of these values, you can determine the rest.**

Say that the area of a circle is 36π. How do you find the other measures? Start with the formula for the area, which involves the radius.

$$36\pi = \pi r^2$$

Solve for the radius by isolating r.

$36\pi = \pi r^2$ Divide by π

$36 = r^2$ Take the square root of both sides

$6 = r$

Now that you know the radius, multiply it by 2 to get the diameter, which is 12. Finally, to find the circumference, simply multiply the diameter by π. The circumference is 12π.

MANHATTAN
GMAT

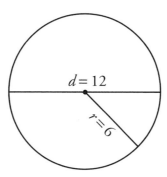

If you...	Then you...	Like this:
Know one thing about a circle	Can find out everything else about the circle by using the standard formulas	If $r = 4$ then $d = 8$, $C = 8\pi$, and $A = 16\pi$

Check Your Skills

1. The radius of a circle is 7. What is the area?
2. The circumference of a circle is 17π. What is the diameter?
3. The area of a circle is 25π. What is the circumference?

Answers can be found on page 469.

Sector: Slice of Pizza

Imagine again that you have a circle with an area of 36π. Now cut it in half and make it a semicircle. Any fractional portion of a circle is known as a **sector**. Think of a sector as a slice of pizza.

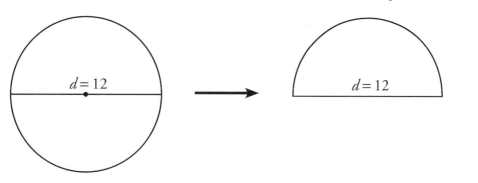

What effect does cutting the circle in half have on the basic elements of the circle? The diameter stays the same, as does the radius. But the area and the circumference are also cut in half. The area of the semicircle is 18π, and the circumference is 6π. When you deal with sectors, you call the remaining portion of the circumference the **arc length.** For this sector, the arc length is 6π.

10

If, instead of cutting the circle in half, you cut it into 1/4's, each piece of the circle would have 1/4 the area of the entire circle and 1/4 the circumference.

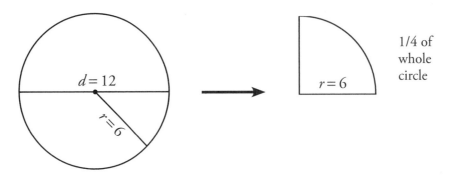

Now, on the GMAT, you're unlikely to be told that you have 1/4th of a circle. Rather, you would be told something about the **central angle**, which is the degree measure between the two radii. Take a look at the quarter circle. Normally, there are 360° in a full circle. What is the degree measure of the angle between the 2 radii? The same thing that happens to area and circumference happens to the central angle. It is now 1/4th of 360°, which is 90°.

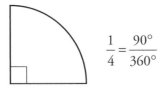

$$\frac{1}{4} = \frac{90°}{360°}$$

Let's see how you can use the central angle to determine sector area and arc length. Imagine that the original circle still has area 36π, but now the sector has a central angle of 60°.

What fractional amount of the circle remains if the central angle is 60°? The whole is 360°, and the part is 60°. So 60/360 is the fraction you're looking for. 60/360 reduces to 1/6. That means a sector with a central angle of 60° is 1/6th of the entire circle. The sector area is 1/6 × (Area of circle), and arc length is 1/6 × (Circumference of circle).

Sector Area = 1/6 × (36π) = 6π

Arc Length = 1/6 × (12π) = 2π

$$\frac{1}{6} = \frac{60°}{360°} = \frac{\text{Sector Area}}{\text{Circle Area}} = \frac{\text{Arc Length}}{\text{Circumference}}$$

In the last example, the central angle told you the fractional amount that the sector represented. But any of the three properties of a sector, namely central angle, arc length and area, could be used.

Consider this example:

A sector has a radius of 9 and an area of 27π. What is the central angle of the sector?

You still need to determine the fraction of the circle that the sector represents. This time, however, you have to use the area. You know the area of the sector, so if you can figure out the area of the whole circle, you can figure out what fractional amount the sector is.

The radius is 9, so now calculate the area of the whole circle. Area $= \pi r^2 = \pi(9)^2 = 81\pi$. $\dfrac{27\pi}{81\pi} = \dfrac{1}{3}$, so the

sector is 1/3 of the circle. The full circle has a central angle of 360°, so multiply that by 1/3. $1/3 \times 360 = 120$, so the central angle of the sector is 120°.

$$\frac{1}{3} = \frac{120°}{360°} = \frac{27\pi \text{ (sector area)}}{81\pi \text{ (circle area)}}$$

Every question about sectors will provide you with enough info to calculate one of the following fractions, which represent the sector as a fraction of the circle:

$$\frac{\text{central angle}}{360} \qquad \frac{\text{sector area}}{\text{circle area}} \qquad \frac{\text{arc length}}{\text{circumference}}$$

All of these fractions have the same value. Once you know this value, you can find any measure of the sector or the original circle.

If you...	Then you...	Like this:
Encounter a sector	Figure out the fraction of the circle that the sector represents	If central angle = 45° and the radius is 5 then fraction = 45°/360° = 1/8 and area = $(1/8)\pi r^2 = (25/8)\pi$

10

Check Your Skills

4. A sector has a central angle of 270° and a radius of 2. What is the area of the sector?
5. A sector has an arc length of 4π and a radius of 3. What is the central angle of the sector?
6. A sector has an area of 40π and a radius of 10. What is the arc length of the sector?

Answers can be found on page 469.

Triangles

Triangles show up all over the GMAT. You'll often find them hiding in problems that seem to be about rectangles or other shapes. Many properties of triangles are tested.

Sum of Any Two Sides > Third Side

The sum of any two side lengths of a triangle will always be greater than the third side length. After all, the shortest distance between two corners of the triangle is the straight line between them, rather than a detour to the third corner.

A related idea is that any side is greater than the *difference* of the other two side lengths. Otherwise, you can't even connect the dots and draw a complete triangle. The pictures below illustrate these two points.

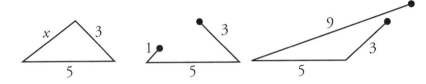

What is the largest number x could be? What's the smallest? Could it be 9? 1?

x must be less than $3 + 5 = 8$

x must be greater than $5 - 3 = 2$

$2 < x < 8$

If you…	Then you…	Like this:
Want to know how long the third side of a triangle could be	Make that side less than the sum of the other two sides, but more than the difference	First side = 6, second side = 4 What could the third side be? It must be less than $6 + 4 = 10$ but greater than $6 - 4 = 2$

Check Your Skills

7. Two sides of a triangle have lengths 5 and 19. Can the third side have a length of 13?

8. Two sides of a triangle have lengths 8 and 17. What is the range of possible values of the length of the third side?

Answers can be found on page 469.

Sum of The Three Angles = 180°

The internal angles of a triangle must add up to 180°. As a result, if you know 2 angles in the triangle, you can find the third angle. Take a look at this triangle:

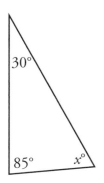

The 3 internal angles must add up to 180°, so you know that $30 + 85 + x = 180$. Solving for x tells you that $x = 65$. The third angle is 65°.

The GMAT can also test you in more complicated ways. Consider this triangle:

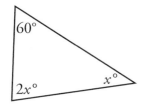

You only know one of the angles. The other two are unknown, but they are both given in terms of x. Again, the 3 angles add up to 180. So $60 + x + 2x = 180$. That means that $3x = 120$. So $x = 40$. The angle labeled $x°$ has a measure of 40° and the angle labeled $2x°$ has a measure of 80°.

The GMAT does not always draw triangles to scale. Don't try to guess angles from the picture, which could be distorted. Instead, solve for angles mathematically.

If you...	Then you...	Like this:
Know two angles of a triangle, or can represent all three in terms of x	Can find all angles using the "sum to 180" principle	First angle = $3x°$ Second angle = $4x°$ Third angle = 40° $3x + 4x + 40 = 180$ $7x = 140$ or $x = 20$

10

Check Your Skills

Find the missing angle(s).

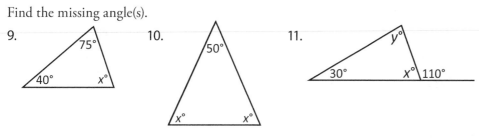

Answers can be found on page 470.

Same Sides = Same Angles, and Vice Versa

Internal angles of a triangle are important on the GMAT for another reason. **Sides correspond to their opposite angles.** That is, the longest side is opposite the largest angle, and the smallest side is opposite the smallest angle. Think about an alligator opening its mouth. As the angle between its upper and lower jaws increases, the distance between top and bottom teeth gets bigger.

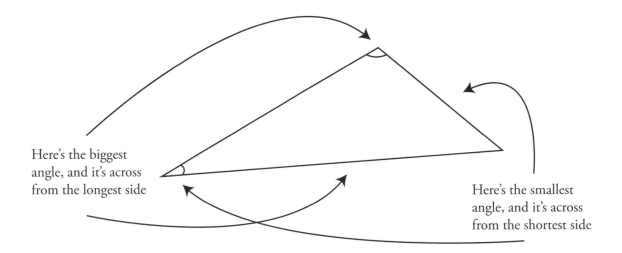

Here's the biggest angle, and it's across from the longest side

Here's the smallest angle, and it's across from the shortest side

This relationship works both ways. If you know the sides of the triangle, you can make inferences about the angles. If you know the angles, you can make inferences about the sides.

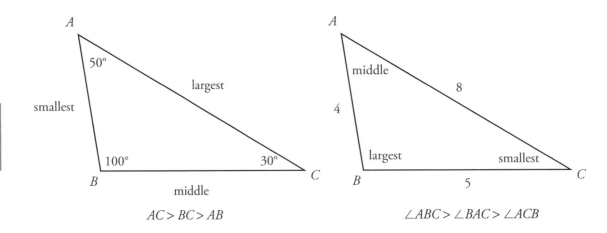

$AC > BC > AB$ $\angle ABC > \angle BAC > \angle ACB$

You frequently encounter a triangle that has 2 or even 3 equal sides. These triangles also have 2 or 3 equal angles. You can classify triangles by the number of equal sides or angles that they have.

- A triangle that has 2 equal angles and 2 equal sides (opposite the equal angles) is an **isosceles triangle.**

- A triangle that has 3 equal angles (all 60°) and 3 equal sides is an **equilateral triangle.**

The relationship between equal angles and equal sides works in both directions. Take a look at these isosceles triangles, and think about what additional information you can infer from them.

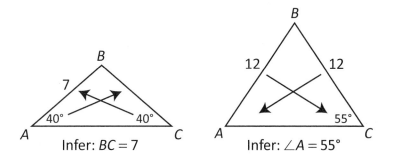

The GMAT loves isosceles triangles. Examine this challenging example:

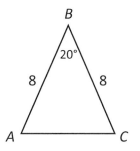

Take a look at the triangle and see what other information you can fill in. Specifically, do you know the degree measure of either *BAC* or *BCA*?

Because side *AB* is the same length as side *BC*, angle *BAC* must have the same degree measure as angle *BCA*. Label each of those angles as *x°* on the diagram.

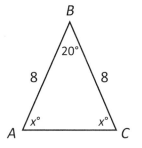

You also know that the 3 internal angles will add up to 180. So $20 + x + x = 180$. $2x = 160$, and $x = 80$. So *BAC* and *BCA* each equal 80°. You can't find the side length *AC* without more advanced math; the GMAT wouldn't ask you for this side length for that very reason.

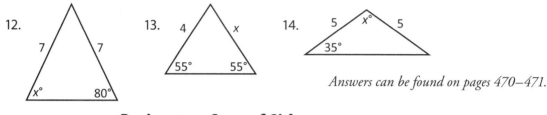

If you…	Then you…	Like this:
See two equal sides in a triangle	Set the opposite angles equal	Two sides both equal 8, so the angles opposite those sides are equal
See two equal angles in a triangle	Set the opposite sides equal	Two angles equal 30°, so the sides opposite those angles are equal

Check Your Skills

Find the value of *x*.

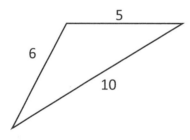

Answers can be found on pages 470–471.

Perimeter: Sum of Sides

The **perimeter** of a triangle is the sum of the lengths of all 3 sides.

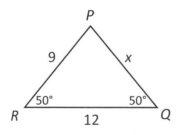

In this triangle, the perimeter is 5 + 6 + 10 = 21. This is a relatively simple property of a triangle, so often it will be used in combination with another property. Try this next problem. What is the perimeter of triangle *PQR*?

To solve for the perimeter, you need to determine the value of *x*. Because angles *PQR* and *PRQ* are both 50°, their opposite sides will have equal lengths. That means sides *PR* and *PQ* must have equal lengths, so side *PQ* has a length of 9. The perimeter of triangle *PQR* is 9 + 9 + 12 = 30.

Check Your Skills

What is the perimeter of each triangle?

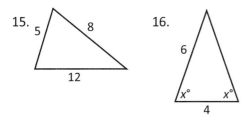

15.   16.

Answers can be found on page 471.

Note: Figures not drawn to scale. You need to be ready to solve geometry problems without depending on exactly accurate figures.

Apply Area Formula: Any Side Can Be the Base

The final property of a triangle to discuss is area, which equals 1/2 (base) × (height). In area formulas for any shape, be clear about the relationship between the base and the height. **The base and the height must be perpendicular to each other.**

In a triangle, one side of the triangle is the base. The height is formed by dropping a line from the third point of the triangle straight down towards the base, so that it forms a 90° angle with the base. The small square located where the height and base meet (in the figure below) is a very common symbol used to denote a right angle. You can also say that the height is **perpendicular** to the base, or vice versa.

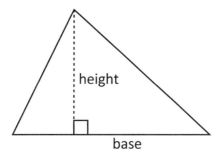

The GMAT often asks you about familiar shapes while presenting them in unfamiliar orientations. Many people think that the base is the "bottom" side of the triangle, but in reality, **any side of the triangle could act as a base.** The three triangles below are all the same triangle, but in each one you have made a different side the base, and drawn in the corresponding height.

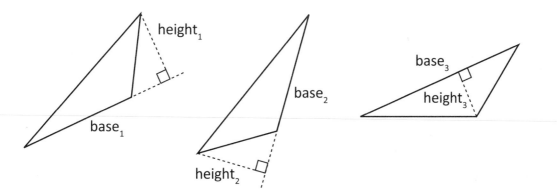

The height can be *outside* the triangle! (You just extend the base.) What matters is that the base and the height are perpendicular to each other. There must be a right angle between the base and the height.

If you...	Then you...	Like this:
Need the area of a triangle	Apply the area formula, using *any* convenient side as the base	$A = 1/2$ (base) (height) Use any side as base

Check Your Skills

What are the areas of the following triangles?

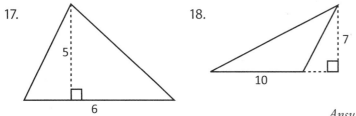

17.

18.

Answers can be found on page 471.

Know Two Sides of a Right Triangle: Find the Third Side

Right triangles are very common on the GMAT. **A right triangle** is any triangle in which one of the angles is a right angle (90°). Consider this example.

What is the perimeter of triangle *ABC*?

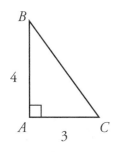

With only two sides of the triangle, how do you get the perimeter? Because this is a right triangle, you can use the **Pythagorean Theorem**, which only applies to right triangles. According to the theorem, the lengths of the 3 sides of a right triangle are related by the equation $a^2 + b^2 = c^2$, where a and b are the lengths of the sides touching the right angle, also known as **legs**, and c is the length of the side opposite the right angle, also known as the **hypotenuse.**

In the triangle above, sides *AB* and *AC* are a and b (it doesn't matter which is which) and side *BC* is c. So $(3)^2 + (4)^2 = (BC)^2$. $9 + 16 = (BC)^2$, so $25 = (BC)^2$, and the length of side *BC* is 5. The triangle looks like this:

10

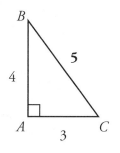

Finally, the perimeter = 3 + 4 + 5 = 12.

Often, you can take a shortcut around using the full-blown Pythagorean Theorem. The GMAT favors a subset of right triangles in which all three sides have lengths that are integer values. The triangle above is an example. The side lengths are 3, 4 and 5—all integers. This group of side lengths is a **Pythagorean triplet**—a 3–4–5 triangle.

A few of these triplets are especially common and should be memorized. For each triplet, the first two numbers are the lengths of the sides that touch the right angle, and the third (and largest) number is the length of the hypotenuse.

3–4–5	5–12–13	8–15–17	6–8–10	10–24–26
			(this is 3–4–5 doubled)	(this is 5–12–13 doubled)

Note that you can double, triple, or otherwise apply a common multiplier to these lengths. 3–4–5 should be thought of as a ratio of 3:4:5.

If you know the triplet, you can save time and effort. Consider this example.

What is the area of triangle *DEF*?

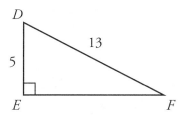

What do you need in order to find the area of triangle *DEF*? The area formula is 1/2 (base) × (height), so you need a base and a height. This is a right triangle, so sides *DE* and *EF* are perpendicular to each other. You can treat one of them as the base and the other as the height.

How do you find the length of side *EF*? First, realize that in theory, **you can always find the length of the third side of a right triangle if you know the lengths of the other two sides.** You can always use the Pythagorean Theorem. In this case, the formula would look like this: $(DE)^2 + (EF)^2 = (DF)^2$. You

know the lengths of two of those sides, so rewrite the equation as $(5)^2 + (EF)^2 = (13)^2$. Solving this equation, you get $25 + (EF)^2 = 169$, so $(EF)^2 = 144$, and finally $EF = 12$.

But these calculations are unnecessary. Once you see a right triangle in which one of the legs has a length of 5 and the hypotenuse has a length of 13, you should recognize the Pythagorean triplet. The length of the other leg must be 12.

However you find the length of side EF, the triangle now looks like this:

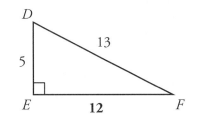

Now you have what you need to find the area of triangle DEF. Area = $\frac{1}{2}(12) \times (5) = \frac{1}{2}(60) = 30$.

If you…	Then you…	Like this:
Know two sides of a right triangle	Can find the third side, either by using the full Pythagorean Theorem or by recognizing a triplet	A leg of a right triangle has length 18, while the hypotenuse has length 30. How long is the third side? $18^2 + x^2 = 30^2$ and solve for x or recognize $3:4:5$ ratio $x = 24$

Check Your Skills

What is the length of the third side of the triangle? For #21, find the area.

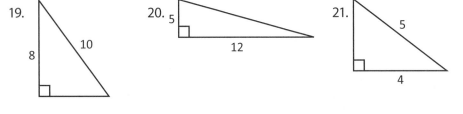

19.

20. 5, 12

21. 5, 4

Answers can be found on page 472.

Quadrilaterals

A quadrilateral is any figure with 4 sides. Three common variations are described below. Before getting to them, realize that **you can always cut up any quadrilateral into two triangles** by slicing across the middle to connect opposite corners. So what you know about triangles could apply in a problem involving quadrilaterals. In many cases, you *shouldn't* cut the quadrilateral that way, but it's good to know you could.

Parallelogram: Cut Into Triangles OR Drop Height

The GMAT frequently deals with **parallelograms**. A parallelogram is any 4 sided figure in which the opposite sides are parallel and equal. Opposite angles are also equal, and adjacent angles add up to 180°.

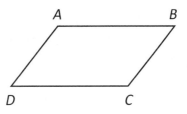

In this parallelogram, sides *AB* and *CD* are parallel and have equal lengths, sides *AD* and *BC* are parallel and have equal length, angles *ADC* and *ABC* are equal and angles *DAB* and *DCB* are equal.

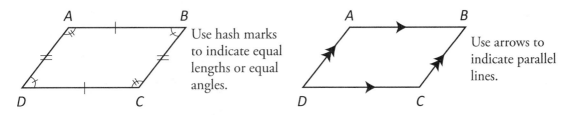

Use hash marks to indicate equal lengths or equal angles.

Use arrows to indicate parallel lines.

An additional property of any parallelogram is that the diagonal will divide the parallelogram into 2 equal triangles.

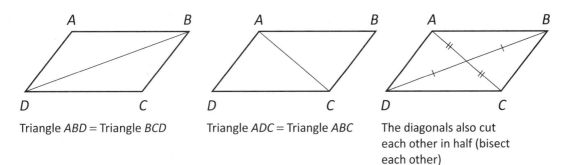

Triangle *ABD* = Triangle *BCD*   Triangle *ADC* = Triangle *ABC*   The diagonals also cut each other in half (bisect each other)

For any parallelogram, the perimeter is the sum of the lengths of all the sides and the area is equal to (base) × (height). With parallelograms, as with triangles, remember that the base and the height *must* be perpendicular to one another.

10

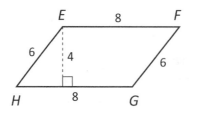

In this parallelogram, what is the perimeter, and what is the area? The perimeter is the sum of the sides, so it's 6 + 8 + 6 + 8 = 28. Alternatively, you can use one of the properties of parallelograms to calculate the perimeter in a different way. You know that parallelograms have two sets of equal sides. In this parallelogram, two of the sides have a length of 6 and two of the sides have a length of 8. So the perimeter equals 2 × 6 + 2 × 8. You can factor out a 2 and say that perimeter = 2 × (6 + 8) = 28.

To calculate the area, you need a base and a height. It might be tempting to say that the area is 6 × 8 = 48. But the two sides of this parallelogram are not perpendicular to each other. The dotted line drawn into the figure, however, is perpendicular to side *HG*. You need to **drop a height** to the base. The area of parallelogram *EFGH* is 8 × 4 = 32.

If you…	Then you…	Like this:
Want the perimeter or area of a parallelogram	Find all sides (for the perimeter) or drop a height (for the area)	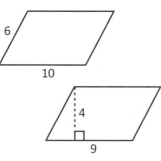 Perimeter = 6 + 8 + 6 + 8 = 28 Area = 8 × 4 = 32

Check Your Skills

22. What is the perimeter of the parallelogram?

23. What is the area of the parallelogram?

Answers can be found on page 472.

Rectangles = Parallelogram + 4 Right Angles

Rectangles are a specific type of parallelogram. Rectangles have all the properties of parallelograms, plus one more—**all 4 internal angles of a rectangle are right angles.** With rectangles, you refer to one pair of sides as the length and one pair of sides as the width. It doesn't matter which is which.

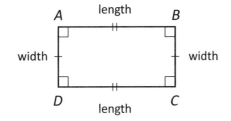

The formula for the perimeter of a rectangle is the same as for the perimeter of a parallelogram. You can add the lengths of the 4 sides, or you can add the length and the width and multiply by 2.

The formula for the area of a rectangle is also the same as for the area of a parallelogram. But for any rectangle, the length and width are by definition perpendicular to each other, so you don't need a separate height. For this reason, the area of a rectangle is commonly expressed as (length) × (width).

For the following rectangle, find the perimeter and the area.

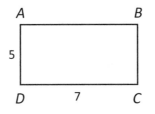

Start with the perimeter. Again, you can either fill in the missing sides and add them all up, or recognize that you have two sides with a length of 5 and two sides with a length of 7.

Therefore, perimeter = 2 × (5 + 7), which equals 24. Alternatively, 5 + 5 + 7 + 7 also equals 24.

Now find the area. The formula for area is (length) × (width). It's irrelevant which side you call the length. Either way, the area = (5) × (7) = 35.

Finally, recognize that the diagonal of a rectangle cuts the rectangle into 2 equal *right* triangles, with all the properties you expect of right triangles.

Check Your Skills
Find the area and perimeter of each rectangle.

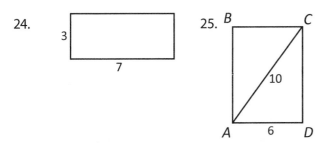

24.   25.

Answers can be found on pages 472–473.

Squares = Rectangle + 4 Equal Sides

The most special type of rectangle is a square. **A square is a rectangle in which all 4 sides are equal.** So knowing only one side of a square is enough to determine the perimeter and area of a square.

For instance, if the length of the side of a square is 3, you know that all 4 sides have a length of 3.

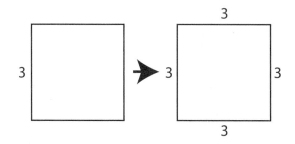

The perimeter of the square is 3 + 3 + 3 + 3, which equals 12. Alternatively, once you know the length of one side of a square, you can multiply that length by 4 to find the perimeter. $3 \times 4 = 12$.

To find the area, you use the same formula as for a rectangle—Area = length × width. But, because the shape is a square, you know that the length and the width are equal. Therefore, you can say that the area of a square is Area = (side)², which is the side length squared.

In this case, Area = $(3)^2 = 9$.

Squares are like circles: if you know one measure, you can find everything. This is because they are both "regular" figures. All circles look like each other, and all squares look like each other. For circles, the most fundamental measure is the radius, and then you can calculate everything else. For squares, the most fundamental measure is the side length.

Geometry: "Word" Problems with Pictures

Now that you know various properties of shapes, such as perimeter and area, how do you use these properties to answer GMAT geometry questions, especially ones with more than one figure? Consider this problem:

Rectangles *ABCD* and *EFGH*, shown below, have equal areas. The length of side *AB* is 5. What is the length of diagonal *AC*?

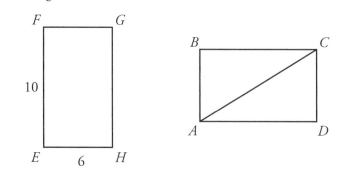

First, **draw your own copies of the shapes and fill in everything you know.** For this problem, redraw both rectangles. Label side *AB* with a length of 5. Also, make note of what you're looking for—in this case you want the length of diagonal *AC*. Draw that diagonal in, and label it with a question mark.

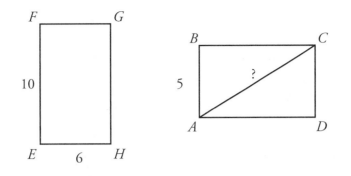

Now turn to the question. Realize that **many geometry questions are similar to the word problems** discussed in Chapter 9. Both types of problems provide you with information, some of which may be disguised. The information is related through common mathematical relationships, which also may be disguised or implied. In word problems, the information is given in words. In geometry, the information is presented visually.

So, has the question above provided you with any information that can be expressed mathematically? Can you create equations?

Yes. The two rectangles have equal areas. So you can say that Area$_{ABCD}$ = Area$_{EFGH}$. You can do even better than that. The formula for area of any rectangle is Area = (length) × (width). So the equation can be rewritten as (length$_{ABCD}$) × (width$_{ABCD}$) = (length$_{EFGH}$) × (width$_{EFGH}$).

The length and width of rectangle *EFGH* are 6 and 10, and the length of *AB* is 5. The equation becomes (5) × (width$_{ABCD}$) = (6) × (10). So (5) × (width$_{ABCD}$) = 60, meaning that the width of rectangle *ABCD* equals 12.

Any time you learn a new piece of information, add that information into your picture.

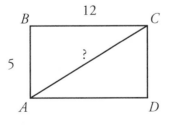

To recap, you've redrawn the shapes and filled in all the given information (such as side lengths, angles, etc.). You've made note of what the question was asking for. Just as you start a word problem by identifying unknowns, creating variables, and writing down givens, the first step for geometry problems is to **draw or redraw figures and fill in all given information.** Of course, **also confirm what you're being asked!**

10

Next, you made use of additional information provided. The question stated that the two rectangles had equal areas. You created an equation to express this relationship, and then you plugged in the values you knew to solve for the width of rectangle *ABCD*. This process is identical to the process used to solve word problems—you **identify relationships and create equations.** After that, you **solve the equations for the missing value** (in this case, the width of *ABCD*).

In some ways, all you have done so far is set up the problem. In fact, aside from noting that you need to find the length of diagonal *AC*, nothing you have done so far seems to have directly helped you actually solve for that value. So far, you have found that the width of rectangle *ABCD* is 12.

So why bother solving for the width of rectangle *ABCD* when you're not even sure why you'd need it? You are *likely* to need that missing value. On the vast majority of GMAT problems, two general principles hold: 1) intermediate steps are required to solve for the value you want and 2) the GMAT almost never provides extraneous information. As a result, something that you *can* solve for is likely to be a stepping stone on the way to the answer.

This doesn't mean that you should run hog-wild and calculate quantities at random. Rather, as you practice these problems, you'll gain a sense of the kinds of stepping stones that the GMAT prefers.

Now that you know the width of *ABCD*, what can you figure out that you couldn't before? Take another look at the value you're looking for: the length of *AC*.

You've already identified a relationship mentioned in the question—that both rectangles have equal areas. But for many geometry problems, there are additional relationships that aren't as obvious.

The key to this problem is to recognize that *AC* is not only the diagonal of rectangle *ABCD*, but is also the hypotenuse of a right triangle. You know this because one property of rectangles is that all four interior angles are right angles.

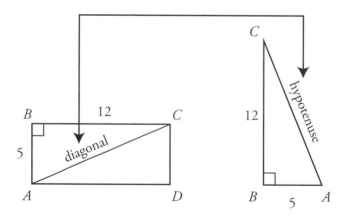

Now that you know *AC* is the hypotenuse of a right triangle, you can use two sides to find the third. One way to get the number is through the Pythagorean Theorem.

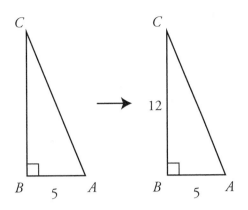

Sides *BC* and *AB* are the legs of the triangle, and *AC* is the hypotenuse, so:

$$(BC)^2 + (AB)^2 = (AC)^2$$
$$(12)^2 + (5)^2 = (AC)^2$$
$$144 + 25 = (AC)^2$$
$$169 = (AC)^2$$
$$13 = AC$$

Alternatively, avoid that work by recognizing that this triangle is one of the Pythagorean triplets: a 5–12–13 triangle. Either way, the answer to the question is *AC* = 13.

Let's recap what happened in the last portion of this question. You needed a non-obvious insight: that the diagonal of rectangle *ABCD* is also the hypotenuse of right triangle *ABC*. Once you had that insight, you could apply "right triangle" thinking to get that unknown side. The last part of this problem required you to **make inferences from the figures.**

Sometimes you need to make a jump from one shape to another through a common element. For instance, you needed to see *AC* as both a diagonal of a rectangle and as a hypotenuse of a right triangle. Here *AC* was common to both a rectangle and a right triangle, playing a different role in each.

These inferences can also make you think about what information you need to find another value.

The process is very similar to that for a word problem:

Step 1: **Draw or redraw figures, fill in all given information, and identify the target.**
         Fill in all known angles and lengths and make note of any equal sides or angles.

Step 2: **Identify relationships and create equations.**
         Start with relationships that are explicitly stated somewhere.

Step 3: **Solve the equations for the missing value.**
         If you can solve for a value, you will almost always need that value to answer the question.

Step 4: **Make inferences from the figures.**

You often need to use relationships that are not explicitly stated.

Try this problem:

Rectangle *PQRS* is inscribed in Circle *O* pictured below. The center of Circle *O* is also the center of Rectangle *PQRS*. If the circumference of Circle *O* is 5π, what is the area of Rectangle *PQRS*?

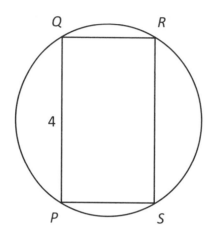

The first thing to do is **redraw the figure** on note paper and **fill in all the given information.** The question didn't explicitly give you the value of any side lengths or angles, but it did say that *PQRS* is a rectangle. That means all 4 internal angles are right angles. This is how the GMAT tests what you know about the key properties of different shapes. Also identify what you're looking for: the rectangle's area.

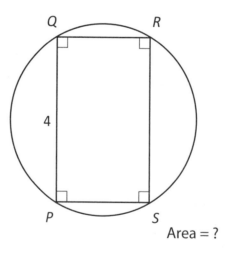

Area = ?

Now **identify relationships and create equations**. The question stated that the circumference of Circle *O* is 5π, and you know the formula for circumference. Circumference equals $2\pi r$, so $5\pi = 2\pi r$.

You only have one unknown (*r*), so **solve the equation for the missing value.** The radius turns out to be 2.5. You also know that $d = 2r$, so the diameter of Circle *O* is 5.

Why do you find the radius and diameter? *Because you can.* And because you'll almost certainly need one of them to answer the question. Now is the time to **make inferences from the figures.**

Ultimately, this question is asking for the area of rectangle *PQRS*. What information do you need to find that value? You have the length of *QP*. If you can find the length of either *QR* or *PS*, you can find the area of the rectangle.

What is the connection between the rectangle and the radius or diameter? Put in a diameter.

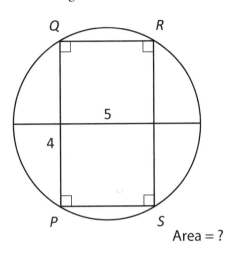

Area = ?

That didn't help much. What if you drew the diameter so that it passed through the center but touched the circle at points *P* and *R*? You know that the line connecting points *P* and *R* will be a diameter, because you know that the center of the circle is also the center of the rectangle.

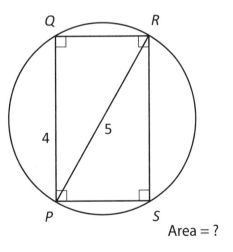

Area = ?

Why draw the diameter this way? Now it's also the diagonal of the rectangle. The circle and the rectangle have a common element. *PR* is the "bridge" between the two figures.

Where do you go from here? You still need the length of either *QR* or *PS* (which are the same, because this is a rectangle). Can you get either one of those values? Yes. *PQR* is a right triangle. Maybe it's not oriented the way you are used to, but all the elements are there: it's a triangle, and one of its internal

10

angles is a right angle. You also know the lengths of 2 of the sides: *QP* and *PR*. So you can use the Pythagorean Theorem to find the length of the third side: *QR*.

$$(QR)^2 + (QP)^2 = (PR)^2$$
$$(QR)^2 + (4)^2 = (5)^2$$
$$(QR)^2 + 16 = 25$$
$$(QR)^2 = 9$$
$$QR = 3$$

Alternatively, you could have recognized the Pythagorean triplet—triangle *PQR* is a 3–4–5 triangle. Either way, you conclude that the length of *QR* is 3.

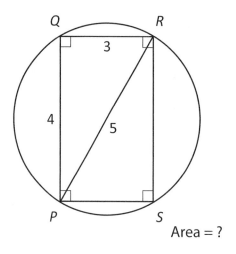

Area = ?

At last, you have what you need to find the area of rectangle *PQRS*. Area = (length) × (width) = (4) × (3) = 12. The answer to the question is 12.

The key insight in this problem was to realize that you could draw a diameter that would also act as the diagonal of the rectangle, linking the two figures as a "bridge." You also had to recognize that *PQR* was a right triangle, even though it may have been hard to see. These kinds of insights will be crucial to success on the GMAT.

10

If you...	Then you...	Like this:
Face a complicated geometry problem, especially one that has more than one figure	Follow the basic 4-step process to solve, finding intermediate unknowns and looking for bridges	1) Redraw, fill in, label target 2) Spot relationships & write equations 3) Solve for what you can 4) Make inferences

Check Your Skills

26. In rectangle *ABCD*, the distance from *A* to *C* is 10. What is the area of the circle inside the rectangle, if this circle touches both *AD* and *BC*? (This is known as an inscribed circle).

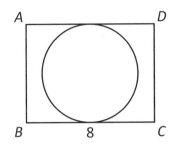

The answer can be found on pages 473–474.

Coordinate Plane—Position Is a Pair of Numbers

Before discussing the coordinate plane, let's review the number line.

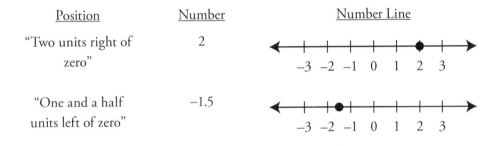

Position	Number	Number Line
"Two units right of zero"	2	
"One and a half units left of zero"	−1.5	

The number line is a ruler or measuring stick that goes as far as you want in both directions. With the number line, you can say where something is with a single number. In other words, you can link a position with a number.

You use both positive and negative numbers to indicate positions both left and right of zero.

You might be wondering "The position of what?" The answer is, a **point**, which is just a dot. When you are dealing with the number line, a point and a number mean the same thing.

If you show me where the point is on the number line, I can tell you the number.   → *the point is at −2*

If you tell me the number, I can show you where the point is on the number line.   *the point is at 0* →

This works even if you only have partial information about the point. If you tell me something about where the point is, I can tell you *something* about the number, and vice-versa.

For instance, if I say that the number is positive, then I know that the point lies somewhere to the right of 0 on the number line. Even though I don't know the exact location of the point, I do know a range of potential values.

The number is positive.
In other words, the number is
greater than (>) 0.

This also works in reverse. If I see a range of potential positions on a number line, I can tell you what that range is for the number.

The number is less than (<) 0.

Everything so far should be familiar. Inequalities were discussed in the last chapter. But now let's make things more complicated. What if you want to be able to locate a point that's not on a straight line, but on a page?

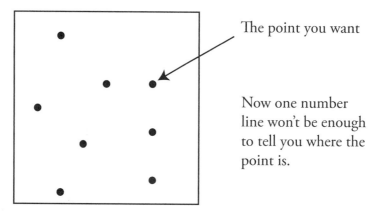

The point you want

Now one number line won't be enough to tell you where the point is.

Begin by inserting the number line into the picture. This will help you determine how far to the right or left of 0 the point is.

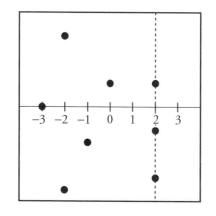

The point is two units to the right of zero.

But all three points that touch the dotted line are two units to the right of zero. You don't have enough information to determine the unique location of the point.

To locate the point, you also need to know how far up or down the dotted line. To determine how far up or down to go, you'll need another number line. This number line, however, is going to be vertical. Using this vertical number line, you can measure how far above or below 0 a point is.

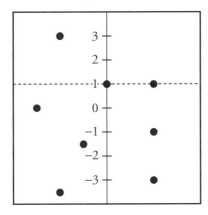

The point is one unit above zero.

Notice that this number line by itself also does not provide enough information to determine the unique location of the point.

But, if you combine the information from the two number lines, you can determine both how far left or right *and* how far up or down the point is.

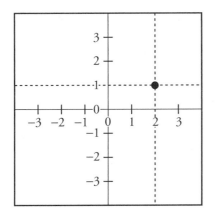

The point is 2 units to the right of 0.

AND

The point is 1 unit above 0.

Now you have a unique description of the point's position. Only one point on the page is BOTH 2 units to the right of 0 AND 1 unit above 0. On a page, you need two numbers to indicate position.

Just as with the number line, information can travel in either direction. If I tell you where the point is located with the two numbers, you can place that point on the page.

The point is 3 units to the left of 0.

AND

The point is 2 unit below 0.

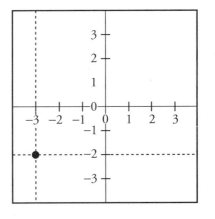

10

If, on the other hand, you see a point on the page, you can identify its location and extract the two numbers.

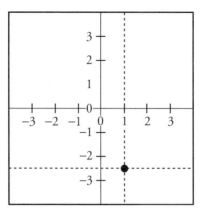

The point is 1 units to the right of 0.

AND

The point is 2.5 units below 0.

Now that you have two pieces of information for each point, you need to keep straight which number is which. In other words, you need to know which number gives the left-right position and which number gives the up-down position.

Some technical terms indicate the difference.

The **x-coordinate** is the left right-number.

> Numbers to the right of 0 are positive.
> Numbers to the left of 0 are negative.

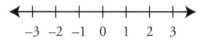

This number line is the **x-axis**

The **y-coordinate** is the up-down number.

> Numbers above 0 are positive.
> Numbers below 0 are negative.

This number line is the **y-axis**

The point where the axes cross is called the **origin**. This is always 0 on both axes.

Now, when describing the location of a point, you can use the technical terms.

The *x*-coordinate of the point is 1 and the *y*-coordinate of the point is 0.

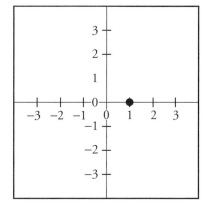

In short, you can say that, for this point, $x = 1$ and $y = 0$. In fact, you can go even further. You can say that the point is at (1, 0). This shorthand always has the same basic layout. The first number in the parentheses is the *x*-coordinate, and the second number is the *y*-coordinate. One easy way to remember this is that *x* comes before *y* in the alphabet. The origin has coordinates (0, 0).

The point is at (−3, −1)

OR

The point has an *x*-coordinate of −3 and a *y*-coordinate of −1.

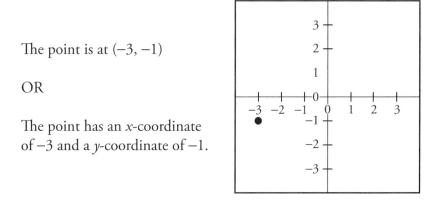

Now you have a fully functioning **coordinate plane:** an *x*-axis and a *y*-axis drawn on a page. The coordinate plane allows you to determine the unique position of any point on a **plane** (essentially, a really big and flat sheet of paper).

And in case you were ever curious about what **one-dimensional** and **two-dimensional** mean, now you know. A line is one dimensional, because you only need one number to identify a point's location. A plane is two-dimensional because you need two numbers to identify a point's location.

If you…	Then you…	Like this:
Want to plot a point on the coordinate plane	Use the *x*-coordinate for right/left of (0, 0) and use the *y*-coordinate for up/down from (0, 0)	(3, 2) is three units right and two units up from the origin

10

Check Your Skills

27. Draw a coordinate plane and plot the following points:

      1. (3, 1)   2. (−2, 3.5)   3. (0, −4.5)   4. (1, 0)

28. Which point on the coordinate plane below is indicated by the following coordinates?

      1. (2, −1)   2. (−1.5, −3)   3. (−1, 2)   4. (3, 2)

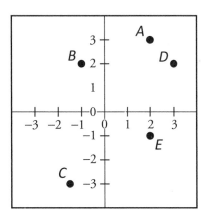

Answers can be found on page 474.

Know Just One Coordinate = Narrow Down to a Line

You need to know both the *x*-coordinate and the *y*-coordinate to plot a point exactly on the coordinate plane. If you only know one coordinate, you can't tell precisely where the point is, but you can narrow down the possibilities.

Let's say that all you know is that the point is 4 units to the right of 0.

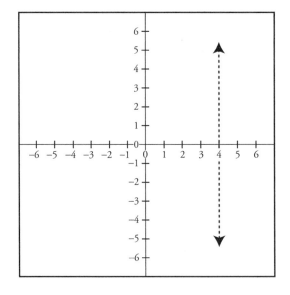

Any point along the vertical dotted line is 4 units to the right of 0. In other words, every point on the dotted line has an x-coordinate of 4. You could shorten that and say $x = 4$. You don't know anything about the y-coordinate, which could be any number. All the points along the dotted line have different y-coordinates but the same x-coordinate, which equals 4.

So, if you know that $x = 4$, then the point can be anywhere along a vertical line that crosses the x-axis at (4, 0). Let's try with another example.

If you know that $x = -3$…

Then we know

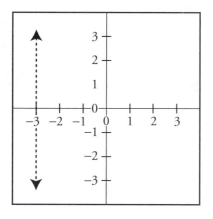

Every point on the dotted line has an x-coordinate of -3.

Points on the dotted line include $(-3, 1)$, $(-3, -7)$, $(-3, 100)$ and so on. In general, if you know the x-coordinate of a point and not the y-coordinate, then all you can say about the point is that it lies on a vertical line.

The x-coordinate still indicates left-right position. If you fix that position but not the up-down position, then the point can only move up and down—forming a vertical line.

Now imagine that all you know is the y-coordinate of a number. Say you know that $y = -2$. How could you represent this on the coordinate plane? In other words, what are all the points for which $y = -2$?

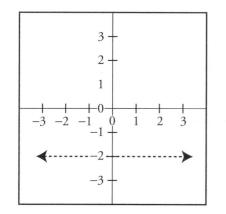

Every point 2 units below 0 fits this condition. These points form a horizontal line. We don't know anything about the x-coordinate, which could be any number. All the points along the horizontal dotted line have different x-coordinates but the same y-coordinate, which equals -2. For instance, $(-3, -2)$, $(-2, -2)$, $(50, -2)$ are all on the line.

Let's try another example. If you know that $y = 1$...

Then we know

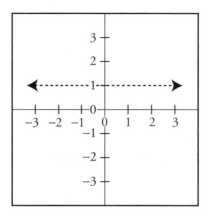

Every point on the dotted line has an y-coordinate of 1.

If you know the y-coordinate but not the x-coordinate, then you know the point lies somewhere on a horizontal line.

If you...	Then you...	Like this:
Know just one coordinate	Let the other coordinate roam free, so that you get a line	The points with a fixed x-coordinate equal to 3 ($x = 3$) form the vertical line through (3, 0), since y is free to run

Check Your Skills

Draw a coordinate plane and plot the following lines.

29. $x = 6$
30. $y = -2$
31. $x = 0$

Answers can be found on page 475.

Knowing Ranges

What do you do if all you know is that $x > 0$? To answer that, return to the number line for a moment. As you saw earlier, if $x > 0$, then the target is anywhere to the right of 0.

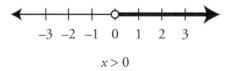

$x > 0$

Now look at the coordinate plane. All you know is that x is greater than 0. And you don't know *any-thing* about y, which could be any number.

How do you show all the possible points? You can shade in part of the coordinate plane: the part to the right of 0.

If you know that $x > 0$...

Then we know

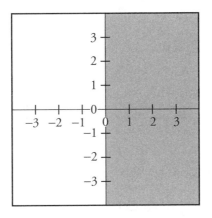

Every point in the shaded region has an x-coordinate greater than 0.

Now say that all you know is $y < 0$. Then you can shade in the bottom half of the coordinate plane—where the y-coordinate is less than 0. The x-coordinate can be anything.

If you know that $y < 0$...

Then we know

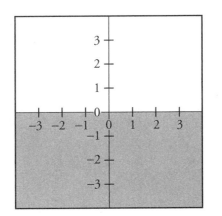

Every point in the shaded region has a y-coordinate less than 0.

Finally, if you know information about both x and y, then you can narrow down the shaded region.

If you know that $x > 0$ AND $y < 0$...

Then we know

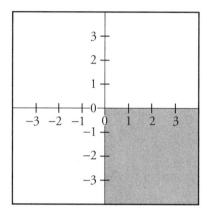

The only place where x is greater than 0 AND y is less than 0 is the bottom right quarter of the plane. So you know that the point lies somewhere in the bottom right quarter of the coordinate plane.

The four quarters of the coordinate plane are called **quadrants.** Each quadrant corresponds to a different combination of signs of x and y. The quadrants are always numbered as shown below, starting on the top right and going counter-clockwise.

If you…	Then you…	Like this:
Only know ranges for a coordinate (or both) because of an inequality or two	Can plot a shaded region corresponding to the proper range	If x is less than 0, then all the points on the left of the y-axis are valid; half the plane is shaded

Check Your Skills

32. Which quadrant do the following points lie in?
     1. $(1, -2)$ 2. $(-4.6, 7)$ 3. $(-1, -2.5)$ 4. $(3, 3)$

33. Which quadrant or quadrants are indicated by the following?
     1. $x < 0, y > 0$ 2. $x < 0, y < 0$ 3. $y > 0$ 4. $x < 0$

Answers can be found on page 476.

Read a Graph = Drop a Line to the Axes

If you see a point on a coordinate plane, you can read off its coordinates as follows. To find an *x*-coordinate, drop an imaginary line down to the *x*-axis (or up to it) and read off the number.

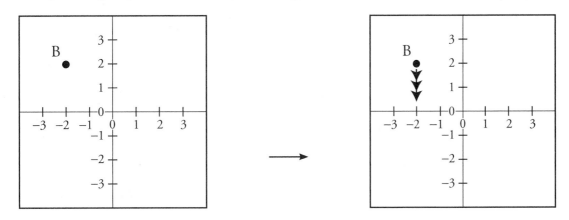

The line hits the *x*-axis at −2, so the *x*-coordinate of the point is −2. Now, to find the *y*-coordinate, you employ a similar technique; only now you draw a horizontal line instead of a vertical line.

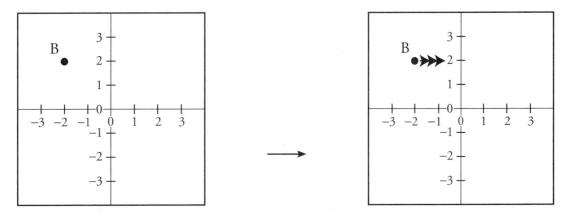

The line touches the *y*-axis at 2, which means the *y*-coordinate of the point is 2. Thus, the coordinates of point B are (−2, 2).

Now suppose that you know the target is on a slanted line in the plane. You can read coordinates off of this slanted line. Try this problem on your own first.

On the line shown, what is the *y*-coordinate of the point that has an *x*-coordinate of −4?

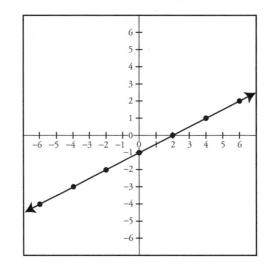

To answer this question, think about reading the coordinates of a point. You went from the point to the axes. Here, you will go from the axis that you know (here, the *x*-axis) to the line that contains the point, and then to the *y*-axis (the axis you don't know).

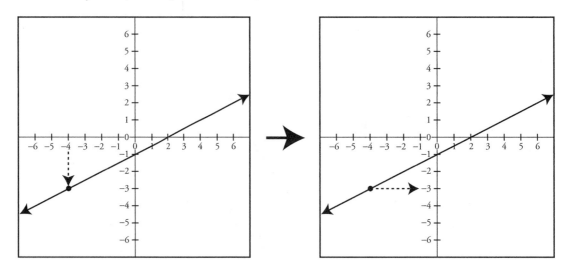

So the point on the line that has an *x*-coordinate of −4 has a *y*-coordinate of −3.

This method of locating points applies equally well to any shape or curve you may encounter on a coordinate plane. Try this next problem.

10

On the curve shown, what is the value of *y* when *x* = 2?

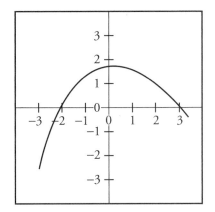

Once again, you know the *x*-coordinate, so you draw a line from the *x*-axis (where you know the coordinate) to the curve, and then draw a line to the *y*-axis.

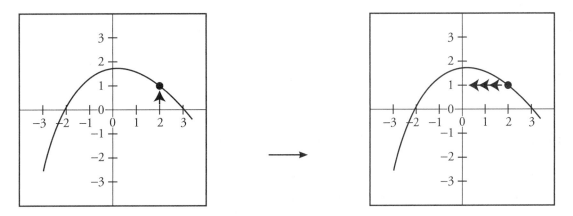

On the curve shown, the point that has an *x*-coordinate of 2 has a *y*-coordinate of 1.

Note that the GMAT will mathematically define each line or curve, so you will never be forced to guess visually where a point falls. This discussion is meant to convey how to use any graphical representation.

10

Check Your Skills

34. On the following graph, what is the *y*-coordinate of the point on the line that has an *x*-coordinate of −3?

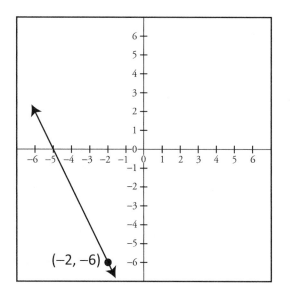

The answer can be found on page 476.

Plot a Relationship: Give Me an *X*, I'll Tell You a *Y*

The most frequent use of the coordinate plane is to display a relationship between *x* and *y*. Often, this relationship is expressed this way: if you tell me *x*, I can tell you *y*.

As an equation, this sort of relationship looks like this:

y = some expression involving *x*   Another way of saying this is you have *y* "in terms of" *x*

Examples: $y = 2x + 1$ If you plug a number in for *x* in any of these
                   $y = x^2 - 3x + 2$ equations, you can calculate a value for *y*.
                   $y = \dfrac{x}{x+2}$

Take $y = 2x + 1$. You can generate a set of *y*'s by plugging in various values of *x*. Start by making a table.

x	$y = 2x + 1$
−1	$y = 2(-1) + 1 = -1$
0	$y = 2(0) + 1 = 1$
1	$y = 2(1) + 1 = 3$
2	$y = 2(2) + 1 = 5$

Now that you have some values, see what you can do with them. You can say that when *x* equals 0, *y* equals 1. These two values form a pair. You express this connection by plotting the point (0, 1) on the coordinate plane. Similarly, you can plot all the other points that represent an *x-y* pair from the table:

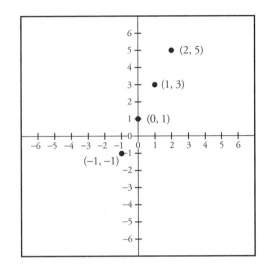

You might notice that these points seem to lie on a straight line. You're right—they do. In fact, any point that you can generate using the relationship $y = 2x + 1$ will also lie on the line.

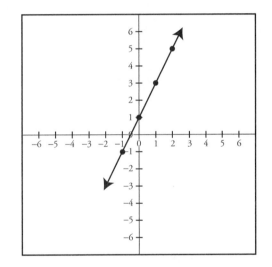

This line is the graphical representation of $y = 2x + 1$

So now you can talk about equations in visual terms. In fact, that's what lines and curves on the coordinate plane are—they represent all the *x–y* pairs that make an equation true. Take a look at the following example:

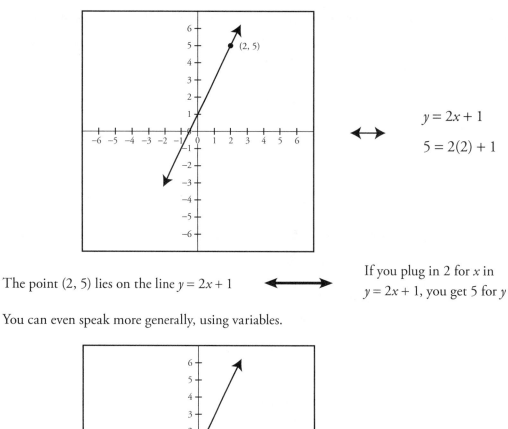

$$y = 2x + 1$$
$$5 = 2(2) + 1$$

The point (2, 5) lies on the line $y = 2x + 1$ ⟷ If you plug in 2 for x in $y = 2x + 1$, you get 5 for y

You can even speak more generally, using variables.

$$y = 2x + 1$$
$$b = 2(a) + 1$$

The point (a, b) lies on the line $y = 2x + 1$ ⟷ If you plug in a for x in $y = 2x + 1$, you get b for y

If you...	Then you...	Like this:
Want to plot a relationship in the x-y plane	Input values of x into the relationship, get values of y back, then plot the (x, y) pairs	Plot $y = 4 - x$ If $x = 0$, then $y = 4$, etc. Then plot $(0, 4)$, etc.

Check Your Skills

35. True or False? The point (9, 21) is on the line $y = 2x + 1$.

36. True or False? The point (4, 14) is on the curve $y = x^2 - 2$.

Answers can be found on page 476.

Lines in the Plane: Use Slope and *Y*-Intercept To Plot

The relationship $y = 2x + 1$ formed a line in the coordinate plane. You can generalize this relationship. Any relationship of the following form represents a line:

$$y = mx + b \qquad\qquad m \text{ and } b \text{ represent numbers (positive or negative)}$$

For instance, in the equation $y = 2x + 1$, you can see that $m = 2$ and $b = 1$.

Lines		Not Lines
$y = 3x - 2$	$m = 3, b = -2$	$y = x^2$
$y = -x + 4$	$m = -1, b = 4$	$y = \dfrac{1}{x}$
These are called linear equations.		These equations are not linear.

The numbers m and b have special meanings when you are dealing with linear equations. $m = $ **slope.** This tells you how steep the line is and whether the line is rising or falling.

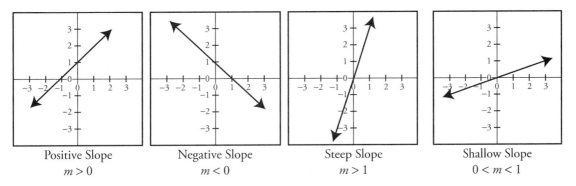

Positive Slope	Negative Slope	Steep Slope	Shallow Slope
$m > 0$	$m < 0$	$m > 1$	$0 < m < 1$

$b = $ **y-intercept.** This tells you where the line crosses the *y*-axis. Any line or curve crosses the *y*-axis when $x = 0$. To find the *y*-intercept, plug in 0 for *x* in the equation.

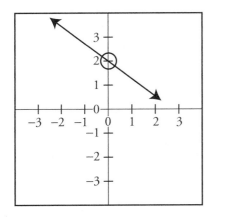
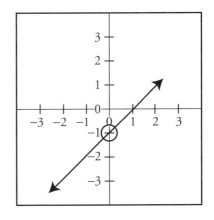

By recognizing linear equations and identifying *m* and *b*, you can plot a line more quickly than by plotting several points on the line.

Check Your Skills

What are the slope and *y*-intercept of the following lines?

37. $y = 3x + 4$
38. $2y = 5x - 12$

Answers can be found on pages 476–477.

How do you use *m* and *b* to sketch a line? Plot the line $y = \frac{1}{2}x - 2$.

The easiest way to begin graphing a line is to begin with the *y*-intercept. You know that the line crosses the *y*-axis at $y = -2$, so begin by plotting that point on the coordinate plane.

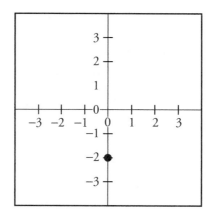

Now you need to figure out how to use slope in order to finish drawing the line. Every slope, whether an integer or a fraction, should be thought of as a fraction. In this equation, the *m* is 1/2. Look at the parts of the fraction and see what they can tell you about the slope.

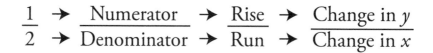

The numerator of the fraction tells you how many units you want to move in the *y* direction—in other words, how far up or down you want to move. The denominator tells you how many units you want to move in the *x* direction—in other words, how far left or right you want to move. For this particular equation, the slope is 1/2, which means you want to move up 1 unit and right 2 units.

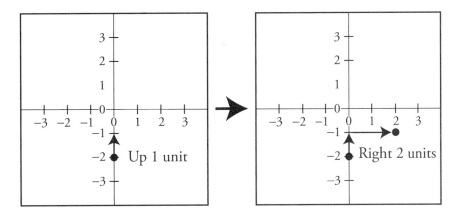

After you went up 1 unit and right 2 units, you ended up at the point (2, –1). What that means is that the point (2, –1) is also a solution to the equation $y = \frac{1}{2}x - 2$. In fact, you can plug in the x value and solve for y to check that you did this correctly.

$$y = \frac{1}{2}x - 2 \rightarrow y = \frac{1}{2}(2) - 2 \rightarrow y = 1 - 2 \rightarrow y = -1$$

What this means is that you can use the slope to generate points and draw the line. If you go up another 1 unit and right another 2 units, you will end up with another point that appears on the line. Although you could keep doing this indefinitely, in reality, with only 2 points you can figure out what the line looks like. Now all you need to do is draw the line that connects the 2 points you have, and you're done.

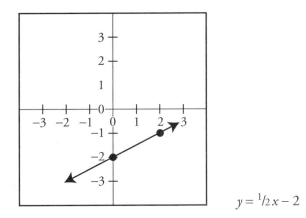

$$y = \frac{1}{2}x - 2$$

That means that this line is the graphical representation of $y = \frac{1}{2}x - 2$.

Let's try another one. Graph the equation $y = (^{-3}/_2)x + 4$.

Once again, the best way to start is to plot the y-intercept. In this equation, $b = 4$, so you know the line crosses the y-axis at the point (0, 4).

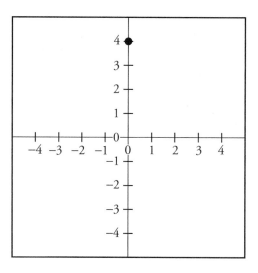

Now you can use the slope to find a second point. This time, the slope is −3/2, which is a negative slope. While positive slopes go up and to the right, negative slopes go down and to the right. To find the next point, you need to go down 3 units and right 2 units.

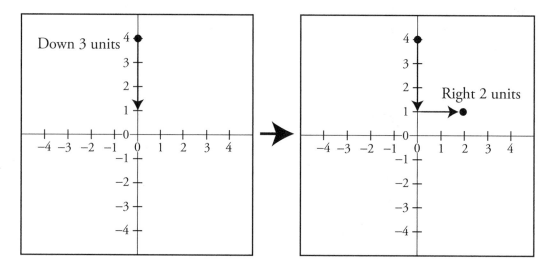

That means that (2, 1) is another point on the line. Now that you have 2 points, you can draw the line.

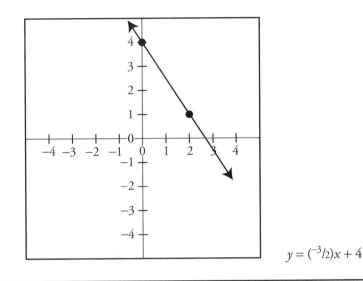

$y = (^{-3}/_2)x + 4$

If you…	Then you…	Like this:
Want to plot a linear equation in the x–y plane	Put the equation in the form of $mx + b$, then use m and b to draw the line	Plot $y = 4 - x$ $y = 4 - x = -1x + 4$ Slope is -1, y-intercept is $(0, 4)$

Check Your Skills

39. Draw a coordinate plane and graph the line $y = 2x - 4$. Identify the slope and the y-intercept.

The answer can be found on page 477.

Check Your Skills Answers

1. The formula for area is $A = \pi r^2$. The radius is 7, so Area $= \pi(7)^2 = 49\pi$.

2. Circumference of a circle is either $C = 2\pi r$ or $C = \pi d$. The question asks for the diameter, so we'll use the latter formula. $17\pi = \pi d$. Divide by π, and we get $17 = d$. The diameter is 17.

3. The link between area and circumference of a circle is that they are both defined in terms of the radius. Area of a circle is $A = \pi r^2$, so we can use the area of the circle to find the radius. $25\pi = \pi r^2$, so $r = 5$. If the radius equals 5, then the circumference is $C = 2\pi(5)$, which equals 10π. The circumference is 10π.

4. If the central angle of the sector is 270°, then it is 3/4 of the full circle, because $\dfrac{270°}{360°} = \dfrac{3}{4}$. If the radius is 2, then the area of the full circle is $\pi(2)^2$, which equals 4π. If the area of the full circle is 4π, then the area of the sector will be $3/4 \times 4\pi$, which equals 3π.

5. To find the central angle, we first need to figure out what fraction of the circle the sector is. We can do that by finding the circumference of the full circle. The radius is 3, so the circumference of the circle is $2\pi(3) = 6\pi$. That means the sector is 2/3 of the circle, because $\dfrac{4\pi}{6\pi} = \dfrac{2}{3}$. That means the central angle of the sector is $2/3 \times 360°$, which equals 240°.

6. We can begin by finding the area of the whole circle. The radius of the circle is 10, so the area is $\pi(10)^2$, which equals 100π. That means the sector is 2/5 of the circle, because $\dfrac{40\pi}{100\pi} = \dfrac{4}{10} = \dfrac{2}{5}$. We can find the circumference of the whole circle using $C = 2\pi r$. The circumference equals 20π. $2/5 \times 20\pi = 8\pi$. The arc length of the sector is 8π.

7. If the two known sides of the triangle are 5 and 19, then the third side of the triangle cannot have a length of 13, because that would violate the rule that any two sides of a triangle must add up to greater than the third side. $5 + 13 = 18$, and $18 < 19$.

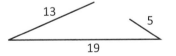   No possible triangle
with these lengths.

8. If the two known sides of the triangle are 8 and 17, then the third side must be less than the sum of the other 2 sides. $8 + 17 = 25$, so the third side must be less than 25. The third side must also be greater than the difference of the other two sides. $17 − 8 = 9$, so the third side must be greater than 9. That means that 9 < third side < 25.

9. The internal angles of a triangle must add up to 180°, so we know that $40 + 75 + x = 180$. Solving for x gives us $x = 65°$.

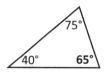

10. The 3 internal angles of the triangle must add up to 180°, so $50 + x + x = 180$. That means that $2x = 130$, and $x = 65$.

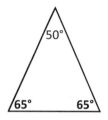

11. In order to determine the missing angles of the triangle, we need to do a little work with the picture. We can figure out the value of x, because straight lines have a degree measure of 180, so $110 + x = 180$, which means $x = 70$.

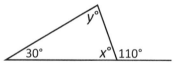

That means our picture looks like this:

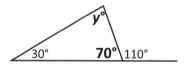

Now we can find y, because $30 + 70 + y = 180$. Solving for y gives us $y = 80$.

12. In this triangle, two sides have the same length, which means this triangle is isosceles. We also know that the two angles opposite the two equal sides will also be equal. That means that x must be 80.

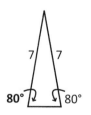

13. In this triangle, two angles are equal, which means this triangle is isosceles. We also know that the two sides opposite the equal angles must also be equal, so x must equal 4.

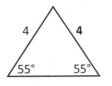

14. This triangle is isosceles, because two sides have the same length. That means that the angles opposite the equal sides must also be equal.

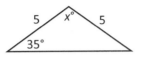

That means our triangle really looks like this:

Now we can find x, because we know $35 + 35 + x = 180$. Solving for x gives us $x = 110$.

15.

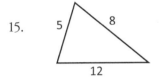

To find the perimeter of the triangle, we add up all three sides. $5 + 8 + 12 = 25$, so the perimeter is 25.

16. To find the perimeter of the triangle, we need the lengths of all three sides. This is an isosceles triangle, because two angles are equal. That means that the sides opposite the equal angles must also be equal. So our triangle looks like this:

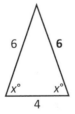

So the perimeter is $6 + 6 + 4$, which equals 16. The perimeter is 16.

17. The area of a triangle is $\frac{1}{2}b \times h$. In the triangle shown, the base is 6 and the height is 5. So the area is $\frac{1}{2}(6) \times 5$, which equals 15.

18. In this triangle, the base is 10 and the height is 7. Remember that the height must be perpendicular to the base—it doesn't need to lie within the triangle. So the area is $\frac{1}{2}(10) \times 7$, which equals 35. The area of the triangle is 35.

19. This is a right triangle, so we can use the Pythagorean Theorem to solve for the length of the third side. The hypotenuse is the side with length 10, so the formula is $(8)^2 + b^2 = (10)^2$. $64 + b^2 = 100$. $b^2 = 36$, which means $b = 6$. So the third side of the triangle has a length of 6. Alternatively, you could recognize that this triangle is one of the Pythagorean triplets—a 6–8–10 triangle, which is just a doubled 3–4–5 triangle.

20. This is a right triangle, so we can use the Pythagorean Theorem to solve for the length of the third side. The hypotenuse is the unknown side, so the formula is $(5)^2 + (12)^2 = c^2$. $25 + 144 = c^2$. $c^2 = 169$, which means $c = 13$. So the third side of the triangle has a length of 13. Alternatively, you could recognize that this triangle is one of the Pythagorean triplets—a 5–12–13 triangle.

21. This is a right triangle, so we can use the Pythagorean Theorem to solve for the third side, or alternatively recognize that this is a 3–4–5 triangle. Either way, the result is the same: The length of the third side is 3.

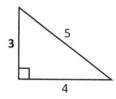

Now we can find the are of the triangle. Area of a triangle is $^1/_2 b \times h$, so the area of this triangle is $^1/_2 (3) \times (4)$, which equals 6. The area of the triangle is 6.

22. In parallelograms, opposite sides have equal lengths, so we know that two of the sides of the parallelogram have a length of 6 and two sides have a length of 10.

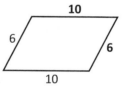

So the perimeter is $6 + 10 + 6 + 10$, which equals 32.

23. Area of a parallelogram is $b \times h$. In this parallelogram, the base is 9 and the height is 4, so the area is $(9) \times (4)$, which equals 36. The area of the parallelogram is 36.

24. In rectangles, opposite sides have equal lengths, so our rectangle looks like this:

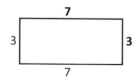

So the perimeter is 3 + 7 + 3 + 7, which equals 20. The area of a rectangle is $b \times h$, so the area is (7) × (3), which equals 21. So the perimeter is 20, and the area is 21.

25. To find the area and perimeter of the rectangle, we need to know the length of either side *AB* or side *CD*. The diagonal of the rectangle creates a right triangle, so we can use the Pythagorean Theorem to find the length of side *CD*. Alternatively, we can recognize that triangle *ACD* is a 6–8–10 triangle, and thus the length of side *CD* is 8. Either way, our rectangle now looks like this:

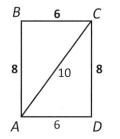

So the perimeter of the rectangle is 6 + 8 + 6 + 8, which equals 28. The area is (6) × (8), which equals 48. So the perimeter is 28 and the area is 48.

26. Redraw the diagram *without* the circle, so you can focus on the rectangle. Add in the diagonal *AC*, since we're given its length.

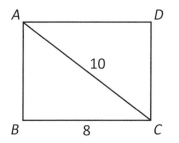

Now we look at right triangle *ABC*. *AC* functions not only as the diagonal of rectangle *ABCD* but also as the hypotenuse of right triangle *ABC*. So now we find the third side of triangle *ABC*, either using the Pythagorean Theorem or recognizing a Pythagorean triplet (6–8–10).

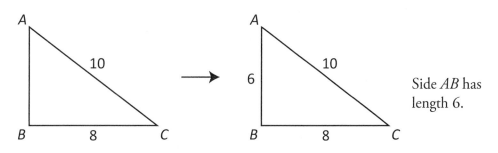

Side *AB* has length 6.

$(AB)^2 + 8^2 = 10^2$

$(AB)^2 + 64 = 100$

$(AB)^2 = 36$

$AB = 6$

Now, we redraw the diagram *with* the circle but without the diagonal, since we've gotten what we needed from that: the other side of the rectangle.

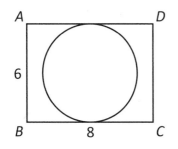

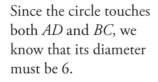
Since the circle touches both *AD* and *BC*, we know that its diameter must be 6.

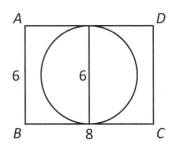

Finally, we find the radius and compute the area:

$d = 6 = 2r$ Area $= \pi r^2$

$3 = r$ $= \pi 3^2$

                  Area $= 9\pi$

27.

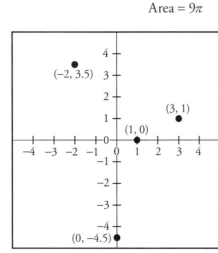

28.   1. (2, −1): **E**

         2. (−1.5, −3): **C**

         3. (−1, 2): **B**

         4. (3, 2): **D**

10

29.

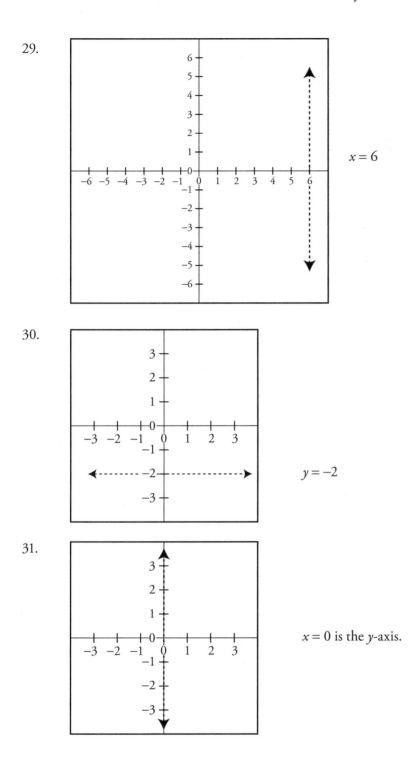

$x = 6$

30.

$y = -2$

31.

$x = 0$ is the y-axis.

32.　1. (1, −2) is in Quadrant IV

2. (−4.6, 7) is in Quadrant II

3. (−1, −2.5) is in Quadrant III

4. (3, 3) is in Quadrant I

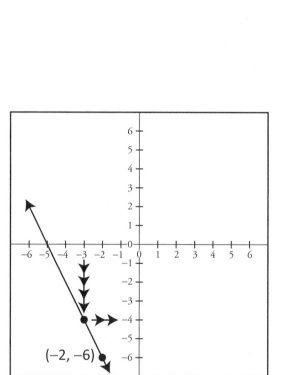

33.　1. $x < 0, y > 0$ indicates Quadrant II

2. $x < 0, y < 0$ indicates Quadrant III

3. $y > 0$ indicates Quadrants I and II

4. $x < 0$ indicates Quadrants II and III

34. The point on the line with $x = -3$

has a y-coordinate of −4.

35. False. The relationship is $y = 2x + 1$, and the point we are testing is (9, 21). So we plug in 9 for x and see if we get 21 for y. $y = 2(9) + 1 = 19$. The point (9, 21) does not lie on the line.

36. True. The relationship is $y = x^2 - 2$, and the point we are testing is (4, 14). So we plug in 4 for x and see if we get 14 for y. $y = (4)^2 - 2 = 14$. The point (4, 14) lies on the curve.

37. The equation $y = 3x + 4$ is already in $y = mx + b$ form, so we can directly find the slope and y-intercept. The slope is 3, and the y-intercept is 4.

38. To find the slope and *y*-intercept of a line, we need the equation to be in $y = mx + b$ form. We need to divide our original equation by 2 to make that happen. So $2y = 5x - 12$ becomes $y = 2.5x - 6$. So the slope is 2.5 (or 5/2) and the *y*-intercept is −6.

39.

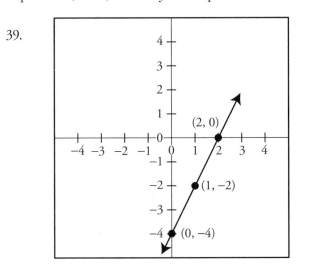

$y = 2x - 4$

slope = 2

y-intercept = −4

10

Chapter Review: Drill Sets

Drill 1

1. The radius of a circle is 4. What is its area?
2. The diameter of a circle is 7. What is its circumference?
3. The radius of a circle is 3. What is its circumference?
4. The area of a circle is 36π. What is its radius?
5. The circumference of a circle is 18π. What is its area?

Drill 2

6. The area of a circle is 100π. What is its circumference?
7. The diameter of a circle is 16. Calculate its radius, circumference, and area.
8. Which circle has a larger area? Circle A has a circumference of 6π and Circle B has an area of 8π.
9. Which has a larger area? Circle C has a diameter of 10 and Circle D has a circumference of 12π.
10. A circle initially has an area of 4π. If the radius is doubled, how many times greater is the new area than the original area?

Drill 3

11. A sector has a central angle of 90°. If the sector has a radius of 8, what is the area of the sector?
12. A sector has a central angle of 30°. If the sector has a radius of 6, what is the arc length of the sector?
13. A sector has an arc length of 7π and a diameter of 14. What is the central angle of the sector?
14. A sector has a central angle of 270°. If the sector has a radius of 4, what is the area of the sector?
15. A sector has an area of 24π and a radius of 12. What is the central angle of the sector?

Drill 4

16. The area of a sector is 1/10th the area of the full circle. What is the central angle of the sector?
17. What is the perimeter of a sector with a radius of 5 and a central angle of 72°?
18. A sector has a radius of 8 and an area of 8π. What is the arc length of the sector?
19. A sector has an arc length of $\pi/2$ and a central angle of 45°. What is the radius of the sector?
20. Which of the following two sectors has a larger area? Sector A has a radius of 4 and a central angle of 90°. Sector B has a radius of 6 and a central angle of 45°.

Drill 5

21. A triangle has two sides with lengths of 5 and 11, respectively. What is the range of values for the length of the third side?
22. In a right triangle, the length of one of the legs is 3 and the length of the hypotenuse is 5. What is the length of the other leg?

23. What is the area of Triangle *DEF*?

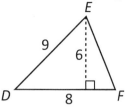

24. Which side of Triangle *GHI* has the longest length?

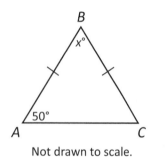

Not drawn to scale.

25. What is the value of *x*?

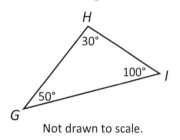

Not drawn to scale.

Drill 6

26. Two sides of a triangle have lengths 4 and 8. Which of the following are possible side lengths of the third side? (More than one may apply)

    a. 2   b. 4   c. 6   d. 8

27. *DFG* is a straight line. What is the value of *x*?

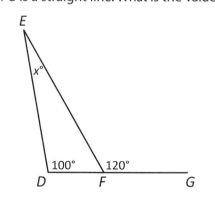

28. Isosceles triangle *ABC* has two sides with lengths 3 and 9. What is the length of the third side?

29. Which of the following could be the length of side *AB*, if $x < y < z$?

      a. 6   b. 10   c. 14

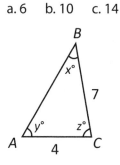

30. What is the area of right triangle *ABC*?

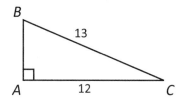

Drill 7

31. What is the perimeter of triangle *ABC*?

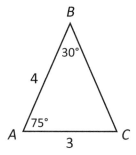

32. The area of right triangle *ABC* is 15. What is the length of hypotenuse *BC*?

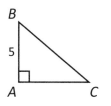

10

33. What is the length of side *HI*?

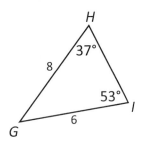

34. Which triangle has the greatest perimeter?

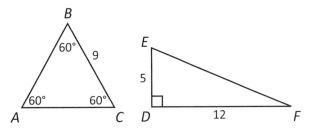

35. *WZ* has a length of 3 and *ZX* has a length of 6. What is the area of Triangle *XYZ*?

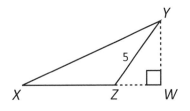

Drill 8

36. What is the perimeter of parallelogram *ABCD*?

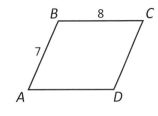

37. What is the area of parallelogram *EFGH*?

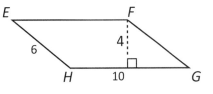

38. The two parallelograms pictured below have the same perimeter. What is the length of side *EH*?

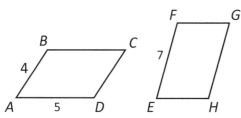

39. In Parallelogram *ABCD*, Triangle *ABC* has an area of 12. What is the area of Triangle *ACD*?

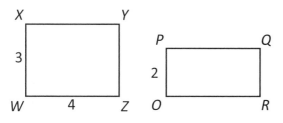

40. Rectangle *WXYZ* and Rectangle *OPQR* have equal areas. What is the length of side *PQ*?

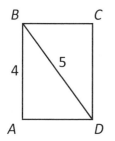

Drill 9

41. What is the area of Rectangle *ABCD*?

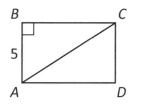

42. In Rectangle *ABCD*, the area of Triangle *ABC* is 30. What is the length of diagonal *AC*?

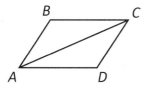

43. Rectangles *ABCD* and *EFGH* have equal areas. What is the length of side *FG*?

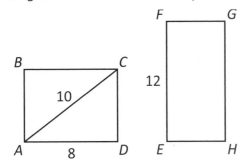

44. A rectangle has a perimeter of 10 and an area of 6. What are the length and width of the rectangle?

45. Right Triangle *ABC* and Rectangle *JKLM* have equal areas. What is the perimeter of Rectangle *JKLM*?

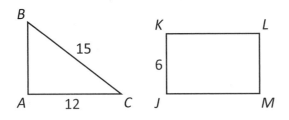

Drill 10

46. What is the perimeter of a square with an area of 25?

47. A rectangle and a square have the same area. The square has a perimeter of 32 and the rectangle has a length of 4. What is the width of the rectangle?

48. A circle is inscribed inside a square, so that the circle touches all four sides of the square. The length of one of the sides of the square is 9. What is the area of the circle?

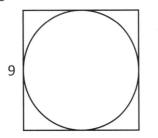

49. Square *ABCD* has an area of 49. What is the length of diagonal *AC*?

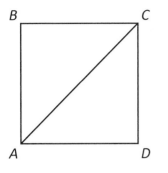

50. Right Triangle *ABC* and Rectangle *EFGH* have the same perimeter. What is the value of x?

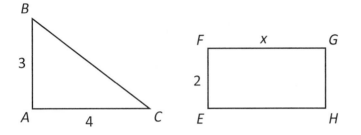

Drill 11

51. Draw a coordinate plane and plot the following points:

1. (2, 3)   2. (−2, −1)   3. (−5, −6)   4. (4, −2.5)

52. What are the *x*- and *y*-coordinates of the following points?

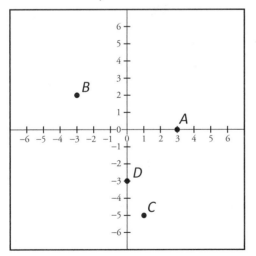

10

53. What is the *y*-coordinate of the point on the line that has an *x*-coordinate of 3?

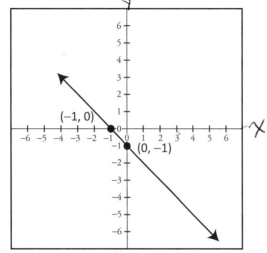

54. What is the *x*-coordinate of the point on the line that has a *y*-coordinate of −4?

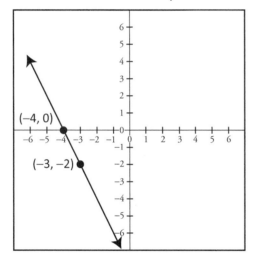

55. Does the point (3, −2) lie on the line $y = 2x - 8$?

Drill 12

56. Does the point (−3, 0) lie on the curve $y = x^2 - 3$?
57. For the line $y = 4x + 2$, what is the *y*-coordinate when $x = 3$?
58. What is the *y*-intercept of the line $y = -2x - 7$?
59. Graph the line $y = \frac{1}{3}x - 4$.
60. Graph the line $\frac{1}{2}y = -\frac{1}{2}x + 1$.

Drill Set Answers

Drill 1

1.   The radius of a circle is 4. What is its area?

Area of a circle is πr^2, so the area of the circle is $\pi(4)^2$, which equals 16π.

2.   The diameter of a circle is 7. What is its circumference?

Circumference of a circle is $2\pi r$, or πd. We have the diameter, so the circumference equals $\pi(7)$, which equals 7π.

3.   The radius of a circle is 3. What is its circumference?

Circumference of a circle is $2\pi r$, or πd. We have the radius, so circumference equals $2\pi(3)$, which equals 6π.

4.   The area of a circle is 36π. What is its radius?

Area of a circle is πr^2, so $36\pi = \pi r^2$. We need to solve for r. Divide both sides by π, so $36 = r^2$. Take the square root of both sides, and $6 = r$. We can ignore the negative solution because distances cannot be negative.

5.   The circumference of a circle is 18π. What is its area?

The connection between circumference and area is radius. We can use the circumference to solve for the radius. $18\pi = 2\pi r$, which means that $9 = r$. That means that Area $= \pi(9)^2$, which equals 81π.

Drill 2

6.   The area of a circle is 100π. What is its circumference?

The connection between circumference and area is radius. $100\pi = \pi r^2$, and solving for r gives us $r = 10$. That means that Circumference $= 2\pi(10)$, which equals 20π.

7.   The diameter of a circle is 16. Calculate its radius, circumference, and area.

$d = 2r$, so $16 = 2r$. Radius $= 8$. Circumference $= 2\pi r$, so Circumference $= 2\pi(8) = 16\pi$. Area $= \pi r^2$, so Area $= \pi(8)^2 = 64\pi$.

8.   Which circle has a larger area? Circle A has a circumference of 6π and Circle B has an area of 8π.

To figure out which circle has a larger area, we need to find the area of Circle A. If we know the circumference, then $6\pi = 2\pi r$, which means $r = 3$. If r $= 3$, then Area $= \pi(3)^2 = 9\pi$. $9\pi > 8\pi$, so Circle A has a larger area.

9.   Which has a larger area? Circle C has a diameter of 10 and Circle D has a circumference of 12π.

We need to find the area of both circles. Let's start with Circle C. If the diameter of Circle C is 10, then the radius is 5. That means that Area $= \pi(5)^2 = 25\pi$.

If the circumference of Circle D is 12π, the $12\pi = 2\pi r$. $r = 6$. If $r = 6$, then Area $= \pi(6)^2 = 36\pi$. $36\pi > 25\pi$, so Circle D has the larger area.

10. A circle initially has an area of 4π. If the radius is doubled, how many times greater is the new area than the original area?

To begin, we need to find the original radius of the circle. $4\pi = \pi r^2$, so $r = 2$. If we double the radius, the new radius is 4. A circle with a radius of 4 has an area of 16π. 16π is 4 times 4π, so the new area is 4 times the original area.

Drill 3

11. A sector has a central angle of 90°. If the sector has a radius of 8, what is the area of the sector?

If the sector has a central angle of 90°, then the sector is 1/4 of the circle, because $\dfrac{9}{360} \times \dfrac{1}{4}$.

To find the area of the sector, we need to find the area of the whole circle first. The radius is 8, which means the area is $\pi(8)^2 = 64\pi$. $1/4 \times 64\pi = 16\pi$. The area of the sector is 16π.

12. A sector has a central angle of 30°. If the sector has a radius of 6, what is the arc length of the sector?

If the sector has a central angle of 30°, then it is 1/12th of the circle, because $\dfrac{30}{360} = \dfrac{1}{12}$. To find the arc length of the sector, we need to know the circumference of the entire circle. The radius of the circle is 6, so the circumference is $2\pi(6) = 12\pi$. That means that the arc length of the sector is $1/12 \times 12\pi = \pi$.

13. A sector has an arc length of 7π and a diameter of 14. What is the central angle of the sector?

To find the central angle of the sector, we first need to find what fraction of the full circle the sector is. We have the arc length, so if we can find the circumference of the circle, we can figure out what fraction of the circle the sector is. The diameter is 14, so the circumference is $\pi(14) =$ 14π. $\dfrac{7\pi}{14\pi} = \dfrac{1}{2}$. So the sector is 1/2 the full circle. That means that the central angle of the sector is $1/2 \times 360° = 180°$. So the central angle is 180°.

14. A sector has a central angle of 270°. If the sector has a radius of 4, what is the area of the sector?

The sector is 3/4 of the circle, because $\dfrac{270°}{360°} = \dfrac{3}{4}$. To find the area of the sector, we need the area of the whole circle. The radius of the circle is 4, so the area is $\pi(4)^2 = 16\pi$. That means the area of the circle is $3/4 \times 16\pi = 12\pi$.

10

15.   A sector has an area of 24π and a radius of 12. What is the central angle of the sector?

We first need to find the area of the whole circle. The radius is 12, which means the area is $\pi(12)^2 = 144\pi$. $\dfrac{24\pi}{144\pi} = \dfrac{1}{6}$, so the sector is 1/6th of the entire circle. That means that the central angle is 1/6th of 360. $1/6 \times 360 = 60$, so the central angle is 60°.

Drill 4

16.   The area of a sector is 1/10th the area of the full circle. What is the central angle of the sector?

If the area of the sector is 1/10th of the area of the full circle, then the central angle will be 1/10th of the degree measure of the full circle. $1/10 \times 360 = 36$, so the central angle of the sector is 36°.

17.   What is the perimeter of a sector with a radius of 5 and a central angle of 72°?

To find the perimeter of a sector, we need to know the radius of the circle and the arc length of the sector.

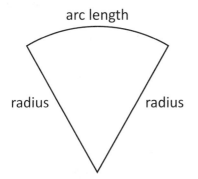

We know the radius is 5, so now we need to find the arc length. Let's begin by determining what fraction of the circle the sector is. The central angle of the sector is 72°, so the sector is 1/5th of the circle, because $\dfrac{72}{360} = \dfrac{1}{5}$. Now we need to find the circumference. The radius is 5, so the circumference of the circle is $2\pi(5) = 10\pi$. The arc length of the sector is 1/5th the circumference. $1/5 \times 10\pi = 2\pi$. So now our sector looks like this. The perimeter of the sector is $10 + 2\pi$.

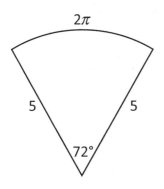

18.   A sector has a radius of 8 and an area of 8π. What is the arc length of the sector?

We first need to find what fraction of the circle the sector is. We can do this by comparing areas. The radius of the circle is 8, so the area of the circle is $\pi(8)^2 = 64\pi$. That means the sector is 1/8th of the circle, because . If we want to find the arc length of the sector, we need to know the circumference. The radius is 8, so the circumference is $2\pi(8) = 16\pi$. The sector is 1/8th of the circle, so the arc length will be 1/8th of the circumference. $1/8 \times 16\pi = 2\pi$. The arc length of the sector is 2π.

19.   A sector has an arc length of $\pi/2$ and a central angle of 45°. What is the radius of the sector?

If the sector has a central angle of 45°, then the sector is 1/8th of the circle, because $\dfrac{45}{360} = \dfrac{1}{8}$. If the sector is 1/8th of the circle, then that means the arc length of the sector is 1/8th of the circumference of the circle. That means that $\pi/2$ is 1/8th of the circumference. If we designate x as the circumference of the circle, then we can say that $\dfrac{\pi}{2} = \dfrac{1}{8}x$. Multiply both sides by 8, and we get $4\pi = x$. That means the circumference is 4π. We know the formula for circumference, so we know that $4\pi = 2\pi r$. Divide both sides by 2π and we get $r = 2$. The radius of the sector is 2.

20.   Which of the following two sectors has a larger area? Sector A has a radius of 4 and a central angle of 90°. Sector B has a radius of 6 and a central angle of 45°.

We need to find the area of each circle. Sector A is 1/4th of the circle, because $\dfrac{90}{360} = \dfrac{1}{4}$. The radius is 4, so the area of the circle is $\pi(4)^2 = 16\pi$. That means the area of Sector A is 1/4th of 16π. $1/4 \times 16\pi = 4\pi$, so the area of Sector A is 4π.

Sector B is 1/8th of the circle, because $\dfrac{45}{360} = \dfrac{1}{8}$. The radius of Sector B is 8, so the area of the full circle is $\pi(6)^2 = 36\pi$. Sector B is 1/8th of the circle, so the area of Sector B is $1/8 \times 36\pi = 4.5\pi$. The area of Sector B is 4.5π.

$4.5\pi > 4\pi$, so the area of Sector B is greater than the area of Sector A.

Drill 5

21.   A triangle has two sides with lengths of 5 and 11, respectively. What is the range of values for the length of the third side?

The lengths of any two sides of a triangle must add up to greater than the length of the third side. The third side must be less than $5 + 11 = 16$. It must also be greater than $11 - 5 = 6$. Therefore, 6 < third side < 16.

22.   In a right triangle, the length of one of the legs is 3 and the length of the hypotenuse is 5. What is the length of the other leg?

If you know the lengths of two sides of a right triangle, you can use the Pythagorean Theorem to solve for the length of the third side. Remember that the hypotenuse must be the side labeled c in the equation $a^2 + b^2 = c^2$. That means that $(3)^2 + (b)^2 = (5)^2$. $9 + b^2 = 25$. $b^2 = 16$, so $b = 4$.

Alternatively, you can recognize the Pythagorean triplet. This is a 3–4–5 triangle.

23.   What is the area of Triangle *DEF*?

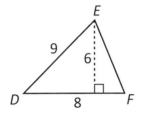

The area of a triangle is $^1/_2$ base × height. Remember that the base and the height must be perpendicular to each other. That means that in Triangle *DEF*, side *DF* can act as the base, and the line dropping straight down from point *E* to touch side *DF* at a right angle can act as the base. Therefore Area = $^1/_2$ (8) × (6) = 24.

24.   Which side of Triangle *GHI* has the longest length?

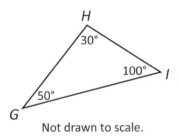

Not drawn to scale.

Although *GI* looks like the longest side, remember that you can't trust what the picture looks like when the question states the picture is not drawn to scale. In any triangle, the longest side will be opposite the larger angle. Angle *GIH* is the largest angle in the triangle, and side *GH* is thus the longest side.

25.   What is the value of *x*?

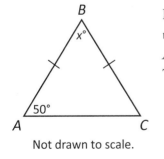

Not drawn to scale.

If you know the other 2 angles in a triangle, then you can find the third, because all 3 angles must add up to 180. In Triangle *ABC*, sides *AB* and *BC* are equal. That means their opposite angles are also equal. That means that angle *ACB* is also 50°.

10

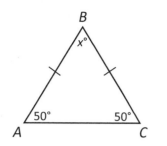

Now that we know the other 2 angles, we can find angle *x*. We know that 50 + 50 + *x* = 180, so *x* = 80.

Drill 6

26.   Two sides of a triangle have lengths 4 and 8. Which of the following are possible side lengths of the third side? (More than one may apply)

a. 2   b. 4   c. 6   d. 8

The lengths of any two sides of a triangle must add up to greater than the length of the third side. The third side must be less than 4 + 8 = 12 and greater than 8 − 4 = 4. So 4 < third side < 12. Only choices c. and d. are in that range.

27.   *DFG* is a straight line. What is the value of *x*?

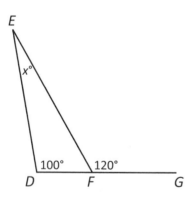

To find the value of *x*, we need to find the degree measures of the other two angles in Triangle *DEF*. We can make use of the fact that *DFG* is a straight line. Straight lines have a degree measure of 180, so angle *DFE* + 120 = 180, which means angle *DFE* = 60.

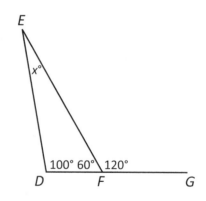

Now we can solve for *x*, because 100 + 60 + *x* = 180. Solving for *x*, we get *x* = 20.

28.   Isosceles triangle *ABC* has two sides with lengths 3 and 9. What is the length of the third side?

It may at first appear like we don't have enough information to answer this question. If all we know is that the triangle is isosceles, then all we know is that two sides have equal length, which means the third side has a length of either 3 or 9. But if the third side were 3, then the lengths of two of the sides would not add up to greater than the length of the third side, because 3 + 3 is not greater than 9.

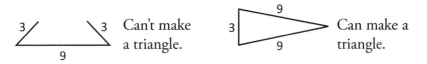

That means that the length of the third side must be 9.

29.   Which of the following could be the length of side *AB*, if $x < y < z$?

a. 6   b. 10   c. 14

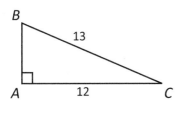

There are two properties of a triangle at play here. The lengths of any two sides of a triangle must add up to greater than the length of the third side. Also, longer sides must be opposite larger angles. Answer choice a. is out because side *AB* is opposite the largest angle, so side *AB* must have a length greater than 7. Answer choice c. is out, because 4 + 7 = 11, so the third side has to be less than 11. The only remaining possibility is b. 10.

30.   What is the area of right triangle *ABC*?

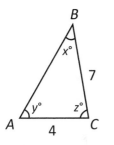

To find the area, we need a base and a height. If we can find the length of side *AB*, then *AB* can be the height and *AC* can be the base, because the two sides are perpendicular to each other.

We can use the Pythagorean Theorem to find the length of side *AB*. $(a)^2 + (12)^2 = (13)^2$. $a^2 + 144 = 169$. $a^2 = 25$. $a = 5$. Alternatively, we could recognize that the triangle is a Pythagorean triplet 5–12–13.

Now that we know the length of side *AB* we can find the area. Area $= \frac{1}{2}(12) \times (5) = 30$.

10

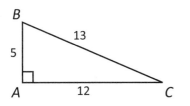

Drill 7

31.   What is the perimeter of triangle *ABC*?

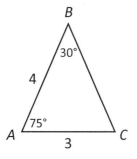

To find the perimeter of Triangle *ABC*, we need the lengths of all 3 sides. There is no immediately obvious way to find the length of side *BC*, so let's see what inferences we can make from the information the question gave us.

We know the degree measures of two of the angles in Triangle *ABC*, so we can find the degree measure of the third. We'll label the third angle *x*. We know that $30 + 75 + x = 180$. Solving for *x* we find that *x* = 75.

Angle *BAC* and angle *BCA* are both 75, which means Triangle *ABC* is an isosceles triangle. If those two angles are equal, we know that their opposite sides are also equal. Side *AB* has a length of 4, so we know that *BC* also has a length of 4.

To find the perimeter, we add up the lengths of the three sides. $4 + 4 + 3 = 11$.

32.   The area of right triangle *ABC* is 15. What is the length of hypotenuse *BC*?

To find the length of the hypotenuse, we need the lengths of the other two sides. Then we can use the Pythagorean Theorem to find the length of the hypotenuse. We can use the area formula to find the length of *AC*. Area = $\frac{1}{2}$ base × height, and we know the area and the height. So $15 = \frac{1}{2}$ (base) × (5). When we solve this equation, we find that the base = 6.

Now we can use the Pythagorean Theorem. $(5)^2 + (6)^2 = c^2$. $25 + 36 = c^2$. $61 = c^2$. $\sqrt{61} = c$. Since 61 is not a perfect square, we know that *c*

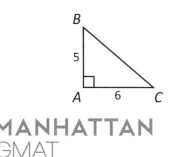

will be a decimal. 61 is also prime, so we cannot simplify $\sqrt{61}$ any further. (It will be a little less than $\sqrt{64} = 8$.)

33.   What is the length of side *HI*?

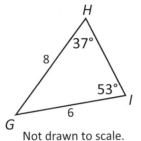

Not drawn to scale.

There is no immediately obvious way to find the length of side *HI*, so let's see what we can infer from the picture. We know two of the angles of Triangle *GHI*, so we can find the third. We'll label the third angle *x*. $37 + 53 + x = 180$. That means $x = 90$. So really our triangle looks like this:

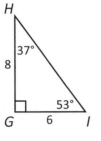

You should definitely redraw once you discover the triangle is a right triangle!

Now that we know Triangle *GHI* is a right triangle, we can use the Pythagorean Theorem to find the length of *HI*. *HI* is the hypotenuse, so $(6)^2 + (8)^2 = c^2$. $36 + 64 = c^2$. $100 = c^2$. $10 = c$. The length of *HI* is 10.

Alternatively, we could have recognized the Pythagorean triplet. Triangle *GHI* is a 6–8–10 triangle.

34.   Which triangle has the greater perimeter?

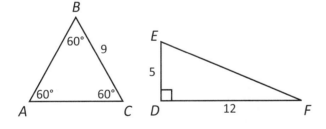

To determine which triangle has the greater perimeter, we need to know the side lengths of all three sides of both triangles. Let's begin with Triangle *ABC*.

There's no immediate way to find the lengths of the missing sides, so let's start by seeing what we can infer from the picture. We know two of the angles, so we can find the third. We'll label the unknown angle *x*. $60 + 60 + x = 180$. $x = 60$.

10

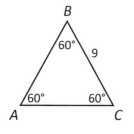

All three angles in Triangle *ABC* are 60°. If all three angles are equal, that means all three sides are equal in this equilateral triangle. So every side of Triangle *ABC* has a length of 9. That means the perimeter = 9 + 9 + 9 = 27.

Now let's look at Triangle *DEF*. Triangle *DEF* is a right triangle, so we can use the Pythagorean Theorem to find the length of side *EF*. *EF* is the hypotenuse, so $(5)^2 + (12)^2 = c^2$. $25 + 144 = c^2$. $169 = c^2$. $13 = c$. That means the perimeter is 5 + 12 + 13 = 30. Alternatively, 5–12–13 is a Pythagorean triplet.

30 > 27, so Triangle *DEF* has a greater perimeter than Triangle *ABC*.

35.   *WZ* has a length of 3 and *ZX* has a length of 6. What is the area of Triangle *XYZ*?

Let's start by filling in everything we know about Triangle *XYZ*.

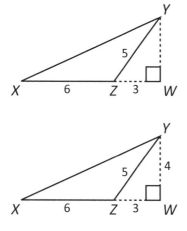

To find the area of Triangle *XYZ*, we need a base and a height. If Side *XZ* is a base, then *YW* can act as a height. We can find the length of *YW* because Triangle *ZYW* is a right triangle, and we know the lengths of two of the sides. *YZ* is the hypotenuse, so $(a)^2 + (3)^2 = (5)^2$. $a^2 + 9 = 25$. $a^2 = 16$. $a = 4$.

Alternatively, we could recognize the Pythagorean triplet: *ZYW* is a 3–4–5 triangle.

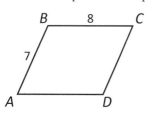

Now we know that the area of Triangle *XYZ* is $\frac{1}{2}b \times h = \frac{1}{2}(6) \times (4) = 12$.

Drill 8

36.   What is the perimeter of parallelogram *ABCD*?

Opposite sides of a parallelogram are equal, so we know that side *CD* has a length of 7 and side *AD* has a length of 8. So the perimeter is 7 + 8 + 7 + 8 = 30.

Alternatively, the perimeter is 2 × (7 + 8) = 30. We can say this because we know that 2 sides have a length of 7 and 2 sides have a length of 8.

MANHATTAN
GMAT

37.   What is the area of parallelogram *EFGH*?

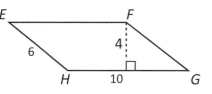

The area of a parallelogram is base × height. In this parallelogram, the base is 10 and the height is 4 (remember, base and height need to be perpendicular). So the area is 10 × 4 = 40.

38.   The two parallelograms pictured below have the same perimeter. What is the length of side *EH*?

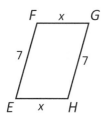

First we can find the perimeter of Parallelogram *ABCD*. We know that 2 sides have a length of 4, and 2 sides have a length of 5. The perimeter is 2 × (4 + 5) = 18. That means Parallelogram *EFGH* also has a perimeter of 18. We know side *GH* also has a length of 7. We don't know the lengths of the other 2 sides, but we know they have the same length, so for now let's say the length of each side is *x*. Our parallelogram now looks like this:

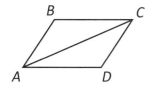

So we know that $7 + x + 7 + x = 18$ → $2x + 14 = 18$ → $2x = 4$ → $x = 2$

The length of side *EH* is 2.

39.   In Parallelogram *ABCD*, Triangle *ABC* has an area of 12. What is the area of Triangle *ACD*?

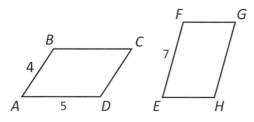

One property that is true of any parallelogram is that the diagonal will split the parallelogram into two equal triangles. If Triangle *ABC* has an area of 12, then Triangle *ACD* must also have an area of 12.

40.   Rectangle *WXYZ* and Rectangle *OPQR* have equal areas. What is the length of side *PQ*?

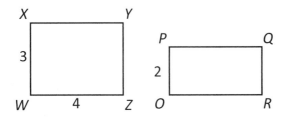

We can start by finding the area of Rectangle *WXYZ*. Area of a rectangle is length × width, so the area of Rectangle *WXYZ* is 3 × 4 = 12. So Rectangle *OPQR* also has an area of 12. We know the length of side *OP*, so that is the width of Rectangle *OPQR*. So now we know the area, and we know the width, so we can solve for the length. l × 2 = 12 → l = 6. The length of side *PQ* is 6.

Drill 9

41.   What is the area of Rectangle *ABCD*?

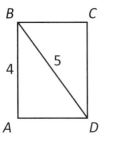

To find the area of Rectangle *ABCD*, we need to know the length of *AD* or *BC*. In a rectangle, every internal angle is 90 degrees, so Triangle *ABD* is actually a right triangle. That means we can use the Pythagorean Theorem to find the length of side *AD*. Actually, this right triangle is one of the Pythagorean Triplets—a 3–4–5 triangle. The length of side *AD* is 3. That means the area of Rectangle *ABCD* is 3 × 4 = 12.

42.   In Rectangle *ABCD*, the area of Triangle *ABC* is 30. What is the length of diagonal *AC*?

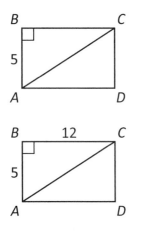

We know the area of Triangle *ABC* and the length of side *AB*. Because side *BC* is perpendicular to side *AB*, we can use those as the base and height of Triangle *ABC*. So we know that ¹/₂(5) × (BC) = 30. That means the length of side *BC* is 12.

Now we can use the Pythagorean Theorem to find the length of diagonal *AC*, which is the hypotenuse of right triangle *ABC*. We can also recognize that this is a Pythagorean Triplet —a 5–12–13 triangle. The length of diagonal *AC* is 13.

43.   Rectangles *ABCD* and *EFGH* have equal areas. What is the length of side *FG*?

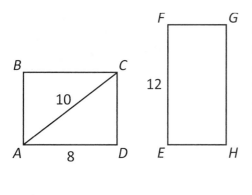

The first thing to notice in this problem is that we can find the length of side *CD*. Triangle *ACD* is a right triangle, and we know the lengths of two of the sides. We can either use the Pythagorean Theorem or recognize that this is one of our Pythagorean Triplets—a 6–8–10 triangle. The length of side *CD* is 6. Now we can find the area of Rectangle *ABCD*. Side *AD* is the length and side *CD* is the width.
$8 \times 6 = 48$.

That means that the area of Rectangle *EFGH* is also 48. We can use the area and the length of side *EF* to solve for the length of side *FG*. $12 \times (FG) = 48$. The length of side *FG* is 4.

44.   A rectangle has a perimeter of 10 and an area of 6. What are the length and width of the rectangle?

In order to answer this question, let's begin by drawing a rectangle. In this rectangle, we'll make one pair of equal sides have a length of *x*, and the other pair of equal sides has a length of *y*.

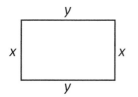

Using the lengths *x* and *y*, we know the perimeter of the rectangle is $2x + 2y$. So we know that:

$2x + 2y = 10$ This can be simplified to **$x + y = 5$**.

We also know the area of the rectangle is $xy = 6$.

$xy = 6$ Area of the rectangle = $l \times w = 6$

Now we can use substitution to solve for the values of our variables. In the first equation, we can isolate *x*.

$x = 5 - y$

Substitute $(5 - y)$ for *x* in the second equation.

$(5 - y)y = 6$
$5y - y^2 = 6$ This is a quadratic, so we need to get everything on one side.
$y^2 - 5y + 6 = 0$ Now we can factor the equation.
$(y - 3)(y - 2) = 0$

So $y = 2$ or 3.

10

When we plug in these values to solve for x, we find something a little unusual. When $y = 2$, $x = 3$. When $y = 3$, $x = 2$. What that means is that either the length is 2 and the width is 3, or the length is 3 and the width is 2. Both of these rectangles are identical, so we have our answer.

45.   Right Triangle *ABC* and Rectangle *JKLM* have equal areas. What is the perimeter of Rectangle *JKLM*?

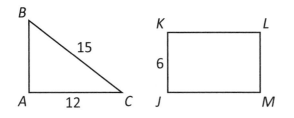

If we can find the length of side *AB*, then we can find the area of Triangle *ABC*. We can use the Pythagorean Theorem to find the length of side *AB*. $(12)^2 + (AB)^2 = (15)^2$ → $144 + (AB)^2 = 225$ → $(AB)^2 = 81$ → $AB = 9$. (A 9–12–15 triangle is a 3–4–5 triangle, with all the measurements tripled.)

Now that we know *AB*, we can find the area of Triangle *ABC*. It's $\frac{1}{2}(12) \times 9 = 54$.

That means that Rectangle *JKLM* also has an area of 54. We have one side of the rectangle, so we can solve for the other. $6 \times (JM) = 54$. So the length of side *JM* is 9. That means that the perimeter is $2 \times (6 + 9) = 30$.

Drill 10

46.   What is the perimeter of a square with an area of 25?

A square has four equal sides, so the area of a square is the length of one side squared. That means the lengths of the sides of the square are 5. If each of the four sides has a length of 5, then the perimeter is $4 \times (5) = 20$.

47.   A rectangle and a square have the same area. The square has a perimeter of 32 and the rectangle has a length of 4. What is the width of the rectangle?

We should start by drawing the shapes that they describe.

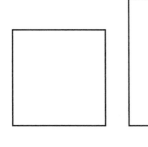

The square has four equal sides, so that means that the perimeter is 4 times the length of one side. If we designate the length of the sides of the square s, then the perimeter is $4s = 32$. That means that s is 8. Now that we know the length of the sides, we can figure out the area of the square. Area = 8^2. So the area of the square is 64.

That means that the area of the rectangle is also 64. We know the length of the rectangle is 4, so we can solve for the width. $4 \times$ (width) = 64. The width is 16.

48.   A circle is inscribed inside a square, so that the circle touches all four sides of the square. The length of one of the sides of the square is 9. What is the area of the circle?

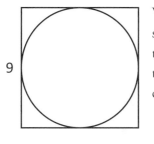

We need to find a common link between the square and the circle, so that we can find the area of the circle. We know that the length of the sides of the square is 9. We can draw a new line in our figure that has the same length as the sides AND is the diameter of the circle.

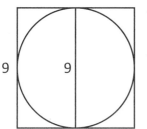

That means that the diameter of the circle is 9. If the diameter is 9, then the radius is 4.5. That means the area of the circle is $\pi(4.5)^2$, which equals 20.25π.

49.   Square *ABCD* has an area of 49. What is the length of diagonal *AC*?

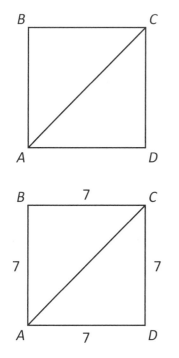

If the square has an area of 49, then (side)^2 = 49. That means that the length of the sides of the square is 7. So our square looks like this:

Now we can use the Pythagorean Theorem to find the length of diagonal *AC*, which is also the hypotenuse of Triangle *ACD*. $x7^2 + 7^2 = (AC)^2$ → $98 = (AC)^2$ → $\sqrt{98} = AC$. But this can be simplified. $AC = \sqrt{2 \times 49} = \sqrt{2 \times 7 \times 7} = 7\sqrt{2}$.

10

50.   Right Triangle *ABC* and Rectangle *EFGH* have the same perimeter. What is the value of *x*?

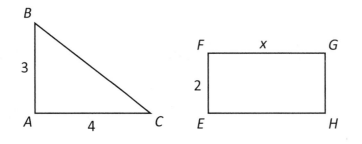

Triangle *ABC* is a right triangle, so we can find the length of hypotenuse *BC*. This is a 3–4–5 triangle, so the length of side *BC* is 5. That means the perimeter of Triangle *ABC* is $3 + 4 + 5 = 12$.

That means the perimeter of Rectangle *EFGH* is also 12. That means that $2 \times (2 + x) = 12$. So $4 + 2x = 12 \rightarrow 2x = 8 \rightarrow x = 4$.

Drill 11

51.   Draw a coordinate plane and plot the following points:
        1. (2, 3)   2. (−2, −1)   3. (−5, −6)   4. (4, −2.5)

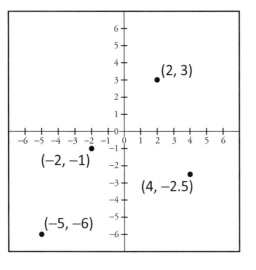

52.   A: (3, 0)   B: (−3, 2)   C: (1, −5)   D: (0, −3)

53.   The *y*-coordinate of the point on the line that has an *x*-coordinate of 3 is −4. The point is
       (3, −4). If you want, you can determine that the line has a slope of −1 from the two labeled
       points that the line intercepts, (−1, 0) and (0, −1).

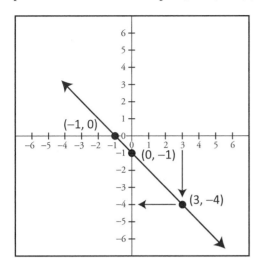

54.   The *x*-coordinate of the point on the line that has a *y*-coordinate of −4 is −2. The point is
       (−2, −4). If you want, you can determine that the line has a slope of −2 from the two labeled
       points that the line intercepts, (−4, 0) and (−3, −2).

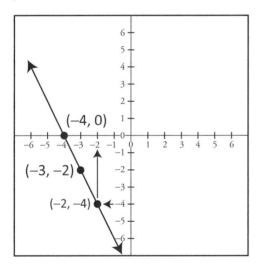

55.   For the point (3, −2) to lie on the line $y = 2x − 8$, *y* needs to equal −2 when we plug in 3 for *x*.

       $y = 2(3) − 8$
       $y = 6 − 8 = −2$
       y does equal −2 when *x* equals 3, so the point does lie on the line.

Drill 12

56.   For the point $(-3, 0)$ to lie on the curve $y = x^2 - 3$, y needs to equal 0 when we plug in -3 for x.

$y = (-3)^2 - 3$
$y = 9 - 3 = 6$
y does not equal 0 when x equals -3, so the point does not lie on the curve.

57.   To find the y-coordinate, we need to plug in 3 for x and solve for y.

$y = 4(3) + 2$
$y = 12 + 2 = 14$
The y-coordinate is 14. The point is $(3, 14)$.

58.   The equation of the line is already in $y = mx + b$ form, and b stands for the y-intercept, so we just need to look at the equation to find the y-intercept. The equation is $y = -2x - 7$. That means the y-intercept is -7. The point is $(0, -7)$.

59.   Graph the line $y = \frac{1}{3}x - 4$

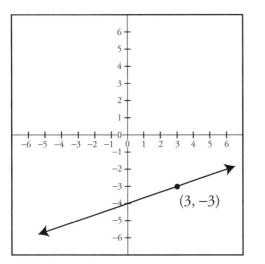

The slope (m) is 1/3, so the line slopes gently up to the right, rising only 1 unit for every 3 units of run.

The y-intercept (b) is -4, so the line crosses the y-axis at $(0, -4)$.

10

60.   Graph the line $\frac{1}{2}y = -\frac{1}{2}x + 1$.

Before we can graph the line, we need to put the equation into $y = mx + b$ form. Multiply both sides by 2.

$y = -x + 2$

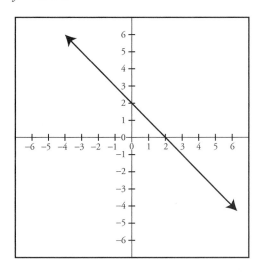

The slope (m) is −1, so the line drops to the right, falling 1 unit for every unit of run.

The y-intercept is 2, so the line crosses the y-axis at (0, 2).

Glossary

absolute value: The distance from zero on the number line for a particular term. E.g. the absolute value of −7 is 7 (written |−7|).

arc length: A section of a circle's circumference.

area: The space enclosed by a given closed shape on a plane; the formula depends on the specific shape. E.g. the area of a rectangle equals *length* × *width*.

axis: one of the two number lines (*x*-axis or *y*-axis) used to indicate position on a coordinate plane.

base: In the expression b^n, the variable b represents the base. This is the number that we multiply by itself n times. Also can refer to the horizontal side of a triangle.

center (circle): The point from which any point on a circle's radius is equidistant.

central angle: The angle created by any two radii.

circle: A set of points in a plane that are equidistant from a fixed center point.

circumference: The measure of the perimeter of a circle. The circumference of a circle can be found with this formula: $C = 2\pi r$, where C is the circumference and r is the radius.

coefficient: A number being multiplied by a variable. In the equation $y = 2x + 5$, the coefficient of the x term is 2.

common denominator: When adding or subtracting fractions, we first must find a common denominator, generally the smallest common multiple of both numbers.

Example:

> Given (3/5) + (1/2), the two denominators are 5 and 2. The smallest multiple that works for both numbers is 10. The common denominator, therefore, is 10.

composite number: Any number that has more than 2 factors.

constant: A number that doesn't change, in an equation or expression. We may not know its value, but it's "constant" in contrast to a variable, which varies. In the equation $y = 3x + 2$, 3 and 2 are constants. In the equation $y = mx + b$, m and b are constants (just unknown).

coordinate plane: Consists of a horizontal axis (typically labeled "*x*") and a vertical axis (typically labeled "*y*"), crossing at the number zero on both axes.

decimal: numbers that fall in between integers. A decimal can express a part–to–whole relationship, just as a percent or fraction can.

Example:

> 1.2 is a decimal. The integers 1 and 2 are not decimals. An integer written as 1.0, however, is considered a decimal. The decimal 0.2 is equivalent to 20% or to 2/10 (= 1/5).

denominator: The bottom of a fraction. In the fraction (7/2), 2 is the denominator.

diameter: A line segment that passes through the center of a circle and whose endpoints lie on the circle.

difference: When one number is subtracted from another, the difference is what is left over. The difference of 7 and 5 is 2, because $7 - 5 = 2$.

digit: The ten numbers 0, 1, 2, 3, 4, 5, 6, 7, 8, and 9. Used in combination to represent other numbers (e.g., 12 or 0.38).

distributed form: Presenting an expression as a sum or difference. In distributed form, terms are added or subtracted. $x^2 - 1$ is in distributed form, as is $x^2 + 2x + 1$. In contrast, $(x + 1)(x - 1)$ is not in distributed form; it is in factored form.

divisible: If an integer x divided by another number y yields an integer, then x is said to be divisible by y.

Example:

> 12 divided by 3 yields the integer 4. Therefore, 12 is divisible by 3. 12 divided by 5 does not yield an integer. Therefore, 12 is not divisible by 5.

divisor: The part of a division operation that comes after the division sign. In the operation $22 \div 4$ (or 22/4), 4 is the divisor. Divisor is also a synonym for factor. See: **factor**

equation: A combination of mathematical expressions and symbols that contains an equals sign. $3 + 7 = 10$ is an equation, as is $x + y = 3$. An equation makes a statement: left side equals right side

equilateral triangle: A triangle in which all three angles are equal; in addition, all three sides are of equal length.

even: An integer is even if it is divisible by 2. 14 is even because 14/2 = an integer (7).

exponent: In the expression b^n, the variable n represents the exponent. The exponent indicates how many times to multiple the base, b, by itself. For example, $4^3 = 4 \times 4 \times 4$, or 4 multiplied by itself three times.

expression: A combination of numbers and mathematical symbols that does not contain an equals sign. xy is an expression, as is $x + 3$. An expression represents a quantity.

factored form: Presenting an expression as a product. In factored form, expressions are multiplied together. The expression $(x + 1)(x − 1)$ is in factored form: $(x + 1)$ and $(x − 1)$ are the factors. In contrast, $x^2 − 1$ is not in factored form; it is in distributed form.

factor: Positive integers that divide evenly into an integer. Factors are equal to or smaller than the integer in question. 12 is a factor of 12, as are 1, 2, 3, 4, and 6.

factor foundation rule: If a is a factor of b, and b is a factor of c, then a is also a factor of c. For example, 2 is a factor of 10. 10 is a factor of 60. Therefore, 2 is also a factor of 60.

factor tree: Use the "factor tree" to break any number down into its prime factors. For example:

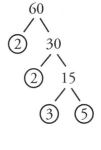

FOIL: First, Outside, Inside, Last; an acronym to remember the method for converting from factored to distributed form in a quadratic equation or expression. $(x + 2)(x − 3)$ is a quadratic expression in factored form. Multiply the First, Outside, Inside, and Last terms to get the distributed form. $x \times x = x^2$, $x \times −3 = −3x$, $x \times 2 = 2x$, and $2 \times −3 = −6$. The full distributed form is $x^2 − 3x + 2x − 6$. This can be simplified to $x^2 − x − 6$.

fraction: A way to express numbers that fall in between integers (though integers can also be expressed in fractional form). A fraction expresses a part-to-whole relationship in terms of a numerator (the part) and a denominator (the whole). (E.g. 3/4 is a fraction.)

hypotenuse: The longest side of a right triangle. The hypotenuse is opposite the right angle.

improper fraction: Fractions that are greater than 1. An improper can also be written as a mixed number. (7/2) is an improper fraction. This can also be written as a mixed number: $3^1/2$.

inequality: A comparison of quantities that have different values. There are four ways to express inequalities: less than ($<$), less than or equal to ($\leq$), greater than ($>$), or greater than or equal to ($\geq$). Can be manipulated in the same way as equations with one exception: when multiplying or dividing by a negative number, the inequality sign flips.

integers: Numbers, such as $−1$, 0, 1, 2, and 3, that have no fractional part. Integers include the counting numbers (1, 2, 3, …), their negative counterparts (−1, −2, −3, …), and 0.

interior angles: The angles that appear in the interior of a closed shape.

isosceles triangle: A triangle in which two of the three angles are equal; in addition, the sides opposite the two angles are equal in length.

line: A set of points that extend infinitely in one direction without curving. On the GMAT, lines are by definition perfectly straight.

line segment: A continuous, finite section of a line. The sides of a triangle or of a rectangle are line segments.

linear equation: An equation that does not contain exponents or multiple variables multiplied together. $x + y = 3$ is a linear equation; $xy = 3$ and $y = x^2$ are not. When plotted on a coordinate plane, linear equations create lines.

mixed number: An integer combined with a proper fraction. A mixed number can also be written as an improper fraction. $3^{1}/_{2}$ is a mixed number. This can also be written as an improper fraction: (7/2).

multiple: Multiples are integers formed by multiplying some integer by any other integer. 12 is a multiple of 12 (12×1), as are 24 ($= 12 \times 2$), 36 ($= 12 \times 3$), 48 ($= 12 \times 4$), and 60 ($= 12 \times 5$). (Negative multiples are possible in mathematics but are not typically tested on the GMAT.)

negative: Any number to the left of zero on a number line; can be integer or non-integer.

negative exponent: Any exponent less than zero. To find a value for a term with a negative exponent, put the term containing the exponent in the denominator of a fraction and make the exponent positive. $4^{-2} = 1/4^2$. $1/3^{-2} = 1/(1/3)^2 = 3^2 = 9$.

number line: A picture of a straight line that represents all the numbers from negative infinity to infinity.

numerator: The top of a fraction. In the fraction, (7/2), 7 is the numerator.

odd: An odd integer is not divisible by 2. 15 is not even because 15/2 is not an integer (7.5).

order of operations: The order in which mathematical operations must be carried out in order to simplify an expression. (See PEMDAS)

the origin: The coordinate pair (0,0) represents the origin of a coordinate plane.

parallelogram: A four-sided closed shape composed of straight lines in which the opposite sides are equal and the opposite angles are equal.

PEMDAS: An acronym that stands for Parentheses, Exponents, Multiplication, Division, Addition, Subtraction, used to remember the order of operations.

percent: Literally, "per one hundred"; expresses a special part-to-whole relationship between a number (the part) and one hundred (the whole). A special type of fraction or decimal that involves the number 100. (E.g. 50% = 50 out of 100.)

perimeter: In a polygon, the sum of the lengths of the sides.

perpendicular: Lines that intersect at a 90° angle.

plane: A flat, two-dimensional surface that extends infinitely in every direction.

point: An object that exists in a single location on the coordinate plane. Each point has a unique *x*-coordinate and *y*-coordinate that together describe its location. (E.g. (1, −2) is a point.

polygon: A two-dimensional, closed shape made of line segments. For example, a triangle is a polygon, as is a rectangle. A circle is a closed shape, but it is not a polygon because it does not contain line segments.

positive: Any number to the right of zero on a number line; can be integer or non-integer.

prime factorization: A number expressed as a product of prime numbers. For example, the prime factorization of 60 is $2 \times 2 \times 3 \times 5$.

prime number: A positive integer with exactly two factors: 1 and itself. The number 1 does not qualify as prime because it has only one factor, not two. The number 2 is the smallest prime number; it is also the only even prime number. The numbers 2, 3, 5, 7, 11, 13 etc. are prime.

product: The end result when two numbers are multiplied together. (E.g. the product of 4 and 5 is 20.

Pythagorean Theorem: A formula used to calculate the sides of a right triangle. $a^2 + b^2 = c^2$, where *a* and *b* are the lengths of the two legs of the triangle and *c* is the length of the hypotenuse of the triangle.

Pythagorean triplet: A set of 3 numbers that describe the lengths of the 3 sides of a right triangle in which all 3 sides have integer lengths. Common Pythagorean triplets are 3–4–5, 6–8–10 and 5–12–13.

quadrant: One quarter of the coordinate plane. Bounded on two sides by the *x*- and *y*-axes.

quadratic expression: An expression including a variable raised to the second power (and no higher powers). Commonly of the form $ax^2 + bx + c$, where *a*, *b*, and *c* are constants.

quotient: The result of dividing one number by another. The quotient of $10 \div 5$ is 2.

radius: A line segment that connects the center of a circle with any point on that circle's circumference. Plural: radii.

reciprocal: The product of a number and its reciprocal is always 1. To get the reciprocal of an integer, put that integer on the denominator of a fraction with numerator 1. The reciprocal of 3 is (1/3). To get the reciprocal of a fraction, switch the numerator and the denominator. The reciprocal of (2/3) is (3/2).

rectangle: A four-sided closed shape in which all of the angles equal 90° and in which the opposite sides are equal. Rectangles are also parallelograms.

right triangle: A triangle that includes a 90°, or right, angle.

root: The opposite of an exponent (in a sense). The square root of 16 (written $\sqrt{16}$) is the number (or numbers) that, when multiplied by itself, will yield 16. In this case, both 4 and −4 would multiply to 16 mathematically. However, when the GMAT provides the root sign for an even root, such as a square

root, then the only accepted answer is the positive root, 4. That is, $\sqrt{16} = 4$, NOT +4 or −4. In contrast, the equation $x^2 = 16$ has TWO solutions, +4 and −4.

sector: A "wedge" of the circle, composed of two radii and the arc connecting those two radii.

simplify: Reduce numerators and denominators to the smallest form by taking out common factors. Dividing the numerator and denominator by the same number does not change the value of the fraction.

Example:

> Given (21/6), we can simplify by dividing both the numerator and the denominator by 3. The simplified fraction is (7/2).

slope: "Rise over run," or the distance the line runs vertically divided by the distance the line runs horizontally. The slope of any given line is constant over the length of that line.

square: A four-sided closed shape in which all of the angles equal 90° and all of the sides are equal. Squares are also rectangles and parallelograms.

sum: The result when two numbers are added together. The sum of 4 and 7 is 11.

term: Parts within an expression or equation that are separated by either a plus sign or a minus sign. (E.g. in the expression $x + 3$, "x" and "3" are each separate terms.

triangle: A three-sided closed shape composed of straight lines; the interior angles add up to 180°.

two-dimensional: A shape containing a length and a width.

variable: Letter used as a substitute for an unknown value, or number. Common letters for variables are x, y, z and t. In contrast to a constant, we generally think of a variable as a value that can change (hence the term variable). In the equation $y = 3x + 2$, both y and x are variables.

x-axis: A horizontal number line that indicates left–right position on a coordinate plane.

x-coordinate: The number that indicates where a point lies along the x-axis. Always written first in parentheses. The x-coordinate of (2, −1) is 2.

x-intercept: The point where a line crosses the x-axis (that is, when $y = 0$).

y-axis: A vertical number line that indicates up–down position on a coordinate plane.

y-coordinate: The number that indicates where a point lies along the y-axis. Always written second in parentheses. The y-coordinate of (2, −1) is −1.

y-intercept: the point where a line crosses the y-axis (that is, when $x = 0$). In the equation of a line $y = mx + b$, the y-intercept equals b. Technically, the coordinates of the y-intercept are (0, b).

ALL TEST PREP IS NOT THE SAME